Fifty Years of Relational,

and Other Database Writings

More Thoughts and Essays on

Database Matters

C. J. Date

Published by:

2 Lindsley Road, Basking Ridge, NJ 07920 USA
https://www.TechnicsPub.com

Cover design by Lorena Molinari

First Printing 2020

Copyright © 2020 C. J. Date. All rights reserved.

Printed in the United States of America.

ISBN, print ed.	9781634628327
ISBN, Kindle ed.	9781634628334
ISBN, ePub ed.	9781634628341
ISBN, PDF ed.	9781634628358

Library of Congress Control Number: 2020942982

Database management isn't so tough
    Set theory, logic—that's all there is to it;
So why are the products so terribly rough?
    Why make such a mess? Why don't they just *do* it?

Part of the answer and part of the blame
    Lies with the language that industry chose—
A travesty, crime, a sin, and a shame
    For something as simple as columns and rows!

—Anon:
Where Bugs Go

Logic,. *n.* The art of thinking and reasoning in strict accordance with the limitations and incapacities of the human misunderstanding.

—Ambrose Bierce:
The Devil's Dictionary (1911)

———— ◆◆◆◆◆ ————

To my friends and personal heroes,
past, present, and future

About the Author

C. J. Date is an independent author, lecturer, researcher, and consultant, specializing in relational database technology. He is best known for his book *An Introduction to Database Systems* (8th edition, Addison-Wesley, 2004), which has sold some 900,000 copies at the time of writing and is used by several hundred colleges and universities worldwide. He is also the author of numerous other books on database management, including most recently:

- From Trafford: *Database Explorations: Essays on The Third Manifesto and Related Topics* (with Hugh Darwen, 2010)

- From Apress: *Date on Database: Writings 2000-2006* (2007); *Database Design and Relational Theory: Normal Forms and All That Jazz* (2nd edition, 2019)

- From Morgan Kaufmann: *Time and Relational Theory: Temporal Databases in the Relational Model and SQL* (with Hugh Darwen and Nikos A. Lorentzos, 2014)

- From O'Reilly: *Relational Theory for Computer Professionals: What Relational Databases Are Really All About* (2013); *View Updating and Relational Theory: Solving the View Update Problem* (2013); *SQL and Relational Theory: How to Write Accurate SQL Code* (3rd edition, 2015); *The New Relational Database Dictionary* (2016); *Type Inheritance and Relational Theory: Subtypes, Supertypes, and Substitutability* (2016)

- From Lulu: *E. F. Codd and Relational Theory: A Detailed Review and Analysis of Codd's Major Database Writings* (2019)

- From Technics: *Logic and Relational Theory: Thoughts and Essays on Database Matters* (2020)

Mr Date was inducted into the Computing Industry Hall of Fame in 2004. He enjoys a reputation that is second to none for his ability to explain complex technical subjects in a clear and understandable fashion.

Contents

Preface

This book is a successor to an earlier one, viz., *Logic and Relational Theory: Thoughts and Essays on Database Matters* (Technics Publications, 2020). Note the present book's subtitle: *More Thoughts and Essays on Database Matters*. As that subtitle suggests, this book is basically "more of the same"—but the point is, I found while putting the earlier book together that there was so much I wanted to say that to have put it all in one volume would simply have been overwhelming. Thus, although each of the books can certainly stand on its own, they're also both part of the same overall project as far as I'm concerned.

Structure of the Book

The book is divided into four parts, as follows:

I. A Bit of History

II. Responding to Criticism

III. Frequently Asked Questions

IV. Interviews

Part I contains a personal account of what happened during the first 50 years of relational history, with the emphasis on theoretical developments (new research results, new discoveries, and so on). Part II consists of a series of responses to technical criticisms, having to do with *The Third Manifesto* in particular. Part III provides an extensive and detailed discussion of a variety of technical questions, covering such topics as relational algebra, missing information, the relationship between the relational model and mathematics and/or logic, relation valued attributes, and more. Finally, Part IV consists of a collection of recent interviews with myself (one of them joint with Hugh Darwen).

The book doesn't have to be read in sequence—most of the chapters are fairly independent of one another. Because they're independent, however, the chapters typically contain references and examples and figures whose numbering is unique only within the chapter in question. For the same reason, there's also a small amount of overlap among certain of the chapters; I apologize for this fact, but I felt it was better to preserve the independence of each individual chapter as much as possible.

Prerequisites

My target audience is database professionals. Thus, I assume you're somewhat familiar with both the relational model and the SQL language. However, certain relational and/or SQL concepts are reviewed briefly here and there (basically wherever I felt such explanations might be needed, or helpful).

A Note on the Text

If you've read this book's predecessor or indeed any of my previous writings, you'll know only too well that I tend to a somewhat excessive use of footnotes ... So you might enjoy, or at least appreciate, the following as much as I did when I came across it recently:

> There are scholars who footnote compulsively, six to a page, writing what amounts to two books at once. There are scholars whose frigid texts need some of the warmth and jollity they reserve for their footnotes and other scholars who write stale, dull footnotes like the stories brought inevitably to the minds of after-dinner speakers. There are scholars who write weasel footnotes, footnotes that alter the assertions in their texts. There are scholars who write feckless, irrelevant footnotes that leave their readers dumbstruck with confusion.

This wonderful piece is from *A Handbook for Scholars*, by M.-C. Van Leunen; I found it quoted in *The Pleasures of Counting*, by T. W. Körner (Cambridge University Press, 1996).

Publishing History

- Chapters 1 and 2, "Fifty Years of Relational: A Personal View," Parts I and II: Previously unpublished—and here let me thank and acknowledge my friends and colleagues Hugh Darwen, François de Sainte Marie, Heli Helskyaho, and Lauri Pietarinen for their review of, and helpful comments on, these two chapters (and Heli in particular for getting me to write them in the first place).

- Chapter 3, "Gödel, Russell, Codd: A Recursive Golden Crowd"; Chapter 4, "To Be Is to Be a Value of a Variable"; and Chapter 5, "And Now for Something Completely Computational": Revised and extended versions of Chapters 13, 14, and 15, respectively, from my book *Logic and Databases* (Trafford, 2007). Those chapters in turn were based on a series of papers with the generic title "A Discussion of Certain Criticisms Concerning *The Third Manifesto*" (*www.thethirdmanifesto.com*, August 2006).

- Chapter 6, "*SQL and Relational Theory*: A Response to Criticism": Previously unpublished.

- Chapter 7, "Terminology Used in the Relational Model": Hugely expanded version of a note originally prepared in response to a question from Jonathan Gennick in 2016.

- Chapter 8, "Drawing Relations as Tables": Revised and extended version of material from Chapter 9 ("Equality Comparisons etc.") from my book *Type Inheritance and Relational Theory: Subtypes, Supertypes, and Substitutability* (O'Reilly, 2016).

- Chapter 9, "Mathematics and the Relational Model"; Chapter 10, "Relational Algebra"; Chapter 11, "Relvar Predicates"; Chapter 12, "Relation Valued Attributes"; Chapter 13, "Normalization and Keys"; Chapter 14, "Missing Information"; Chapter 15, "Values, Variables, Types, and Constraints"; and Chapter 16, "SQL Criticisms": Revised and hugely expanded version of sections from an appendix to my book *Logic and Databases* (Trafford, 2007).

- Chapter 17, "No to SQL! No to NoSQL!": Originally published in *NoCOUG Journal 27*, No. 3 (August 2013). Republished here with minor revisions by permission of Iggy Fernandez and Hugh Darwen.

- Chapter 18, "The SimpleTalk Interview": Originally published online at *http://www.red-gate.com/simple-talk/* (August 22nd, 2014) under the title "Chris Date and the Relational Model." Republished here with minor revisions by permission of Richard Morris.

- Chapter 19, "Looking Backward, Looking Forward": Originally published in *NoCOUG Journal 33*, No. 4 (November 2019) under the title "Down Memory Lane with C. J. Date." Republished here with minor revisions by permission of Iggy Fernandez.

C. J. Date
Healdsburg, California
2020

Part I

A BIT OF HISTORY

Chapter 1

Fifty Years of Relational:

A Personal View

Part I

Those who cannot remember the past are condemned to repeat it.
Often quoted in the form:
Those who don't know history are doomed to repeat it.
—George Santayana:
The Life of Reason (1905)

This chapter and the next together consist of the script for a live presentation on the history of relational databases and the relational model. I originally wrote them in 2019—a fairly auspicious date as far as we're concerned, because it was both

- The 50th anniversary, or in other words the golden jubilee, of the birth of the relational model, and

- The 25th anniversary, or in other words the silver jubilee, of the birth of *The Third Manifesto* (about which I'll have quite a bit more to say in Chapter 2).

So I've divided the presentation into two parts accordingly, corresponding to the first 25 years and the second 25 years, respectively, of relational history—or my own view of that history, at any rate. The first part is based on a presentation I gave as an opener at the various conferences that were held in 1994-1995 to celebrate the relational model's own silver jubilee;[1] the second part is new.

So the relational model was born in 1969—on August 19th, 1969, to be precise, when Ted Codd's very first paper on the relational model was published:

■ E. F. Codd: "Derivability, Redundancy, and Consistency of Relations Stored in Large Data Banks," IBM Research Report RJ599 (August 19th, 1969)

(That date happened to be Ted's own 46th birthday, by the way.) The following year, he beefed the paper up slightly, changed its title, and republished it in *Communications of the ACM*:

■ E. F. Codd: "A Relational Model of Data for Large Shared Data Banks," *Communications of the ACM 13*, No. 6 (June 1970)

And basically because it was published outside IBM—and published, moreover, in such a widely respected and widely disseminated journal—that 1970 paper is much better known than its 1969 predecessor. However, that doesn't alter the fact that it was really 1969 that marked the start of the relational era.[2]

As for myself, I was in almost at the beginning. In 1970, like Ted, I was working for IBM—actually at the IBM development lab in Hursley, England, where I'd been given the job of figuring out what to do about database support in the language PL/I. (The Hursley lab had "the PL/I mission" within IBM at that time.) So I studied, and experimented with, IBM's own database product, the hierarchic system IMS; and I studied the CODASYL network proposals, which were a hot item at the time; and I studied Ted's relational stuff. And to me it was plain as a pikestaff that Ted's relational way was the way to go! My own background is in mathematics (primarily pure mathematics), and here for the first time in my computing career was something that actually made use of some of the stuff I'd learned at university. So I jumped on the relational bandwagon, you might say, almost at once. In other words, my own role in relational database—

---

[1] Boston, June 1994; Chicago, December 1994; Toronto, March 1995; London, Stockholm, and Rome, all in October 1995.

[2] Of course Ted had been thinking about this stuff for quite a while before he published his 1969 paper—I think he probably began work on it sometime in the summer of 1968. By the way, I'd like to stress the fact that he did do all of that work singlehanded! Ted was indeed the sole inventor and "onlie begetter" of the original relational model.

and in particular my role, I think it's fair to say, as one of Ted's earliest and strongest supporters—dates back to 1970, the year his ideas first began to be widely promulgated in the database community at large. (Such as it was!—I mean, there wasn't much of a "database community," as such, at that time anyway.)

One further preliminary remark: This presentation is very much a theoretician's view of the history; I'm not going to say all that much about products or implementations. But then the relational model *is* theory! What's more, as I've argued for years, *theory is practical* ... The whole point of that theory is to allow us to build products that are 100% practical. Let me elaborate. It's a sad commentary, on our modern education system not least, that people often want to dismiss or avoid theory; there seems to be a widespread perception that if something is theoretical, it can't be practical. ("Don't bother me with that theoretical stuff, I'm a practical guy.") My own position is exactly the opposite: namely, that if something isn't based on solid theory, it's likely to be very unpractical indeed—not least because it'll probably be hard to understand.

Here's another way to say the same thing (or a similar thing, or a related thing, or *something*): In the database world there are model people and there are implementation people. Of course, the model people—and I'm proud to be one of them—certainly need the implementation people, in order to get their abstract theoretical ideas realized in concrete practical terms. But the implementation people need the model people too, in order to have some hope of implementing something that works properly. In this connection, I'd like to draw your attention to one of my favorite quotes. It's from Leonardo da Vinci, and thus dates back over 500 years (!):

> Those who are enamored of practice without theory are like a pilot who goes into a ship without rudder or compass and never has any certainty where he [*sic*] is going. **Practice should always be based upon a sound knowledge of theory.** (*Italics and boldface added.*)

Aside: Of course, one of the great things about theory is that it helps you think about things *clearly* and *precisely*. But that reminds me of a story ... As you might know, for many years I made my living teaching seminars and classes on all of this relational stuff ... And people would sometimes ask me: "Don't you get bored, teaching the same stuff over and over again?" To which my reply was always the same: First, it isn't the same stuff—it's growing all the time—and what's more my understanding of it is growing all the time too (I'm always learning myself); and in any case, second, even if it *were* the same stuff over and over, you can still get questions you never heard before, which makes it interesting. And here's an example. I was teaching one of my classes, and hammering away on this point about the importance of theory, and in particular on how it helps you *think precisely* ... And this guy puts up his hand and says: "Why is it important to think precisely?"

That was right out of left field! I mean, that was certainly a question I'd never heard before. So I said: "Well, I don't know exactly"—which I thought was a pretty damn good answer, on the spur of the moment.

Some people in the audience got the point and laughed, but I don't think the guy who asked the question did. *End of aside.*

STRUCTURE OF THE PRESENTATION

Let me now begin my survey of the first 25 years (i.e., from 1969 to 1994, more or less). Now, I don't want to say too much about what I personally did during that time; in other words, I don't want this to be too self-indulgent. (Some people might think it is anyway—and if you're one of them, then I apologize ahead of time.) However, I do just want to mention my book *An Introduction to Database Systems*, which I believe did help to spread the relational message in the early days. The first edition of that book was published in 1975, and in fact I think it was the first book of any kind, anywhere, on database technology.

By the way, that book was actually written in the period late 1971 to early 1972, and by rights it should have been published in 1972. However, it was delayed for nearly three years by all kinds of obstructionism on the part of certain persons inside IBM. No names, no pack drill!—but if you want to buy me a beer sometime I might tell you more about it all.

Anyway, here's the way I've structured this first half of the presentation. Basically I've divided it up into four main sections:

- *Original contributions:* Here I'll briefly survey the major early relational papers by Ted Codd and others.

- *The historical context:* These days we take relational ideas so much for granted that it's hard for some people—especially (ahem) people who might be a little younger than I am, and perhaps have more hair—to appreciate just what the world was like before Ted came along.

- *The battles for acceptance:* Here the title says it all, pretty much.

■   *Milestones:* And here I'll summarize what seem to me to be some of the most significant events during those first 25 years.

ORIGINAL CONTRIBUTIONS

OK, let me begin with a list, in chronological order, of what I regard as Codd's most important relational papers. There are six of them:

1. "Derivability, Redundancy, and Consistency of Relations Stored in Large Data Banks" (1969)

2. "A Relational Model of Data for Large Shared Data Banks" (1970)

3. "A Data Base Sublanguage Founded on the Relational Calculus" (1971)

4. "Relational Completeness of Data Base Sublanguages" (1972)

5. "Further Normalization of the Data Base Relational Model" (1972)

6. "Interactive Support for Nonprogrammers: The Relational and Network Approaches" (1974)

These papers were absolutely staggering in their originality. Among other things, they changed, and changed permanently, the way database management was perceived in the IT world. More specifically, they transformed what had previously been nothing but a ragbag of tricks and ad hoc techniques into a solid scientific endeavor.

Now, I've already said a little about the first two papers in the list.[3] Let me just say a few quick words about the other four:

---

[3] Though I should note that no. 2, the 1970 paper, was subsequently republished in *Communications of the ACM*'s own silver jubilee issue as one of a very select list of "Milestones of Research." To give some idea of the caliber of the items in that list, here are some of the others: Dijkstra's paper on the THE operating system and his first paper on concurrency control; Tony Hoare's papers "An Axiomatic Basis for Computer Programming" and "Communicating Sequential Processes"; Niklaus Wirth's paper on program development by stepwise refinement; Ritchie and Thompson's paper on UNIX; Rivest, Shamir, and Adleman's paper on public key encryption; and so on.

■ No. 3 was the one where Ted defined what was probably the very first relational language, "Data Sublanguage ALPHA." ALPHA was based on relational calculus; it was never implemented as such, but it was quite influential on the design of various other languages that were, including QUEL, and QBE, and also (though to a lesser extent) SQL.

■ No. 4—much the hardest to understand, incidentally—was the one where he formally defined the relational algebra and relational calculus and defined an algorithm ("Codd's Reduction Algorithm") for mapping any expression in the calculus into an equivalent one in the algebra.

■ No. 5 was the one where he introduced the fundamental ideas of normalization and defined the first three normal forms.

■ And no. 6—well, I'll have a bit more to say about no. 6 later, so let me skip that one for now.

And here's a summary of what I regard as Ted's major contributions, based on these six papers:

■ His biggest overall achievement was to make database management into a science. In other words, he put the field on a solid scientific footing, by providing a theoretical framework, the relational model, within which a variety of important problems could be addressed in a scientific manner. Thus, the relational model really serves as the basis for a *theory* of data. (Indeed, the term "relational theory" is preferable in some ways to the term "relational model," and it might have been nice if Ted had used it. But he didn't.)

■ As a consequence of the previous point, he introduced a welcome and sorely needed note of clarity and rigor into the database field.

■ He introduced not only the relational model in particular, but the whole idea of a data model in general.

■ He stressed the importance of the distinction—regrettably still widely misunderstood, even today—between model and implementation.

- He saw the potential of using predicate logic as a foundation for database management.

- He defined both a relational algebra and a relational calculus as a basis for dealing with data in relational form.

- He defined (albeit only informally) that first relational language, "Data Sublanguage ALPHA."

- He introduced the crucial concept of functional dependence and defined the first three normal forms accordingly.

- He defined the key notion of essentiality. (That's what paper no. 6 is all about. As I've said, I'll come back to that paper later—but I'm afraid details of essentiality as such are beyond the scope of this presentation.)

However, there's one thing I must make very clear before I go any further. Of course I admire and am hugely grateful for the work Ted did in the late 1960s and early 1970s—and so should we all be; indeed, we all of us owe our very livelihood to him and that work! But it's important not to be blinded by such feelings into uncritical acceptance of everything he said or wrote, and it's important not to accept him as the sole authority on relational matters. Indeed, it's to his credit that Ted himself is on record as agreeing with this position. In an interview in *Data Base Newsletter 10*, No. 2 (March 1982), he stated explicitly that "I see relational theory as simply a body of theory to which many people are contributing in different ways." And many people have indeed made contributions to relational theory since it was first introduced, and in my view some of those contributions have been of major importance. In fact, let me mention a few of them right away:

- *System R:* System R was a relational prototype built in the IBM research lab in San Jose, California, in the mid 1970s. The broad objective was to show that a system could be relational and yet still deliver reasonable performance, something a lot of people were skeptical about at the time. In this aim they succeeded admirably—in particular, they pioneered various optimization and compilation techniques—and in fact I think it's probably true that, more than any other single project, System R is responsible for getting relational technology to start its move into the mainstream.[4]

Of course, something else that System R pioneered (most unfortunately, in my opinion!) was its use of SQL as the user language—so that qualifier "relational" should probably be set in quotation marks every time it appears in the previous paragraph. Now, I really don't want to say much about SQL in this presentation. After all, this is supposed to be a *relational* presentation, and one of the most obviously noticeable things about SQL is how unrelational it is.[5] However, I do want to say that, in my opinion, SQL is one of the worst designed languages I've ever seen. Its huge commercial success and its general influence on the database world are certainly not due to its technical merits—such as they are—but are instead a rather damning commentary on the power exerted, back in the 1970s and 1980s, by a certain large corporation on the way we did business at the time.

Be all that as it may, here are a couple of important System R publications:

1. M. M. Astrahan et al.: "System R: Relational Approach to Database Management" (June 1976). This paper describes System R as it was originally conceived.

2. M. W. Blasgen et al.: "System R: An Architectural Overview" (February 1981). And this one describes System R as it became by the time it was fully implemented.

■ *INGRES:* There were two "big" prototypes back in the mid 1970s, System R and INGRES (pronounced *in'gress*). INGRES was also done in California, at UC Berkeley, so System R and INGRES were kind of competitors for a while (and as a matter of fact INGRES had a lot of influence on products too for several years). Also INGRES had a much

---

[4] So perhaps System R's contribution had more to do with practice than theory. But its pioneering work on optimization (among other things) certainly had its theoretical side, so I think it's fair to include System R in the present list. *Note:* Analogous remarks apply to INGRES also, the next item in my list.

[5] But if SQL isn't relational, how then can we reasonably say that SQL systems are relational systems? Good question! I have a good answer to it, too, but I don't want cause unnecessary offense, so I think it's better if I don't give that answer here.

better user language!—namely, QUEL—but (sadly) QUEL eventually lost out to SQL, at least in the commercial world. Publications:

1. M. R. Stonebraker, E. Wong, P. Kreps, and G. D. Held: "The Design and Implementation of INGRES" (September 1976)

2. Michael Stonebraker (ed.): *The INGRES Papers: The Anatomy of a Relational Database Management System* (1986)

- *IS/1 and PRTV:* I'll say more about these prototypes (which were done at the IBM Scientific Centre in Peterlee, England) when I get to the "milestones," later. Here let me just note a couple of publications:

1. P. A. V. Hall, P. Hitchcock, and S. J. P. Todd: "An Algebra of Relations for Machine Computation" (January 1975)

2. S. J. P. Todd: "The Peterlee Relational Test Vehicle—A System Overview" (1976)

- *Query-By-Example (QBE):* This one was also done in IBM, at the research lab in Yorktown Heights, New York. The nice thing about it was this: Many people were scared off by Codd's relational calculus, thinking it all looked rather terrifyingly mathematical. But the concepts involved are actually very simple, and what QBE showed was that it was possible to wrap a layer of syntactic sugar around those concepts and make them very palatable indeed. Here's the first of many papers on the subject by QBE's designer, Moshé Zloof:

1. Moshé M. Zloof: "Query-By-Example" (May 1975)

- *Optimization:* Optimization is both a challenge for and a strength of relational systems—a challenge, because it must be done in order to achieve reasonable performance ("if you don't do it, you're dead"); a strength, because user requests in a relational system (unlike other systems) are at a sufficiently high semantic level that they're optimizable in the first place. And the very first paper on such matters, so far as I'm aware, was written by Frank Palermo, a protégé of Ted Codd's at the IBM research lab in San Jose, California:

1. Frank Palermo: "A Data Base Search Problem" (1972)

■ *Dependency theory:* The following are two crucial papers out of what's since become a pretty large field in its own right:

1. W. W. Armstrong: "Dependency Structures of Data Base Relationships" (August 1974)

2. Ronald Fagin: "Normal Forms and Relational Database Operators" (May/June 1979)

I'll elaborate on them briefly here. First, Armstrong's paper abstracted from Ted's notion of functional dependence and began the study of dependency theory as a branch of—well, mathematics, really, or maybe logic—in its own right. Second, Fagin's paper is the definitive statement— the last word, if you like—on what might be called "classical" normalization (in particular, it's the paper that defined fifth normal form, 5NF).

THE HISTORICAL CONTEXT

No matter what field you work in, you really owe it to yourself to know something of the history of that field. As Santayana said (more or less), those who don't know history are doomed to repeat it. And in fact I do have some concerns in this connection, which I'll touch on later, in Part II of this presentation.

Anyway, we're so used to relational technology these days, and think of it as so "obvious" and "natural," that I suspect that many people don't even know what the database scene was like before Ted Codd came along. So I want to spend a few minutes talking about "the bad old days."

Actually, talking of Ted Codd: You might not know this, but in fact there are some people who dispute Ted's claim to be the inventor of the relational model ... Indeed, there's considerable evidence to suggest that the true founder of the field was *William Shakespeare*. Yes! Here's Shakespeare's sonnet no. 122:

Thy gift, thy tables, are within my brain
Full charactered with lasting memory,
Which shall above that idle rank remain
Beyond all date, even to eternity;
Or at the least so long as brain and heart
Have faculty by nature to subsist,
Till each to razed oblivion yield his part
Of thee, thy record never can be missed.
That poor retention could not so much hold,
Nor need I tallies thy dear love to score;
Therefore to give them from me was I bold,
To trust those tables that receive thee more.
　　To keep an adjunct to remember thee
　　Were to import forgetfulness in me.

(With acknowledgments to Pam McFarland, who first brought to my attention the fact that the Bard was relational hip.)

On closer examination, however, we can see that Shakespeare isn't really claiming proprietorship over the relational model, but is in fact addressing Ted and admitting that it was all really Ted's doing—

Thy gift, *thy* tables, are within my brain ...

So the Dark Lady of the sonnets is clearly Ted Codd (?).

I'm not sure about that "beyond all Date," however! (I've added an initial cap.)

On a more serious note, here's an extended quote from the IMS manuals as they were back in those days (it's from the IMS Database Administration Guide, to be precise):

Logically deleting a logical child prevents further access to the logical child using its logical parent. Unidirectional logical child segments are assumed to be logically deleted. A logical parent is considered logically deleted when all its logical children are physically deleted. For physically paired logical relationships, the physical child paired to the logical child must also be physically deleted before the logical parent is considered logically deleted.

Physical Parent of a Virtually Paired Logical Child: When ... all physical children that are virtually paired logical children are logically deleted, the physical parent segment is physically deleted.

You see the kind of thing we used to have to put up with?

Mind you, I'm not sure things have improved all that much ... Here's a quote from the SQL standard:

> However, because global temporary table contents are distinct within SQL-sessions, and created local temporary tables are distinct within <module>s within SQL-sessions, the *effective* <schema name> of the schema in which the global temporary table or the created local temporary table is instantiated is an implementation-dependent <schema name> that may be thought of as having been effectively derived from the <schema name> of the schema in which the global temporary table or created local temporary table is defined and the implementation-dependent SQL-session identifier associated with the SQL-session.[6]

By the way, I hope you're paying attention. There's going to be a short quiz later.

Anyway, this sentence (yes, it's all one sentence!) is taken from a section of the standard titled—and intended, believe it or not, to explain the concept of—"Tables." I never realized tables were so complicated.

But let's get back to the historical context. My next example is taken from "The Great Debate," which was held in 1974 and was basically a debate over relations vs. networks (or more specifically the network model, à la CODASYL).[7] First let me explain the background.

During the week of July 23rd-27th, 1973, while I was still working for IBM in England, Ted Codd and I both attended a database conference in Montreal, Canada. I remember an awful lot of nonsense being talked at that event!—a state of affairs that made me realize that the database field was most certainly still in its infancy at that time. What made it interesting, though, was that Charlie Bachman had just been named the 1973 ACM Turing Award winner, and he did a dry run for us of his Turing Award lecture, "The Programmer as Navigator."

Now, Charlie was the lead designer behind a system called IDS, which the CODASYL proposals were largely based on, and so Ted and I already had a good idea of what he, Charlie, was going to say. We also both knew Charlie's

---

[6] In the interest of accuracy I should note that the offending text is taken from an early (1992) version of the standard—it's been revised in subsequent versions. Observe that I say *revised*, though; I don't say *improved*.

[7] "The Great Debate" isn't my title—I got it from a report on the debate by Robert L. Ashenhurst that appeared the following month (i.e., in the June 1974 issue) of *Communications of the ACM*, of which Ashenhurst was Editor in Chief at the time.

"navigational" ideas were *not* the way to go—Ted's relational ideas were. So of course Ted wanted to engage Charlie, and the audience, in an argument on the relative merits of the two schemes, right then and there. I wasn't too happy about that idea, though, because I knew that to do the job properly (a) we'd need more time to prepare our position, and moreover (b) we'd need more time to present our position, too—certainly more time than we could reasonably expect to be given, or would even be appropriate, in that conference setting. So I suggested to Ted that he not attempt to debate with Charlie then and there, but rather that he issue a challenge to hold a *proper* debate at some future time. And Ted agreed.

So Charlie gave his talk. I could feel Ted almost quivering with anticipation in the seat next to me, waiting to leap up to the microphone the second Charlie finished. Of course, we both knew everyone expected him to say *something*—probably offering some detailed technical criticism of what Charlie had presented. But what Ted actually did say was as follows, more or less: "First let me congratulate Charlie on his Turing Award. It couldn't happen to a nicer guy" (and so on and so forth) ... Then he continued: "But none of that alters the fact that on this issue Charlie is, unfortunately, *dead wrong*." And he went on to say that a Q&A session following a presentation wasn't the right forum for the kind of discussion that was really needed on these matters, and that therefore he and Chris Date would like to issue a challenge (etc., etc.). And that was the origin of what came to be called The Great Debate, which was held at the ACM SIGMOD conference in Ann Arbor, Michigan, the following May (1974), and was regarded by many people as one of the defining moments in the ongoing battle between the old way of doing things and Ted's new relational way.

Now, Ted and I took this debate very seriously, and we prepared a couple of detailed technical papers to support the arguments we planned to make. In particular, Ted wrote the paper that appeared as no. 6 in that list of papers I showed earlier, and as part of that paper he included the following example ("the machine shop scheduling example"). I should make it very clear, though, that Ted didn't invent the example—he took it from a tutorial paper on CODASYL.[8] The application is as follows:

---

[8] R. L. Frank and E. H. Sibley: "The Data Base Task Group Report: An Illustrative Example," ISDOS Working Paper No. 71, U.S. National Technical Information Service Document AD-759-267 (February 1973). *Note:* The Data Base Task Group (abbreviated DBTG) mentioned in Frank and Sibley's title was a task group of CODASYL (Conference on Data Systems Languages). CODASYL in turn was the organization behind the original development of COBOL; however, when people use the name CODASYL in a database context, what they're referring to is the DBTG Report, which was published in April 1971— over eighteen months, be it noted, *after* the publication of Codd's first relational paper.

Given a machine X, a job number Y, the desired start date A for the job, and the desired stop date B, find a person who can operate machine X and is not scheduled at all between date A and date B, and schedule this person.

Here then is the CODASYL solution. First the schema:

```
SCHEMA NAME IS EMPLOYEE-BASE;
    PRIVACY LOCK IS SCHED-SCHEMA
        OR PROCEDURE SECURE-SCHEDULE;
    AREA NAME IS PANDJ-AREA.
    AREA MED-AREA;
    PRIVACY FOR UPDATE IS PROCEDURE MED-DEPT.
    AREA SECRET; ON OPEN CALL SECURE-PROC;
    ON CLOSE CALL LOCK-PROC.
    AREA REST; PRIVACY IS PROCEDURE SCHED-DEPT
        OR PROCEDURE SECURE-PROC.
    AREA XP; AREA IS TEMPORARY; PRIVACY TEMP-AREA.
RECORD NAME IS PERSON;
    LOCATION MODE IS CALC EMP-HASH USING
        IDENTIFICATION-NUM DUPLICATES ARE NOT ALLOWED;
    WITHIN PANDJ-AREA;
    ON DELETE CALL MICROFILM-RECORDER;
    PRIVACY LOCK FOR DELETE ONLY IS PROCEDURE EMP-LEFT.
        NAME; PICTURE IS "A(20)".
        IDENTIFICATION-NUM; PICTURE IS "9(6)".
        DATE-OF-BIRTH; PICTURE IS "99X99X99".
    1 AGE; PICTURE "99V9"; IS VIRTUAL RESULT OF
        AGE-CALC USING DATE-OF-BIRTH, TODAYS-DATE.
    1 SALARY; TYPE IS FIXED 7,2; CHECK IS RANGE OF
        8000.00 THRU 75000.00.
    1 EDUCATION; TYPE FIXED 2.
    1 EDUCATION-INFO; OCCURS EDUCATION TIMES.
        2 DEGREE; PICTURE "AA".
        2 START-DATE; PICTURE "99X99X99".
        2 COMPLETION-DATE; PICTURE "99X99X99", CHECK
            NOT-BEFORE USING EDUC-OK, START-DATE.
        2 DEGREE-RECEIVED-FROM PIC "A(20)".
RECORD NAME JOB;
    LOCATION IS VIA JOBSET SET;
    WITHIN PANDJ-AREA.
    1 JOB-CODE; PIC "X(4)".
    1 START-DATE; PIC "99X99X99".
    1 FINISH-DATE; PIC "99X99X99".
    1 PERFORMANCE-RATING; PIC "99V9".
RECORD IS MEDICAL;
    LOCATION MODE CALC USING DISEASE
        DUPLICATES ARE ALLOWED;
    WITHIN MED-AREA.
    1 ABSENCE-DATES; PICTURE "99X99X99X99X99X99".
    1 DISEASE; PICTURE IS "A(30)".
    1 NOTE-PAGES; TYPE IS REAL FIXED DECIMAL 2.
```

```
       1 NOTES; OCCURS NOTE-PAGES TIMES.
            2 NOTE-PAGE; PICTURE "A(500)".
RECORD NAME IS MACHINE; LOCATION MODE IS CALC
       MACH-HASH USING MACH-NUMBER
       DUPLICATES NOT ALLOWED;
       WITHIN REST, SECRET AREA-ID MACH-LOCATOR;
       PRIVACY LOCK PROCEDURE IS-IT-SECURE.
       1 MACH-TYPE; PICTURE "999".
       1 MACH-NUMBER; PICTURE "9(5)".
       1 SCHEDULE; PICTURE "99".
       1 SCHEDULED-USE; OCCURS SCHEDULE TIMES.
            2 JOB-CODE; PICTURE "9(8)".
            2 SCHEDULE-COMPLETION; TYPE IS DATE.
            /* NOTE IMPLEMENTOR-TYPE DATE. */
            2 SCHEDULE-START; TYPE IS DATE.
            2 WORKER-IDENTIFICATION; PICTURE "9(6)".
       /* NOTE THERE WOULD BE OTHER ELEMENTS,
          BUT IRRELEVANT TO THIS EXAMPLE */
RECORD SKILL-LINK; LOCATION MODE IS CALC
       USING SKILL-CODE, DUPLICATES ALLOWED;
       WITHIN REST.
       1 SKILL-CODE; PICTURE "999".
       1 SK-SALARY;
            VIRTUAL SOURCE IS SALARY OF OWNER OF HAS-SKILL.
       1 JOB-RATE; PICTURE "9(2)V9(2)";
            IS VIRTUAL RESULT OF AVERAGE-RATE
            USING SK-SALARY.
       1 MACH-SK; VIRTUAL SOURCE IS MACH-TYPE
            OF OWNER OF NEEDS-SKILL.
RECORD NAME IS CHECK-PERSON;
       LOCATION MODE IS CALC USING CHECK-PERSON-ITEM
            DUPLICATES NOT ALLOWED;
       WITHIN XP.
       /* NOTE: THIS IS THE TEMPORARY AREA. */
       01 CHECK-PERSON-ITEM;
            TYPE IS DATABASE-KEY.
       /* NOTE: THIS ASSUMES THAT A CALC-KEY
          CAN BE A DATABASE-KEY. */
RECORD NAME IS CHECK-MACHINE;
       LOCATION MODE IS CALC USING CHECK-PERSON-ITEM;
            DUPLICATES NOT ALLOWED;
       WITHIN XP.
       01 CHECK-MACHINE-ITEM;
            TYPE IS DATABASE-KEY.
SET NAME IS JOBSET;
       ORDER IS NEXT;
       OWNER IS PERSON.
       MEMBER IS JOB, MANDATORY, AUTOMATIC;
       SET OCCURRENCE SELECTION IS THRU CURRENT OF SET.
SET NAME IS MEDSET;
       ORDER IS LAST;
       OWNER IS PERSON.
       MEMBER IS MEDICAL, OPTIONAL, AUTOMATIC,
```

```
            SET OCCURRENCE SELECTION IS THRU CURRENT OF SET.
    SET NEEDS-SKILL;
        ORDER IS SORTED DUPLICATES ARE ALLOWED;
        OWNER IS MACHINE.
        MEMBER IS SKILL-LINK OPTIONAL MANUAL
            LINKED TO OWNER;
        DESCENDING KEY SKILL-CODE;
        SET SELECTION THRU CURRENT OF SET.
    SET NAME IS HAS-SKILL;
        ORDER IS SORTED DUPLICATES ARE FIRST;
        OWNER IS PERSON.
        MEMBER IS SKILL-LINK OPTIONAL MANUAL
            LINKED TO OWNER;
        ASCENDING KEY SKILL-CODE;
        SELECTION IS LOCATION MODE OF OWNER.
    SET NAME IS WORKING-ON;
        ORDER LAST;
        OWNER IS PERSON.
        MEMBER IS MACHINE OPTIONAL MANUAL LINKED TO OWNER
        DUPLICATES NOT ALLOWED FOR SCHEDULE-START;
        SEARCH KEY IS SCHEDULE-START, MACH-NUMBER USING INDEX
            NAME IS MACH-WORK-INDEX DUPLICATES ARE NOT ALLOWED;
        SET OCCURRENCE SELECTION IS THRU
            LOCATION MODE OF OWNER.
        /* NOTE THIS IS CALC. */
    SET SYS-MACHINE;
        ORDER IS SORTED INDEXED NAME IS MACHINE-INDEX
        DUPLICATES ARE NOT ALLOWED;
        ON REMOVE CALL SINKING-FUND;
        PRIVACY LOCK FOR REMOVE IS PROCEDURE MACH-AWAY;
        OWNER IS SYSTEM.
        MEMBER IS MACHINE OPTIONAL AUTOMATIC;
        ASCENDING KEY IS MACH-NUMBER.
        /* NOTE NO SELECTION CLAUSE FOR SINGULAR SETS. */
```

And here's the sample application as such:

```
IDENTIFICATION DIVISION.
    PROGRAM-ID. SCHEDULE-PERSON-TO-MACHINE.
    PRIVACY KEY FOR COMPILE IS 'START-SCHEMA';
    PRIVACY KEY OF REST AREA IS PROCEDURE 'DEPT-SCHED'.
    AUTHOR. R.L.FRANK AND E.H.SIBLEY.
    DATE-WRITTEN. JANUARY 1973.
ENVIRONMENT DIVISION.
DATA DIVISION.
SCHEMA SECTION.
    INVOKE SUB-SCHEMA
        SCHEDULE-ID OF SCHEMA EMPLOYEE-BASE.
FILE SECTION.

WORKING-STORAGE-SECTION.
```

```
PROCEDURE DIVISION.
    OPEN PANDJ-AREA, WITH-HOLD, REST.
    OPEN non DBTG files.
FIND-MACHINE.
    OPEN XP.
    MOVE MACHINE-NUMBER TO MACH-NUMBER.
    FIND MACHINE RECORD VIA SYS-MACHINE USING
        MACH-NUMBER.
    IF ERROR-STATUS = 326 GO TO
        NOT-IN-DATA-BASE.
FOUND-REC.
    MOVE CURRENCY STATUS FOR MACHINE RECORD TO
        SAVE-MACHINE.
GET-NEXT-SKILL.
    FIND NEXT SKILL-LINK RECORD OF NEEDS-SKILL SET.
    IF ERROR-STATUS = 326 OR = 307 GO TO NO-ONE-AVAILABLE.
    FIND OWNER IN HAS-SKILL OF CURRENT OF SKILL-LINK RECORD.
    IF ERROR-STATUS = 322 THEN GO TO GET-NEXT-SKILL.
    MOVE CURRENCY STATUS FOR PERSON RECORD
        TO SAVE-PERSON.
    MOVE CURRENCY STATUS FOR
        PERSON RECORD TO CHECK-PERSON-ITEM.
    STORE CHECK-PERSON.
    IF ERROR-STATUS = 1205
        GO TO GET-NEXT-SKILL.
CHECK-PERSONS-SCHEDULE.
    FIND NEXT SKILL-LINK RECORD OF HAS-SKILL SET;
        SUPPRESS NEEDS-SKILL CURRENCY UPDATES.
    IF ERROR-STATUS = 307 GO TO PERSON-IS-FREE.
    FIND OWNER IN NEEDS-SKILL OF
        CURRENT OF SKILL-LINK RECORD;
        SUPPRESS NEEDS-SKILL CURRENCY UPDATES.
    IF ERROR-STATUS = 322
        GO TO CHECK-PERSONS-SCHEDULE.
    MOVE CURRENCY STATUS FOR MACHINE RECORD
        TO CHECK-MACHINE-ITEM.
    STORE CHECK-MACHINE.
    IF ERROR-STATUS = 1205 GO TO CHECK-PERSONS-SCHEDULE.
    GET MACHINE.
    MOVE 1 TO AVAILABLE.
    PERFORM SEE-IF-SCHEDULED THRU SEE-EXIT VARYING
        SCHEDULE-COUNT FROM 1 BY 1 UNTIL SCHEDULE-COUNT
        IS GREATER THAN SCHEDULE.
    IF AVAILABLE = 0 GO TO GET-NEXT-SKILL.
    GO TO CHECK-PERSONS-SCHEDULE.
SEE-IF-SCHEDULED.
    /* NOTE: HERE WE WILL MARK AS NOT BEING AVAILABLE
        ANYONE WHO IS SCHEDULED FOR THAT TIME. */
    IF SCHEDULE-DATE-START IS GREATER THAN SCHEDULE-START
        IN MACHINE (SCHEDULE-COUNT) AND LESS THAN
        SCHEDULE-COMPLETION IN MACHINE (SCHEDULE-COUNT)
        GO TO PERSON-NOT-AVAILABLE.
    IF SCHEDULE-DATE-END IS GREATER THAN SCHEDULE-START
```

```
            IN MACHINE (SCHEDULE-COUNT) AND LESS THAN
            SCHEDULE-COMPLETION IN MACHINE (SCHEDULE-COUNT)
            GO TO PERSON-NOT-AVAILABLE.
      GO TO SEE-EXIT.
PERSON-NOT-AVAILABLE.
      FIND PERSON USING SAVE-PERSON,
            SUPPRESS ALL CURRENCY UPDATES.
      GET PERSON.
      IF IDENTIFICATION-NUM IN PERSON IS EQUAL
            WORKER-IDENTIFICATION IN MACHINE
            (SCHEDULE-COUNT) MOVE 0 TO AVAILABLE,
            GO TO SEE-EXIT.
      MOVE WORKER-IDENTIFICATION IN MACHINE
            (SCHEDULE-COUNT) TO IDENTIFICATION-NUM IN PERSON.
      FIND PERSON RECORD, SUPPRESS HAS-SKILL
            CURRENCY UPDATES.
      MOVE CURRENCY STATUS FOR PERSON RECORD
            TO CHECK-PERSON-ITEM.
      STORE CHECK-PERSON.
SEE-EXIT. EXIT.
PERSON-IS-FREE.
/* NOTE: HERE WE GET THE MACHINE WE WANTED TO SCHEDULE. */
      FIND MACHINE USING SAVE-MACHINE.
      GET MACHINE.
      FIND PERSON USING SAVE-PERSON.
      GET PERSON.
      ADD 1 TO SCHEDULE IN MACHINE.
      MOVE IDENTIFICATION-NUM IN PERSON
            TO WORKER-IDENTIFICATION
            IN MACHINE (SCHEDULE IN MACHINE).
      MOVE SCHEDULE-DATE-START TO SCHEDULE-START IN MACHINE
            (SCHEDULE IN MACHINE).
      MOVE SCHEDULE-DATE-END TO SCHEDULE-COMPLETION IN MACHINE
            (SCHEDULE IN MACHINE).
      MOVE SCHEDULE-TASK TO JOB-CODE IN MACHINE (SCHEDULE IN
            MACHINE).
      MODIFY MACHINE.
      IF ERROR-STATUS = 803
            GO TO PERSON-IS-FREE.
      CLOSE XP.
      GO TO GET-NEW-MACHINE.
```

In his paper, Ted showed this CODASYL solution, and then went on to give a relational solution for the same problem, using his own ALPHA language. First the schema:[9]

---

[9] The schema part of the comparison isn't totally fair, because the relational schema shows only items that are pertinent to the sample application, while the network schema contains a great deal of additional (but irrelevant) material.

```
DOMAIN JOBNO    PIC X(4)
DOMAIN PNO      PIC 9(6)
DOMAIN MACHNO   PIC 9(5)
DOMAIN DATE     PIC 99X99X99
DOMAIN SKILLNO PIC 999

RELATION SCHED ( JOBNO , PNO , MACHNO ,
                 SCHED_START_DATE , SCHED_STOP_DATE )
         KEY ( JOBNO )
RELATION PERSON_SKILL ( PNO , SKILLNO )
         KEY ( PNO ,SKILLNO )
RELATION MACH_SKILL ( MACHNO , SKILLNO )
         KEY ( MACHNO , SKILLNO )
```

And here's the application proper:[10]

```
INSERT INTO SCHED ( PNO , MACHNO , JOBNO , START , STOP )
SELECT PNO , X , Y , A , B FROM PERSON_SKILL WHERE
EXISTS ( SELECT * FROM MACH_SKILL WHERE
         MACHNO = X AND SKILLNO = PERSON_SKILL.SKILLNO AND
         NOT EXISTS ( SELECT * FROM SCHED WHERE
                      PNO = PERSON_SKILL.PNO AND
                      START_DATE < B AND STOP_DATE > A ) ) ;
```

It's just one statement! And then, as Ted goes on to say (with, I presume, tongue firmly in cheek), "some comparative statistics may be of interest":[11]

	DBTG	SQL
GO TO	15	0
PERFORM UNTIL	1	0
currency indicators	10	0
IF	12	0
FIND	9	0
GET	4	0
STORE / INSERT	2	1
MODIFY	1	0
MOVE CURRENCY	4	0
other MOVEs	9	0
SUPPRESS CURRENCY	4	0
total statements (etc.)	>60	1
logic errors	≥ 2	0

---

[10] For reasons of familiarity I've replaced Ted's ALPHA solution by an SQL solution. Also, there's one slight piece of fudging in that solution—the statement shown will actually find and schedule *all* persons capable and available, not just one—but this state of affairs doesn't materially affect the big picture.

[11] For reasons not important here, the table of statistics as I give it differs in certain minor respects from that given in Ted's paper.

Note the last line in particular! The fact is, the DBTG "solution" actually contains at least two currency errors[12]—by which I mean errors in logic, not just simple syntax errors, of which there does also seem to be at least one. Here's another quote from Ted's paper:

> These statistics should not be interpreted as a criticism of [the authors Frank and Sibley]. Their objective was to provide a tutorial on the application of DBTG, and in this respect they succeeded rather well. The important thing to note is the elimination in the ALPHA code of branching, explicit iteration, and cursor control—an essential step toward providing general support for the nonprogramming user, and a desirable step toward removing a large burden of irrelevant decision making by the programmer.

By the way, that comment of Ted's that "they succeeded rather well" can be interpreted in at least two ways, can't it? Myself, I think he meant *exactly* what he said here.

And by the way again, one of the reviewers of an early draft of this script had this to say:

> The amount of code in [the CODASYL solution] is mind boggling ... And it's basically the same amount of code you need for current XML / Jason / MongoDB solutions.

If that's really true (and I have no reason to doubt it), then what an indictment of our field!

> *Aside:* While we're on the subject of comparing relational and nonrelational ways of doing things, there's another story I'd like to tell quickly. In the 1970s I was working on the design of a language called UDL (Unified Database Language), which was at least partly relational. And in 1978, I think it was, I was asked to give a presentation on that language at a GUIDE meeting in Albuquerque (GUIDE being one of the IBM user associations). I met with my session chairperson, Linda Jones, for a beer the night before, and she said I shouldn't just give UDL solutions to my various examples, I should give DL/I solutions too for comparison. (DL/I is the user language for IMS, of course.) "Good idea," I said, and started to write out such DL/I solutions then and there in the bar ... And of course I kept

---

[12] Simplifying somewhat, a currency error occurs in DBTG when the implicit "current position" in the database isn't what the application programmer thinks it is.

making mistakes, and having to start over, and then starting over *again*, and generally cursing and swearing and banging the table, etc., etc. ... And I looked up, and Linda was falling about laughing, and she said, "All we need do is show a video of you doing exactly what you're doing right now, and you'll have made your point." *End of aside.*

But this all touches on something else, something important. To spell it out: *The relational model isn't just "a better CODASYL."* In a way, us early relational advocates (and I certainly include myself in that camp, of course) did ourselves a major disservice in the early days. You see, we had to try and convince the world at large that relations were really a viable technology and could solve the same kinds of problems that hierarchies and networks could solve—and so we necessarily got into the business of doing comparisons between relational solutions and solutions using those older, prerelational technologies. And in so doing, we unwittingly reinforced the idea that relations and hierarchies and networks could sensibly *be* compared in such a way—with

a. The implication that relations and hierarchies and networks were all the same kind of animal, as it were, and with

b. The further implication that if relations did replace hierarchies and networks, then something else could come along and replace relations in their turn.

Well, I'd like to make it very clear now that such a perception is *wrong*. Relational really is different. It's the foundation. It's the principles. It's ... Well, what I'm trying to say is this: Even if (for whatever reasons) the system doesn't look particularly relational on the outside, it certainly ought to be relational on the inside. A DBMS that didn't support join, at least internally, would be like a computer that didn't support addition, at least internally. Relational is *fundamental*.

THE BATTLES FOR ACCEPTANCE

Anyway, as I hope you can see, the historical context was a mess. And you'd think that anyone like Ted with a good and reasonable proposal for getting out of that mess would be welcomed with open arms. Right? Well, you'd be wrong.

Yes, you'd be wrong. Ted spent a huge amount of his time fighting for his ideas, both in the community in general and—in a way, much more significant!—inside IBM in particular ... You see, IBM was the major player in the database marketplace at the time. (Life was different in those days.) Thus, Ted and I both felt that if we could only get IBM moving in the right direction, then everyone else would move in the right direction too. With hindsight, in fact, I wonder if IBM's early failure to strike out strongly on a relational front was the beginning of the end for IBM in this arena ... Certainly they let the relational market slip away from them—not 100%, of course, but certainly to a significant degree. Hmmm ... Interesting to speculate.

Anyway, to get to the battles: They were all very much uphill. I'll focus first on the battles inside IBM. Exhibit A is a letter (still in my possession, by the way) that Ted received in August 1975 from the IBM manager responsible for data systems products marketing and planning. Ted had written to him suggesting he should seriously consider relational databases as a part of IBM's long term database and software strategy, and this is that manager's response:[13]

My staff and I have found [your comments] interesting. In order to provide a more thorough and in depth analysis on their applicability as a requirement for future DB systems, we respectfully request that you provide the following:

1) A clear definition of relational data bases: their structure, access technique, programming methods, compatibility, and comparison with our current database standard DL/I.

2) Economic justification of a business case

3) Account scenarios and experience of users in today's environment, with names, descriptions, performance, and function provided.

4) Account of application descriptions of user in the future, by industry and application type, if possible.

5) Description of compatibility with CODASYL

All of this, in *August 1975*!

---

[13] As a general rule, you can take it that quotes in this presentation (both parts) from this point forward are lightly edited for reasons of consistency, continuity, and the like. In the case at hand, however, apart from very minor editing as indicated in the first line the quote is absolutely verbatim, down to and including the apparently random use of periods.

The point is, of course, that IMS was IBM's database strategy at the time, and relational very definitely wasn't. But I often wonder what happened to that manager ... I expect he got promoted.

Here's another example (Exhibit B). This is a quote from an article that Ted himself wrote ("Relational Database Management: IBM's Counter-Strategic Launch") discussing IBM's release of its flagship product DB2:[14]

> Early during the development of DB2 [*i.e., in 1977 or so*], the planning and design team were alerted to the fact that several important features of the relational model [*keys, foreign keys, etc.*] were missing from the specifications ... The response from the designers was devoid of careful thinking and lacking in technical foundation. The features in question were ridiculed as "religious" and "academic" [*i.e., unpractical and useless*]. An additional response was "We couldn't have met our June deadline"—this, after IBM had wasted six years before beginning to develop a relational product !!!

Here's another example (Exhibit C), this time from my own experience: In May 1974, I attended a working meeting of the GUIDE Database Programming Languages Project in Anaheim, California. My attendance was at the invitation of the IBM representative to the project, and I was there in order to answer questions about this new thing called relational database. Participants in the project had defined a set of five sample problems, and individual members had coded solutions to those problems using a variety of existing database products—IMS, TOTAL, IDS, and so on—which they took turns to present to the rest of the group. Needless to say, the solutions were all quite complicated, each of them involving several pages of detailed code. So then I got up and was able to demonstrate that the five problems—which I'd come to cold (I mean, I'd never seen them prior to that afternoon)—could each be formulated as *a single line of code* in relational calculus.

Well, everyone in the group was seriously impressed, and indeed pretty excited at the possibilities. At that point the IBM rep called a coffee break and took me out into the hallway, and the following conversation ensued:

> IBM rep: "Look, I don't want you coming on too strong about this relational stuff."

---

[14] I have in my possession a draft copy of this article dated September 22nd, 1986 (i.e., well after DB2 was first announced).

Me: "Why ever not?"—a reasonable question, I think, given that the whole reason for his inviting me in the first place was precisely to talk about the said relational stuff, and given too that I was beginning to be known by that time as a relational advocate.

IBM rep: "Because IBM doesn't have a product."

Me: "Well, then, maybe IBM should get a product!"

And it did, too, only seven years later.

I'll give you one more IBM example (Exhibit D): In 1971-1972 I was still in England, working for IBM U.K., but also active in a British Computer Society (BCS) Working Group on database management. And that BCS group decided, partly at my instigation, to run a one day conference in London on relational databases—it must have been one of the first, if not *the* first, conferences to be devoted to the subject, as a matter of fact—and we invited Ted to come over from California to be our star speaker.

Now, IBM U.K. management was very concerned about the possible impact of this event on its efforts to sell IMS in Europe. (As a matter of fact I believe they'd recently lost two important IMS accounts in the U.K. Perhaps they were looking for a scapegoat.) After much transatlantic correspondence, therefore—the details of which I'll leave to your imagination—they even went so far as to take Ted and myself out to dinner the night before the conference to shape our heads (sorry!—I mean: to caution us to be diplomatic in what we might say).[15] Well, during the conference the next day—that would be April 5th, 1973—the inevitable question came up:

"Dr Codd, what are the implications of these ideas of yours for IMS?"

Everyone held their breath. You could have heard a pin drop. The IBM thought police at the back of the hall arranged themselves into some kind of damage control stance. And Ted looked at the questioner through his glasses— and took them off—and put them back on again—and then he said:

---

[15] Of course I was going to be one of the speakers too; in fact I was giving the very first presentation the next morning. By the way, my name was printed in the conference program as "C. J. Data"—the first time this particular mistake appeared in print but not the last, not by a long chalk. PS: A similar mistake occurred with Ted's name too on at least one subsequent occasion, when it was given as "E. F. Code." Code and data, eh? Interesting!

"I did not fly 6,000 miles across the Atlantic to talk about IMS."

As I recall, this response drew a round of applause.[16]

> *Aside:* Ted did have a rather—well, rather *special*—way of dealing with questions at conferences. I could cite many examples, but I'll limit myself to just one here. In 1972, Ted and I were both on a database panel at a conference in Miami Beach, Florida, and someone asked a question. Ted said: "Oh, I just happen to have a transparency here that will answer your question"—and he pulled a transparency out of his briefcase and showed it on the overhead projector [*that was state of the art technology at the time!*], but covering the lower part of the slide and exposing just the top three lines, which said:
>
> > *blah blah blah blah blah ...*
> > *blah blah blah blah blah ...*
> > *blah blah blah blah blah ...*
>
> I mean, I don't remember *exactly* what they said, but the point was, they did address the question. Then in answer to another question he showed a bit more of the transparency (exposing another three lines):
>
> > *blah blah blah blah blah ...*
> > *blah blah blah blah blah ...*
> > *blah blah blah blah blah ...*
>
> And so on and so on, until ultimately he'd shown every part of the transparency except the bottom line, which said in big black letters:
>
> ***** IBM Confidential *****
>
> *End of aside.*

---

[16] By the way, I still have the attendance list from that BCS conference. It makes for very interesting reading, including as it does a large number of people who went on to make a name for themselves in the database world (or in a few cases already had). Here are some of them: Barry Aldred; Chris Bird; Tony Brown; Rod Cuff; Alex d'Agapeyeff; Hugh Darwen; Peter Dearnley; Ed Dee; David Gradwell; Jane Grimson; Patrick Hall; Doug Hembry; Derek Howe; Adrian Norman; Chris Reynolds; Terry Rogers; Geoff Stacey; Ronald Stamper; Peter Stocker; Mike Sykes; Ed Tozer; Bill Waghorn; Maurice Wilkes.

I turn now to battles outside IBM.[17] The most visible example was The Great Debate that I mentioned earlier. I still have in my possession the handbill that was produced by a certain attendee, who shall remain nameless here, at the Montreal conference meeting where the debate was first proposed (it was surreptitiously passing from hand to hand among members of the audience, but when it got to me I snagged it):

Tag Team Championship of the World !!!

Careful Codd and Up-to-Date

vs.

Boxer Bachman and Slippery Tax

Get your tickets early—sellout expected !!!

As it turned out, though, the actual speakers at the event were as follows:

- For the relational side, Ted Codd, plus seconds Dennis Tsichritzis and Kevin Whitney;

- For the network side, Charlie Bachman, plus seconds Ed Sibley and Jim Lucking.[18]

As I've said, Ted and I prepared very carefully for this debate and wrote a couple of papers ahead of time, one of them (written by Ted) comparing the approaches from an end user perspective and the other (written by me)

---

[17] I talk of battles outside IBM, but it's only fair to add that those battles weren't with users, or customers. Users and customers were much easier to persuade that relational was a good idea (I wonder why?). No, the people we had battles with were, of course, people who had some kind of vested interest in the status quo—which is to say the vendors, primarily, and especially IBM. In fact, Ted and I had a strategy ... We felt that if we could get the customers on our side, then the customers would turn around and put pressure on IBM to get something done. And that's pretty much what happened. (It also explains why I did everything I could in those days to give presentations outside of IBM, which in fact I did do a lot of.)

[18] I was supposed to be one of Ted's seconds but had visa problems and was unable to get to the meeting (it all happened at almost exactly the time I was moving from England to California). Dennis Tsichritizis stood in for me. Similarly, "Slippery Tax"—i.e., Tax Metaxides, who was chairman of the CODASYL Data Base Task Group at the time, as I recall, and was also at the Montreal conference—didn't act as a Bachman second, either; his place was taken by Ed Sibley, who was also present at that Montreal event. PS: I once wrote a clerihew about Ed Sibley, but I think I'd better not publish it here.

comparing them from an application programming perspective. (The paper Ted wrote was his essentiality paper, which I did mention briefly earlier.) What's more, we had these two papers carefully reviewed ahead of time by several interested parties, both pro and con. Our adversaries, by contrast, didn't seem well prepared at all, and they certainly didn't have the same kind of documentary support for their position. The net result was that some people in the audience switched from CODASYL to relational, no one switched the other way, and everybody got something to think about.

Well, there were plenty of other battles both inside and outside IBM, but I think I've said enough for you to get the general picture. At least you should have some idea by now of the kind of battles Ted got himself involved in at that time. Thank goodness, he won. And so did we all. So did society at large.

MILESTONES

In thinking about major milestones along the way—during the first 25 years, that is—it's a little difficult to say which events were major and which not so much. IBM's 1983 announcement of DB2, for example, was obviously major in some ways, but perhaps not so major as the internal IBM meeting at which the decision was made to devote resources to building that product. Thus, some "major" events weren't very visible at the time, or weren't very obviously major at the time they occurred ... For another example, I feel my own presentations and publications did help in some way toward Ted's ultimate success, and my jumping on the bandwagon in 1970 might thus be regarded as a fairly minor "major event"! Likewise the publication of my book in 1975, which I've already mentioned ... The longest journey begins with a single step.

All of that being said, however, I don't think anybody would quarrel with the following perhaps rather conservative list.

1970: Publication of Codd's paper in Communications of the ACM

In my professional opinion, this was **the single most important event in the entire history of the database field**. In particular, of course, this paper of Codd's, plus his next few, together served, not incidentally, to show the fundamental importance of theory. Well, you already know this is one of my hot button issues ... but I'd like to take a moment to expand on the point a little bit here.

First of all, as I've more or less said already, it's common to decry theory as "not practical"—and yet here we have an entire *practical* multibillion dollar industry made possible by theory.[19] Indeed, it seems to me that today's database products are at their least attractive, and cause real practical problems, precisely at those points where they depart from the theory. Database practitioners (implementers in particular) ignore the theory at their own peril.

Anyway, it was Ted's 1970 paper that really got the ball rolling. That was the paper that put database research on what earlier I called "a solid scientific footing." In fact, prior to the publication of this paper, there scarcely *was* any database research. I think there were two reasons for this state of affairs. The first was that the research community regarded database as "just commercial I/O files," and therefore *boring* ... The second was that in fact the whole problem was just too damn difficult! What Ted did was provide a framework in which problems could be precisely stated ... and articulating a problem precisely is a significant step toward solving that problem, of course (or, turning that statement around, if you can't even *state* the problem, you have very little chance of solving it).

The commercial world didn't pay much attention at first, of course, but the academic world latched on to the ideas fairly quickly, and a huge amount of research began on such topics as database languages; database design; integrity; security; concurrency; data independence; optimization; data distribution; database system architecture; semantic modeling and the nature of data in general; and of course implementation.

Mind you, I do need to make some disclaimers here. First of all, I'm not saying (and nor would Ted) that nobody else contributed to relational development during the 1970s—of course not! And I'm not saying, and nor would Ted, that his 1970 paper got every last detail exactly right. And I'm not saying, and nor would Ted, that he foresaw every last implication of his invention. But all of this is normal and typical with such a major contribution. For example, think of the automobile, or television—or the computer itself, come to that. Though I'm tempted to say in some of these cases that if the parties concerned *had* seen all of the implications they might have suppressed their inventions ... But I digress.

> *Aside:* I was very inclined, while thinking about this list of milestones, to include *all* of the papers by Ted that I mentioned earlier; what's more, I don't it would be

---

[19] Currently estimated at around $50 billion a year, according to an article in the Autumn 2019 issue of the BCS magazine *IT Now*.

all that unreasonable to do so, either. At the same time, I didn't want the presentation to be too repetitive, and so I decided, a trifle reluctantly, not to do so after all. But to a small extent I'd like to have my cake and eat it too ... That is, I do think I should say just a little bit about normalization. Ted began what became the theory of normalization in 1972 with his paper "Further Normalization of the Data Base Relational Model" (No. 5 in my original list). That theory isn't part of the relational model as such, of course; rather, it's a separate theory that builds on top of that model. But it's become such a large field in its own right, and it's one that has such obvious practical importance, that I felt I really should mention it, even though in some ways it sits at right angles to the main theme of this section. And it has its own milestones, of course, the most important of which (apart from Ted's 1972 paper) I think would be the publication of the papers I mentioned earlier, by Armstrong (1974) and Fagin (1979), respectively. Just to remind you, Armstrong showed how dependencies could be treated as objects of formal study in their own right, and Fagin provided a definitive treatment of "classical" normalization, all the way up to and including the new fifth normal form (5NF). *End of aside.*

Let me get back to my main theme. After the publication of Ted's 1970 paper, numerous prototype implementations quickly got under way. I've already mentioned several of these, but there's one I didn't mention before, and that's MacAIMS:

1970-71: MacAIMS (Goldstein & Strnad)

I mention the MacAIMS prototype mainly for historical interest. It was built at MIT around 1970-1971. It's an interesting example of that phenomenon whereby ideas seem to float around the stratosphere and get picked up by several people independently at pretty much the same time—as with, for example, the almost simultaneous development of the differential calculus by Leibniz and Newton (around 1700), or the almost simultaneous discovery of Neptune by Leverrier and Adams (1845), or the almost simultaneous creation of the theory of evolution by Wallace and Darwin (1850s). Thus, MacAIMS was a relational system developed in parallel with, and at least partly independently of, Ted's original work. However, the MacAIMS people didn't seem to realize what they had—at least, not fully—and they never really followed through. Nevertheless, it would be wrong of me to ignore their pioneering efforts here.

My next milestone is perhaps a little tongue in cheek:

1971: Suppliers and parts, Version 1

Where would we be without the famous suppliers-and-parts database? (Where would *I* be?) PS: What I'm here calling "Version 1" is the version first introduced to the world in Ted's ALPHA language paper. Later versions, refined and extended and simplified compared with Version 1, were defined by me in various subsequent publications.

1971-1975: IS/1 and PRTV (Todd and others)

IS/1 ("Information System One") was a prototype, built as I said previously at the IBM U.K. Scientific Centre in Peterlee, England. It became operational in January 1972 and was one of the very first relational prototypes anywhere; only MacAIMS predated it, I think, and IS/1 (which later grew into PRTV) was much more sophisticated than MacAIMS in many respects, especially with regard to optimization. More to the point, perhaps, is this: IS/1 and PRTV predated System R and SQL—and IS/1 and PRTV did so many things right with their language interface ISBL (Information System Base Language) that System R and SQL later did wrong. For example, they supported all of the following:

- Proper relations (duplicates not allowed, proper attribute names)

- User language cleanly based on relational algebra, with proper closure and proper expression nesting

- Lazy evaluation

- User defined operators

- Sophisticated expression transformation and other optimizations

This isn't the place to go into technical details on these matters, so I won't. But I do want to say this: The IS/1 and PRTV people had the great misfortune to be in the wrong part of IBM, with the result that their ideas—through no fault of their own—were not as widely disseminated or as widely influential as they ought to have been, and deserved to have been. A great pity, in my opinion, and we're all paying the price.

Aside: Incidentally, we also see here another instance of the overall shabby history of relational technology in IBM.[20] First of all, IBM management objected strongly to the name "IS/1," on the grounds that it sounded too much like a product, and they made the team change it to "PRTV" (Peterlee Relational Test Vehicle), a name that was deliberately chosen for its unmemorable quality. And the whole PRTV project was eventually squashed by IBM management anyway ... The code was "covered by a frontend oriented toward urban planning and then marketed (in Europe only) as an urban planning tool, its relational interior being carefully ignored by IBM salespeople" (this quote is from that paper of Ted's I mentioned earlier, regarding "IBM's Counter-Strategic Launch").

And while I'm on the topic of "shabby history," I'd like to draw your attention to another example: viz., product naming. Look at "SQL/DS," a name deliberately chosen to suggest that the product was not a database manager at all (not to mention the fact that the SQL/DS announcement was deliberately accompanied by—indeed, effectively made to take second place to—a simultaneous announcement of a new release of DOS DL/I). Look at "DB2," a name that has absolutely nothing to recommend it whatsoever, and in particular says nothing about the fact that the product was, or at least was supposed to be, relational![21] IBM's competitors didn't have the same qualms; in fact, the two most important early competitors actually put "relational" in their company names. I refer here to Relational Software Inc., RSI, which later became Oracle Corporation, and Relational Technology Inc., RTI, which later became Ingres Corporation.[22] *End of aside.*

Next milestone:

---

[20] Given that "shabby history," it's somewhat ironic these days to see IBM now pushing the technology so hard, and indeed trumpeting the fact that the relational model was invented in IBM. Bit of a cheek, really, considering how the powers that be in IBM in those days fought so hard against Ted and his ideas, and indeed against everything relational.

[21] Talking of product naming: Some years later IBM came to realize that it would look much better, at least from a marketing perspective, if it pretended that all of its various SQL products were part of one big happy family, even though the truth is that they were all developed quite independently of one another, with different "code bases." So SQL/DS became Db2 for VSE [*sic lowercase b*]; SQL/400 became Db2 for i [*sic*]; the original mainframe DB2 became Db2 for z/OS; and so on. By the way, I love that switch from "DB2" to "Db2." Can you imagine the time and effort that went into *that* decision? PS: SQL/DS in particular has changed its name several times—first as just indicated to "Db2 for VSE," then to "Db2 for VSE and VM," and then to "Db2 Server for VSE and VM." I think that's it for now.

[22] Originally ORACLE and INGRES (all caps), respectively, but at some point the style changed to initial caps only. See the previous footnote!

1974: The Great Debate

I've already said enough about this one. Onward.

Early to mid 1970s: System R (many people, especially Chamberlin and Traiger)

I've already said quite a lot about this one too ... Let me just add one thing (this might be another "invisible" major event): Around 1978 or so, the System R prototype began to be used internally in IBM as the DBMS for online financial and schedule control for various software development projects ... *one of which was IMS!* I could elaborate on this point if we had time (in particular, on how and why it happened), but I certainly think there's a lesson to be learned here. Of some kind. Don't you?

  To continue with the milestones:

Early to mid 1970s: INGRES (many people, especially Stonebraker and Wong)

The "other" big 1970s prototype, as I've said. INGRES was quite influential in the academic world for a while (and of course it too, like System R, led fairly directly to a commercial product), but it suffered from the misfortune of not being built in IBM. I'll say it again: Its user language QUEL was, in the opinion not just of myself but of many other people also, far superior to IBM's query language SQL.[23] Oh well ... Next:

1979+: Early product announcements (Oracle, Ingres, DB2 ...)

I skip further details here as being too obvious. Not really much I want to say. Oh, except perhaps that Oracle was the first to be announced (that was in 1979) ... What actually happened was that the System R team, being research people, published a whole long list of papers in the open research literature in the second half of the 1970s, describing what they were doing ... and Larry Ellison assumed, correctly, that IBM would eventually build a product based on System R, and

---

[23] I have a story here too. In 1983 (the year I left IBM) I wrote what became the first edition of my book *A Guide to DB2*, and included as an appendix a BNF grammar for SQL as it then was. Three or four years later I wrote a companion book, *A Guide to INGRES*, and included as an appendix a BNF grammar for QUEL. The SQL grammar was five pages of text, the QUEL grammar three—which was obviously a plus for QUEL, of course, but that's not all: The fact is, there was more functionality in those three pages of QUEL than there was in those five pages of SQL.

decided to jump the gun by building something himself based on those published System R papers.

PS: A few interesting "tales out of school" here, too, if we had time, having to do with (a) the origin of the product name "Oracle" and (b) the name of the first release of the product and (c) the hardware platforms the product ran on and (d) a bug in the original System R security mechanism ... and several others too. Onward!

1981: Codd's ACM Turing Award

The ACM Turing Award is, of course, the top award in computer science—not quite a Nobel Prize, but certainly up there. In those days it came with $250,000 cash (that amount has recently been upped to a million dollars). Anyway, I can tell you that nobody was more pleased than me when Ted got that award, in 1981. (Well, maybe Ted was.) He really deserved it, and the recognition—recognition in the academic world, at least—that came with it.[24]

By the way, in this connection I'd like to mention the piece I wrote about Ted some years later for the Turing Award winners section of the ACM website (*amturing.acm.org*).[25] Among other things you can find a brief bio of Ted there, if you're interested.

1986, 1989, 1992: First three versions of the SQL Standard

Before I say anything about this item, there's something I need to face up to, something that I'm afraid is a little unpleasant. The fact is, you might be surprised to note a certain chronological omission here ... To be specific, you might have expected to see a "milestone" entry along the lines of *1985: Publication of Codd's Computerworld articles*—by which I mean the articles in which:

a. Ted gave a definition, albeit a very informal one, of what later became known as "the relational model version 1" (RM/V1), and

b. He also first published his famous—or infamous—"twelve rules."

---

[24] And I have a couple of stories in connection with Ted's Turing award, too (see Chapter 12).

[25] Republished as Appendix A of my book *E. F. Codd and Relational Theory: A Detailed Review and Analysis of Codd's Major Database Writings* (Lulu Press, 2019).

Well, I'm afraid the omission is deliberate. It's my honest opinion that the 1985 RM/V1 definition was quite horrible. Not because it was informal, I hasten to add—nothing wrong with that, especially given the context in which it appeared—but rather because of (a) the many things it omitted and (b) some of the things it included. I don't want to get into details here; I've published an extended critique elsewhere,[26] and in any case such details would be out of place in a presentation like this; so I'm afraid you're just going to have to take my word for it.

It's also my opinion that the twelve rules were fairly horrible too. Certainly they received far more attention, and caused far more brouhaha, than they merited. I've published a critique of those rules too (actually as part of the published critique of RM/V1 just mentioned).

More generally—I'm really sorry to have to say this, I'm afraid it's going to sound very harsh; but we have to face facts—I don't believe anyone who performs a candid comparison between Ted's first few papers (I mean the ones he published in the period 1969-1974, the ones I singled out for comment earlier in this presentation) and these 1985 *Computerworld* articles can fail to notice how the total brilliance of the former is replaced by what can only be described as muddle and confusion in the latter. That's why—at least, partly why—I said earlier that it's important not to be blinded by the originality and brilliance of those early papers into uncritical acceptance of everything Ted said or wrote, and it's important not to accept Ted as the sole authority on relational matters. And it's also why there's no entry in my list of milestones for Ted's 1985 articles and his twelve rules.

What's more, for very similar reasons, there's also no entry in the list along the lines of *1990: Publication of Codd's book on RM/V2*. In my opinion, that book is even worse—much worse, in fact—than those 1985 articles.[27]

My apologies for this sorry state of affairs, but there it is. Don't blame me.

Let me get back to what I'm supposed to be talking about under this line item— namely, the first three versions of the SQL standard, which I can briefly characterize as follows:

---

[26] See Chapter 7 ("The Relational Model Version 1") of the book mentioned in footnote 25.

[27] An extended critique of that book appears as Chapter 8 of the book mentioned in footnote 25.

- SQL/86: Basically the intersection of existing implementations at the time (so the vendors could all claim compliance, even though the functionality included was grossly inadequate for writing real applications)

- SQL/89: Added keys and foreign keys (but these features were optional, so the vendors could all claim instant compliance with the new version of the standard *without making any change at all* to their products—and even with those optional features, the functionality was still inadequate)

- SQL:1992 (note the new naming style): Added a *huge* number of new features (further discussion to follow)

Personally I regard these developments not so much as milestones but rather as *millstones*.[28] For example, the first version, SQL/86, omitted support for keys, and so (thanks to what Hugh Darwen calls *The Shackle of Compatibility*) keys must forever remain optional in the SQL world, instead of being mandatory as they should be. Languages do "live forever," even bad ones (though I do have to say SQL is one of the worst),[29] and that's why it's so important to get them right the first time. I mean, the mistakes live forever too.

As for SQL:1992, I regard it not just as a millstone but in effect as a kind of confidence trick[30]—it suffers from so many errors (of both omission and commission), and contradictions, and inconsistencies that in fact, in the final analysis, it's actually unimplementable. As a consequence, no one does (implement it, I mean); rather, everyone implements what might be described as a proper superset of a proper subset of the standard, and no two SQLs are the same. In fact, I believe this is even true of IBM's own implementations in particular ... I haven't investigated recently, but there was certainly a time when no two IBM SQLs were the same, and I'd take a fairly large wager that matters

---

[28] And here you *can* blame me, somewhat, if you want to. When the pertinent standardization activities first began, it wasn't at all a done deal that SQL was going to be the direction—some of the people involved felt they should be designing a brand new relational language from scratch, and there was even talk of trying to define some kind of "relational Algol." For my sins, however, the IBM rep to the committee, Phil Shaw (who was my manager in IBM for a couple of years, though I don't recall if that was the case at the time in question), brought me along to one of the meetings to give a presentation on SQL ... And the rest, as they say, is history.

[29] Old joke: What's the second worst computer language ever invented? *Answer:* OS/360 JCL.

[30] The same goes for all later versions too.

are still that way today. Even though they're all supposed to be part of one big happy family, as discussed earlier.

1987: Tandem NonStop SQL

Let me move on to something much more pleasant and positive. First I need to give a little background. Early relational systems, while certainly providing great improvements in usability, flexibility, data independence, productivity, ease of development, etc., over prerelational systems, didn't provide the kind of performance needed for high volume production applications. And some people claimed they never would. Here are some typical quotes from those early days:

- Practically speaking, relational systems can handle far less data and far less processing than operational systems

  > —William Inmon: "What Price Relational?"
  > *Computerworld* (November 28th, 1983)

  Well, that was true at the time, but it wasn't *inherently* true. By the way, I could tell you a few things about Mr Inmon if we had time ... He used to be an IMS consultant and was vigorously and vociferously opposed to relational ideas until he saw which way the wind was blowing; then he became a DB2 "expert" (overnight, it seemed). He even wrote a book about DB2. He used the suppliers-and-parts example. He had a suppliers table, and a parts table ... and another table to show which suppliers supplied which parts ... *and another, separate table to show which parts were supplied by which suppliers!* To my mind, that betrayed a truly profound understanding of relational technology.[31]

- Relational is inherently slow.

  > —Frank Sweet: "What, If Anything, Is a Relational Database?"
  > *Datamation 30*, No. 14 (July 15th, 1984)

  "Inherently"? No. By the way, I'd like to quote something else from Mr Sweet's article:

---

[31] In case you might be tempted to take this sentence too literally, let me make it clear that I'm being ironic, and by "understanding" I mean *lack* of same.

COBOL can no more access a relational database than a circle can have corners. It's simply a contradiction in terms ... There's no such thing as a relational database. When you get right down to it, "relational database" is as meaningless as "plaid music" or "scratchy color." The adjective describes languages or processes, not data. The database itself, the pool of shared business data, can be neither procedural nor relational [*sic*].

Your comments here.[32]

■   Nonrelational and relational DBMSs are working toward different and irreconcilable design objectives—performance vs. ease of ad hoc use.

—Hugh Ryan
Computerworld (September 1984)

"Different objectives" is certainly not true now, if it ever was. More to the point, why on earth should those objectives be irreconcilable?

■   Relational databases are powerful and flexible but are slow performers.

—Bao Nguyen
Computerworld (September 1985)

The usual sad confusion between model and implementation.

■   Right now the performance of SQL-based systems is atrocious.

—Michael Braude
Computerworld (January 1986)

Well, that wasn't entirely true even at the time.

■   Why Large On-Line Relational Systems Don't (And May Not Ever) Yield Good Performance" (title of paper).

—William Inmon
System Development (April 1986)

---

[32] Here are mine, for what they're worth: What we have here is *a total failure to abstract*. Of *course* there's such a thing as a relational database; it's a database that's perceived by the user as a collection of relations—in other words, a database that *at a certain level of abstraction* consists of relations. To suggest that there's no such thing as a relational database, just because what's fundamentally stored on the disk is not relations but merely bits and bytes, is like suggesting that there's no such thing as human thought, because what's fundamentally going on inside the brain is merely neurons firing. It's all a question of the level of abstraction at which the construct in question is viewed. "When you get right down to it," COBOL is an abstraction too, and so too are bits and bytes, and so too are magnetized spots on the disk, ..., and so on, ad infinitum (?).

Mr Inmon obviously wrote this paper before he became a born again DB2 expert!

Aside: It's a bit of a digression, of course, but I'd like to give a somewhat lengthy quote from Inmon's paper here, together with the response I wrote at the time. Here first is the quote:

> One of the great mystiques proclaimed by the relational theorists is that relational theory has a firm mathematical foundation and that is supposed to give relational systems a long term basis for stability. If we are to accept the fact that a nonprocedural language is the only means to manipulate relational data, then relational theory is at odds with queueing theory, which also has a firm mathematical foundation. An interesting question then becomes, which is more relevant in the real world—queueing theory or relational theory? Queueing theory is a daily fact of life—on the crowded freeways, in the supermarket, at the lunch counter, in the bank, in the bathroom in the morning, and so forth. Applied queueing theory is observable 100 times a day in the life of modern man [*sic*]. Where then is relational theory observable and relevant?

My response (or series of responses, rather) at the time:

> First, it's absurd to label the fact that "relational theory has a firm mathematical foundation" a "mystique"; it's only detractors who don't understand the technology who like to decry theory and claim that relational databases are somehow mysterious. Second: Yes, that firm mathematical foundation does provide "a long term basis for stability," for numerous sound and well known reasons. Third, the point about relational theory being "at odds with queueing theory" (a) isn't demonstrated in Inmon's paper, and much more important (b) is a complete red herring! (Which do you prefer, Thursdays or porridge? The comparison is about as meaningful.) Fourth, *queues* are a "daily fact of life," but queueing theory regrettably isn't; indeed, if it were, we might see fewer queues. Fifth, relational theory is certainly "observable and relevant," because it consists in large part of elements from set theory and logic, which form the basis of much of mathematics (or is Inmon arguing that mathematics is not observable and relevant?). Furthermore, a knowledge of logic enables people to pinpoint the errors in arguments such as Inmon's, which I think makes it very relevant indeed.

Finally, the entire quote from Inmon's paper is an illustration of what's sometimes known as *ignoratio elenchi*—the fallacy of arguing to the wrong point.

End of aside.

To get back to Tandem NonStop SQL: In March 1987 I wrote a short article for *Computerworld* based on that product, titled "R.I.P. the Relational Performance Myth (1970-1987)." Here's a quote from that article:

> The relational performance myth has finally been exposed for what it is—a myth. A genuine relational DBMS has finally demonstrated transaction rates equal to or better than the rates of the fastest nonrelational DBMSs—rates in the hundreds or even thousands of transactions / second.

In other words, Tandem had in my view provided a convincing refutation of the claims articulated in the foregoing quotes from Inmon and the rest (and many others like them).

By the way, let me point out explicitly that Tandem is, of course, a parallel processor system. And relational systems and parallel processing are such an obviously good match! I mean, there's so much in the relational model that's inherently parallelizable (if that's a word) ... Not only running transactions in parallel, but also statements within transactions (maybe) and operations within statements (definitely) ... And as a special case of the foregoing, consider distributed databases. Relational database technology is a clear prerequisite for good, genuine, transparent, general purpose, distributed database technology.

Late 1980s to mid 1990s: Postgres / PostgreSQL (Stonebraker and others)

On to my final "milestone" ... The next few years (from the mid 1980s on) were in many respects mainly a period of consolidation. However, one major new development appeared on the scene in the late 1980s and early to mid 1990s: namely, the so called object / relational systems. There were several prototypes, and later several products (most of which, though not all, were enhanced versions of existing SQL products such as Oracle and DB2); but Postgres, done at UC Berkeley, was new, and was certainly one of the pioneers.

Now, "object / relational" was much ballyhooed at the time, in the trade press and elsewhere, as "the next great wave." It was described as a marriage between object systems and relational systems (as of course the name suggests), one that would provide the benefits of both technologies. As so often, however, I'm afraid I have a slightly jaundiced view of what was really going on here ... Let me explain.

First of all, we're talking about something that happened at least 25 years ago. Indeed, the term *object / relational* sounds a little quaint now; but I can assure you that object / relational databases were a pretty hot topic at the time, and it wasn't long before all of the mainstream DBMS vendors were describing their products as, or claiming their products to be, object / relational, to a greater or lesser extent. ***But:*** This state of affairs notwithstanding, it was my opinion at the time, and still is, that a true "object / relational" system would be nothing more nor less than a true *relational* system—which is to say, it would be a system that supports the relational model, with all that such support entails. After all, the whole point about an object / relational system from the user's point of view is simply that it allows attributes of relations to be of arbitrarily complex types. In other words, a proper object / relational system is really just a relational system with proper type support (including proper user defined type support in particular)—which just means it's a proper relational system, no more and no less. Thus, what some people are pleased to call "the object / relational model" is, likewise, really just the relational model, no more and no less. In my opinion, therefore, *object / relational* is essentially just a marketing term, dreamt up by the so called "relational" DBMS vendors at the time to disguise the fact that their original "relational" products really weren't very relational at all.[33]

CONCLUDING REMARKS

Well, that brings me to the end of my "milestones" list, and indeed to the end of the first half of this history. Just to remind you, here are the topics I've covered:

- *Original contributions:* Here I took a brief look at various early papers by Codd and others, and I tried to summarize what was achieved with those papers.

- *The historical context:* Here I tried to give some idea of how horrible life was in the database trenches before Ted Codd came along, with examples

---

[33] They still aren't, but that's another story.

from IMS (hierarchies) and CODASYL (networks) in particular. (Also from SQL, unfortunately!)

■ *The battles for acceptance:* Here I talked about the fights inside IBM (mostly, because that's where Ted and I were both working) and, to some extent, outside IBM as well.

■ *Milestones:* And here I gave a kind of overview, or summary, of what happened in the first 25 years.

On to the next 25 years!

Chapter 2

Fifty Years of Relational:

A Personal View

Part II

I would like to see computer science teaching set deliberately in a historical framework ... Students need to understand how the present situation has come about, what was tried, what worked and what did not, and how improvements in hardware made progress possible. The absence of this element in their training causes people to approach every problem from first principles. They are apt to propose solutions that have been found wanting in the past. Instead of standing on the shoulders of their precursors, they try to go it alone.

—Maurice Wilkes: "Software and the Programmer"
Communications of the ACM 34, No. 5 (May 1991)

Welcome to Part II of this presentation! Now, I think I should begin by offering an apology right up front ... The fact is, this part is really going to put the personal into that "personal view," as you'll soon see. Well, I guess you might think Part I already did that, but it's only fair to warn you that Part II is going to do it too but a lot more so, and I just hope you're OK with that.

All right: So what happened in the second 25 years of relational? Of course, the products got better in various ways—in particular they performed better, thanks in part to improved optimization—and they became more and more accepted as the standard way of doing business in the commercial world. They also began to branch out into new application areas and new technologies, such as AI. As far as I'm concerned, however, "relational" means first and foremost relational *theory*, and so what I mostly want to focus on in Part II is *theoretical* developments—especially ones that I myself had some kind of hand in. In other words, I want to talk about how we went on to build on the foundations that were laid in the first 25 years, which I talked about in Part I.

First of all, however, there's one sad thing that happened during this period: namely, Ted Codd died in 2003. I wrote several memorial pieces for him at the time that appeared in various newspapers and other publications, but the one I'd most like to draw your attention to here is the piece I did some years later for the ACM Turing Award winners section of the ACM website (*amturing.acm.org*).[1] It includes a brief bio of Ted that I put together "with a little help from his friends." (And relations. If you see what I mean.)

STRUCTURE OF THE PRESENTATION

Here's what I plan to cover in this second half of the presentation:

- *Replacing relational?* The battles continue ... Still staving off ignorant attacks!

- *Why relational won't be replaced:* The relational model is rock solid and won't be replaced—but what exactly is it?

- *The Third Manifesto:* An attempt led by Hugh Darwen, with enthusiastic support and assistance from myself, to inject some rigor into the mess and thereby provide a proper basis for further investigations.

- *Research topics and successes:* Building on the *Manifesto* (the title says it all).

First of all, though, I'd like to step back for a moment and consider the question of why we should pay attention to relational history anyway. Of course, the epigraph to this chapter—the quote from Maurice Wilkes—gives one good general answer, and so does the Santayana quote from Part I ("Those who don't know history are doomed to repeat it"). However, there are some more specific reasons for studying relational history in particular. The fact is, Codd's

---

[1] I mentioned that piece in Part I of this presentation. It was republished as Appendix A of my book *E. F. Codd and Relational Theory: A Detailed Review and Analysis of Codd's Major Database Writings* (Lulu Press, 2019).

introduction of the relational model some 50 years ago represented a genuine paradigm shift[2]—much more so, I venture to suggest, than a number of other innovations, or developments, that have been described as paradigm shifts over the years. As I said in Part I, relational really is different; it's not just "a better CODASYL," it's truly *foundational*. In fact, I've presented arguments elsewhere[3] to show that in order to be properly general purpose—in particular, to be properly application neutral—a database simply has to be relational.

To repeat, relational really is different. The relational model has been with us now for over 50 years, as you know; and I for one think it's very telling that in all that time no one has managed to invent any new kind of theory that might supplant or even seriously be considered as superior to the relational model in any way. In my opinion, in fact, no one has even come close to coming up with such a theory. Of course, there have been many attempts, as I'm sure you also know, but as far as I'm concerned those attempts have universally failed.

None of which (I'm sorry to say) alters the fact that ever since relational technology first appeared on the scene in 1969 and the early 1970s, us relational folks have found ourselves spending an inordinate amount of time staving off ignorant attacks. Further details to follow immediately!

REPLACING RELATIONAL?

Mind you, there *is* a problem (and this is certainly one area where studying the history can help): namely, not too many people know exactly what the relational model is.[4] And precisely because of that widespread lack of proper understanding, unscrupulous—or, at best, uneducated—vendors and other such people, with various vested interests, are able to get away with claiming that they do have something new, something that's "better than the relational model." Here's a typical quote:

- ■ Computer science has seen many generations of data management, starting with indexed files, and later, network and hierarchic DBMSs ... and more recently

---

[2] Defined by Thomas Kuhn in his book *The Structure of Scientific Revolutions* as "a fundamental change in the basic concepts and experimental practices of a scientific discipline."

[3] See, e.g., Chapter 1 ("What's a Relational DBMS?") of the book mentioned in footnote 1.

[4] It's certainly not SQL! Indeed, it's precisely part of the problem here that people do tend to equate the relational model with SQL—and then, knowing very well that SQL suffers from all kinds of defects, they go on to assume that the defects in question are defects of the relational model, which they're not.

relational DBMSs ... Now, we are on the verge of another generation of database systems ... that provide *object management*, supporting much more complex kinds of data.

—Rick Cattell: "Next Generation Database Systems"
Communications of the ACM 34, No. 10 (October 1991)

The talk of "generations" here (not to mention the overall tenor of the quote) suggests rather strongly that just as the old hierarchic and network systems were made obsolete by relational systems, so relational systems in turn are about to be made obsolete by object oriented systems (object systems, or just OO systems, for short). Now, it might be argued in Cattell's defense that what he's really saying is that it's *object / relational* systems, not object systems as such, that'll be that "next generation"—but even if so, it doesn't really affect my main point. I'll have more to say about object / relational systems later in this presentation.

Here's another quote that suggests the same thing—i.e., that object systems will be "the next generation":[5]

■ It is hard for relational advocates, having been on the leading edge for 10 to 12 years, to wake up and find that fashion has moved on to something else. The temptation is to tell the upstarts they don't know what they're talking about.

—Charles Babcock: "Relational Backlash"
Computerworld (June 28th, 1993)

This quote doesn't mention object systems directly, but it's clear from the rest of the article that it's object systems it's referring to.

Quotes like these first two remind me of the old joke: "But am I being paranoid if everyone really *is* out to get me?"[6] Because the fact is, the upstarts *don't* know what they're talking about, at least as far as the relational model is concerned. Indeed, I think Babcock unwittingly puts his finger on it when he mentions the word *fashion*; I mean, I think what he's talking about *is* just fashion. The next quote says as much, rather eloquently:

■ I am, I regret to say, resigned to the transient triumph of OO: Fashion is more powerful than reason, for reason is not the property of any vested interest. We

---

[5] By the way, it's interesting to see that this quote and the previous one, both of which are quite negative in tone, are both from near the end of the *first* 25 years of relational. So people were already saying relational was over, before it even got seriously under way!

[6] I have a great quote in this connection: *Paranoia is having all the facts* (William Burroughs).

should count ourselves lucky that for some while now, fashion and reason have coincided in relational. But—once again—we have failed to learn from our successes.

—Adrian Larner:
Private communication (mid 1990s)

I like this quote very much! Background: Adrian Larner was a close friend of Hugh Darwen's (and an acquaintance of mine also) in the U.K. When I was struggling to make sense of OO—this was sometime in the mid 1990s, when I was working on what became the 6th edition of my book *An Introduction to Database Systems*—Adrian wrote me a very long letter to explain all about objects[7] (26 pages, I think it was), and the quote above was the whole of the final paragraph from that letter.

> *Aside:* It was in that 6th edition of my book that I first complained—not for the last time—that OO concepts generally seem to be pretty fuzzy. In particular, I said, you mustn't expect the kind of crispness, precision, and clarity that we're accustomed to in the relational world. And I continued as follows:
>
>> Many object concepts are quite imprecise, and there's little true consensus and much disagreement, even at the most basic level ... In particular, there's no abstract, formally defined "object data model," nor is there even consensus on an informal model ... In fact, there seems to be much confusion over levels of abstraction: specifically, over the crucial distinction between model and implementation.
>
>> Well, one of my reviewers (an object aficionado, needless to say) took great exception to these comments, complaining that my characterization of OO concepts as imprecise and fuzzy just wasn't fair. It's not the *concepts* that are fuzzy, he said, it's just their *definitions* ... I rest my case. *End of aside.*

Of course, object systems never did replace relational systems after all—that didn't happen, and we know that now. Indeed, we don't hear much about object DBMSs at all these days. But it's hard to argue with, or resist, suggestions like "OO will take over" when you first meet them, if you don't really know what the relational model is in the first place.

---

[7] I nearly said "on the subject of objects." What is it about OO that makes people want to make silly jokes all the time?

That same lack of knowledge also makes it hard to argue with or resist ideas that (as Maurice Wilkes puts it) "have been found wanting in the past." As an example here, I could cite the heavy reliance in object systems on *pointers* (years after Ted Codd showed us why pointers were bad news)—not to mention the subsequent introduction of pointers into, of all things, the standard "relational" language SQL!

> *Aside:* In connection with pointers in SQL, I remember a conversation I had with Don Chamberlin—widely recognized as "the father of SQL"— back in 1996, at a conference on object / relational systems. Don wanted to know what was wrong with an SQL table having a column whose values were pointers—he called them "references," but he meant pointers—to rows somewhere else. Heresy! I didn't do a very good job of answering his question at the time, because it took me so much by surprise (as far as I was concerned it was right out of left field) ... I mean, I thought Codd had answered it pretty well a quarter of a century before. But what I did do was go away and write a paper—"Don't Mix Pointers and Relations!"—in which I tried to answer the question in detail, and definitively.[8] Of course, I sent a review copy of that paper to Chamberlin before publishing it, and he requested the right to reply. As a consequence, his paper "Relations and References—Another Point of View" appeared alongside mine in the journal in which mine was first published.[9] However, reading that reply merely made me realize that Chamberlin had completely failed to understand my arguments, and so I wrote a follow-up paper, "Don't Mix Pointers and Relations—*Please!*"
>
> What this episode finally convinced me of was something I'd suspected for a long time: namely, that the inventor of SQL never really understood the relational model. *End of aside.*

Here's a list of approaches, or technologies, or—well, schemes (I don't really know what the right generic label is)—that have been proposed from time to time as being somehow "better than relational." Of course, some of these (like

---

[8] I said Codd had already given a good answer to Chamberlin's question a quarter of a century before, but I think I should say too that in my opinion my own paper gave at least one much better one: namely, that (a) pointer values are addresses and (b) variables have addresses but values don't, and so (c) the "rows" that are pointed to must be row variables specifically, not row values. And row variables represent a huge departure from—in fact, a major violation of—the relational model. PS: Actually, "row variables" (at least as such things are meant to be understood in the present context) don't just violate the relational model, they don't really make any sense at all. But this isn't the place to get into details of why they don't.

[9] *InfoDB 10*, No. 6 (April 1997). *Note:* My paper and the one I refer to as "a follow-up paper" in the next sentence (the next sentence of the main text, I mean) were both republished in the book *Relational Database Writings 1994-1997*, by Hugh Darwen, David McGoveran, and myself (Addison-Wesley 1998).

OO) we don't hear so much about any more, but others are still very much with us, and I'm sure more will be proposed in the future:

- The associative model

- E/R (i.e., as a DBMS technology as such, not just as an aid to design)

- OO (i.e., for databases, not just programming)

- XML (i.e., for databases, not just documents)[10]

- The semistructured model

- NoSQL[11]

- Key-value stores

- Graph databases

And doubtless others. By the way—I really have to say this—as far as I'm concerned "the XML model," such as it is, is basically just the old IMS-style hierarchic model warmed over, and "the OO model," such as it is, is basically just the old CODASYL-style network model warmed over. Those who don't know history are doomed to repeat it?

Actually I have a nice quote in connection with all of this stuff (and it makes a nice coda for the section as a whole):

- All of these schemes attempt to solve through technical means a nontechnical problem: namely, *the reluctance of talented people to master the relational model,*

---

[10] Three points here. 1. Well after XML first appeared, an attempt was made to define an "XML algebra"—an attempt that was doomed from the start, because if X is an XML document, X MINUS X isn't. 2. A quote from an XML tutorial paper: "XML avoids the fundamental question of what we should do, by focusing entirely on how we should do it" (this is one of my all time favorite quotes). 3. As you might know, XML has its own query language, called XQuery (and as I once heard someone say, "if you like SQL, you'll love XQuery"). Indeed, one of the XQuery designers was Don Chamberlin ... who subsequently wrote a paper all about it—"XQuery: An XML Query Language," *IBM Systems Journal 41*, No. 4 (2002)—in which he said the following among other things: "Iteration is an important part of a query language." This was written some 30 years after Codd first stated almost the exact opposite, viz., that a query language should "not involve branching, iteration, or cursors."

[11] If this literally meant "No SQL" I might be in favor of it. But I believe it actually stands for "Not only SQL."

and thus benefit from its data consistency and logical inferencing capabilities. Rather than exploit it and demand more relational functionality from DBMS vendors, they seek to avoid and replace it, unwittingly advocating a return to the fragile, unreliable, illogical systems of the 1960s, minus the greenbar fanfold paper.

—James K. Lowden: letter to the editor
Communications of the ACM 54, No. 7 (July 2011)

WHY RELATIONAL WON'T BE REPLACED

In my opinion the relational model is rock solid, and "right," and will endure. It will never be replaced. A hundred years from now, I fully expect database systems still to be based on Codd's relational model. Why? Because the foundations of that model are themselves rock solid in turn. Let me elaborate.

First, I've said, or at least strongly implied, that the relational model is the right and proper foundation for database systems. But of course the relational model has still deeper foundations of its own: namely, set theory and logic. Concerning which, consider the following:

- Set theory goes back some 150 years, to Cantor (whose work began in 1870 or so).

- Logic goes back well over 2000 years, at least as far as Aristotle (384-322 BCE).

In fact, set theory and logic are the foundation for much of mathematics!—and they've both been studied by a lot of very smart people for a very great length of time. Of course, that's not to say there's nothing wrong with them; however, if there *is* something wrong with them ... Well, let me just say that if there is, then we can forget about databases, we have much bigger problems. But of course I don't think there is anything wrong with them. Mind you, however, once again there *are* some problems (problems with relational, I mean) ... The first is that the implementations—considered as implementations of the relational model as such, that is—are so poor (thank you, SQL), which makes them subject to fair and legitimate criticism. As I've said, however, those criticisms need to be understood for what they are: namely, legitimate criticisms of the implementations as implementations, *not* legitimate criticisms of what they're supposed to be implementing, which is the relational model.

The second problem is that the relational model is something of a moving target (or as some of our critics have put it, a little unkindly, we keep moving the goalposts). Now, in one way this state of affairs isn't unreasonable. After all, the relational model is really just a small part of mathematics, and mathematics isn't a static thing—it grows and evolves as new discoveries are made and new theorems are proved. And the same is true (though to a much lesser extent, of course) of the relational model in particular.

On the other hand, I have to admit that the picture isn't quite as rosy or scientifically respectable as I'm pretending. The sad fact is, not all of that moving of the goalposts has been done for legitimate, purely scientific reasons. Ted Codd in particular kept changing his definition of what the relational model was. What's more, some of his changes were "silent" (i.e., they were made without any acknowledgment that they'd even been made, let alone with any kind of accompanying rationale); worse, some of them were, to say the least, rather hard to justify scientifically. As Mike Stonebraker says in his introduction to *Readings in Database Systems* (2nd edition, Morgan Kaufmann, 1994), "one can think of four different versions" of the model:

1. Defined by Codd's paper in *Communications of the ACM* (1970)

2. Defined by Codd's Turing Award paper (1981)

3. Defined by Codd's twelve rules and scoring system (1985)

4. Defined by Codd's book (1990)

> *Aside:* Stonebraker refers to "four versions," but actually I think it should be *at least* four. For example, Codd's paper "Extending the Database Relational Model to Capture More Meaning" (*ACM Transactions on Database Systems 4*, No. 4, December 1979) contains a definition—admittedly not very formal, but then nor are the ones Stonebraker mentions—that differs from *all* of those listed above.
>
> As a matter of fact I don't think Codd ever gave a formal definition of the relational model. In fact I don't think he ever gave an informal definition, either!—at least, not one that was anywhere close to being precise. In particular (and very surprisingly), no such definition, either formal or informal, appears in either his pioneering 1970 paper or his 1990 book—which is certainly odd, considering the titles of those publications. For the record, here are those titles (and note the subtle shift from "A" to "The," by the way!):

- ■   (1970 paper) "A Relational Model of Data for Large Shared Data Banks"

- ■   (1990 book) *The Relational Model for Database Management Version 2*

End of aside.

Well, for reasons I've explained in detail elsewhere,[12] I certainly don't agree with all of the moving of the goalposts that the definitions mentioned by Stonebraker reflect. Which could serve as a convenient segue into my next topic ... except that first I want to mention, and debunk, another set of (allegedly) changing definitions of what the relational model is. In his book *Joe Celko's Data and Databases: Concepts in Practice* (Morgan Kaufmann, 1999), the author, Joe Celko, says this:

> There is no such thing as *the* relational model for databases anymore [*sic*] than there is just one geometry.

And to bolster this—on the face of it, absurd—position, he goes on to identify what he calls six "different relational models," which he refers to as follows (the labels are Celko's and I quote them here absolutely verbatim):

1.   Chris Date = No Duplicates, No NULLs

2.   E. F. Codd, RM Version I

3.   E. F. Codd, RM Version II

4.   SQL-92 = Duplicates, One NULL

5.   Duplicates, One NULL, Non-1NF Tables

6.   Rick Snodgrass = Temporal SQL

Now, I wrote an immediate response to these claims of Celko's when I first encountered them,[13] and I don't want to repeat that response here. All I want to do here is say that (a) those claims don't have much to do with moving the

---

[12] In the book mentioned in footnote 1 in particular.

[13] That "immediate response" appeared in my book *Database in Depth: Relational Theory for Practitioners* (O'Reilly, 2005). Later I beefed it up somewhat, and it now appears as Appendix A of my book *SQL and Relational Theory: How to Write Accurate SQL Code* (3rd edition, O'Reilly, 2015).

goalposts, they're just nonsense and obfuscation, and as a consequence (b) they really don't *help*.[14]

Enough of Joe Celko. As I've said, I don't agree with all of that moving of the goalposts (at least, not unless it's done for good scientific reasons), and that state of affairs can serve as a convenient segue into my next topic.

THE THIRD MANIFESTO

The Third Manifesto ("the *Manifesto*," or just *TTM* for short), by Hugh Darwen and myself, is among other things our own attempt at providing a definitive statement of what the relational model really is. As I've written elsewhere:[15]

> Perhaps because we're a trifle sensitive to criticisms such as Stonebraker's, Hugh Darwen and I have tried to provide, in our book *Databases, Types, and the Relational Model: The Third Manifesto*, our own careful statement of what the relational model is ... Indeed, we'd like our *Manifesto* to be seen as a definitive statement in that regard. I refer you to the book itself for the details; here just let me say that we see our contribution in this area as primarily one of dotting a few *i*'s and crossing a few *t*'s that Codd himself left undotted or uncrossed in his own work. We most certainly don't want to be thought of as departing in any major respect from Codd's original vision; indeed, the entire *Manifesto* is very much in the spirit of Codd's original ideas and continues along the path that he originally laid down.[16]

Note, therefore, that we're definitely talking about evolution, not revolution. We don't think the world wants revolution.

> *Aside:* In his book *The Mathematical Universe* (Wiley, 1994), William Dunham says this:

---

[14] In case it's not obvious, what I mean is, they don't help the cause of genuine understanding.

[15] E.g., in that same Appendix A mentioned in footnote 13.

[16] The qualifiers "original" and "originally" are important here! Probably the biggest overall difference between Codd's position and the *Manifesto*'s is that Codd wanted nulls to be supported and the *Manifesto* doesn't. But nulls weren't part of the relational model as Codd originally saw it, either—he didn't spell out what he meant by "null support" until 1979, in his paper "Extending the Data Base Relational Model to Capture More Meaning" (*ACM Transactions on Database Systems 4*, No 4, December 1979).

> Jakob Bernoulli's productive years coincided with Gottfried Wilhelm Leibniz's discovery of calculus, and Jakob was one of the chief popularizers of this immensely fruitful subject. As with any developing theory, calculus benefited from those who followed in its creator's footsteps, scholars whose brilliance may have fallen short of Leibniz's but whose contributions toward tidying up the subject were indispensable. Jakob Bernoulli was one such contributor.

Well, we see our *Manifesto* as fulfilling a role with respect to Codd and his relational model that's similar to that of Jakob Bernoulli with respect to Leibniz and his calculus. *End of aside.*

Let me back up a little. Here first is a brief *TTM* timeline:

- Hugh Darwen, first handwritten *Manifesto* draft (1994)

Hugh has always been the prime mover in this effort, and I'll say more about that first draft of his later. Do note, however, that (as I said in Part I of this presentation) 2019 was indeed the *Manifesto*'s 25th birthday, though of course we'd been thinking about these matters for some time prior to 1994 ... In fact, I think we first discussed the idea in very general terms as far back as 1989, at an IBM conference Hugh was attending in Palo Alto, California. (I left IBM back in 1983, but I was still one of the speakers at that IBM conference.)

- "Introducing ... *The Third Manifesto*" (*DBP&D 8*, No. 1, January 1995)

The first appearance in print of anything to do with the *Manifesto*.

- *"The Third Manifesto"* (ACM *SIGMOD Record 24*, No. 1, March 1995)

The first appearance in print of the *Manifesto* as such (the previous item wasn't the *Manifesto* as such, it was just "the view from 20,000 feet").

And then a book, which has been through three editions and (for reasons that aren't important here) confusingly keeps changing its title:

- *Foundation for Object/Relational Databases: The Third Manifesto*, 1st edition (Addison-Wesley, 1998)

- *Foundation for Future Database Systems: The Third Manifesto*, 2nd edition (Addison-Wesley, 2000)

- *Databases, Types, and the Relational Model: The Third Manifesto*, 3rd edition (Addison-Wesley, 2007)

All of these publications except the very first (the handwritten draft) are joint productions by Hugh Darwen and myself. *Note:* For the most up to date information on the *Manifesto* and related matters, please refer to the website *www.thethirdmanifesto.com*.

———— ◆ ◆ ◆ ◆ ◆ ————

Before going any further I'd like to summarize some of those evolutionary changes (what I called "dotting a few *i*'s and crossing a few *t*'s") that the *Manifesto* represents:

- We've clarified the logical difference between relations and relvars (more on this one later).

- We've added relational comparisons.

- We have a better understanding of the nature of relational algebra, including the relative significance of various operators and an appreciation of the importance of relations of degree zero,[17] and we've identified certain useful new operators, such as EXTEND and MATCHING.

- We've added image relations.

- We've clarified the concept of first normal form; as a consequence, we've embraced the concept of relation valued attributes in particular.

- We have a better understanding of updating, including view updating in particular.

---

[17] To understand why those relations are so important, consider the fact that they perform a role in the relational algebra that's analogous to the role performed by zero in ordinary arithmetic.

- We have a better understanding of the fundamental significance of integrity constraints in general, and we have some good theoretical results regarding certain important special cases.

- We've clarified the nature of the relationship between the relational model and logic (more specifically, predicate logic).

- Finally, we have a clearer understanding of the relationship between the relational model and type theory (more specifically, we've clarified the nature of domains).

I'd like to elaborate briefly on this last item. The basic point is this: Relations have attributes, and those attributes have types; thus, relations are "defined over" types (also known, especially in early relational writings, as domains). It follows that the theory of relations requires a supporting theory of types. Now, Ted Codd never provided any such thing;[18] so one of the things we took it on ourselves to provide in our *Manifesto* was exactly that, a theory of types. And we did.

In connection with that theory of types, by the way, there's one important point I'd like to spell out explicitly (because it's often not properly understood). The point is this: *The question of what types are supported is orthogonal to the question of support for the relational model as such.* Or more catchily:

Types are orthogonal to tables.

In other words, the relational model does say there have to be some types, because relations are defined over them. But it doesn't say what those types have to be! The relational model has *never* prescribed types as such.[19] Beliefs to the contrary—e.g., that the relational model can deal with numeric types and string

---

[18] Actually Ted always resisted the claim that types and domains were the same thing. However, he never offered any good scientific reasons for his resistance, and as far as I'm concerned his position on the matter was simply wrong. PS: I do believe I know *why* he held the position he did, too, but I don't intend to say anything further about it here.

[19] With one exception, type BOOLEAN (truth values). But that exception doesn't materially affect my point, and I don't want to discuss it any further here. PS: For the record, though, there are a couple of things that are explicitly *pro*scribed. The first proscription, simplifying somewhat, says that if relation *r* is of type *T*, then no attribute of *r* can itself be of type *T*. The second says that no relation in the database can have an attribute of any pointer type. (The first of these proscriptions is a logical necessity; the second is a deliberate limitation imposed by the relational model.)

types, but not much else—are often expressed but are simply mistaken, and wrong.

What exactly led us to do this work? In fact there were several motivations, though they're all very much tangled up with one another. I'll list them first, then elaborate on each in turn in a subsection of its own.

- Frustration over lack of understanding of the relational model

- Frustration over "the relational backlash"

- Frustration over SQL (Darwen's "last straw")

- Frustration over two previous manifestos

- Frustration over **The Great Blunder**

Lack of Understanding of the Relational Model

In some ways I don't blame people for being a little confused as to what the relational model really is. I've already talked about moving the goalposts and such matters ... As a matter of fact Hugh and I were quite perturbed at Ted Codd's goalpost moving activities—along with quite a lot else!—in his 1985 *Computerworld* articles and his 1990 book. To elaborate on these points:

- We were perturbed by—among other things—the generally prescriptive tone of those articles and that book. Many of the specific ideas in the book in particular are controversial, to say the least (in some cases they're clearly wrong); and it doesn't seem appropriate to state categorically that the system *must* adopt a particular approach to some issue when the approach in question is demonstrably flawed, and superior approaches have already been described in the literature. And even where the ideas aren't wrong or controversial, it still seems undesirable to be excessively prescriptive, for fear of stifling invention.

■ We were also perturbed by the lack of understanding of relational theory among people who really ought to know better—by which I mean, for example, (a) university professors who are supposed to teach this stuff, (b) implementers who are responsible for actually building DBMS products, and (c) various other self-proclaimed "experts" (consultants, technical journalists, and the like).

Here by way of illustration are a few horrible—but genuine!—examples of this latter point:

■ Your instructor probably told you that the relational view was not only mathematically correct, provably correct, or something similar, but also far more flexible than anything that preceded it. That explanation is fairly simple and perhaps a little embarrassing for the computer world, because **the relational theory of data is wrong**. Data cannot always be represented in terms of entities, attributes, and relationships.[20] (*Boldface added.*)

—Robin Bloor: "The End of Relational"
DBMS 5, No. 7 (July 1992)

There are many things I could say in response to Mr Bloor here, but I'll limit myself to just this: If "the relational theory of data is wrong," does that mean that set theory and logic are wrong too? Because, as I hope you understand by now if you didn't before, the relational model is really just an applied form of set theory and logic. Come off it, Mr Bloor!

■ A newer form of database manager, the *relational model*, ... removes information about complex relationships from the database ... Although the relational model is much more flexible than its predecessors, it extracts a steep price for this flexibility. The information about complex relationships that was removed from the database must be expressed as procedures in every program that accesses the database, a clear violation of the independence required for modularity.

—David A. Taylor:
Object Technology: A Manager's Guide, 2nd edition
(Addison-Wesley, 1998)

---

[20] Of course, relational theory doesn't really say it can. I mean, what it does say—implicitly perhaps—is that data can always be represented in terms of *relations*, not "entities, attributes, and relationships." Perhaps Mr Bloor was muddling levels, confusing the relational model with the so called entity / relationship model? (That said, however, I'd love to see an example of data that can't be represented in terms of "entities, attributes, and relationships.")

Oh *dear* ... There are so many things wrong with this one, on so many different levels, I don't know where to begin. I think I'll leave it to you. (But how on earth does a book this bad get published—let alone get into a *second edition*?)

- It is important to make a distinction between stored relations, which are *tables*, and virtual relations, which are *views* ... We shall use *relation* only where a table or a view could be used. When we want to emphasize that a relation is stored, rather than a view, we shall sometimes use the term *base relation* or *base table*.
    —Hector Garcia-Molina, Jeffrey D. Ullman, and Jennifer Widom:
    Database Systems: The Complete Book
    (Prentice Hall, 2002)

Again I'll say just one thing, out of the numerous responses this piece cries out for ... Actually, it's very important *not* to make a distinction between "stored relations" and views! (I'm assuming here that by "stored relations" the authors really mean *base* relations. Though if they do, then that's another problem right there.) The *whole point* about a view is that it's supposed to look and feel just like a base relation. (Or a base relvar, rather, but that's another point that desperately needs a proper response. As I've already said, however, I'll be talking about the whole business of relations vs. relvars later on, so let me just leave it for now.)

By the way, notice that this terrible piece of nonsense is from a *textbook*! No wonder the level of understanding is so bad in the population at large, if this is typical of the teaching—which I'm horribly afraid it is.[21]

- Don't use joins ... Oracle and SQL Server DBMSs ... have fundamentally different approaches to the concept ... You can end up with unexpected result sets ... You should understand the basic types of join clauses ...Equijoins are formed by retrieving all the data from two separate sources and combining it into one large table. Inner joins are joined on the inner columns of two tables. Outer joins are joined on the outer columns of two tables. Left joins are joined on the left columns of two tables. Right joins are joined on the right columns of two tables. There are also other kinds of joins ...

---

[21] In this connection it's pertinent to remind you of Celko's book (also a textbook, of a kind) and his "six relational models." Pity the poor student who's just trying to make sense of all this stuff.

The important thing to remember about joins is to not use them if you want your application to work well with different database servers.
—Sanders Kaufman: "Database Design for Platform Independence"
www.zdnet.com (June 27th, 2002)

This *pièce de résistance* is a direct quote from a document purporting to give advice to SQL users. Believe it or not.

Anyway, you can see what we were up against (indeed, still are) ... and so we thought we could provide a useful service by giving a complete, precise, and fairly formal definition of the relational model, and that's one thing we tried to do with our *Manifesto*.

"The Relational Backlash"

We wanted to respond to all this nonsense, too ("objects are the next generation," and so on and so forth). In particular, we wanted to show that a relational system could do all of the things its detractors said it couldn't, such as supporting "complex objects" and user defined operators.

SQL

It really is a crying shame that as far as all too many people are concerned, "relational" means SQL. And strange, too, given that (as I said in Part I of this presentation) one of the most immediately noticeable things about SQL is how unrelational it is ... Indeed, we believe that any attempt to move forward, if it's to stand the test of time, must *reject SQL unequivocally*. Our reasons for taking this position are too many and too varied to spell them out in detail here; in any case, we've described them in depth in many places, and you can go to those places if you want more specifics. Of course, we're not so naïve as to think that SQL will ever disappear; rather, it's our hope that some other language, perhaps based on our *Manifesto*, will be sufficiently superior to SQL that it'll become the database language of choice (i.e., by a process of natural selection), and SQL will become "the database language of last resort." In fact, we see a parallel with the world of programming languages, where COBOL has never disappeared and never will; but COBOL has become "the programming language of last resort" for developing applications, because much better alternatives exist. We see SQL as a kind of database COBOL, and we'd like a new, *Manifesto* conforming language to become a preferable alternative to it.

Given that SQL databases and SQL applications are going to be with us for a long time, however, we do have to pay some attention to the question of what to do about today's "SQL legacy" (I love that phrase). And the *Manifesto* does include some specific suggestions in this connection. I don't want to get into details of those suggestions here, but the broad message is: *We're in this for the long haul.*

Another way of saying all of the above is: The situation is a real mess right now. If we do nothing, then nothing will happen. If we do something, then something might happen. In other words, we're optimists and, to say it again, we're in it for the long haul.

Anyway, this line item in my original list of frustrations included the phrase "Darwen's last straw." Let me elaborate. As I've said, Hugh Darwen was always the prime mover in this effort ... Well, let him explain in his own words:[22]

In 1993 the U.K. Open University's course on relational databases included a question on a test paper in which the students were asked to state the meaning, in real world terms, of the following SQL query:

```
SELECT  NAME
FROM    CITY AS C1
WHERE   4 >
        ( SELECT COUNT(*)
          FROM    CITY AS C2
          WHERE   C1.POPULATION < C2.POPULATION )
```

I was one of the tutors who had to mark these test papers. I struggled with this question and so did most of the students. My difficulty was caused mainly by the perverse way in which the two comparisons were written, causing me to translate the query, word for word, into something like this:

Get names of all cities C1 where four is greater than the number of other cities C2 where the population of C1 is less than the population of C2.

This seemed to me a bit like asking somebody trying to purchase alcohol if seventeen was less than their age.[23] I tried inverting the two comparisons:

---

[22] What follows is a lengthy extract (edited slightly here) from Hugh's article "How *TTM* Got Off the Ground." The original can be found on the *Manifesto* website.

[23] Twenty in the U.S., of course, not seventeen.

```
SELECT NAME
FROM    CITY AS C1
WHERE ( SELECT COUNT(*)
        FROM    CITY AS C2
        WHERE   C2.POPULATION > C2.POPULATION ) < 4
```

Now my translation became:

> *Get names of all cities C1 where the number of other cities C2 whose population is greater than the population of C1 is less than four.*

And the real meaning became clear. I thought it was a bit unkind of the test paper deviser to set the question that way—after all, we were supposed to be testing the students' understanding of relational stuff, not their mental agility—and I told Chris Date about the question, asking him if he agreed that the way in which the comparisons were written made it more difficult than it ought to have been. He readily agreed but added, "I think I know why they set it that way. Many SQL products won't let you write it the other way—and that includes your own company's product, DB2!" I was flabbergasted by that information. I had come across many funny quirks in programming languages during my career but never one that allowed certain expressions to appear on one side of a comparison and not on the other. Was there some problem, perhaps, with handling comparisons having "scalar subqueries" on the left side? I checked the 1992 version of the SQL standard and found no such restriction mentioned.

Now, at that time I was IBM's U.K. representative to the SQL standard committee. Perceiving a point of nonconformance in DB2, therefore, I got on the phone to my U.S. colleague Nelson Mattos, who was IBM's U.S. representative on the committee and the person from whom other IBM representatives took guidance. I told him about the nonconformance and suggested that he might wish to get on to the DB2 development people to advise them to address the discrepancy. What actually happened was not the outcome I had envisaged. It turned out that the previous version of the standard had indeed included the restriction in question—no subqueries on the left side of a comparison. At the next meeting (January 1994) of the committee in Munich, Germany, a change proposal appeared from the U.S., authored by Nelson Mattos, reinstating that restriction! Now, the aim of an IBM representative on the committee is to align the standard with DB2—just as it's the aim of Oracle's representatives to align it with Oracle, and so on.[24] Thus, it was my IBM duty to try to persuade my non IBM colleagues on the U.K. committee that the U.K. should support this proposal; so I swallowed my pride and did just that, and the proposal was accepted.

---

[24] There are those, like me, who might have thought it should surely be the other way around; but of course such silly idealists would be wrong.

Well, there's such a thing as the last straw—the one that breaks the camel's back—and that was the last straw for me. Ever since the publication of *The Object-Oriented Database System Manifesto* in 1989 and the response *Third Generation Database System Manifesto* in 1990, Chris and I had been wondering if we might attempt a response of our own to both documents, and we had been using "The Third Manifesto" as a provisional title for communication between the two of us. And I was so ashamed of my participation in the skulduggery described above that during the interim weekend of that meeting, while other delegates went off to ski in the Austrian Alps (which I could see from my hotel room window), I put pencil to paper and wrote the first draft—nine pages—of the *Manifesto* and faxed it to Chris for comments.[25]

And that's where it all began. But what an indictment of the standardization process! *Cui bono?*

The Two Previous Manifestos

As that "last straw" text of Hugh's indicates, one reason we wanted to write our *Manifesto* was to respond to two others that had been published not all that long before (actually in 1989 and 1990, respectively):

1. "The Object Oriented Database System Manifesto," by Malcolm Atkinson, François Bancilhon, David DeWitt, Klaus Dittrich, David Maier, and Stanley Zdonik (Proc. 1st International Conference on Deductive and Object-Oriented Databases, Kyoto, Japan, 1989)

2. "Third Generation Database System Manifesto," by Michael Stonebraker, Lawrence A. Rowe, Bruce G. Lindsay, James Gray, Michael Carey, Michael Brodie, Philip Bernstein, and David Beech (*ACM SIGMOD Record 19*, No. 3, September 1990)

    Aside: Let me say a word about the title of the second of these manifestos. The general idea was as follows: Basically, first generation database systems were the old hierarchic and network (CODASYL) systems, such as IMS and IDMS; second generation systems were today's relational (or at least SQL) systems; and third generation systems were whatever comes next. Here's a direct quote: "Second generation systems made a major contribution in two areas,

---

[25] Those nine handwritten pages can also be found on the *Manifesto* website.

nonprocedural data access and data independence, and these advances must not be compromised by third generation systems." (By the way, do you think that's all that relational systems did?) *End of aside*.

Like our own *Manifesto*, these two previous ones both proposed a basis on which future DBMSs might be built; however, it seemed to us that they both suffered from some very serious defects. As we wrote in the first edition of our own *Manifesto* book:

■ The first [*i.e., of those prior manifestos*] essentially ignores the relational model. In our opinion, this flaw is more than enough to rule it out as a serious contender. In any case, it seems to us that it fails to give firm direction.

■ The second does correctly embrace the relational model, but fails to emphasize (or indeed even mention) the hopelessness of continuing to follow a commonly accepted perversion of that model—namely, SQL—in pursuit of relational ideals. In other words, it simply assumes that SQL, with all its faults, is an adequate realization of the relational model and hence an adequate foundation on which to build.

Aside: I can't resist giving another quote here (this time from the first of those earlier manifestos), and a rather appalling quote at that:

> With respect to the specification of the system, we are taking a Darwinian approach: We hope that, out of the set of experimental prototypes being built, a fit model will emerge. We also hope that viable implementation technology for that model will evolve simultaneously.

What this quote seems to be saying is this (paraphrasing considerably):

> Write the code first; then develop a model later (maybe) by abstracting from that code.

I find this position quite extraordinary; I mean, surely it's better to know what we're doing before we try to do it?[26] *End of aside*.

---

[26] Of course, writing the code first and defining the model later was exactly what happened with hierarchies and networks (at least, insofar as "models" can even be said to exist in those cases). A similar remark applies to XML also (see the first of the three points mentioned in footnote 10.) That's why I said in Part I of this presentation that Ted Codd not only invented the relational model in particular, he actually invented the concept of a data model in general. Indeed, I believe it's still the case today that relational DBMSs are the only kind for which an abstract model was defined first, prior to any implementation.

So we wanted to respond to these two manifestos. More specifically, we wanted to deal with the object / relational issue, which was a hot topic at the time (it was addressed by the second of the earlier manifestos, though not the first). More specifically still, we wanted to deal with something we called **The Great Blunder**.

The Great Blunder

As I've just indicated, **The Great Blunder** has to do with that business of "object / relational" systems (O/R systems for short). Let me back up for a moment. As I've said, Hugh's original handwritten *TTM* draft was very short. Being so short, it was of course very terse: so terse, in fact, that we had to write an entire book of over 500 pages to explain it! That was our first edition, of course, and its title was *Foundation for Object / Relational Databases: The Third Manifesto*.[27] Note the explicit reference to O/R databases. Here's a quote from the preface that explains the point:

> *The Third Manifesto* is a detailed proposal for the future direction of data and database management systems (DBMSs). Like Codd's original papers on the relational model, it can be seen as an abstract blueprint for the design of a DBMS and the language interface to such a DBMS. In particular, it lays the foundation for what we believe is the logically correct approach to integrating relational and object technologies, a topic of considerable interest at the present time ... Perhaps we should say that we don't regard this idea as just another fad, soon to be replaced by some other briefly fashionable idea. On the contrary, we think object / relational systems are in everyone's future—a fact that makes it even more important to get the logical foundation right, of course, while we still have time to do so.

Well, it's certainly true that there was a lot of interest at the time in integrating OO and relational technologies. The trouble was, it seemed to us that many people were going after that objective in a fatally flawed way. To be specific, they were assuming that the relational concept that corresponded most closely to the OO *class* concept was the concept of a relation as such[28]—a

---

[27] Our original title had it the other way around—*The Third Manifesto: Foundation for Object / Relational Databases*—but Addison-Wesley made us change it. Further explanation available on request.

[28] Or a relvar, rather (see the next subsection), but this latter term wasn't in wide use at the time. Not that it is now either, of course—but it should be.

mistake that we referred to, rather rudely, as **The Great Blunder**. To us, by contrast, it was perfectly plain that the true relational analog of an object class was a *type* (*aka* a domain).[29] Thus, part of our goal in writing the book was simply to push for what we regarded as the right way to go about building O/R systems—in particular, to help the community avoid that "great blunder," if we could.

> *Aside:* Later we realized there was a second great blunder, too: viz., allowing database relations to contain pointers. Committing **The First Great Blunder** leads inevitably to committing **The Second Great Blunder** as well; however, what we didn't fully realize at the time was that it was possible to commit the second without committing the first. Well ... it would be more accurate to say we never dreamt that someone might commit the second and not the first—but that was before I had the conversation I mentioned earlier with Don Chamberlin. (Actually, Chamberlin's reason for wanting to commit the second blunder was probably to pave the way for committing the first as well—but even if so, it doesn't materially affect my point: namely, that it's at least possible to commit the second without committing the first.) *End of aside.*

By the way, if it's not obvious to you that **The First Great Blunder** is indeed a blunder, I'm going to have to ask you to take it on trust—this isn't the place to get into the technical details. If you want a detailed explanation, I refer you to my book *An Introduction to Database Systems* (8th edition, 2004). Here I just want to repeat and stress the following points from near the end of Part I of this presentation:

- A relational system that did types (domains) right would be able to do all of the things that OO advocates claim their systems can do and relational systems can't.

- The whole reason we were hearing so much about OO systems at the time was because the relational vendors had failed to step up to the mark (i.e., they'd failed to implement the relational model as such).

---

[29] I've said there's little consensus on the meanings of terms in the object world, and this criticism applies to the term *class* in particular (examples supplied on request). Thus, the claim I'm making here—viz., that a class is just a type—might meet with resistance in certain quarters. But I stand by it; I mean, I don't want to argue the point here.

- That failure stemmed from a failure to understand what the relational model really was.

- In fact, the "O/R model" is really nothing more nor less than the relational model, and a "true O/R system" would be nothing more nor less than a true relational system![30]

In other words, "object / relational" is really nothing more than a marketing term, dreamt up by the "relational" DBMS vendors to disguise the fact that their "relational" products weren't really very relational at all.[31] This field we all toil in—how shabby it can be ...

Relation Values vs. Relation Variables

There's one particular *Manifesto* contribution I'd like to emphasize in this discussion—namely, its introduction of the important term *relvar* (short for relation variable). To elaborate: Historically there's been a lot of confusion over the difference between relations as such and relation *variables*. Forget about databases for a moment; consider instead the following simple programming language example. Suppose I say in some programming language:

```
VAR N INTEGER ... ;
```

Then N here isn't an integer; rather, it's a *variable*, whose *values* are integers as such (different integers at different times). We all understand that. Well, in exactly the same way, if I say in SQL—

```
CREATE TABLE T ... ;
```

—then T *is not a table*; rather, it's a variable, a table variable or (as I'd prefer to call it, ignoring various SQL quirks such as duplicate rows and left to right column ordering) a relation variable, whose values are relations as such (different relations at different times).

Consider the famous suppliers-and-parts database. Now, I'm sure you're familiar with this example—you've probably seen it before, probably many

---

[30] And that's why we sincerely hope that what we wrote in the preface to our book—namely, that we think O/R systems are in everyone's future—turns out to be true.

[31] To repeat from Chapter 1: They still aren't, but that's another story.

times. Just to review briefly, though, S is suppliers; P is parts; and SP is shipments of parts by suppliers. Here's a picture (the various attributes—SNO, PNO, CITY, and so on—I take to be all pretty much self-explanatory):

S

SNO	SNAME	STATUS	CITY
S1	Smith	20	London
S2	Jones	10	Paris
S3	Blake	30	Paris
S4	Clark	20	London
S5	Adams	30	Athens

P

PNO	PNAME	COLOR	WEIGHT	CITY
P1	Nut	Red	12.0	London
P2	Bolt	Green	17.0	Paris
P3	Screw	Blue	17.0	Oslo
P4	Screw	Red	14.0	London
P5	Cam	Blue	12.0	Paris
P6	Cog	Red	19.0	London

SP

SNO	PNO	QTY
S1	P1	300
S1	P2	200
S1	P3	400
S1	P4	200
S1	P5	100
S1	P6	100
S2	P1	300
S2	P2	400
S3	P2	200
S4	P2	200
S4	P4	300
S4	P5	400

Now, what the picture shows is one possible value for this database, made up of three relations. Well, more precisely, what it shows is three relation *values*: namely, the relation values that happen to exist in the database at some particular time. But if we were to look at the database at some different time, we'd probably see three different relation values appearing in their place. In other words, S, P, and SP here are really *variables*: relation variables, to be precise. For example, suppose the relation variable S currently has the value shown in the picture, and suppose we delete the tuples for suppliers in London:

```
DELETE S WHERE CITY = 'London' ;
```

Or if you prefer SQL:[32]

---

[32] By the way, you might think the inclusion of the keyword FROM in the SQL version makes the syntax a little more user friendly, but actually it just muddies the issue. S WHERE CITY = 'London' is a relational expression, and it denotes the set of tuples to be deleted. So what the SQL formulation says is logically equivalent to DELETE FROM *<set of tuples to be deleted>*. But that makes no sense! What it *ought* to say is something like DELETE S WHERE CITY = 'London' *FROM S*. But then that *FROM S* is redundant (I mean, what else could those tuples possibly be deleted from?)—and so I think my original formulation is clearer, and for that reason more user friendly. *Note:* For the record, that formulation is expressed in the language **Tutorial D**, which I'll be discussing later.

```
DELETE FROM S WHERE CITY = 'London' ;
```

Here's the result:

SNO	SNAME	STATUS	CITY
S2	Jones	10	Paris
S3	Blake	30	Paris
S5	Adams	30	Athens

Conceptually, what's happened here is that the old value of S has been replaced in its entirety by a new value. Of course, the old value (with five tuples) and the new one (with three) are somewhat similar, in a sense, but they certainly are different values. In fact, the DELETE just shown is logically equivalent to, and indeed shorthand for, the following *relational assignment*:

```
S := S WHERE NOT ( CITY = 'London' ) ;
```

As with all assignments, the effect here is as follows: The source expression on the right side is evaluated, and then the result of that evaluation—a relation value in the case at hand, since the source expression is a relational expression—is assigned to the target variable on the left side (a relation variable, of course), with the overall result already explained.

So DELETE is shorthand for a certain relational assignment. And an analogous remark applies to INSERT and UPDATE also, of course: They too are basically just shorthand for certain relational assignments. Thus, relational assignment is the only update operator we really need, logically speaking, and it's the only one that's included in the relational model.

We see, therefore, that there's a logical difference between relation values and relation variables. The trouble is, the relational community has historically used the same term, *relation*, to stand for both. (Of course, SQL makes an exactly analogous mistake, using *table* to mean sometimes a table value and sometimes a table variable.) And that practice has certainly led to confusion. In the *Manifesto*, therefore, we distinguish very carefully between the two—we talk about relation values when we mean relation values and relation variables when we mean relation variables. (And I'd like to suggest rather strongly that you do the same! We've found that being careful over this important logical difference is a huge aid to clarity in thinking.) However, we also abbreviate *relation value*, most of the time, to just *relation*—exactly as we abbreviate *integer value* most of the time to just *integer*. And we abbreviate *relation variable* most of the time to **relvar**; for example, we say the suppliers-and-parts database contains three *relvars*.

It was our hope that *The Third Manifesto* would inspire people to use it as a basis for investigating numerous further areas of R&D in database technology, and indeed that's exactly what's happened. Here's a list of some of the fields—fields, I stress, of considerable practical as well as theoretical interest—in which such investigations have been carried out:

- Implementation

- Language design

- Business rules, constraints, and predicates

- View updating

- Type inheritance

- Temporal data

- Database design

- Missing information

I'd like to say too that these topics are all very much interconnected. Here are some examples to illustrate this point: (a) type inheritance turns out to be important in connection with temporal data; (b) constraints and predicates are the key to doing view updating right; and (c) proper relational design can help with the missing information problem.

By the way, in case you think I'm puffing up the importance of our *Manifesto* too much here, I really don't mean to. Partly I'm just using it as a kind of organizing principle ... but I do want to talk about what seem to me the interesting events in the second quarter century of relational history, and as far as

I'm concerned many of those events do stem from the *Manifesto* (which is, to say it again, exactly as we'd hoped; just like Ted Codd's papers 25 years before, in fact). In any case, I think the issues I'm going to be talking about are significant, regardless of whether you think the *Manifesto* has anything to do with them.

IMPLEMENTATION

There've been some 15 to 20 implementations of the ideas in the *Manifesto*, depending on how you count. I'll mention just a few of them here:

- *Rel* (Dave Voorhis): An ongoing and fairly complete implementation of **Tutorial D** (see later), developed at the University of Derby, U.K. Available through the *Manifesto* website *www.thethirdmanifesto.com*.

- D4 (Alphora): The first known attempt at a commercial implementation. Intended among other things as an application development frontend for various SQL backends (Oracle, DB2, etc.). Unfortunately the Alphora team eventually had to add SQL-style null support in order to achieve acceptable performance with those backends (which of course do already include such support). Regretfully, therefore, we had to withdraw our official Seal of Approval, as it were ... but D4 is otherwise highly *TTM* conformant, if that's a word. (Actually it is.)

- SIRA_PRISE (Erwin Smout): Meant as a full function, true relational DBMS. Provides efficient support for arbitrarily complex integrity constraints; multiple assignment; intervals (temporal data); user defined types and operators; and so on.

- Ingres Project D (Ingres Corp. and others): Meant as a high-performance true relational DBMS, to support everything in *TTM* via a **Tutorial D** interface living alongside the existing QUEL and SQL interfaces. Unfortunately this project has now been abandoned.

- DuroDBMS (René Hartmann): An open source relational DBMS with a **Tutorial D** interface, supporting nested transactions, user defined types, and declarative integrity constraints (including transition constraints).

There's one further project I'd like to mention here:

- The TransRelational^{TM} Model(Required Technologies Inc.): Now this one is not, and was never meant to be, a *TTM* project as such—it was developed independently—but in many ways it's a superlatively good fit with *TTM* ideas. Unfortunately the company later went under (not for technical reasons), but the technology lives on elsewhere. See my book *Go Faster! The TransRelational^{TM} Approach to DBMS Implementation*, available from *http://bookboon.com/en/go-faster-ebook* (2002, 2011) as a free download.

LANGUAGE DESIGN

The Third Manifesto isn't a language definition; all it does is lay down the functionality that any *TTM* conformant language must support and a set of principles that any such language must abide by. However, it does need a way of referring generically to any such language, and it uses the name **D** for that purpose. So **D** isn't a language, it's a family of languages, and there could be any number of individual languages all qualifying as a valid member of that family. **Tutorial D** is one such.[33] **Tutorial D** is based on the relational algebra; it's defined more or less formally in the *TTM* book, and it's used throughout that book and elsewhere as a basis for examples. In fact, I and others have been using that language for such purposes in books and presentations for many years now, and I think our experience in that regard has shown that it's both well designed and fairly self-explanatory. I'll give just one example here (deliberately a slightly nontrivial one) to illustrate the point. Suppose the shipments relvar SP has just two attributes, SNO and PNO (i.e., ignore quantities for simplicity). Then the expression

```
SP GROUP { PNO } AS PNO_REL
```

evaluates to a relation with one tuple for each distinct supplier, containing (a) that supplier's supplier number and (b) a unary "nested" relation containing part numbers for all parts supplied by that supplier (i.e., it maps a relation without a relation valued attribute into one with one). For example, if SP has as its current value the relation shown on the left in the following picture, the result is the relation shown on the right:

---

[33] By contrast, SQL very definitely isn't.

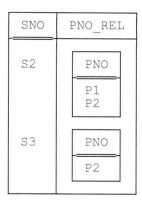

Here for interest is what I *think*—but I wouldn't stake good money on it—is an SQL analog of the foregoing **Tutorial D** expression:

```
SELECT DISTINCT X.SNO ,
                CAST ( TABLE ( SELECT Y.PNC
                               FROM   SP AS Y
                               WHERE  Y.SNC = X.SNO )
                     AS ROW ( PNO VARCHAR(6) ) MULTISET )
                AS PNO_REL
FROM    SP AS X
```

By the way, a **Tutorial D** expression for "going the other way," as it were (i.e., mapping the relation on the right—let's call it SPP—to the one on the left) is also straightforward:

```
SPP UNGROUP PNO_REL
```

This time I'll leave the SQL analog to you!

Aside: With reference to the simplicity of the foregoing **Tutorial D** expressions vs. the complexity of their SQL counterparts, here are two nice quotes:

■ For what is clear and easily comprehended attracts; the complicated repels.

—David Hilbert

■ Sometimes one has to say difficult things, but one ought to say them as simply as one knows how.

—G. H. Hardy

It's worth noting in passing that Hilbert and Hardy were both mathematicians, and very great ones at that (German and English, respectively). *End of aside.*

There's something else I want to say about language design: namely, I want to talk about a design principle we call *syntactic substitution*. It works like this. Suppose you're trying to design some new language from scratch. In our view, then, the right way to proceed is as follows:

- First you need to decide what basic concepts your language needs to support. The concepts in question, or *primitives*, should be chosen very carefully: Ideally, they should be (a) few in number; (b) mutually independent, or *orthogonal*, as far as is reasonably possible; (c) agreed to by all parties concerned; and of course (d) agreeable, not disagreeable, in nature.
  Note: This collection of primitives might reasonably be called a *model*. Certainly the relational model provides an appropriate collection of primitives if the language you're supposed to be defining is a database language specifically.

- Next you need to choose some good syntax for those basic or primitive concepts.

- Now you have a language!—in fact, a *complete* language, in the sense that it supports everything in your model. But if that's it in its entirety—if that's all you have—then your language will probably be quite hard to use; that is, in all but the simplest cases the statements and expressions needed to solve problems will probably be quite hard to formulate. For example, I for one would prefer not to have to formulate all relational update operations in terms of explicit relational assignment.

- So the next step is to define some good syntactic shorthands. The trick here is to recognize commonly occurring patterns—combinations of concepts and/or operations that occur over and over again—and then come up with some well thought out and well defined shorthands for those patterns. In the database case, examples include INSERT, DELETE, and UPDATE; foreign key constraints; the MATCHING and NOT MATCHING operators; image relations; and many, many others. In each of these examples, the syntax commonly used to express them is basically just shorthand for something that provides the same functionality but is typically much more longwinded.

- Those shorthands thus obviously save a great deal of writing. More to the point, they effectively raise the level of abstraction, by allowing the user to think about those commonly occurring bundles of concepts as single things (a bit like macros in a conventional programming language). What's more, they also offer the chance of improved performance, because they allow the implementation to recognize those bundles of concepts more readily and give them some kind of special-case treatment. And, of course, they can be used as the basis for defining still higher level shorthands.[34]

- In other words, as Hugh Darwen has written,[35] development of the language should proceed where possible by defining new language constructs in terms of ones already defined. That's the basic idea of syntactic substitution. However, Hugh also cautions:

> Importantly, syntactic substitution does *not* refer to an imprecise principle such as might be expressed as "*A* is something like (possibly very like) *B*," where *A* is some proposed new syntax and *B* is some expression using previously defined operators. If *A* is close in meaning to *B* but can't be specified by true syntactic substitution, then we have a situation that is disagreeable and probably unacceptable[36]—in stark contrast to true syntactic substitution, which can be very agreeable and acceptable indeed.

In sum, we believe the principle of syntactic substitution is a good basis for designing languages, and we've used it extensively in the design of **Tutorial D**.

---

[34] For example, Chapter 14, "Quota Queries," of my book *Logic and Relational Theory: Thoughts and Essays on Database Matters* (Technics Publications, 2020) contains a proposal for a new operator called IS_NTH_LARGEST, which is defined in terms of another proposed operator called QUOTA, which is defined in terms of still another proposed operator called RANK, which is defined in terms of the existing **Tutorial D** operators EXTEND, RENAME, and restriction (and as a matter of fact RENAME isn't primitive either, though EXTEND and restriction are).

[35] In his paper "Valid Time and Transaction Time Proposals: Language Design Aspects," in Opher Etzion, Sushil Jajodia, and Suryanaryan Sripada (eds.): *Temporal Databases: Research and Practice* (Springer Verlag, 1998).

[36] As I've shown elsewhere, SQL provides several examples of such a disagreeable situation. See, for example, Chapter 4 ("Redundancy in SQL") in the planned follow-on to the present book, viz., *Stating the Obvious, and Other Database Writings*.

One last point, though: I mustn't mislead you—**Tutorial D**, though we do believe it's a pretty good language as far as it goes, is in a sense only a toy language. In particular, it has no I/O and no exception handling. Thus, one thing we'd like to do is beef it up and turn it into some kind of **Industrial D**, thereby turning it into a serious contender for commercial implementation—though if we did that we'd probably want to give it a fancier name, like Java or Python! Some preliminary thoughts in this direction can be found in Chapter 16, "Toward an Industrial Strength Dialect of **Tutorial D**," in our book *Database Explorations: Essays on The Third Manifesto and Related Topics* (Trafford, 2010).

BUSINESS RULES, CONSTRAINTS, AND PREDICATES

Our work on the *Manifesto* led us—eventually, and a trifle painfully at times—to a proper understanding of these topics and how they're interrelated. It wouldn't be appropriate to go into details here, so I won't; instead, I'll just point you to a few relevant publications:

- "Constraints and Predicates" (Chapter 4 of my book *Logic and Relational Theory: Thoughts and Essays on Database Matters*, Technics Publications, 2020)

- "What *Is* Database Design, Anyway?" (Appendix A of my book *Database Design and Relational Theory: Normal Forms and All That Jazz*, 2nd edition, Apress, 2019)

- My (very informal!) book *WHAT Not HOW: The Business Rules Approach to Application Development* (Addison-Wesley, 2000)

VIEW UPDATING

View updating has been a thorny problem ever since the relational model first saw the light of day. Many, many papers and articles have been written on the subject over the years, and most of them have been quite depressing and/or negative in tone. Now, I don't claim the problem is 100% solved, either; however, I do believe the ideas of *The Third Manifesto* have allowed us to get much closer to a solution than anyone has managed before, as far as I'm aware.

In particular, our improved understanding of integrity constraints and predicates (see the previous section) has allowed us to make significant strides in the right direction. For further details, I refer you to my book *View Updating and Relational Theory: Solving the View Update Problem* (O'Reilly, 2013).

TYPE INHERITANCE

Under this heading, by contrast, I do want to get into a certain amount of technical detail. But it's a tricky area, and all I can do here is just touch on a few of the basic ideas.

To begin at the beginning: As I've already said, our *Manifesto* includes a theory of types. In fact, we regard the provision of that theory as one of the *Manifesto*'s main contributions. But thinking about types in general quickly leads to thinking about type inheritance in particular ... and we did that, and what we came up with was basically a whole new inheritance model, or theory, that's separate from the *Manifesto* as such but grafted on top of it, as it were. Which I'll now very briefly describe.

First of all, I should explain what we mean by the term *type inheritance*, or just *inheritance* for short. Basically, we use that term to refer to that phenomenon according to which we can sensibly say, for example, that every circle is an ellipse, and hence that all properties that apply to ellipses in general apply to—i.e., *are inherited by*—circles in particular. Equivalently (though loosely): All circles are ellipses, but "most" ellipses aren't circles.

Now, I need to explain immediately that there's no consensus in this field, and some people would dispute even the foregoing apparent truism (i.e., that circles are ellipses). By way of illustration, here's a verbatim quote from the book *The C++ Programming Language*, by Bjarne Stroustrup (3rd edition, Addison-Wesley, 1997):

> In mathematics a circle is a kind of an ellipse, but in most programs a circle should not be derived from an ellipse or an ellipse derived from a circle. The often heard arguments "because that's the way it is in mathematics" and "because the representation of a circle is a subset of that of an ellipse" are not conclusive and most often wrong. This is because for most programs, the key property of a circle is that it has a center and a fixed distance to its perimeter. All behavior of a circle (all operations) must maintain this property ... On the other hand, an ellipse is characterized by two focal points that can be changed independently of each other. If those focal points coincide, the ellipse looks like a circle, but it is not a circle

because its operations do not preserve the circle invariant. In most systems, this difference will be reflected by having a circle and an ellipse provide sets of operations that are not subsets of each other.

Well, we say to hell with all that! ... In our approach, in very striking contrast, (a) a circle most certainly is an ellipse—just as it is "in mathematics," in fact, as Stroustrup rightly says, and also (and more to the point) just as it is in the real world—and (b) ellipse properties most certainly are inherited by circles. By which we mean, for example, that every ellipse has an area, and therefore every circle has an area also. More precisely:

a. Types ELLIPSE and CIRCLE are such that type ELLIPSE is a *supertype* of type CIRCLE and type CIRCLE is a *subtype* of type ELLIPSE.

b. There's an operator—AREA_OF, say—that, given an argument of type ELLIPSE returns the area of that ellipse, and that operator can be invoked with an argument of type CIRCLE, because circles *are* ellipses.

Of course, the converse is false—the subtype will have properties of its own that don't apply to the supertype. For example, circles have a radius, but ellipses in general don't; in other words, there's an operator that returns the radius of a given circle, but that operator can't be invoked with an argument that's "just an ellipse," because such ellipses aren't circles.

So operators are inherited.[37] But constraints are properties too, of a kind, and therefore they're inherited too.[38] For example, any constraint that applies to ellipses in general also applies to circles in particular (for otherwise some circles wouldn't be ellipses). By way of example, suppose ellipses are subject to the constraint that the length a of their major semiaxis is greater than or equal to the length b of their minor semiaxis; then that same constraint must be satisfied by circles also. (For circles the semiaxes coincide in the radius, and this particular constraint is satisfied trivially.)

Again, of course, the converse is false—there'll be constraints that apply to circles specifically but not to ellipses in general. In fact, the constraint $a = b$ is an example of one that applies to circles specifically but not to ellipses in general.

---

[37] By *operators* here, I really mean read-only operators specifically.

[38] By *constraints* here, I really mean type constraints specifically.

Well, from simple ideas such as the foregoing—all of which, let me stress, are really nothing more than logical consequences of the even more fundamental notion that *types are sets*—we've constructed a complete and rigorous inheritance model, one that supports:

a. Both single and multiple inheritance

That is, a given subtype can have any number of supertypes (loosely speaking). For example, type CIRCLE has just one, ELLIPSE—that's single inheritance—but type SQUARE might have two, RECTANGLE and RHOMBUS[39]—that's multiple inheritance. Of course, the former is just a special case of the latter. But you need to understand that support for the latter is quite unusual! Many inheritance schemes described in the literature deal with single inheritance only. That's the way SQL is, for example.

b. Scalar, tuple, and relation inheritance

That is, the subtypes and supertypes we're talking about can be tuple or relation types as well as scalar types. For example, the relation type

```
RELATION { E CIRCLE , R SQUARE }
```

is a subtype of the relation type

```
RELATION { E ELLIPSE , R RECTANGLE }
```

And again such support is quite unusual—most inheritance schemes deal with scalar inheritance only. Again, that's the way SQL is, for example.[40]

---

[39] In other words, every square is both a rectangle (the four contained angles are all right angles, which is the defining property of a rectangle) and a rhombus (the four sides are all the same length, which is the defining property of a rhombus).

[40] Two points here. First, believe it or not, SQL tables don't even have types, and so the idea that one table type might be a subtype of another simply doesn't arise (in fact, it *can't* arise), in SQL. Second, it's true that SQL does support something it calls supertables and subtables (and also, in connection with that support, something it calls subrows and superrows), but I for one regard these constructs with considerable suspicion. They certainly don't have anything to do with type inheritance as such. For further explanation, I refer you to Chapter 22 ("Inheritance in SQL") of my book *Type Inheritance and Relational Theory: Subtypes, Supertypes, and Substitutability* (O'Reilly, 2016).

And, very importantly (but uniquely, and controversially!), our model also supports:

c. "Specialization by constraint" (S by C for short)

That is, if an ellipse has $a = b$ then it's a circle, and if it's a circle then it has $a = b$, and *the system is aware of both of these facts.* In particular, therefore, the fact that a given value of type ELLIPSE has $a = b$ means that the value in question is "specialized"—in effect, by the system—to type CIRCLE.

Now, the idea that an ellipse is a circle if and only if it has $a = b$ is in strict accordance with the way the world works, of course, but—rather incredibly—*nobody* except us has an inheritance scheme that supports it (as far as we know). Certainly SQL doesn't. Here's another quote to illustrate the point (actually this quote talks about classes instead of types, and squares and rectangles instead of circles and ellipses, but I'm sure you won't need me to translate for you):

> Is SQUARE a subclass of RECTANGLE? ... Stretching the x dimension of a rectangle is a perfectly reasonable thing to do. But if you do it to a square, then the object is no longer a square. This is not necessarily a bad thing conceptually. When you stretch a square you *do* get a rectangle ... But ... most object languages do not want objects to change class ... This suggests a design principle for classification systems: *A subclass should not be defined by constraining a superclass.*
> —James Rumbaugh: "A Matter of Intent: How to Define Subclasses"
> *Journal of Object Oriented Programming* (September 1996)

Notice the rationale—"most object languages don't want objects to change class." By contrast, we say "Let's get the model right first, then worry about designing a language to support it afterward." And in our model, stretching a square does produce a rectangle (if you see what I mean). That's S by C. (Or G by C, to be more precise—G for generalization. S by C and G by C are two sides of the same coin, and we use "S by C" as a shorthand label for both considered together. Stretching a square produces a rectangle—OK, that's G by C. By the same token, squashing a rectangle produces a square—OK, that's S by C! Speaking pretty loosely, of course, in both cases.)

By the way, you might be wondering *why* object languages don't want objects to change class and therefore don't support S by C, since it seems so obviously the right thing to do. The answer, believe it or not, is because they support *pointers* ... The issue is far too arcane to get into details on here, but the fact is that pointers and S by C turn out to be simply, but fundamentally, incompatible. If we're right on this (and we think we are), then we say tough—it's just too bad for pointers, and they'll have to go.[41]

Be that as it may, our inheritance model, and as a matter of fact SQL's too, are both described in detail in my book *Type Inheritance and Relational Theory: Subtypes, Supertypes, and Substitutability* (O'Reilly, 2016). And I'd like to call your attention here to something I say in that book:

> There's no consensus on a formal, rigorous, and abstract type inheritance model. In our work on *The Third Manifesto*, therefore, we were more or less forced to develop an inheritance model of our own ... We're very serious about that model. We'd like it *not* to be seen as just an academic exercise. Rather, we'd like it to be considered by the community at large as a serious contender for filling the gap (i.e., as a candidate for the role that *is* "formal, rigorous, and abstract" and can be generally agreed upon by that "community at large"). We offer it here in that spirit.

Of course, you might have noticed that so far I haven't said anything as to why inheritance is worth supporting in the first place! There seem to be at least two answers to this question:

- First, the ideas of subtyping and inheritance do seem to arise naturally in the real world (as with ellipses and circles, or rectangles and squares). Thus, subtyping and inheritance look as if they might be useful tools for "modeling reality."

- Second, if we can recognize such general patterns—patterns of subtyping and inheritance, that is—and build intelligence regarding them into our application and system software, we might be able to achieve certain practical economies. For example, a program that works for ellipses might work for circles too, even if it was originally written with no thought for circles at all (perhaps type CIRCLE hadn't even been defined at the time the program in question was written).

---

[41] And if they do, then—since support for objects seems to *require* support for pointers—it follows that objects (as that term is usually understood) will have to go too. Interesting conclusion!

That said, I should say too that most of the existing literature seems more concerned—I'm tempted to say, *much* more concerned—with the second of these goals than it is with the first; in other words, it seems to be principally interested in inheritance as a mechanism for designing, building, and (re)using *programs*. Our own focus, by contrast, is more on the first than the second; that is, we're interested in inheritance as a conceptual tool for designing, building, and (re)using *data structures*. (After all, we're database people, and data structures are important to us.) In other words, what we're looking for is an inheritance model that can be used to "model reality"—certain aspects of reality, at any rate—much as the relational model itself can also be used to model certain aspects of reality.

TEMPORAL DATA

Here's another really big issue that I'd like to say a little more about. This time I'll start with the pertinent reference:

- C. J. Date, Hugh Darwen, and Nikos A. Lorentzos: *Time and Relational Theory: Temporal Databases in the Relational Model and SQL* (Morgan Kaufmann, 2014)

Nikos is the prime mover in this work (he began working on this topic in the late 1980s).

Now, much of the research in the temporal database field seems to assume that the relational model is incapable of dealing with temporal data, and hence that it needs extensions of some kind. Consider by way of example the following (genuine) research paper titles:

- "A Temporally Oriented Data Model"

- "The Time Relational Model"

- "The Historical Relational Data Model (HRDM) Revisited"

- "Temporal Extensions to the Relational Model and SQL"

And so on. What these titles (and many others like them) all tend to suggest is that something radical is needed: major surgery to the relational model, at least, or possibly even something entirely new. Our position, by contrast, is: No, don't do *anything* to the relational model! We believe, and we demonstrate in our book, that the relational model needs no *EXTENSION*, and no *CORRECTION*, and no *SUBSUMPTION*—and above all no *PERVERSION*—for it to be able to support temporal data.

> *Aside:* Actually I'm touching here on an issue that's bigger—much bigger—than just temporal data as such. The fact is, the relational model needs no extension, no correction, no subsumption, and above all no perversion, for it to be able to support *any* of the "new" things I'm talking about in this part of my presentation. *End of aside.*

Now, once again I don't want to mislead you here—we do define a bunch of new "temporal" operators, for example—but everything we "add" to the relational model is, in the final analysis, just shorthand for something the relational model can already do. In other words, we make heavy use (actually very heavy use) of that principle of syntactic substitution I talked about earlier. That's the way to make progress in these various fields I'm talking about ... But let me get back to temporal data specifically. Consider the following relation:

SNO	DURING
S1	[*d04*:*d07*]
S1	[*d05*:*d10*]
S1	[*d09*:*d09*]
S2	[*d05*:*d06*]
S2	[*d03*:*d03*]
S2	[*d07*:*d08*]

The intended meaning here—the *predicate*—is this: *Supplier SNO was under contract throughout interval DURING.*[42] For example, we see among

---

[42] The fact that every relation, and also every relvar, has an associated predicate, which is an informal statement of what the relation or relvar in question "means"—i.e., what the *intended interpretation* is for that relation or relvar—is something else I'd like to discuss in more depth if we had time, but I'm afraid you're just going to have to trust me once again. A detailed discussion of such matters can be found in many places, though; see, for example, my book *SQL and Relational Theory: How to Write Accurate SQL Code*, 3rd edition (O'Reilly, 2015).

other things that supplier S1 was under contract throughout the interval from "day 4" (*d04*) to "day 7" (*d07*), inclusive.

> *Aside:* So yes, we do introduce something new: namely, we introduce interval types. (More precisely, we introduce an interval *type generator*, which allows for the definition of any number of specific interval types.) But introducing new types doesn't change the relational model! In particular, therefore, we're definitely not "extending" the relational model. Remember the catchphrase: *Types are orthogonal to tables. End of aside.*

In our book, then, we define all kinds of "new" constructs for dealing with relations like the one just shown, including:

- Two new operators, PACK and UNPACK

- Generalized versions ("U_ operators") of regular projection, join, etc.

- Generalized join dependencies ("U_JDs")

- New constraints, PACKED ON and WHEN / THEN

And on and on. Now, I can't possibly get into details of all of this stuff here; I'll just say one thing, to give a slight hint. Let SD be the relation in the picture on the previous page. Then I can think you can see some problems with that relation:

- *Redundancy:* For example, relation SD tells us twice that supplier S1 was under contract on day 6.

- *Circumlocution:* For example, relation SD takes three tuples to tell us what it could have told us with just one, viz., that supplier S1 was under contract throughout the interval [*d04:d10*].

Well, we can get rid of these problems by "packing" relation SD "on attribute DURING," thus:

```
PACK SD ON ( DURING )
```

Here's the result:

SNO	DURING
S1	[d04:d10]
S2	[d03:d03]
S2	[d05:d08]

As you can see, this relation doesn't suffer from either the redundancy problem or the circumlocution problem that SD suffers from. But let me stress again that all of these "new" things (PACK and all the rest) are, in the last analysis, just shorthand for combinations of things that can already be done—albeit not very easily, in some cases—by means of features already present in the relational model.

DATABASE DESIGN

As you know, there's more to relational theory than just the relational model as such. Design theory in particular isn't part of the model; rather, it's a separate theory that builds on top of that model. As an obvious illustration of the point, the concept of normalization is based on certain more fundamental notions—in particular, the projection and join operators of the relational algebra—that *are* part of the model. And there are a few recent developments in the design theory field that I want to say something about here. Though I have to admit up front that their connections with *The Third Manifesto* as such aren't all that direct, except inasmuch as *Manifesto* concepts proved very helpful in providing the framework for doing the pertinent research.

First I want to talk about a couple of new normal forms. Now, I assume you're familiar with the classical normalization hierarchy, which looks like this:

```
1NF
2NF
3NF
BCNF
4NF
5NF
```

I assume you know too that (in a sense) 5NF is the ultimate normal form. What this means, a little more precisely, is that if relvar R is in 5NF, then it's guaranteed to be free of redundancies that can be removed by taking projections.

That is, it might be possible to replace R by projections (just as we do when we step from 2NF to 3NF, for example), but that replacement won't eliminate any redundancies—if there were any redundancies in R, those redundancies will still be present in the projections.

I also need to assume you know something about join dependencies (JDs)—though I realize that might be a pretty big assumption! Here's a rough definition: Basically, the JD ✪$\{X1, ..., Xn\}$ (pronounced "star $X1$, ..., Xn") holds in relvar R if and only if R is equal to its projections on $X1, ..., Xn$—in other words, if and only if R can be nonloss decomposed into those projections. For example, the following JD—

```
✪{ { SNO , SNAME } , { SNO , STATUS , CITY } }
```

—clearly holds in the suppliers relvar S, because {SNO} is a key for that relvar. So we could decompose that relvar accordingly, if we wanted to. (I'm not saying we *must* decompose it; I'm just saying we could if we wanted to, that's all.)

Now, it's always the case that (as in the foregoing example) certain JDs are implied by the keys of the pertinent relvar. We can never get rid of those. It's if any *other* JDs hold that we might have a problem.

> *Aside:* If you happen to be familiar with this topic, you might realize that I'm playing pretty fast and loose with it here. In particular, I'm conflating the notion of *being implied by a key*, singular, with the notion of *being implied by keys*, plural. The difference is significant, but not all that important for my purposes in this presentation, which is why I feel justified in indulging in a little bit of what a friend of mine once called "creative lying." *End of aside.*

Here then is a definition of 5NF:

Definition (fifth normal form): Relvar R is in fifth normal form, 5NF, if and only if every JD that holds in R is either trivial or implied by the keys of R[43]—where a JD ✪$\{X1, ..., Xn\}$ is trivial if and only if one of the Xi components is equal to the entire heading.

5NF is generally understood and believed to be "the end of the normalization road." Well, I'm here to tell you now that there are at least two senses in which it isn't! To be specific, I want to tell you about two new normal

---

[43] Actually that "either trivial or" could be dropped, because trivial JDs *are* implied by keys, trivially.

forms, 6NF and ETNF, one of which, 6NF, is really important (the other, ETNF, is perhaps less so).

6NF

I mentioned that in connection with our temporal work we defined generalized versions of the relational operators—of projection and join in particular, but in fact of all of the other relational operators as well—that we called U_ operators. Using U_projection and U_join in particular, we then defined a generalized form of JD (a U_JD) and a generalized form of relational equality (U_equality).[44] Now, I must stress that these generalizations truly are all generalizations—by which I mean that regular projection is just a special case of U_projection, regular join is just a special case of U_join, and so on. Anyway, we were then able to use those generalized concepts to define a new normal form, 6NF, that turns out to be really important in connection with temporal data:

> **Definition (sixth normal form for temporal data):** Relvar *R* is in sixth normal form, 6NF, if and only if the only U_JDs that hold in *R* are trivial ones; in other words, the only U_JDs that hold in *R* have *H* as a component, where *H* is the heading of *R*.

Now, to explain this definition in detail would take us much further afield than I want to go here. All I want to do here is point out that a reduced form of the definition, in which U_JDs are replaced by ordinary "vanilla" JDs (which are just a special case), applies to regular data as well:

> **Definition (sixth normal form for regular data):** Relvar *R* is in sixth normal form, 6NF, if and only if the only JDs that hold in *R* are trivial ones; in other words, the only JDs that hold in *R* have *H* as a component, where *H* is the heading of *R*.

Thus, going back to the example of the suppliers relvar S, we can see it's not in 6NF, because the following JD (among others) holds in that relvar—

    ⋈{ { SNO , SNAME } , { SNO , STATUS , CITY } }

---

[44] It might help to note here for the record that the two relations depicted on pages 85 and 87, respectively, though they're clearly not equal, are in fact U_equal.

—and this JD is obviously not trivial. By contrast, the projections

```
S { SNO , SNAME }
S { SNO , STATUS }
S { SNO , CITY }
```

are in 6NF, all three of them. And S can be replaced by them, because the JD

```
 ☼{ { SNO , SNAME } , { SNO , STATUS } , { SNO , CITY } }
```

also holds in S.

Why would we want to perform such a replacement? More generally, why would we want relvars to be in 6NF? What are the benefits? Well, there are several answers to this question:

1. The first is that the predicate, the intended meaning, for such a relvar is clean and simple—in particular, it involves no ANDs. (Note that the predicate for the original suppliers relvar does involve a bunch of ANDs: *Supplier SNO is under contract* **AND** *has name SNAME* **AND** *has status STATUS* **AND** *is located in city CITY.*) Thus, the tuples in a 6NF relvar at any given time correspond to what might reasonably be called "atomic facts," or (perhaps better) "irreducible facts."

2. The second has to do with temporal data specifically. I can't go into details here; let me just say that 6NF is really important in the temporal context (perhaps more so than in the nontemporal context), because it's of major help with dealing with the old design problems of data redundancy and the update anomalies caused by such redundancy—with the particular redundancy and update problems, that is to say, that arise in connection with temporal data specifically.

3. The third answer is tied up with our next topic, missing information, so I'll defer the details until we get to that topic.

References: For a discussion of 6NF in the temporal context, see the book where it was defined:

- C. J. Date, Hugh Darwen, and Nikos A. Lorentzos: *Time and Relational Theory: Temporal Databases in the Relational Model and SQL* (Morgan Kaufmann, 2014)[45]

And for a discussion of 6NF for regular data, as well as a gentle introduction to its use in the temporal context, see:

- C. J. Date: *Database Design and Relational Theory: Normal Forms and All That Jazz* (2nd edition, Apress, 2019)

Now I'd like to move on to ETNF.

ETNF

I'll begin with a quote from "the jazz book" (i.e., the second of the references just mentioned):

> We generally want our databases to be as free of redundancy as possible, where by *redundancy* I mean more specifically any redundancy that can be removed by taking projections. And of course we use the normalization discipline to help us reach that goal. Now, for many years it was believed that a relvar had to be in 5NF in order for it to be free of redundancy in the foregoing sense. Somewhat surprisingly, however, it turns out that this belief was incorrect—that is, it turns out that several other normal forms can be defined, all of them both weaker than 5NF and stronger than 4NF, and all of them just as effective as 5NF at eliminating redundancy. The normal forms in question are:
>
> - Essential tuple normal form, ETNF
>
> - Redundancy free normal form, RFNF (also known as key complete normal form, KCNF)
>
> - Superkey normal form, SKNF
>
> The normal form hierarchy now looks like this:

---

[45] Actually this book is a major revision of an earlier one by the same authors—*Temporal Data and the Relational Model* (Morgan Kaufmann, 2003)—and 6NF first saw the light of day in that earlier book.

```
                            1NF
                            2NF
                            3NF
                            BCNF
                            4NF
                            ETNF
                       RFNF / KCNF
                            SKNF
                            5NF
                            6NF
```

Of the three new normal forms—ETNF, RFNF (or KCNF), and SKNF, I mean—the most important one, and the only one I want to discuss any further, is ETNF. And I'm not going to say much about that one either!—the details are much too complicated for an overview presentation like this one. In fact, I'm not even going to define it. What I will do, though, is state some theorems that provide practical tests for ETNF:

Theorem: Relvar R is in ETNF if and only if it's in BCNF and, for every JD J that holds in R, at least one component of J is a superkey for R.[46]

Theorem: Relvar R is in ETNF if it's in BCNF and at least one of its keys is noncomposite.

Theorem: Relvar R is in ETNF if it's in 3NF and all of its keys are noncomposite.

References: This is the paper where ETNF was first defined and various associated theorems proved:

■ Hugh Darwen, C. J. Date, and Ronald Fagin: "A Normal Form for Preventing Redundant Tuples in Relational Databases," Proc. 15th International Conference on Database Theory, Berlin, Germany (March 26th-29th, 2012)

And for a tutorial discussion of such matters, see the jazz book again:

---

[46] In case you're not familiar with the concept of a superkey, here's a definition: A superkey is a subset of the heading of the pertinent relvar that includes a key of that relvar. For example, {SNO,CITY} is a superkey for relvar S. Note that it follows from this definition that all keys are superkeys, but "most" superkeys aren't keys. *Exercise:* How many superkeys does the suppliers relvar S have?

■ C. J. Date: *Database Design and Relational Theory: Normal Forms and All That Jazz* (2nd edition, Apress, 2019)

Now I'd like to move on to the last of my design topics, orthogonality.

Orthogonality

Here now is a sample value for another possible design for suppliers:

SNC

SNO	SNAME	CITY
S1	Smith	London
S2	Jones	Paris
S3	Blake	Paris
S4	Clark	London
S5	Adams	Athens

STC

SNO	STATUS	CITY
S1	20	London
S2	30	Paris
S3	30	Paris
S4	20	London
S5	30	Athens

Now, this design is obviously bad—note in particular that the fact that any given supplier is located in a given city appears twice—and yet it abides by all of the usual normalization principles:

■ Both projections are in 5NF.

■ The decomposition is nonloss.

■ Dependencies are preserved.[47]

■ Both projections are needed in the reconstruction process.

It follows that the usual normalization principles by themselves aren't enough—we need something else to tell us what's wrong with the design (something else *formal*, that is; we all know what's wrong with it informally). To put it another way, normalization provides a set of formal principles to guide us in our attempts to reduce redundancy, but that set of principles by itself is inadequate, as the example plainly shows. We need another principle; in other

---

[47] I don't want to get into too much detail about preserving dependencies here. However, I'll just note in particular that every *functional* dependency (FD) that holds in relvar S also holds in—i.e., is *preserved* in— at least one of the two projections, and possibly in both.

words, as I've said on many occasions and in many places, ***we need more science***. And orthogonality is just that—another little piece of science, to add to the science already available to us in the form of normalization theory.

Now, there's quite a lot to this notion of orthogonality, and I'm not even going to attempt to cover it all here. All I want to do here is give a very much simplified definition of *The Principle of Orthogonal Design* that does at least take care of the foregoing example. Here it is:

> **Definition (*The Principle of Orthogonal Design*, hugely simplified version):** Let *R1* and *R2* be relvars. Then there must not exist a JD *J* that holds in *R1* such that (a) some component *X* of *J* is equal to some subset of the heading of *R2*, and (b) the projections on *X* of *R1* and *R2* are equal.

In the case at hand, for example, the JD

```
☼{ { SNO , SNAME } , { SNO , CITY } }
```

holds in relvar SNC; the component {SNO,CITY} of that JD is a subset of the heading of relvar STC; and the projections of SNC and STC on those attributes {SNO,CITY} are indeed equal. So the design violates orthogonality. So don't do it!

Now, the foregoing discussion doesn't illustrate the point, but orthogonality actually takes care of issues arising from decomposition via restriction, too (normalization, of course, has to do with decomposition via projection). An example might be to replace the parts relvar P by two restrictions, one for light parts and one for heavy parts. Of course, this latter design would require appropriate definitions of "light" and "heavy"—and orthogonality would then tell us to make sure those definitions don't overlap (i.e., no part is allowed to be both light and heavy).[48]

References: Orthogonality was first described in:

■ C. J. Date and David McGoveran: "A New Database Design Principle," *Database Programming & Design 7*, No. 7 (July 1994)

---

[48] Pretty obvious stuff, you might be forgiven for thinking. But the principles of normalization are obvious too! The obviousness isn't the point. Rather, the point lies in stating what "obvious" means in formal and precise terms, so that a machine can understand.

However, don't read this paper!—it's both confusing and confused. (All my fault, I hasten to add. Please don't blame David.)

A much more extensive discussion of orthogonality—possibly still confusing, but I hope much less confused—can be found in the jazz book:

- C. J. Date: *Database Design and Relational Theory: Normal Forms and All That Jazz* (2nd edition, Apress, 2019)

MISSING INFORMATION

What a horrible topic to finish up with! Well, I shouldn't say that ... The topic is certainly important, even if it's currently such a mess. Here's what I say about it by way of introduction in my book *An Introduction to Database Systems*:

> Information is often missing in the real world; examples such as "date of birth unknown," "speaker to be announced," "present address not known," and so on, are common and familiar to all of us. Clearly, therefore, we need some way of dealing with such missing information in our database systems. And the approach to this problem most commonly adopted in practice (in SQL in particular) is based on *nulls* and *three-valued logic* (3VL). For example, we might not know the weight of some part, say part P7, and so we might say, loosely, that the weight of that part "is null"—meaning, more precisely, that (a) we do know the part exists, and of course (b) we also know it has a weight, but (c) to repeat, we don't know what that weight is.
>
> To pursue this example a little further, consider the tuple that represents part P7 in the database. Obviously we can't put a genuine WEIGHT value in that tuple. So what we do instead is *mark* or *flag* the WEIGHT position in that tuple as "null," and then we interpret that mark or flag to mean, precisely, that we don't know what the genuine value is. Now, we might think, informally, of that WEIGHT position as "containing a null," or of that WEIGHT value as "being null," and indeed we often talk in such terms in practice. But it should be clear that such talk *is* only informal, and indeed not very accurate; to say that the WEIGHT component of some tuple "is null" is really to say that *the tuple contains no WEIGHT value at all*. That's why the expression "null value," which is heard very frequently, is deprecated: The whole point about nulls (or a large part of the point, at any rate) is precisely that they're not values—they are, to repeat, marks or flags.

Now, you probably already know what I think about this nulls business: In my opinion (and in that of many other people too, I hasten to add), nulls and 3VL are and always were a serious mistake, and they have no place in a respectable formalism like the relational model.[49] For example, to say that a certain part tuple contains no WEIGHT value is to say, by definition, that the tuple in question isn't a part tuple after all. In fact, it isn't a tuple at all, not even of any kind!—as can be seen from the very definition of the term *tuple* (basically as a set of attribute / value pairs). The truth is, the very act of trying to state precisely what the nulls scheme is all about is sufficient to show why the idea isn't exactly coherent ... As a consequence, it's hard to explain it coherently, too.[50] As David Maier says in this connection in his book *The Theory of Relational Databases* (Computer Science Press, 1983): "It all makes sense if you squint a little and don't think too hard."

> *Aside:* In fact, the only person I ever met who (a) could credibly claim to understand the relational model, ***and*** (b) thought that nulls were a good idea, was Ted Codd! Indeed, you might be aware that Ted and I actually got into a debate in print on this issue. It appeared in *Database Programming & Design 6*, No. 10 (October 1993),[51] under the title "Much Ado about Nothing." (One of the things I hate about this topic is that people always seem to want to make feeble jokes ... But I digress.) Anyway, during that debate Ted came up with the following absolutely priceless remark:
>
> > Database management would be simpler if missing values didn't exist.
>
> Unfortunately I don't think he did mean this as a joke. *End of aside.*

Anyway: So what we have so far is that (a) the problem is important, and (b) nulls and 3VL don't solve it. Now what?

---

[49] Indeed, nulls and 3VL were Ted Codd's one big mistake. Now, perhaps we can forgive him for that mistake, considering that he gave us his wonderful relational model—but I do have to say I wish that mistake hadn't been one of such epic proportions. PS: To repeat something I already said (more or less) in footnote 16, there weren't any nulls in Ted's relational model at all when he originally defined it, back in 1969. In fact, he didn't add them (at least, not officially) until ten years later, in 1979. So the relational model managed perfectly well without them for ten years—and I'd frankly prefer to keep it that way. Which is what *The Third Manifesto* does, of course.

[50] Chris Date's *Principle of Incoherence*: It's hard to criticize something coherently if what's being criticized is itself not very coherent in the first place.

[51] And was subsequently republished in my book *Relational Database Writings 1991-1994* (Addison-Wesley, 1995).

Well, the sad truth is that *nobody* has a perfect solution to this problem. Nevertheless, a certain amount of progress toward such a solution has been made, as I'd now like to explain.

No nulls in the database: First of all, 6NF gives us the obvious way to avoid nulls completely, at least in the database as such. For example, consider suppliers and parts once again—in fact, for simplicity, let's focus just on parts. A 6NF design for parts would replace the original relvar P by its projections PP, PL, PW, and PC on {PNO,PNAME}, {PNO,COLOR}, {PNO,WEIGHT}, and {PNO,CITY}, respectively. (We'd probably want a unary relvar PN too, whose purpose would be simply to list the part numbers for every part that's currently of interest.)

Suppose now that some part, say part P7, has no known weight; then that part will simply have no tuple in relvar PW—and similarly for parts with no known name or no known color or no known city, mutatis mutandis. Hey presto: No nulls!

More generally, if there are two or more properties, like name and color, that every part does always have, then separating those properties out into distinct projections is probably not worth it; but if some property is "optional"— in other words, if it has the potential to be "missing" or unknown for some reason—then placing that property in a relvar of its own is probably a good idea.

> *Aside:* By the way, you might be thinking, especially if you're steeped in the kinds of SQL implementations to be found on the market today (where each base relvar maps to its own stored file, pretty much), that the kind of 6NF design I'm talking about here is bound to perform horribly. All those joins, right? But here's another place where that TransRelational™ idea—see the section "Implementation," earlier—really shows its strength. Let me abbreviate TransRelational™ to just TR. Then 6NF and TR are actually a perfect marriage, not least because, in TR, *join costs are linear.* That is, joining two relations of a million tuples each takes $O(2M)$ time, whereas in classical implementations it takes $O(1T)$ time—i.e., it's 500,000 times slower. Now, I'm not going to explain, here, how this can be; if you want to know more, I'm afraid I'm just going to have to point you to the *Go Faster!* book I mentioned earlier. (But perhaps you can begin to see why I gave the book that title!) Do notice, however, how all this is another example of the interrelatedness of all of these developments that I've been talking about in this presentation. *End of aside.*

No nulls in results: I show in the following paper how we can get "don't know" answers—when "don't know" is the appropriate answer, of course!—out of a database without nulls, without straying from good old two-valued logic, 2VL (in other words, there's no need for 3VL or 4VL, etc.):[52]

- C. J. Date: "*The Closed World Assumption*" (Chapter 5 in this book's predecessor, *Logic and Relational Theory: Thoughts and Essays on Database Matters*, Technics Publications, 2020)

   Aside: Of course, SQL expressions in particular do often "evaluate to null" (pardon the solecism), meaning we can get nulls in results—but that's simply a mistake in the design of SQL. For example, SQL says the sum of an empty set of numbers is null, whereas it should of course be zero. *End of aside.*

Suggestions for consideration: The following book—

- C. J. Date and Hugh Darwen: *Database Explorations: Essays on The Third Manifesto and Related Topics* (Trafford, 2010)

—contains several chapters suggesting various possible "null free" approaches to the missing information problem, of which the most ambitious and most carefully thought out is probably this one:

- Hugh Darwen: "The Multirelational Approach" (Chapter 24)

But I hasten to add that neither Hugh nor I would actually recommend adopting this scheme—especially since it effectively replaces, or at least hugely expands, the entire relational model by something else (namely, something that might be called "the multirelational model"). To quote Hugh's paper:

   I feel bound to say that, if the scheme overall is seen principally as an approach to the "missing information" problem—a problem to which, I say again, purely relational solutions already exist—then it does seem to involve a degree of complexity out of proportion to the problem it's meant to address.

---

[52] Codd actually wanted not just 3VL, for dealing with one kind of null, but 4VL, for dealing with two different kinds ("value unknown" and "value not applicable"). I discuss such matters in detail in Chapter 18, "Why Three- and Four-Valued Logic Don't Work," of my book *Date on Database: Writings 2000-2006* (Apress, 2006).

But at least it's good to see such a scheme worked out in so much detail (though, as Hugh also says, "there are quite a few loose ends to be tidied up" and "there are many topics that need further investigation").

CONCLUDING REMARKS

Well, I have another quote for you:

> The only thing we learn from history is that we learn nothing from history.
> —Georg Wilhelm Friedrich Hegel (considerably paraphrased):
> *Lectures on the Philosophy of World History* (1830)

I even toyed with the idea of making this into an epigraph to the presentation as a whole but decided not to, partly because of its self-referential and thereby paradoxical nature. (I mean, if it's true, then it's false—right?) Be that as it may, I hope very much that, *pace* Herr Hegel, you have in fact managed to learn something from this presentation ... Just to remind you, here's an outline of what we've covered in this second part:

- *Replacing relational?* I talked about the battles we had to fight, and in some cases still have to fight—all of them coming down (in my view) to a failure to understand what the relational model is really all about.

- *Why relational won't be replaced:* The relational model is rock solid ... but what exactly is it? I talked about moving the goalposts. The fact is, definitions do change over time as we improve our own understanding, and I did summarize (under the *Third Manifesto* umbrella) what some of the *good* changes have been.

- *The Third Manifesto:* I talked about what the *Manifesto* is and why we wrote it. In particular I talked about our introduction of the (as far as we're concerned, very important) term *relvar*, and I emphasized that "types are orthogonal to tables."

- *Research topics and successes:* And then I gave "the view from 20,000 feet" for a number of research and development directions and successes, based in most cases rather directly on the *Manifesto*.

In closing, I very much doubt whether it'll be me who does Part III of this presentation, covering the *next* 25 years—but I certainly hope somebody does, and I hope it'll be even more positive and, frankly, even more exciting. Thank you for listening.

Part II

RESPONDING TO

CRITICISM

Chapter 3

Gödel, Russell, Codd:

A Recursive Golden Crowd

A paradox? A paradox!
A most ingenious paradox!

—W. S. Gilbert:
The Pirates of Penzance (1879)

As explained in Chapter 2, *The Third Manifesto* (the *Manifesto* for short) is a proposal by Hugh Darwen and myself, solidly grounded in classical two-valued logic, for a foundation for data and database management systems (DBMSs). Like Codd's original papers on the relational model, it can be seen as an abstract, logical blueprint for the design of a DBMS. It consists in essence of a rigorous set of principles, stated in the form of a series of prescriptions, proscriptions, and "very strong suggestions," that we—i.e., Hugh and myself—require adherence to on the part of a hypothetical database programming language that we call **D**. The various prescriptions and proscriptions and suggestions are described in detail in our book *Databases, Types, and the Relational Model: The Third Manifesto*, 3rd edition (Addison-Wesley, 2007), referred to throughout this part of the present book as "the *Manifesto* book" for short.

Now, any serious scientific endeavor is quite properly the subject of careful scrutiny and questioning, and the *Manifesto* and its language **D** are no exception in this regard. Indeed, some of the improvements we've been able to make to the *Manifesto* over the years have been the direct result of criticisms we've received at various times. In other cases, we've been able to show that the criticisms were invalid for some reason; in still others, the jury is still out, in the sense that it's not yet clear whether changes are needed or not. This chapter and the next two

have to do with certain criticisms that fall at least partly into this third category.[1]
In essence, the criticisms in question allege that:

1. **D** permits the formulation of paradoxical, and hence undecidable, expressions.

2. **D** is required to be computationally complete.

3. **D** is required to support relation variables (or *relvars*) and relational assignment.

Let me say immediately that the second and third of these allegations are certainly true, and the first is probably true too[2] (at any rate, it doesn't hurt to assume for present purposes that it is). In each case, therefore, what's at issue isn't so much the allegation, or claim, itself; rather, it's the consequences of that claim. Thus, the intent of this chapter and the next two is to spell out the details of the three claims and, perhaps more important, to consider some of their implications.

Note: These chapters are almost certainly not the last word on the subject; they're merely my own current best shot at responding to the criticisms (in particular, at bringing various relevant issues to the surface, as it were, so they can be carefully examined). The chapters are somewhat interrelated; however, I've written them in such a way as to allow each to stand on its own—partly because I think the issues can be treated separately to some degree but also, and more important, because I think it makes the arguments a little more digestible than might otherwise be the case. However, I have to warn you that this decision on my part does mean the chapters involve a small amount of overlap.

There are a couple more preliminary remarks that I need to get out of the way before we can get down to the substance of the first criticism. The first has to do with **Tutorial D** (which has already been discussed to some extent in Part I of this book, of course) and how it relates to the language **D**. The name **D** is meant to be generic—it refers to any language that conforms to the principles

---

[1] Most of the criticisms in question arose in the course of a private correspondence in late 2005 – early 2006 between Hugh Darwen and two other parties deliberately left unnamed here. All of the criticisms examined in these three chapters arise from that correspondence (which I'll refer to from this point forward as "the critical letters"), except where explicitly noted otherwise.

[2] At least, the second is certainly true. The third is also true so long as we assume, as the *Manifesto* book explicitly does, that the language **D** is imperative in style, and might be true even if it isn't.

laid down in the *Manifesto*. Thus, there could be any number of distinct languages all qualifying as a valid **D**. **Tutorial D** is one such; it's defined more or less formally in the *Manifesto* book itself, and it's used throughout that book and elsewhere as a basis for examples. Unfortunately, however, our critics often don't properly distinguish between **D** and **Tutorial D**, even though there's a clear logical difference between the two. As a result, it's sometimes hard to tell whether a given criticism is aimed at the *Manifesto* in general or at **Tutorial D**, considered as a specific and possibly flawed attempt at defining a valid **D**, in particular—a state of affairs that can make it hard to respond properly, sometimes, to the criticism in question.

As for the second of my additional "preliminary remarks," I'll begin with a lightly edited extract from the *Manifesto* book itself (repeated in part from Chapter 2):

> We must stress that what we're *not* doing is proposing some kind of "new" or "extended" relational model. Rather, we're concerned with what might be called the "classical" version of that model; we've tried to provide as careful and accurate a description of that classical model as we possibly can. It's true that we've taken the opportunity to dot a few *i*'s and cross a few *t*'s (i.e., to perform a few minor tidying activities here and there); however, the model as we describe it departs in no essential respects from Codd's original vision as documented in [his earliest relational papers] ... The ideas of the *Manifesto* are in no way intended to supersede those of the relational model, nor do they do so; rather, they use the ideas of the relational model as a base on which to build ... We see our *Manifesto* as being very much in the spirit of Codd's original work and continuing along the path he originally laid down. We're interested in evolution, not revolution.

The reason I quote this passage again here is because of a phenomenon—one that shows up in Chapter 4 in particular—that we've observed repeatedly in criticisms of our work: namely, a tendency to complain that something we propose conflicts with something in Codd's own writings (presumably with the implication that what we're proposing must therefore be wrong, ipso facto). We reject the existence of such conflict as sufficient justification for criticism, and we reject the presumed implication. Our admiration for Codd's genius in inventing the relational model in the first place, and for the extraordinary series of papers he wrote on the subject in the years 1969-1974, is second to none. However, it doesn't follow that we agree with all of Codd's relational writings unreservedly, and indeed we don't. Thus, there are indeed aspects of the *Manifesto* where our ideas depart from Codd's—not many, I hasten to add, but some. Support for nulls is a case in point; Codd required it (albeit not in his original papers, i.e., the ones mentioned above that appeared in the years 1969-1974), but the *Manifesto* categorically rejects it.

With all of that preamble out of the way, let me move on to the main point of the present chapter, which is to examine the following specific criticism:

■ *The Third Manifesto* in general, and **Tutorial D** in particular, both permit the formulation of expressions that are paradoxical, and hence undecidable.

THE PARADOX OF EPIMENIDES

Consider the following example:

■ Let *p* be the predicate "There are no true instantiations of predicate *p*." Assume for now that *p* is indeed a valid predicate (I'll examine this assumption in the next section); then in fact it's not only a predicate but a proposition, because it has no parameters.

■ Let *r* be the relation corresponding to *p* (i.e., the relation whose body contains all and only those tuples that correspond to true instantiations of *p*). Since *p* has no parameters, *r* has no attributes (i.e., it's of degree zero), and so it must be either TABLE_DEE or TABLE_DUM.

    Note: In case you're not familiar with the important relations TABLE_DEE and TABLE_DUM, I should explain that (a) TABLE_DEE is the unique relation with no attributes and just one tuple (necessarily the empty tuple, also known as the 0-tuple), and (b) TABLE_DUM is the unique relation with no attributes and no tuples at all. These two are the only relations—the only possible relations—of degree zero.

■ Suppose *r* is TABLE_DEE. Then the interpretation of the sole tuple in *r* is that *p* is true—in which case, by definition, there are no true instantiations of *p*, and *r* shouldn't contain any tuples after all. In other words, *r* should be TABLE_DUM.

■ Conversely, suppose *r* is TABLE_DUM. Then the interpretation of the fact that there aren't any tuples in *r* is that *p* is false—in which case, by definition, there must be at least one (actually, exactly one) true instantiation of *p*, and *r* should therefore contain at least one (actually, exactly one) tuple after all. In other words, *r* should be TABLE_DEE.

Of course, I'm sure you've realized that this example is basically just the well known Paradox of Epimenides ("This statement is false") in relational form. As you can surely also see, the root of the problem is the self reference: Predicate *p* refers to itself.

In case you're not comfortable with arguments that rely on the special relations TABLE_DEE and TABLE_DUM, let me give another example that illustrates the same general point. This one is a greatly simplified version of an example originally due to David McGoveran and documented by myself in a couple of early installments of my regular column in the magazine *Database Programming & Design*:[3]

- Let *r* be a relation with a single attribute, N, of type INTEGER, and let the predicate for *r* be "The cardinality of *r* is N."[4]

- If *r* is empty, then the cardinality of *r* is zero, so the tuple *t* = TUPLE {N 0} should appear in *r*, so *r* shouldn't be empty after all.

- But then if tuple *t* = TUPLE {N 0} does appear in *r*, then *r* isn't empty and its cardinality clearly isn't zero, and so tuple *t* shouldn't appear in *r* after all.

Again, therefore, we appear to have some kind of paradox on our hands.

---

[3] "How We Missed the Relational Boat" (*DBP&D* 6, No. 9, September 1993); and"Answers to Puzzle Corner Problems, Installments 13-17" (*DBP&D* 7, No. 1, January 1994). Both installments were republished in my book *Relational Database Writings 1991-1994* (Addison-Wesley, 1995).

[4] If we call this predicate *q*, then it can equivalently be stated in the form "There are exactly N true instantiations of predicate *q*"—a formulation that serves to highlight both the self reference as such and the similarity to the predicate *p* in the previous example.

DISCUSSION

For the remainder of this chapter I revert for definiteness to the first example, the one involving TABLE_DEE and TABLE_DUM. Now, I said in connection with that example that p was a predicate, and in fact a proposition—but is it? By definition, a proposition is a statement that's unequivocally either true or false. (More precisely, it's a statement that makes an assertion that's unequivocally either true or false.) But p is clearly neither true nor false—because if it's true it's false and vice versa—so perhaps I was wrong to say as I did previously that it was a proposition in the first place.

More fundamentally, though, I don't think we need to argue over whether p is a predicate, or more specifically a proposition; what we do need to do is decide whether our formal system—whatever system we happen to be talking about—treats it as such. If it does, then we have a problem. Note very carefully, however, that:

- The problem isn't a problem with **Tutorial D** specifically; in fact, I don't see how it could be, since I didn't appeal to **Tutorial D** at all in the example.

- Nor is it a problem with *The Third Manifesto* specifically, since I didn't appeal to the *Manifesto* at all in the example, either; all I did was appeal to the well known fact that any given predicate has a corresponding relation—namely, that relation whose body contains all and only those tuples that correspond to true instantiations of the predicate in question. (Equivalently, the corresponding relation is that relation whose body effectively represents the *extension* of the predicate in question.)

- Nor is it a problem with the relational model specifically, for essentially the same reason.

- Nor is it a problem that arises from the fact that *The Third Manifesto* requires **D**, and therefore **Tutorial D** (indirectly), to be computationally complete. I mention this point because the *Manifesto* has been criticized on precisely these grounds: the grounds, that is, that computational completeness "creates a language with logical expressions ... that are provably not decidable." Note carefully that I'm not saying here that this criticism is incorrect; I'm merely pointing out that the lack of decidability in the specific example under discussion, regarding whether relation *r* contains a tuple or not, doesn't seem to have anything to do with the fact that **D** is required to be computationally complete (and hence that the same is true of **Tutorial D** in particular).

So it seems rather that the problem, if problem there is, must be with *logic*. To spell the point out: Either logic admits *p* as a predicate or it doesn't. If it does, there's a problem with logic. If it doesn't, then the problem with logic goes away, and hence the problems (if any) with the relational model, *The Third Manifesto*, and **D** and **Tutorial D** all go away too, a fortiori.

Note: I believe Bertrand Russell's theory of types might have something to do with the idea that *p* and constructs like it might need to be rejected as legal predicates.[5] Even if so, however, this state of affairs doesn't invalidate my point, which is (to repeat) that if there's a problem in this area, then it's intrinsic—it isn't the fault of either *The Third Manifesto* (or **D**) in general or **Tutorial D** in particular.

A REMARK ON TUTORIAL D

Now let me concentrate on **Tutorial D** specifically for a moment. It might be thought, at least superficially, that the following is a formulation of the Paradox of Epimenides in **Tutorial D** terms (and if it is, it might therefore be thought that there's indeed a problem with **Tutorial D** after all):

```
VAR R BASE RELATION { } KEY { } ;

CONSTRAINT EPIMENIDES COUNT ( R ) = 0 ;
```

More specifically, it might be thought that constraint EPIMENIDES here is a formal expression of predicate *p* ("There are no true instantiations of predicate *p*," or equivalently "The number of true instantiations of predicate *p* is zero"). But it isn't. The reason it isn't is that *The Closed World Assumption* doesn't apply to constraints. *The Closed World Assumption* says (in general, and

---

[5] Note the parallels with Russell's Paradox. Here for the record is one formulation of that paradox: Let *S* be the set of all sets that aren't members of themselves. Does *S* contain itself as a member? If it does, then by definition it doesn't; conversely, if it doesn't, then by definition it does. As I understand it, Russell's theory of types avoids this paradox by, in effect, prohibiting constructs such as "set *S*" from being regarded as sets in the first place —possibly even from being defined.

speaking rather loosely) that relvar R should contain all and only the tuples at a given time that satisfy the predicate for R at that time. But **Tutorial D** isn't aware, and can't be aware, of relvar predicates; all it can be aware of is relvar constraints. And there's no requirement—nor can there be a requirement, in general—that relvar R contain all and only the tuples at a given time that satisfy the constraints that apply to R at that time. So the fact that (in the example) the specified relvar is always empty—i.e., its value is always TABLE_DUM—doesn't of itself lead to any paradox.[6]

To put the matter another way, the fact that some relvar R is constrained to be empty at all times merely means that the relvar predicate for R must be one that always evaluates to FALSE. (In the example, since the relvar has no attributes, its predicate has no parameters—i.e., it's just a proposition—and the proposition in question must be logically equivalent to the degenerate proposition FALSE. For example, it might be the proposition $1 = 0$.)

I switch now to another tack. Here's another attempt to formulate the Paradox of Epimenides in **Tutorial D** terms:

```
VAR R BASE RELATION { } KEY { } ;

CONSTRAINT EPIMENIDES
        IF COUNT ( R ) > 0 THEN COUNT ( R ) = 0 AND
        IF COUNT ( R ) = 0 THEN COUNT ( R ) > 0 ;
```

Constraint EPIMENIDES here is logically equivalent to the following:

If there exists a tuple in relvar R, then relvar R is empty, and if relvar R is empty, then there exists a tuple in relvar R.

Or perhaps more strikingly:

Relvar R contains a tuple if and only if it doesn't contain a tuple.

In other words, the constraint is a contradiction. (Please note that I'm using the term *contradiction* here in its formal logical sense. In general, a contradiction in logic is a predicate such that, no matter what arguments are substituted for its parameters, the corresponding instantiation—i.e., the corresponding

---

[6] As an aside, consider the constraint COUNT$(R) \neq 0$. Naturally we would expect this constraint to be violated if and only if R is empty. In SQL, however, if the constraint happens to have been specified by means of a CHECK clause on the pertinent base table definition (i.e., the CREATE TABLE for R) instead of by means of CREATE ASSERTION, then it'll be considered to be *satisfied* if R is empty!

proposition—is guaranteed to evaluate to FALSE.) But if a constraint is a contradiction, then there's no way—at least, there should be no way—to introduce it into the system in the first place![7] More generally, if some user attempts to define some new constraint for some database, the first thing the system must do is check that the database in question currently satisfies it. If that check fails, then the constraint must obviously be rejected; and if that constraint is a contradiction, then there's no way the database can currently satisfy it.

Of course, I'm assuming here for the sake of the argument that the system is indeed able to detect the fact that the database fails to satisfy some proposed constraint. What happens if this assumption is invalid is discussed, implicitly, in Chapter 5. For completeness, however, I give here a brief sketch of what should happen in a properly designed system when some user attempts to define some new integrity constraint *C*:

1. The system evaluates *C* against the current state of the database.

2. If the result of that evaluation is TRUE, the system accepts *C* as a legitimate constraint and enforces it from this point forward, until such time as it's dropped again.

3. If the result of that evaluation is FALSE, the system rejects *C* as not being legitimate at this time.

4. If the evaluation fails to terminate after some prescribed period of time, a time out occurs and the system rejects *C*—not because it knows it's not legitimate, but because it's too complex for the system to handle.

A REMARK ON *THE THIRD MANIFESTO*

Since it's essentially rather simple, the Paradox of Epimenides as such doesn't illustrate the point, but in general the idea of "predicates referencing predicates" corresponds in relational terms to relations having relation valued attributes (RVAs). In particular, a directly self-referencing predicate—i.e., a predicate *p* that includes a direct, explicit reference to *p* itself—would correspond to a

---

[7] I hope I don't need to stress the point that I'm talking about relvar constraints here, not relvar predicates. As we've already seen, there's no problem with a relvar *predicate* being a contradiction (no logical problem, that is, though it does mean the pertinent relvar will always be empty).

relation of some type *T* that has an attribute of that same type *T*. A type like *T* here is a *recursively defined* type, or just a recursive type for short. The *Manifesto* book has the following to say on such matters (observe that the extract quoted covers indirectly defined recursive types as well as directly defined ones). *Note:* I've modified the text somewhat, but I haven't changed the meaning in any important respect. You can ignore the reference to "possreps" if you don't know what they are.[8]

> It's an open question as to whether any relation type can be defined, either directly or indirectly, in terms of itself. More precisely, let RELATION *H* be a relation type, and let *S*(1), *S*(2), ... be a sequence of sets defined as follows:
>
> $S(1)$ = { *t* : *t* is the type of some attribute in *H* }
>
> $S(i)$ = { *t* : *t* is the type of some component of some possrep for some scalar type, or the type of some attribute of some relation or tuple type, in S(*i*-1) } (*i* > 1)
>
> If there exists some *n* (*n* > 0) such that RELATION *H* is a member of *S*(*n*), then that type RELATION *H* is recursively defined. (This definition requires a slight extension if type inheritance is supported, but this detail needn't concern us here.) Thus, the open question is whether such recursively defined types should be permitted. We don't feel obliged to legislate on this question so far as our model is concerned; for the purposes of [the *Manifesto* book], however, we follow *The Principle of Cautious Design* and assume, where it makes any difference, that such types aren't permitted.[9]

It seems to me that the arguments of the present chapter make it desirable to strengthen the foregoing position. Specifically, I now think that recursively defined relation types should be explicitly prohibited. Points arising from this position:

■ Please understand that I'm *not* saying that relation valued attributes (RVAs) should be prohibited. I mention this point because *The Third Manifesto* has

---

[8] They're explained, briefly in Chapter 4 ("Constraints and Predicates") in this book's predecessor *Logic and Relational Theory: Thoughts and Essays on Database Matters* (Technics Publications, 2020).

[9] *The Principle of Cautious Design* can be stated as follows: Given a design choice between options *A* and *B*, where *A* is upward compatible with *B* and the full consequences of going with *B* aren't yet known, the cautious decision is to go with *A*.

been criticized by many people for supporting RVAs, on the basis that they take us into the realms of second (or higher) order logic. This latter claim might or might not be true; but if it is, then nobody has yet demonstrated a specific problem that's caused by that fact (meaning that fact alone)—at least, nobody has demonstrated such a problem to us, the authors of the *Manifesto*. See Chapter 12 for further discussion of such matters.

■ The extract quoted above from the *Manifesto* book says, to repeat, that for the purposes of that book we assume that recursively defined types aren't permitted. However, **Tutorial D** as described in that same book does permit such types to be defined, possibly indirectly, through its SAME_TYPE_AS construct. Here's a simple example:

```
VAR RX BASE
    RELATION { A1 INTEGER , A2 SAME_TYPE_AS ( RX ) } ;
```

Here's a slightly more complex example:

```
VAR RX BASE
    RELATION { A1 INTEGER , A2 SAME_TYPE_AS ( RY ) } ;
VAR RY BASE
    RELATION { A3 INTEGER , A4 SAME_TYPE_AS ( RX ) } ;
```

So maybe **Tutorial D** as described in the *Manifesto* book does suffer from a lack of decidability. I presume, however, that the implementation could be designed to reject any attempt to make use of this "feature" by rejecting (preferably at compile time) any attempt to define, either directly or indirectly, a type *T* in terms of itself—much as the system should reject any attempt to define a constraint that can't be shown to evaluate to TRUE at the time it's defined.

Chapter 4

To Be Is to Be

a Value of a Variable

To be is to be a value of a variable
(or to be some values of some variables).

—George Boolos:
Logic, Logic, and Logic (1998)

If we want things to stay as they are,
things will have to change.

—Giuseppe di Lampedusa:
The Leopard (1957)

"Change" is scientific, "progress" is ethical;
change is indubitable, whereas progress is a matter of controversy.

—Bertrand Russell:
Unpopular Essays: Philosophy and Politics (1950)

In what I'm calling for the purposes of these three chapters "the critical letters," two writers, who I'll refer to as Critic A and Critic B (both male, incidentally), criticize *The Third Manifesto*—the *Manifesto* for short—for its support for relation variables and relational assignment. This chapter is a response to that criticism. Readers are expected to be familiar with the following *Manifesto* concepts and terminology:

- A relation variable (*relvar* for short) is a variable whose permitted values are relation values (*relations* for short).

- Relational assignment is an operation by which some relation value *r* is assigned to some relation variable *R*.

The *Manifesto* book explains these notions in detail, using the language **Tutorial D** as a basis for examples.

WHY WE WANT RELVARS

To repeat, *relvar* is short for relation variable. The term was coined by Hugh Darwen and myself and first appeared in writing in 1995, in the first published version of our *Third Manifesto*.[1] Ted Codd, inventor of the relational model, never used the term (nor its longhand form, relation variable), but in his first two papers he did use the term "time-varying relation," and—as far as the present chapter is concerned, at any rate—I take a "time-varying relation" to be nothing but a relvar by another name.[2] Thus, Hugh and I certainly don't claim to be the first to recognize the logical difference between (a) relations or relation values, on the one hand, and (b) relvars or relation variables, on the other;[3] however, we do believe we were the first to draw wide attention to that difference. We also believe that relvars and the related notion of relational assignment are essential if we're to be able to update the database (!). Note carefully that variables and assignment go hand in hand (we can't have one without the other): To be a variable is to be assignable to, to be assignable to is to be a variable. Note further that "assignable to" and "updatable" mean exactly the same thing; hence, to object to relvars is to object to the idea that we need to be able to update the database. Thus, we believe that relvars are logically required.[4]

Perhaps a little more explanation is needed here. Most people, if they think about relational updating at all, probably think about the conventional INSERT,

---

[1] Hugh Darwen and C. J. Date: *"The Third Manifesto," ACM SIGMOD Record 24*, No. 1 (March 1995).

[2] The two papers in question were "Derivability, Redundancy, and Consistency of Relations Stored in Large Data Banks," IBM Research Report RJ599 (August 19th, 1969) and "A Relational Model of Data for Large Shared Data Banks," *CACM 13*, No. 6 (June 1970). Even in those first two papers, however, he usually used just the unqualified term *relation*, and it often wasn't clear whether the relation in question was meant to be time-varying or otherwise.

[3] In particular, the 1980 paper "Tables, Table Variables, and Static Integrity Constraints," by E. O. de Brock (University of Technology, Eindhoven, Netherlands), which predated the first version of *The Third Manifesto* by some 15 years, also clearly distinguished between relations and relvars (though it called them tables and table variables, respectively). However, it did so only as a direct consequence of comments by myself on an earlier draft, which didn't. In other words, I'd been thinking about this issue for many years prior to our work on the *Manifesto* as such.

[4] Well ... they *are* required, but only in the sense explained in more detail in the section "Database Values and Variables," later.

DELETE, and UPDATE operators, not about relational assignment as such—especially as SQL in particular doesn't support it, though it does support INSERT, DELETE, and UPDATE, of course. But INSERT, DELETE, and UPDATE are all in the final analysis just shorthand for certain relational assignments. For example, consider the usual suppliers-and-parts database (see page 70 for a sample value). Given that database, the **Tutorial D** INSERT statement

```
INSERT SP RELATION
        { TUPLE { SNO SNO('S3') , PNO PNO('P1') ,
                                  QTY QTY(150) } ,
          TUPLE { SNO SNO('S5') , PNO PNO('P1') ,
                                  QTY QTY(500) } } ;
```

is really just shorthand for the relational assignment

```
SP := SP UNION ( RELATION
        { TUPLE { SNO SNO('S3') , PNO PNO('P1') ,
                                  QTY QTY(150) } ,
          TUPLE { SNO SNO('S5') , PNO PNO('P1') ,
                                  QTY QTY(500) } } ) ;
```

Likewise, the **Tutorial D** DELETE statement

```
DELETE S WHERE CITY = 'Athens' ;
```

is shorthand for the relational assignment

```
S := S MINUS ( S WHERE CITY = 'Athens' ) ;
```

And the **Tutorial D** UPDATE statement

```
UPDATE P WHERE CITY = 'London' :
        { WEIGHT := 2 * WEIGHT , CITY := 'Oslo' } ;
```

—a little trickier, this one—is shorthand for the relational assignment

```
P := ( P WHERE CITY ≠ 'London' )
      UNION
      ( EXTEND P WHERE CITY = 'London' :
              { WEIGHT := 2 * WEIGHT , CITY := 'Oslo' } ) ;
```

Aside: Actually there's a little more that needs to be said about each of the foregoing operators. First, INSERT. As you can see from the corresponding expansion in terms of explicit assignment, the **Tutorial D** INSERT statement doesn't consider it an error to attempt to insert a tuple that's already present. If we want an exception to be raised in such a situation, we should use D_INSERT ("disjoint INSERT") instead of INSERT, in which case the UNION in that expansion will be replaced by D_UNION ("disjoint union"). See, e.g., my book *SQL and Relational Theory: How to Write Accurate SQL Code*, 3rd edition (O'Reilly, 2015) for further explanation.

A similar remark applies to DELETE also. To be specific, as again you can see from the corresponding expansion, the **Tutorial D** DELETE statement doesn't consider it an error to attempt to delete a tuple that's not currently present. If we want an exception to be raised in such a situation, we should use I_DELETE ("included DELETE") instead of DELETE, in which case the MINUS in that expansion will be replaced by I_MINUS ("included minus," also known as "included difference"). Again see, e.g., the *SQL and Relational Theory* book for further explanation.

Finally, I note that the UPDATE example shown above could safely be formulated as a DELETE plus an INSERT (i.e., as what's called a multiple assignment), thus:[5]

```
DELETE P WHERE CITY = 'London' ,
INSERT P ( EXTEND P WHERE CITY = 'London' :
         { WEIGHT := 2 * WEIGHT , CITY := 'Oslo' } ) ;
```

What's more, the DELETE and INSERT here could safely be replaced by appropriate I_DELETE and D_INSERT operations (why?). See the section "Multiple Assignment," later in this chapter, for further explanation. *End of aside.*

Anyway, it should be clear from all of the above that relational assignment is the only relational updating operator we really need, logically speaking. For that reason, I'll focus on relational assignment as such for the remainder of this chapter. Also, I'll take the unqualified term *assignment* from this point forward

---

[5] *A note on syntax:* The DELETE in that multiple assignment is logically equivalent to the following: DELETE P (P WHERE CITY = 'London'). To elaborate: The general form of DELETE is DELETE *R rx*, where *R* is a relvar name and *rx* is a relational expression. If *rx* is of the form "*R* WHERE *bx*," however, DELETE *R rx* becomes DELETE *R R* WHERE *bx*, which in the interest of simplicity we allow to be abbreviated to just DELETE *R* WHERE *bx*. Thus, our original DELETE example, DELETE S WHERE CITY = 'Athens', is shorthand for DELETE S S WHERE CITY = 'Athens'.

to mean relational assignment specifically. As already mentioned, I'll also take the unqualified term *relation* to mean a relation value specifically, except occasionally when I'm quoting from other writers.

CRITIC A'S OBJECTIONS

What I'm calling "the critical letters" include several objections by Critics A and B to the relvar and assignment notions (objections to which Hugh Darwen responded at the time, because the letters were addressed to him in the first instance). Those objections were triggered by a remark by a third party on a separate issue, only tangentially related to the matter at hand (and I'll ignore the substance of that issue here for that reason). In commenting on that third party's remark, Critic A said this:[6]

> I and [the third party] do not subscribe to relvars and think Codd did not either.

Hugh responded:

> I'm baffled by your nonsubscription to relvars ... Don't you subscribe to INSERT, DELETE, UPDATE, and relational assignment? Codd certainly did. The target operand for all of these operations is a relation variable (relvar for short).

To which Critic A replied:

> More precisely, we don't subscribe to explicit relvars and Codd used "time-varying relations" to avoid them ... Bearing in mind that simplicity was one of Codd's main objectives, we think he may have refrained intentionally from introducing relvars. He was obviously aware of the time dimension of databases, yet as far as we have been able to determine, he never included time-variance semantics in his formal model. Had he done so, the language of sets and mathematical relations would have been rather strained because, as Date himself points out, every object in the language has a fixed value. Since relationships within and among Codd's relations are evaluated at a point in time, this permits the use of set semantics ... While conceptually Codd's "time-varying relation" has to be something like a relvar, the "gloss" permitted Codd to stick to simple sets (which cannot change), yet still contend with updates ... It is, perhaps, significant

---

[6] For reasons of clarity and flow I've edited most of the quotes in this chapter, sometimes drastically so.

that later, in his RM/T paper, he referred to insert-update-delete as "transition rules," not operations.

And in a subsequent email the same critic went on to say:

> Please note that it is not claimed there are no relvars involved. The only claim is that it is not a good idea to deal with them explicitly in the data language, because it creates complexity due to problems with unfixed sets. It's hard to believe that Codd did not think about variables, and that he used the term "time-varying relation" lightly.

——— ♦ ♦ ♦ ♦ ♦ ———

Well, now I'd like to offer some blow by blow responses of my own to these various remarks of Critic A's. I've repeated those remarks (but set them in italics) and numbered them for purposes of subsequent reference.

1. *More precisely, we don't subscribe to explicit relvars.*

    This statement seems to suggest that Critic A does subscribe to "implicit" relvars, whatever they might be. If so, then apparently relvars are bad only if they're explicit. I don't understand this position.

2. *Codd used "time-varying relations" to avoid [explicit relvars].*

    There are two ways to interpret this remark. The first is: Codd used the *concept* of "time-varying relations" in order to avoid having to deal with the *concept* of relvars (explicit or otherwise). If this interpretation is the intended one, then I'd like to know exactly what the difference is between these two concepts; our two critics claim a difference exists, but they never seem to come out and say what it is.

    The second interpretation is: Codd used the *term* "time-varying relations" in order to avoid having to use the *term* "relvars" (again, explicit or otherwise). If this interpretation is the intended one, then I can assure you the suggestion is incorrect. I worked with Codd for many years and knew him well, and I had many discussions with him on this very point. While I don't think I can do complete justice to his position on the matter (because, frankly, I don't think it made sense), I can at least state with some authority that there was no hidden agenda behind his use of the term "time-varying relation"; it was just the term he used, that's all, and I don't think he attached any great significance to it. Certainly he never had very much to say about it in any of his publications after 1970; for example, his book *The Relational Model for Database Management Version 2* (Addison-Wesley, 1990) doesn't even mention it.

More particularly—and contrary to both of the foregoing possible interpretations of Critic A's remark—the 1969 and 1970 papers in which Codd first mentioned "time-varying relations" contain not the slightest hint that he introduced that term in order to avoid discussing variables and/or updating. *Au contraire*, in fact: In both of those papers, he explicitly discussed the question of relational updating. For example, here's a direct quote from the 1970 paper:

> Insertions take the form of adding new elements to declared relations ... Deletions ... take the form of removing elements from declared relations.

And in case you might be wondering exactly what Codd meant by the term *declared relation*, the 1969 and 1970 papers both make it clear that a declared relation is a named relation ("time-varying," of course) that:

- Is explicitly declared as such to the system;

- Is described in the system catalog;

- Can be updated (so the declared name denotes different relations—that is, different relation *values*—at different times); and

- Can be referenced in updates, as well as in retrievals and constraints.

Well, that all looks like a relvar to me, and an explicit one to boot.

3. *Bearing in mind that simplicity was one of Codd's main objectives, we think he may have refrained intentionally from introducing relvars.*

I find no evidence in any of his writings of such "intentional refraining." In fact, I find numerous counterexamples—not only in the remarks just quoted regarding insertions and deletions and declared relations, but in remarks elsewhere as well (e.g., in his paper on the ALPHA language, which I'll have a bit more to say about later).

4. *He was obviously aware of the time dimension of databases, yet as far as we have been able to determine, he never included time-variance semantics in his formal model.*

If "time-variance semantics" merely means that Codd's time-varying relations vary over time (and I don't know what else it might mean), then there's clear evidence—not solely in the name—that he did include such semantics. In particular, he certainly did include a kind of (explicit) relational assignment "in his formal model," another issue that I'll come back to later.

5. *Had he done so, the language of sets and mathematical relations would have been rather strained because, as Date himself points out, every object in the language has a fixed value.*

It's not important, but I don't know what writings of my own Critic A is referring to here. More to the point, I don't understand the significance of his criticism. "The language of sets and mathematical relations" still applies 100% to the state of the database at any given time. Updating the database merely replaces one such state of the database by another. Where's the problem?[7]

6. *Since relationships within and among Codd's relations are evaluated at a point in time, this permits the use of set semantics.*

I'm not quite sure what this means, but I *think* Critic A is agreeing with the point I've just made in my previous response. As for the phrase "set semantics": That phrase and a slight variant, "set theoretic semantics," appear repeatedly in the critical letters, but I don't really know what they mean. Presumably they refer to something that includes set operators such as union and intersection but excludes assignment; but then why not talk about (e.g.) "arithmetic semantics," meaning something that includes arithmetic operators such as "+" and "×" but excludes arithmetic assignment? I mean, why not just talk in terms of set operators and be done with it? (I won't repeat these questions every time one of those unclear

---

[7] And in any case, relvars are surely "objects in the language," and they obviously don't have "fixed values."

phrases occurs but will let this one paragraph do duty for all.) Overall, I don't think Critic A means anything here other than that the value of a given relvar at a given point in time is a relation (whose body is a set, of course: namely, a set of tuples). If that's indeed what he means, then of course I agree with him; but so what? Or more politely: What's wrong with this state of affairs?

7. *While conceptually Codd's "time-varying relation" has to be something like a relvar, the "gloss" permitted Codd to stick to simple sets (which cannot change), yet still contend with updates.*

I wholeheartedly agree with Hugh's response to this one:

> Well, somebody will have to explain to me what the difference is [*i.e., between a relvar and a "time-varying relation"*] ... If it walks like a duck, swims like a duck, flies like a duck, and quacks like a duck, what is it?

See also my own earlier comments on this same issue. *Note:* I might add that I don't really understand what's meant by the term "gloss" as used here, either, but perhaps it's not important.

8. *It is, perhaps, significant that later, in his RM/T paper, he referred to insert-update delete as "transition rules," not operations.*

No, he didn't. In fact, the term *transition* doesn't appear anywhere in the RM/T paper![8] What he actually said was as follows (this is a direct quote from that paper):

> All insertions into, updates of, and deletions from ... relations are constrained by the following two rules [*and he goes on to give definitions of the entity and referential integrity rules. Then he explicitly states that the relational model includes those two rules, and he refers to them generically as*] the insert-update-delete rules.

Note the explicit text referring to "insertions into, updates of, and deletions from" relations (i.e., "time-varying" relations, obviously).

---

[8] "The RM/T paper" is E. F. Codd: "Extending the Database Relational Model to Capture More Meaning," *ACM TODS 4*, No. 4 (December 1979).

9.   *Please note that it is not claimed there are no relvars involved. The only claim is that it is not a good idea to deal with them explicitly in the data language, because it creates complexity due to problems with unfixed sets.*

To the extent that I understand these remarks (which isn't very far), they just look like arm waving to me. See my response above to Critic A's remark no. 1.

10.   *It's hard to believe that Codd did not think about variables, and that he used the term "time-varying relation" lightly.*

Actually it's not hard to believe at all. See my responses above to Critic A's remarks nos. 2 and 4.

———— ♦ ♦ ♦ ♦ ♦ ————

I've already quoted part of Hugh's response to Critic A's remarks. That response continues:

> I thought "relational assignment" was Codd's term, and one of his twelve rules ... Codd's accounts of assignment, insert, update, and delete on pp 87-94 of the RM/V2 book look indistinguishable from those of **Tutorial D** ...

Well, I can confirm that Codd did use the term *relational assignment* in "the RM/V2 book," though it isn't actually one of his twelve rules.[9] (One of those rules does have to do with INSERT, DELETE, and UPDATE, but there's no rule regarding assignment as such.) But he certainly referred to the *concept* of assignment, and even showed explicit syntax for it, much earlier than that; for example, it's mentioned in the RM/T paper, which appeared in 1979.
It's not true to say, however (*pace* Hugh), that RM/V2's facilities in this area are "indistinguishable from those of **Tutorial D**." For example, the RM/V2 facilities include the idea that certain deletes can cause the introduction of nulls into the database, which **Tutorial D** certainly doesn't support. At the same time

---

[9] "The RM/V2 book" is the book mentioned earlier, *The Relational Model for Database Management Version 2* (Addison-Wesley, 1990). The twelve rules were described in Codd's articles "Is Your DBMS Really Relational?" and "Does Your DBMS Run by the Rules?" (*Computerworld*, October 14th and 21st, 1985, respectively).

they don't include support for multiple assignment, which **Tutorial D** does support (see the section after next). What's more, the text on pages 87-94 of the RM/V2 book contains much material not directly related to the semantics of the operators as such, including many details that surely don't belong in an abstract model at all. Here are a couple of examples:

> Whenever rows are withheld by the DBMS from insertion (to avoid duplicate rows in the result), the *duplicate row indicator* is turned on.

> If one or more indexes exist for the target relation, the DBMS will automatically update these indexes to support the inserted rows.

And so on. It also contains several prescriptions that are in direct conflict with *The Third Manifesto*. For example:

> The domain of any column ... in which the values are derived by means of a function is identified [in the catalog] as *function-derived*, because the DBMS usually cannot be more specific than that.

> The relational model includes the *cascading option* in some of its manipulative operators.[10]

Again, and so on! All of that being said, however, I do agree with Hugh that the general functionality being defined in this part of the RM/V2 book is at least somewhat similar to that found in the analogous portions of **Tutorial D**.

To all of the above I add that as early as 1971 Codd was proposing explicit support for INSERT, DELETE, and UPDATE (albeit not for assignment as such); I refer to his paper on Data Sublanguage ALPHA,[11] in which 12 examples (out of a total of 32, or in other words nearly 40 percent) were updating examples specifically.

---

[10] *The Third Manifesto* doesn't prohibit "cascading options" that are specified declaratively (it doesn't prescribe them, either). However, Codd is suggesting here that they might be specified procedurally instead.

[11] E. F. Codd: "A Data Base Sublanguage Founded on the Relational Calculus," Proc. 1971 ACM SIGFIDET Workshop on Data Description, Access and Control, San Diego, Calif. (November 1971).

CRITIC B'S OBJECTIONS

After the exchanges between Critic A and Hugh discussed above, Critic B joined in the debate (effectively taking over from Critic A, who bowed out and didn't contribute any further). In his first message, Critic B said this among other things:

> The conflation of set theoretic language (which has only equivalence) and a computational language (which has both assignment and equivalence) results in muddy semantics, which neither Hugh nor Chris [has] discussed or even acknowledged. Furthermore, neither [seems] to have applied any of the vast literature on nondecidability and incompleteness to *The Third Manifesto*.

Well, it's true that *The Third Manifesto* prescribes, and **Tutorial D** (like every other imperative language I know) supports, "both assignment and equivalence." In fact, the *Manifesto* prescribes, and **Tutorial D** supports, all three of the following:

■ *Logical equivalence*, also known as *truth functional equivalence* ("$\equiv$"): If p and q are truth valued expressions, the equivalence $p \equiv q$—not meant to be actual **Tutorial D** syntax—is such an expression also, evaluating to TRUE if and only if p and q both evaluate to the same truth value.[12]

■ *Value equality* ("="): Values $v1$ and $v2$ are equal (i.e., the comparison $v1 = v2$ evaluates to TRUE) if and only if they're the very same value.

■ *Assignment* (":="), relational or otherwise: The assignment $V := v$ causes the specified value v to be assigned to the specified variable V (after which—assuming the assignment succeeds—the comparison $V = v$ is required to evaluate to TRUE).

I'd like to elaborate on value equality in particular, since certain subsequent remarks of Critic B's suggest there might be some breakdown in communication in this area. As I've said, values $v1$ and $v2$ are equal if and only if they're the very same value (and I note in passing that the term *identity* might reasonably be

---

[12] Actually, logical equivalence ("$\equiv$") as I understand it is merely value equality ("=") as it applies to truth values specifically; that is, the equivalence $p \equiv q$ is equivalent (!) to the equality $/p/ = /q/$. See Chapter 2 ("Some Operators Are More Equal than Others") of my book *Logic and Relational Theory: Thoughts and Essays on Database Matters* (Technics Publications, 2020) for an extensive discussion of such matters.

used instead of equality for this concept; indeed, it often is, especially in the context of formal logic). In other words, it's our position, reflected in the *Manifesto*, that:

■ Any given value—the integer three, for example—exists (a) for all time and (b) exactly once in the universe, as it were.

■ However, any number of distinct *appearances*, or *occurrences* (or, perhaps better, *representations*), of that given value can exist, at the same time or at different times, and possibly in different places.

And if two such "different places" happen to contain appearances of the same value at the same time, then comparing those two "places" for equality will give TRUE—i.e., they'll "compare equal"—at that time. (So I suppose we could say we have here an example of yet another kind of equality, which we might call *appearance equality*. No such term is used in the *Manifesto*, however.) Here's an extended extract from my book *The New Relational Database Dictionary* (O'Reilly, 2016) that explains the overall situation:

> Observe that there's a logical difference between a value as such and an appearance of that value in some context—for example, an appearance as the current value of some variable or as an attribute value within the current value of some relvar. Of course, every appearance of a value has an implementation that consists of some internal or physical representation of the value in question (and distinct appearances of the same value might have distinct physical representations). Thus, there's also a logical difference between an appearance of a value, on the one hand, and the physical representation of that appearance, on the other; there might even be a logical difference between the physical representations used for distinct appearances of the same value. All of that being said, however, it's usual to abbreviate *physical representation of an appearance of a value* to just *appearance of a value*, or (more often) to just *value*, so long as there's no risk of ambiguity. Note, however, that *appearance of a value* is a model concept, whereas *physical representation of an appearance* is an implementation concept—users certainly might need to know whether (for example) two variables contain appearances of the same value, but they don't need to know whether those two appearances use the same physical representation.
>
> *Example:* Let N1 and N2 be variables of type INTEGER. After the following assignments, then, N1 and N2 both contain an appearance of the integer value 3. The corresponding physical representations might or might not be the

same (for example, N1 might use a base two representation and N2 a base ten representation), but either way it's of no concern to the user.

```
N1 := 3 ;
N2 := 3 ;
```

What if anything is wrong with the foregoing state of affairs? *Note:* If (as Critic B's next sentence—"neither [Hugh nor Chris seems] to have applied any of the vast literature on nondecidability and incompleteness to *The Third Manifesto*"—might suggest) the answer to this question is that it gives rise to undecidability, then I've already dealt with that issue in Chapter 3 (and there's more to come in Chapter 5 also), so I won't discuss it further here. But I can't tell from the quoted extract whether the problem that Critic B is referring to is indeed that one.

I'd also like to know exactly what's "muddy" about the semantics of **Tutorial D**. Hugh asked the same question:

> Please justify by showing concrete examples in **Tutorial D** where our "semantics" are "muddy." Please also explain what you think it takes for semantics to be muddy. I understand indeterminacy (as found in SQL), but I believe we have none of that.

Critic B never explicitly responded to these requests, as far as I can tell, unless the following (part of a lengthier set of comments, to be discussed further below) is a response:

> Your request that I explain what **Tutorial D** does wrong through examples in **Tutorial D** is absurd! You cannot give examples in any language of what that language does NOT do!

As promised, I'll come back to these particular remarks of Critic B's a little later. For the moment, however, I want to stay with Hugh's reactions to Critic B's complaints overall. Indeed, Hugh wrote a long response to Critic B, of which the following is the substance:

> If the database language has no named relvars, how are updates expressed in it, and how are constraints expressed? And how are queries expressed? ... The answers must be accompanied by examples in some concrete syntax. This requirement is a stringent one and I might not respond to a response that does not

attempt to address it. The syntax should be based, where appropriate, on relational algebra ...

    We have assignment so that the database can be updated. As far as the database is concerned, assignment is restricted to relational assignment only, because relation variables are the only kind allowed in the database ... A proposal to do away with relation variables needs to demonstrate two very important things: first and foremost, an alternative way of updating the database; second, the advantages of this alternative way over assignment to relvars.

Critic B returned to the fray:

> To clarify, I have NOT proposed doing away with the concept of relation variables per se ...
>
>   Your question goes to the heart of the very great difference in semantics between set theoretic and computational languages ... The set theoretic analog of "updating" semantics is two sets (e.g., A and B) connected by a "set transformation" or "transition" rule ... Semantically, this is VERY different from saying that A becomes B via some update operator because—in set theoretic language—B does not replace A and so there is no assignment of values to some variable. Instead both always exist but are merely related in a known way.
>
>   The problem created by combining set theoretic language and computational language semantics in some completely unspecified manner makes *The Third Manifesto* as flawed as the NULL problems in SQL!
>
>   Your request that I explain what **Tutorial D** does wrong through examples in **Tutorial D** is absurd! You cannot give examples in any language of what that language does NOT do!
>
>   In **Tutorial D**, I do not know how to interpret "equivalence"—sometimes you seem to want the set theoretic concept (i.e., an assertion of identity) and sometimes you seem to want the computational concept (an assertion of value equivalence). If the first is not intended, then how does **Tutorial D** support inference? And if it is, how do you square this with assignment, which is obviously at odds with the set theoretic semantics for which there is no concept of variable?

I have some blow by blow responses of my own to all this:

1. *To clarify, I have NOT proposed doing away with the concept of relation variables per se.*

This claim seems to be related to Critic A's remark to the effect that (apparently) explicit relvars are bad but implicit ones might be OK. I still fail to understand what exactly is being proposed here, or what exactly it is that's being objected to.

2. *Your question goes to the heart of the very great difference in semantics between set theoretic and computational languages.*

The question referred to is, I presume, the one in which Hugh asks how updates are to be done without relvars (if it isn't, then I don't understand). But Critic B doesn't *answer* that question! I can accept that there might be some merit in thinking of the "old" state of the database immediately before some update and the "new" state immediately after that update as somehow coexisting (living alongside one another, as it were). But the real world fact is that the "new" state does have to replace the "old" one,[13] and so our formalisms, whatever they might be, have to be prepared to deal with that state of affairs. The notion of variables allows us to do exactly that (deal with that state of affairs, that is). And if "set theoretic languages" don't, well, then so much the worse for them.

3. *The set theoretic analog of "updating" semantics is two sets (e.g., A and B) connected by a "set transformation" or "transition" rule.*

I think my response to the previous point takes care of this point as well. Here I merely add that Critic A also referred to transition rules, though in fact what he said about them was incorrect.

4. *Semantically, this is VERY different from saying that A becomes B via some update operator because—in set theoretic language—B does not replace A and so there is no assignment of values to some variable. Instead both always exist but are merely related in a known way.*

Again I think I've already dealt with this point. However, I'd like to say a little more about it here:

---

[13] At least conceptually, inasmuch as the "new" state must now be understood to be the current state. It's true that in a system in which nothing is ever actually deleted the "old" state might be kept around as well—but so what? Note in particular that there must be a way of referring to both the "new" (or current) state and the "old" (or previous) state, an issue discussed in some detail by Hugh and myself in our book with Nikos Lorentzos, *Time and Relational Theory: Temporal Databases in the Relational Model and SQL* (Morgan Kaufmann, 2014). Note further that our temporal proposals most definitely do rely on the relvar concept.

- First, *The Third Manifesto* never talks in terms of "one set becoming another"; rather, it talks in terms of a *variable* which has one *value* at one time and another value at another time. (In particular, it talks in terms of a *relation* variable having one *relation* value at one time and another at another.)

- Second, the *Manifesto* also never talks in terms of one set replacing another. As already explained, all values "always exist"; thus, it follows that all sets also "always exist," a fortiori, because sets *are* values. However, the *Manifesto* does talk in terms of a variable being updated, which means the *appearance* of one value (in that variable) is replaced by an *appearance* of another. In fact, it tries very hard to be precise over such matters—over the logical difference, in particular, between a value as such and an appearance of such a value in some context, as I tried to explain on pages 127-128—and it's truly frustrating to be so roundly misunderstood.

Overall, these two sentences of Critic B's just look like an attempt to state fuzzily what the *Manifesto* states very precisely.

5. *The problem created by combining set theoretic language and computational language semantics in some completely unspecified manner makes The Third Manifesto as flawed as the NULL problems in SQL!*

What exactly is it in *The Third Manifesto* that's "completely unspecified"? If anything's unspecified here, I'd have to say it's the meaning of "computational language semantics"—not to mention "set theoretic semantics," a notion I've already commented on. Also, what exactly does "as flawed as the NULL problems in SQL" mean? Nulls give rise to some kind of many-valued logic, which most authorities agree causes horrible problems in the database context; but the *Manifesto*'s insistence on "computational language semantics" certainly necessitates no departure from conventional two-valued logic. At best, therefore, the reference to nulls is a red herring, and the claim that the *Manifesto* is "as flawed as the NULL problems in SQL" is an apples and oranges comparison.

Note added later: It occurs to me that the phrase "the problem created by combining set theoretic language and computational language semantics" might refer to something we categorically prohibit: namely, the possibility that (a) a new value might be assigned to some variable during (b) the process of evaluating some expression that involves that very same variable. (I mean, part (a) here might be regarded as an application of "computation language semantics," and part (b) might be regarded as an application of "set theoretic language semantics.") If that's indeed what it refers to, then we agree that allowing such a possibility could have adverse consequences (though I believe some languages do in fact permit it). For that reason, any language that's supposed to conform to *The Third Manifesto* is required to satisfy the following conditions among others (and of course **Tutorial D** does so):

■   Syntactically, no assignment is an expression; more generally, no update operator invocation is an expression.

■   Syntactically, therefore, no expression (no relational expression in particular) is allowed to include either an assignment or, more generally, an update operator invocation of any kind.

■   By contrast, an expression (a relational expression in particular) is certainly allowed to include a read-only operator invocation. Syntactically, however, such an invocation is itself just another expression; by definition, therefore, it includes no assignments and no update operator invocations of any kind.[14]

It follows from all of the above that if a given relational expression *exp* includes any references to some relvar *R*, then throughout evaluation of *exp* those references all denote the same thing: namely, the relation *r* that's the value of *R* immediately before evaluation of *exp* begins.

---

[14] Two comments here. First, it's true that the code that implements a given read-only operator might be written in such a way as to update certain variables that are purely local to the operator in question; however, such updates have no lasting effect. In fact, that implementation code is always logically equivalent to a single RETURN statement, the operand to which is itself formulated as an expression. Thus, such an operator cannot and does not update anything in its environment; in particular, it cannot and does not update anything in the database.

Second, it's also true that the syntax for expressing a given read-only operator invocation might include a WITH clause, whose effect can be understood in terms of assignments to certain variables that are local to the operator invocation in question. However, the first comment applies in this situation also, mutatis mutandis.

6. *Your request that I explain what **Tutorial D** does wrong through examples in **Tutorial D** is absurd! You cannot give examples in any language of what that language does NOT do!*

To me, this response looks suspiciously like a cop-out on Critic B's part. I thought the point at issue (see Chapters 3 and 5) was that **Tutorial D** allows expressions that can't be evaluated. If so, it must be possible to give an example of such an expression. Now, I agree this might be difficult to do—I mean, the expression might be extremely complex—but Critic B is saying it's impossible. So perhaps Critic B is referring to something else that **Tutorial D** "does wrong." In fact, I think he must be—since he goes on to suggest that there's something the language "does NOT do," and allowing expressions that can't be evaluated is something that it does do (at least according to Critic B).

When the foregoing points are clarified, I'd then like to know why analogous criticisms don't apply to the hypothetical language described in Codd's 1969 and 1970 papers or to his ALPHA language. And assuming I'm right in thinking those criticisms do apply, then I'd also like to see a language to which they don't.

7. *In **Tutorial D**, I don't know how to interpret "equivalence"; sometimes you seem to want the set theoretic concept (e.g., an assertion of identity) and sometimes you seem to want the computational concept (an assertion of value equivalence). If the first is not intended, then how does **Tutorial D** support inference? And if it is, how do you square this with assignment, which is obviously at odds with the set theoretic semantics for which there is no concept of variable?*

I'm afraid I'm far from fully understanding these remarks. Let me see if I can clarify matters a little:

■ I *think* that what Critic B is here calling "assertion of identity" is what we call value equality.

■ I *think* that what Critic B is here calling "assertion of value equivalence" is what I suggested earlier might be called "appearance equality."

I've already tried to explain these constructs (i.e., value equality and "appearance equality"), and I believe the *Manifesto* is perfectly explicit on when and where they can be used and what their semantics are. As for "[the *Manifesto*] supporting inference": I *think* what Critic B is referring to here is the process of determining the value of a relational expression (in particular, the process of responding to a query). If so, then I believe the *Manifesto* is perfectly explicit on what's involved in that process. What's more, I fail to see how assignment and "the concept of variable" come into the picture, since—as I've already tried to explain a little while back— neither has any role to play in that process.

———— ◆ ◆ ◆ ◆ ———

In a subsequent message, Critic B said this:

> My desire is not to introduce a database language with no variable names, etc., but that **Tutorial D** should cleanly separate set theoretic semantics and computer language semantics. You want a single language which has both, but I don't believe this is possible unless (for example and at least) truth value equivalence is distinct from cardinal and ordinal value equivalence.

> As I said earlier, **Tutorial D** has:

a. Logical equivalence, also known as truth functional equivalence (which I assume is the same as what Critic B here calls truth value equivalence), together with

b. Value equality (and possibly "appearance equality" too), together with

c. Assignment (which Critic B previously at least suggested might also be considered a kind of equivalence).

But now he (i.e., Critic B) additionally talks about "cardinal and ordinal value equivalence." I have no idea whether or not this is one of the three kinds **Tutorial D** has; I don't know whether "cardinal and ordinal value equivalence" is one kind or two; and I don't even know whether Critic B thinks it would be good or bad if **Tutorial D** supported it (or them). Anyway, Hugh responded:

I have explained what we mean by "equals," in response to certain statements from you that indicated you were worried that we had two different kinds. (I didn't understand both of the two kinds, but our only kind appears to be the one you want. See RM Prescription 8.)

What Hugh here calls "our only kind" is specifically value equality, the semantics of which are precisely specified in *The Third Manifesto*'s RM Prescription 8 (RM for Relational Model).[15] Critic B replied (a trifle impolitely, I would have said):

I realize you don't understand that there are two (actually many) kinds of "equal" ... As best I can guess, your ability to think in purely set theoretic terms when talking about **Tutorial D** is mentally blocked. Let me simply say that value equivalence is not the same as identity. Value refers to a comparison of measures of a quantitative property, while identity pertains to what mathematicians often call entities ("things").

Well, I'm going to have to repeat here some things I've already said (and I apologize up front for the repetition) ... but I strongly suspect from these remarks of Critic B's that he hasn't taken on board exactly what *The Third Manifesto* means by the term *value*. I also suspect that what he calls "value equivalence" is what we mean when we talk of equality of distinct *appearances* of the *same* value. (To say it again, in our view of the world, any given value simply exists— as I've put it elsewhere, it has no location in time or space—but such a value can have any number of distinct appearances, at distinct locations in time and space.) And I further suspect that these misunderstandings on his part have led him into a criticism that has no basis in fact. I also think, contrary to what Critic B is saying here, that—to use his term—what *we* might call "value equivalence" (which is to say "value equality") is indeed "the same as identity." Thus, two appearances are equal if and only if they're appearances of the identical value.

As for the notion that there are many kinds of equality: Well, it might be true (I really don't know) that many kinds can be defined, but I think the important one is the one we define in RM Prescription 8—and that's the one we

---

[15] For the record, here's the text of that prescription: **D** shall support the **equality** comparison operator "=" for every type *T*. Let *v1* and *v2* be values, and consider the equality comparison *v* = *v2*. The values *v1* and *v2* shall be of the same type *T*. The comparison shall return TRUE if and only if *v1* and *v2* are the very same value. *Note:* It follows from this prescription that if (a) there exists an operator *Op* (other than "=" itself) with a parameter *P* of declared type *T* such that (b) two successful invocations of *Op* that are identical in all respects except that the argument corresponding to *P* is *v1* in one invocation and *v2* in the other are distinguishable in their effect, then (c) *v1* = *v2* must evaluate to FALSE.

appeal to, explicitly or implicitly, whenever we talk about equality as such in the context of *The Third Manifesto*.

In the same message, Critic B also says this:

> I have not stated how I think updates to the database should be expressed, except that we can safely use the set theoretic representation as having both a "canonical" method and a "canonical" semantics. I object to assignment because I see it as being at odds with the set theoretic representation and importing [*imputing?*] a "before and after semantics" which is inherently procedural.

Here are my responses:

1. *I have not stated how I think updates to the database should be expressed.*

   Well, as I said earlier (quoting Hugh), a proposal to do away with relation variables needs to demonstrate two very important things: first and foremost, an alternative way of updating the database; second, the advantages of this alternative way over relvar assignment. It's truly frustrating to be told over and over that our approach doesn't work—especially without being told clearly *why* it doesn't work, and especially when it's essentially the same as the approach supported by all imperative languages since programming languages were first invented—without at the same time being told about some alternative approach that does work.

2. *We can safely use the set theoretic representation as having both a "canonical" method and a "canonical" semantics.*

   The significance of these observations escapes me. Do they add anything to what has gone before?

3. *I object to assignment because I see it as being at odds with the set theoretic representation and importing [imputing?] a "before and after semantics" which is inherently procedural.*

   Assume for the sake of the discussion that (a) it's true that set theory has no notion of assignment and that (b) it's true that updates are a requirement. (For my part I have no difficulty in accepting either of these assumptions.) Then the obvious conclusion isn't that assignment is inherently flawed; rather, it's that set theory by itself is inadequate as a theoretical basis for a database programming language. However, Critic B asserts that assignment and set theory (or "the set theoretic representation") are actually at odds with each other—i.e., they're actually in conflict, suggesting that if we support one we can't support the other. If that's true, then so much the worse for set theory, as I said before; but frankly, I don't see why it should be true. *Note:* Replace "set theory" by "logic" throughout the foregoing remarks, and the resulting argument is also something I would sign on to.

What's more, the notion of "before and after semantics" is indeed implied by assignment. More significantly, however, it's implied by— *derives from* might be a better way of putting it—the fundamental way time works in our universe! (I suppose we might say that being "inherently procedural" derives from the way time works in our universe, too, if we could agree that "procedural" just means performing one action after another, in sequence; but the problem here is that the label "procedural" is usually taken to mean "*low level* procedural" and hence is used, almost always, in a pejorative sense.) If set theory can't deal with "before and after semantics," then (to say it one more time) so much the worse for set theory. *Note:* Again, replace "set theory" by "logic" throughout the foregoing remarks and the resulting argument is also something I would sign on to.

MULTIPLE ASSIGNMENT

The Third Manifesto prescribes not just assignment per se but what it calls *multiple* assignment. In essence, multiple assignment is simply an operation that allows several individual assignments all to be performed simultaneously (as it were), without any integrity checking being done until all of those individual assignments have been executed in their entirety. For example, the following "double DELETE" is, logically, a multiple assignment operation:

```
DELETE S  WHERE SNO = SNO('S1') ,
DELETE SP WHERE SNO = SNO('S1') ;
```

Note the comma separator after the first DELETE, which indicates syntactically that the end of the overall statement has not yet been reached.

Critic B raises several questions in connection with the foregoing notion. To quote:

I am uncertain as to how you intend multiple assignment to be implemented. If there are, e.g., five individual assignments, are they processed in order as stated from top to bottom or is the order arbitrary or are they expected to be processed in parallel? Your rewrite algorithm for eliminating multiple references to the same variable raises more issues than it solves. At best, it seems to assume there are no side effects among the individual assignments, so that order does not matter. If this is the assumption, then clearly there are certain ordered sets of assignments (normally coded as transactions) that cannot be rewritten as a multiple assignment because they will produce a result different than that which was originally intended ... I like the idea of multiple assignment but not at the expense of transactions and therefore not at the expense of deferred constraint checking.

Once again I find I need to offer some blow by blow responses:

1. *I am uncertain as to how you intend multiple assignment to be implemented.*

   We expect it to be implemented as specified. The semantics are specified in the *Manifesto* book (actually in the *Manifesto* itself, of course), and are also described in detail in a paper by Hugh and myself in my book *Date on Database: Writings 2000-2006* (Apress, 2006).

2. *If there are, e.g., five individual assignments, are they processed in order as stated from top to bottom or is the order arbitrary or are they expected to be processed in parallel?*

   This question is fully answered in the references just mentioned. For the record (and simplifying slightly), the basic idea is that (a) the expressions on the right sides of the individual assignments are evaluated (in arbitrary order, because the order makes no difference) and then (b) the individual assignments to the variables on the left sides are executed in sequence as written. *Note:* This explanation requires some slight refinement if two or more of the individual assignments involve the same target variable. The details can be found in the references mentioned above.

3. *Your rewrite algorithm for eliminating multiple references to the same variable raises more issues than it solves.*

The references mentioned above do include a "rewrite algorithm" for combining—not eliminating!—"multiple references to the same variable." Now, we frankly don't believe the algorithm does "raise more issues than it solves"—but if it does, then it would be helpful to be given some specifics. Certainly it's hard to respond to this criticism without them.

4. *At best, it seems to assume there are no side effects among the individual assignments, so that order does not matter.*

The point of the rewrite algorithm—which I assume is what "it" refers to here—is simply to make sure that intended updates are never lost. It achieves this desirable effect by combining individual assignments to the same target variable in such a way as to ensure that those assignments all contribute appropriately to the overall result. The net effect is that order does matter, but only insofar as assignments to the same target variable are concerned. *Note:* Critic B's term *side effects* is misleading, though. Indeed, side effects as such can't occur.

5. *If this is the assumption, then clearly there are certain ordered sets of assignments (normally coded as transactions) that cannot be rewritten as a multiple assignment because they will produce a result different than that which was originally intended ... .*

I can't resist twitting Critic B slightly here on his use of the phrase "ordered sets" ... More important, however, we would like to see an example of a sequence of assignments that can't be rewritten as a multiple assignment. The obvious suggestion would seem to be something along these lines:

```
X := exp ; Y := f ( X ) ;
```

But the following multiple assignment will achieve what's presumably intended:

```
X := exp , Y := f ( exp ) ;
```

So will the following sequence, which avoids the need to write out that possibly complicated expression *exp* twice:

```
Temp := exp ;
X := Temp , Y := f ( Temp ) ;
```

6. *I like the idea of multiple assignment but not at the expense of transactions and therefore not at the expense of deferred constraint checking.*

We like multiple assignment, too; in fact, we regard it as a sine qua non. Please note, however, that we don't propose it as a replacement for transactions. In his responses to the critical letters Hugh says the following (and I agree with these remarks):

> I believe that transactions can theoretically be dispensed with but I prefer to keep them for what I believe are strong and possibly compelling reasons of convenience. I know people who disagree with me here and would prefer to get rid of transactions altogether. I respond to them by agreeing that that might be nice but I need to see some specific language proposals to address the inconvenience that transactions currently address.

However, I must add that we still insist on immediate constraint checking, even within the confines of an individual transaction.

DATABASE VALUES AND VARIABLES

Despite everything I've said in this chapter so far, there's one sense in which relvars and relational assignment are and always were a mistake after all, as I'll now try to explain.

We want to be able to update the database. Now, I said earlier that "updatable" and "assignable to" mean exactly the same thing; I also said that to be assignable to is to be a variable, and to be a variable is to be assignable to. Doesn't it follow from these remarks that the database is a variable? And since the notion of variables containing variables is a logical absurdity, doesn't it follow further that the database, being a variable, can't possibly contain relation variables?

The answer to both of these questions is in fact *yes*: The database is a variable, and it can't contain other variables (neither relation variables nor any other kind) nested inside itself. Here's a quote from Appendix D of the *Manifesto* book:

> The first version of *The Third Manifesto* drew a distinction between database
> values and database variables, analogous to that between relation values and
> relation variables. It also introduced the term *dbvar* as shorthand for *database
> variable*. While we still believe this distinction to be a valid one, we found it had
> little direct relevance to other aspects of the *Manifesto*. We therefore decided, in
> the interest of familiarity, to revert to more traditional terminology.

And after elaborating slightly on these remarks, that appendix goes on to say the
following:

> Now this bad decision has come home to roost! With hindsight, it would have
> been much better to "bite the bullet" and adopt the more logically correct terms
> *database value* and *database variable* (or dbvar), despite their lack of familiarity.

It then goes on to show that (a) any given database variable is really a *tuple*
variable, with one attribute—a relation valued attribute—for each "relation
variable" contained in that database variable, and hence that (b) relation variables
are really *pseudovariables*, which allow update operations to "zap" individual
components of the containing database variable.[16] As Hugh put it in his
responses to the critical letters:

> Chris and I contemplated the idea of regarding the database as a single variable
> [but] we were unable to devise convenient syntax for the usual kinds of ...
> updating that are expected (assignment of the complete database for every
> required update being obviously unthinkable). Or rather, the only convenient
> syntax we could come up with involved dividing the database up into the named
> "portions" that we call relation variables.

Now, I mention all this merely for completeness and to head off at the pass, as
it were, certain criticisms of our position that might occur to some readers.
The fact is, even though the database is really a variable and relvars are really
pseudovariables, it's my belief that this state of affairs doesn't undermine any of
the arguments I've been making earlier in this chapter in any material respect.

---

[16] This argument is amplified in a planned successor to the present book, viz., *Stating the Obvious, and
Other Database Writings*. See also Appendix D of the *Manifesto* book.

CONCLUDING REMARKS

I'd like to conclude with a couple of final observations:

1. First and foremost, the position of Critics A and B with regard to relvars remains extremely unclear: They seem to think relvars are fundamentally flawed, and yet at the same time they seem to want to retain them, at least "implicitly" (?). They also fail to explain what the logical difference is between a relvar as such and a "time-varying relation."

2. It's true that certain programming languages—specifically, the so called logic languages (e.g., Prolog) and functional languages (e.g., LISP)—do apparently manage to exist without assignment: indeed, without any notion of "persistent memory" at all. When it comes to updating the database, however, then as far as I know all such languages simply cheat; in effect, they perform some kind of assignment, possibly as a side effect, even though assignment as such isn't part of the logic or functional programming style.

Chapter 5

And Now for Something

Completely Computational

Myself when young did eagerly frequent
Doctor and Saint, and heard great Argument
About it and about: but evermore
Came out by the same Door as in I went.

—Edward Fitzgerald:
The Rubáiyát of Omar Khayyam (1859)

The Third Manifesto, by Hugh Darwen and myself ("the *Manifesto*" for short), lays down a set of prescriptions and proscriptions regarding the design of a database programming language it calls **D**. One of those prescriptions in particular—"OO Prescription 3" (OO for Other Orthogonal)—reads as follows:

> **D** shall be **computationally complete**. That is, **D** may support, but shall not require, invocation from so called host programs written in languages other than **D**. Similarly, **D** may support, but shall not require, the use of other languages for implementation of user defined operators.

However, one particular critic, in what for the purposes of this chapter and its two predecessors I'm calling "the critical letters," argues that this prescription implies that the *Manifesto* is deeply flawed. To quote:[1]

> It's an error to make **Tutorial D** computationally complete because it creates a language with logical expressions that are provably not decidable—yet a decision procedure must exist for any logical expression to be evaluated.

---

[1] For reasons of clarity and flow I've edited most of the quotes in this chapter, sometimes drastically so.

Note: As you can see, this quote refers to **Tutorial D**, not **D** as such, so I need to explain how **Tutorial D** and **D** relate to each other. To begin with, the name **D** is generic—it's used to refer generically to any language that conforms to the principles laid down in *The Third Manifesto*. Thus, there could be any number of distinct languages all qualifying as a valid **D**. **Tutorial D** is one such; it's defined more or less formally in the *Manifesto* book, and it's used throughout that book and elsewhere as a basis for examples. Just to be definite I'll concentrate on **Tutorial D** myself (mostly) in the present chapter, since that's what our critic does, but the discussions and arguments are equally applicable to any valid **D**.

DECIDABILITY

To repeat, our critic claims that **Tutorial D** suffers from a lack of decidability, or more precisely that certain **Tutorial D** logical expressions (also known as boolean expressions) aren't decidable. What does this mean?

Well, first, any given expression denotes a value; to put it another way, it can be thought of as a rule for computing the value in question. Hence, a logical expression in particular can be thought of as a rule for computing a logical value, or in other words a truth value. So a logical expression is an expression, formulated in some language L, that's supposed to denote either TRUE or FALSE.[2] Let *exp* be such an expression. To say *exp* is undecidable, then, is to say that although it's well formed—meaning it's constructed in full accordance with the syntax rules of L (it must be well formed, of course, for otherwise it wouldn't be an expression of L in the first place)—there doesn't exist an algorithm that can determine in finite time whether *exp* evaluates to TRUE. By extension, the overall language L itself is said to be undecidable if and only if there exists at least one L expression that's undecidable. I remark in passing that predicate calculus is undecidable in this sense, while propositional calculus is decidable.

If language L is decidable, then by definition there exists a general purpose algorithm (a "decision procedure") for determining in finite time whether an arbitrary logical expression of L evaluates to TRUE. By contrast, if L is undecidable, then no such algorithm exists. What's more, if L is undecidable, there isn't even an algorithm for determining ahead of time, as it were, whether a

---

[2] Naturally I limit my attention here to two-valued logic only.

given logical expression of L is decidable (if there were, the system could sidestep the problem, in effect, by not even attempting to evaluate expressions that are undecidable).

It follows from the foregoing that if **Tutorial D** in particular is undecidable, there'll be certain **Tutorial D** logical expressions that the system won't be able to deal with satisfactorily. On the face of it, then, the fact that **Tutorial D** is undecidable, if it is a fact, looks like a serious flaw.

COMPUTATIONAL COMPLETENESS

Our critic doesn't just claim that **Tutorial D** is undecidable, he—the critic is male—goes on to claim more specifically that it's the fact that **Tutorial D** is computationally complete that makes it so:

> If a given language incorporates predicate logic *and is computationally complete*, it's a logical consequence that [some] syntactically correct expressions of that language ... will be undecidable [*italics added*].

So what exactly does it mean for a language to be computationally complete?

Oddly enough, I was unable to find a good, simple definition of the term *computational completeness* in any of the fairly large number of computing references I examined. But many of them did include a definition of the term *computable function*, and I think it's a reasonable guess that a language is computationally complete if and only if it supports the computation of all computable functions. I'll take that as my working definition, anyway. So what's a computable function? Here are a couple of definitions from the literature:

- (From Sybil P. Parker, ed., *The McGraw-Hill Dictionary of Mathematics*, McGraw-Hill, 1994): A computable function is a function that can be computed by a Turing machine in a finite number of steps.

- (From Eric W. Weisstein, *CRC Concise Encyclopedia of Mathematics*, Chapman & Hall / CRC, 1999): A computable function is a function that can be coded using WHILE loops.

COMPUTATIONAL COMPLETENESS IMPLIES UNDECIDABILITY

As I've said, our critic claims that it's specifically the fact that **Tutorial D** is computationally complete that makes it undecidable. Here's an extended version of the extract I quoted near the beginning of the previous section:

> The problem is simply this: If a given language incorporates predicate logic and is computationally complete, it's a logical consequence that the set of syntactically correct expressions of that language will include self-referential expressions, and some of those will be undecidable. This is what Gödel showed in the process of constructing his first incompleteness theorem ... So, if **Tutorial D** is computationally complete, the set of syntactically correct **Tutorial D** expressions includes self-referential, undecidable expressions. I merely apply Gödel to **Tutorial D**.

The same critic appeals to Gödel's second incompleteness theorem, too. Here's an extended version of the extract I quoted near the beginning of this chapter:

> It's an error to make **Tutorial D** computationally complete because it creates a language with logical expressions that are provably not decidable—yet a decision procedure must exist for any logical expression to be evaluated (see Gödel's second incompleteness theorem). Is an example in **Tutorial D** more convincing than a proven theorem? Codd carefully avoided this trap, but *The Third Manifesto* does not!

I'll come back to the question of whether Codd "avoided this trap" in the next section. First, however, let me state for the record Gödel's two incompleteness theorems. *Note:* Actually those theorems can be stated in many different forms; the versions I give here are somewhat simplified—in fact, oversimplified—but they're good enough for present purposes. Note too that for the purposes of this discussion I'm regarding the terms *expression* and *statement* as interchangeable, even though they're not usually so regarded in programming language contexts.

> **Gödel's First Incompleteness Theorem:** Let S be a consistent formal system that's at least as powerful as elementary arithmetic; then S is incomplete, in the sense that there exist statements in S that are true but can't be proved in S.

Gödel's Second Incompleteness Theorem: Let *S* be a consistent formal system that's at least as powerful as elementary arithmetic; then the consistency of *S* can't be proved in *S*.

I confess I don't directly see the relevance of the second of these theorems to our critic's arguments, but the first clearly does support them. What's more, since Gödel's proof of his first theorem (a) involves the explicit construction of a self-referential statement—in effect an arithmetic analog of the statement "This statement can't be proved in *S*"—and then (b) proves that precisely that statement can't be proved either true or false in *S*, it follows more specifically that the set of undecidable expressions in *S* includes certain self-referential expressions. So all right, then: I'll accept for the sake of the argument that if **Tutorial D** is computationally complete, then it's undecidable, in the sense that its expressions do include ones that are self-referential and undecidable.

DOES CODD "AVOID THE TRAP"?

So far we've seen that our critic claims, apparently correctly, that **Tutorial D**, being computationally complete, is undecidable. What's more, he also claims, at least implicitly, that Codd's relational algebra and relational calculus are decidable; in fact, they surely must be, since Codd's calculus is essentially an applied form of propositional calculus, which is decidable, and Codd's algebra is logically equivalent to his calculus.

> *Aside:* A couple of points here:
>
> ■ First, relational calculus is usually thought of as being an applied form of predicate calculus, not propositional calculus; however, the fact that we're dealing with finite systems means that it is indeed propositional calculus that we're talking about, at least from a logical point of view.
>
> ■ Second, Codd's original calculus was actually less expressive than his algebra (i.e., there were certain algebraic expressions that had no equivalent in the calculus), but this deficiency in the calculus was subsequently remedied. The details need not concern us further in this chapter.
>
> *End of aside.*

As we've seen, our critic also claims that Codd "avoids the trap" of requiring computational completeness and thereby getting into the problem of undecidability. Now, he never actually comes out and states exactly how this goal—i.e., avoiding the trap—is or can be achieved, but he does imply rather strongly that it's a matter of drawing a sharp dividing line between the database and computational portions of the language:

> My desire is that **D** should cleanly separate set theoretic semantics and computer language semantics[3] ... OO Prescription 3 should be restated to say that **D**'s application sublanguage shall be computationally complete and entirely procedural and **D**'s database sublanguage shall not be computationally complete, shall be entirely nonprocedural, and shall be decidable (though I would still be concerned about how these sublanguages interact with each other) ...

> [*Another attempt, later:*] Separate **D** into **RD** (the relational, nonprocedural part) and **CD** (the computational, procedural part). Then OO Prescription 3 should be restated to say that **RD** shall not be computationally complete and shall not invoke any operator that cannot be implemented in **RD** ... A relational database language **RD** must be decidable. It follows that it must not be computationally complete, nor should it invoke any procedure that cannot, in principle, be implemented in **RD**.

So do Codd's own language proposals abide by such restrictions? Absolutely not! Here's a quote from Codd's famous 1970 paper (and please note the last two sentences in particular):[4]

> Let us denote the data sublanguage by *R* and the host language by *H* ... *R* permits the specification for retrieval of any subset of data from the [database] ... [The] class of qualification expressions which can be used in a set specification must have the descriptive power of the class of well formed formulas of an applied predicate calculus ... Arithmetic functions may be needed in the qualification or other parts of retrieval statements. Such functions can be defined in *H* and invoked in *R*.

And here's a quote from Codd's paper on his proposed ALPHA language:

---

[3] On that business of "set theoretic semantics vs. computer language semantics," see Chapter 4.

[4] That paper's less well known 1969 predecessor—which was in fact Codd's very first paper on the relational model—contains essentially identical text.

All computation of functions is defined in host language statements; all retrieval and storage operations in data sublanguage statements. A data sublanguage statement can, however, contain a use of a function defined in host statements ... An expandable library of functions which can be invoked in queries provides a means of extending the selective capability of data sublanguage ALPHA.

The ALPHA paper then goes on to give several examples of the use of such functions, in both the "target list" and "qualification" portions of queries. So I would say that, in these papers at least, Codd didn't just fail to "avoid the trap," he didn't even seem to think there might be a trap to avoid in the first place.

Note: In commenting on an earlier draft of the present chapter, our critic claimed that Codd's separation of the languages *R* and *H* was sufficient to "avoid the trap." In particular, he claimed that (a) one effect of that separation was that an invocation in *R* of a function defined in *H* could be regarded as a constant so far as *R* was concerned, and (b) the trap was avoided because functions defined in *H* had no access to the variables of *R*. I don't understand these claims. In particular, the specific functions Codd uses in examples in the ALPHA paper most certainly do have access to "the variables of *R*"—the functions in question include (but aren't limited to) analogs of the familiar aggregate operators COUNT, SUM, AVG, MAX, and MIN, all of which are of course explicitly defined to operate on relations (meaning relvars, rather, and those relvars are precisely "the variables of *R*"). And if the point is that these functions only read their operands and don't update them, then a precisely analogous remark could be made with respect to **Tutorial D**, so presumably that isn't the point.

As an aside, I'd like to add that, for reasons it would be invidious to go into detail on here, I've never been much of a fan of the data sublanguage idea anyway[5] (which is partly why the *Manifesto*'s OO Prescription 3 reads the way it does). As I've written elsewhere:[6]

Personally, I've never been entirely convinced that factoring out data access into a separate "sublanguage" was a good idea, [although it's] been with us, in the shape of embedded SQL, for a good while now. In this connection, incidentally, it's interesting to note that with the addition in 1996 of the PSM feature ("Persistent

---

[5] I mean, I prefer the idea of a single, integrated language that provides both database functionality and conventional programming language functionality—in other words, a language like **Tutorial D**.

[6] E.g., in my book *The Database Relational Model: A Retrospective Review and Analysis* (Addison-Wesley, 2001).

Stored Modules") to the SQL standard, SQL has now become a computationally complete language in its own right!—meaning that a host language as such is no longer logically necessary (with SQL, that is).

In the interests of fairness and accuracy, however, I should add that SQL doesn't include any I/O capabilities, so a host language might still be needed to provide that functionality.

WHY WE WANT COMPUTATIONAL COMPLETENESS

Here again is OO Prescription 3 as originally stated:

> **D** shall be **computationally complete**. That is, **D** may support, but shall not require, invocation from so called host programs written in languages other than **D**. Similarly, **D** may support, but shall not require, the use of other languages for implementation of user defined operators.

Our critic commented on this prescription as follows:

> I don't understand the text beginning "That is"—it isn't a definition of what it would mean for a language to be computationally complete. Being invocable from, or being able to invoke, programs written in other languages does not make a language computationally complete.

Of course I agree that the text beginning "That is" isn't a definition of computational completeness; it wasn't meant to be, and some rewording might be desirable (perhaps replace the phrase "That is" by "Therefore"?). Rather, that text was meant to spell out certain consequences that follow if **D** is computationally complete—in other words, it was meant to explain why we thought computational completeness was a good idea. As Hugh wrote in his own response to our critic:

> I hope the justification for our inclusion of computational completeness is clear. It is partly so that applications can be written in **D**, to avoid the problems inherent in writing them in some other language, and partly to allow implementations of user defined operators to be coded in **D**.

Later in the correspondence, in response to the criticisms I've already discussed, Hugh said this:

We could perhaps have said something like this instead: **D** shall include comprehensive facilities for the implementation of database applications and user defined operators. A computationally complete language would suffice for these purposes but **D** is not required to be computationally complete; nor are applications and user defined operators required to be written in **D**.

But if we agree to back off from computational completeness, how far do we go?—i.e., where do we draw the line? How much computation can we safely support? If it's true that computational completeness just means being able to compute all computable functions, and a computable function just means a function that can be coded using WHILE loops, do we have to prohibit WHILE loops? If so, where does that leave us? *Note:* These questions are rhetorical, of course. My point, in case it isn't obvious, is that I don't think we *can* back off from computational completeness. What's more, Hugh agrees with me; his suggestion that **D** might not need to be computationally complete was never meant as more than a straw man (sorry, straw person).

But there's another issue I need to address under the rubric of why we wanted **D** to be computationally complete. Computational completeness implies among other things that relational expressions can include invocations of user defined, read-only, relation valued operators—operators whose implementation might be coded in **D** itself, perhaps using loops or other procedural constructs—and some critics seem to think that such a state of affairs is contrary to Codd's original intent that queries and the like should all be expressed declaratively. However, we would argue that all read-only operator invocations are equally "declarative," regardless of where, how, by whom, and in what language(s) those operators are implemented (and regardless of whether they're relation valued). By way of illustration, consider the following example:

```
OPERATOR TABLE_NUM ( K INTEGER )
        RETURNS RELATION { N INTEGER } ;
        ... implementation code ...
END OPERATOR ;
```

When invoked, this operator returns a relation representing the predicate "*N* is an integer in the range 1 to *K*, inclusive."[7] Surely, then, an invocation such as

---

[7] In other words, that relation contains a tuple for every integer from 1 to *K*, inclusive. The utility of such an operator is demonstrated in the paper "A Constant Friend" (by Hugh, writing as Andrew Warden) in my book *Relational Database Writings 1985-1989* (Addison-Wesley, 1990).

TABLE_NUM (9999) is equally "declarative" regardless of whether the implementation code (a) is written in **D** by the user doing the invoking, or (b) is written in **D** by some other user, or (c) is written by some user in some other language, or (d) is provided as part of the DBMS.

DOES IT ALL MATTER?

Here's our critic once more:

> If **Tutorial D** is undecidable, sooner or later, whether by human user accident or by machine generation, an attempt will be made to evaluate an undecidable statement and the implementation will fail. You might object by pointing out that this does not happen in computationally complete languages such as Ada or Pascal or Fortran or Java. However, you would be quite wrong. It is actually quite easy to code an infinite procedural loop which no compiler can detect.[8]

More specifically, as we've seen, our critic claims that a relational language must have an associated decision procedure ("a decision procedure must exist for any logical expression to be evaluated"). But is this claim correct? Predicate calculus has no decision procedure, but at least it's possible to come up with a procedure that does some of what's required and is sound and complete. To paraphrase some remarks from a book on logic and programming:[9]

> Given a well formed formula of predicate calculus, if that formula evaluates to TRUE, then such a procedure will eventually return TRUE; however, if the formula evaluates to FALSE, either the procedure will eventually return FALSE or it will run forever. Thus, if the procedure has failed to terminate after some given period of time, we can't say whether the formula is TRUE.

In practice, therefore, we can surely incorporate such a procedure into the system implementation. Moreover, we can incorporate a time-out mechanism into that procedure, such that if evaluation of some given expression fails to halt after some predetermined period of time, the system can terminate evaluation and

---

[8] I agree with this last sentence!—but it seems to me to be an argument *against* the author's own position (?), since all it seems to be saying is that **Tutorial D** is no worse than any other programming language as far as decidability is concerned.

[9] Zohar Manna and Richard Waldinger, *The Logical Basis for Computer Programming, Volume 2: Deductive Systems* (Addison-Wesley, 1990), page 596.

return a message to the user, along the lines of *Expression too complex to evaluate*. What it mustn't do, of course, is return either TRUE or FALSE in such a situation! To do that would be to return what Codd—albeit writing in a very different context—once called a "severely incorrect" result.[10]

To summarize, therefore:

■ Clearly we would like a system in which all possible expressions can be evaluated in finite time.

■ This objective apparently can't be achieved if we insist on computational completeness.

■ However, we are at least aware of this fact, and so we can plan for it.

■ In particular, we can build code into the system that allows it to respond to certain requests by saying, in effect, "I can't process this request because it's too complex."

In conclusion, I'd like to point out that:

■ Inability to respond definitively to certain requests is a common occurrence in ordinary human discourse. We deal with such situations all the time. So having the system occasionally respond with the message *Expression too complex to evaluate* doesn't necessarily mean the system is useless.

■ In any case, even without computational completeness, it seems likely that there'll exist requests that, though answerable in finite time in principle, might take so long to answer in practice that they're effectively unanswerable after all. In other words, the undecidability problem exists, in a sense, even without computational completeness. And our pragmatic fix for that problem (implementing a time-out mechanism) is therefore presumably needed anyway.

---

[10] The context was the debate ("Much Ado About Nothing") between Codd and myself on nulls and three-valued logic. I mentioned that debate in passing in Chapter 2. It originally appeared in *Database Programming & Design* 6, No. 10 (October 1993) and was later republished in my book *Relational Database Writings 1991-1994* (Addison-Wesley, 1995).

■ Finally, if computational completeness leads to a lack of decidability, then it follows that conventional programming languages are undecidable. But we've lived with this problem for many years now, and as far as I know it hasn't led to any insuperable difficulties. Why should database languages be any different in this regard?

APPENDIX A: COMPUTABLE FUNCTIONS

In the body of this chapter, I quoted the *CRC Concise Encyclopedia of Mathematics* as saying that a computable function is one that can be coded using WHILE loops. Following this definition, that reference goes on to say:

> FOR loops (which have a fixed iteration limit) are a special case of WHILE loops, so computable functions can also be coded using a combination of FOR and WHILE loops. The Ackermann function is the simplest example of a function which is computable but not primitive recursive.

I'd like to elaborate briefly on these remarks:

■ First, a function is said to be *recursive* if and only if it "can be obtained [*i.e., defined, and therefore implemented*] by a finite number of operations, computations, or algorithms." (This definition is from *The McGraw-Hill Dictionary of Mathematics*. Note that the term "recursive" isn't being used here in the usual programming language sense; in fact, it seems to mean nothing more nor less than computable, as that term was previously defined.)

■ Second, a function is said to be *primitive recursive* if and only if it can be coded using FOR loops only. (This definition is from the *CRC Concise Encyclopedia of Mathematics*.)

Now, I don't know in what sense exactly the Ackermann function can be said to be "the simplest example" of a function that's "recursive [*or at any rate computable*] but not primitive recursive." For interest, however, I give the definition of that function here (and I note that this definition in particular is certainly recursive in the usual programming language sense). Here it is:

Definition (Ackermann function): Let x and y denote nonnegative integers. Then the Ackermann function $ACK(x,y)$ can be defined thus:

```
OPERATOR ACK ( X NONNEG_INT, Y NONNEG_INT )
        RETURNS NONNEG_INT ;
        RETURN ( CASE
                    WHEN X = 0 THEN Y + 1
                    WHEN Y = 0 THEN ACK ( X - 1, 1 )
                    ELSE ACK ( X - 1, ACK ( X, Y - 1 ) )
                 END CASE ) ;
END OPERATOR ;
```

Warning: Please don't try to execute this algorithm on a real machine, not even for fairly small x and y.

Chapter 6

SQL and Relational Theory

In accordance with their textbooks, they are always in motion; but as for dwelling upon an argument or a question, and quietly asking and answering in turn, they can no more do so than they can fly ... If you ask any of them a question, he will produce, as from a quiver, sayings brief and dark, and shoot them at you; and if you enquire the reason of what he has said, you will be hit with some other newfangled word, and you will make no way with any of them. Their great care is, not to allow of any settled principle either in their arguments or in their minds ... for they are at war with the stationary, and do what they can to drive it out everywhere.

—Plato (the speaker, Theodorus, is talking about the Ephesians),
quoted in the essay "Sayings Brief and Dark" by Richard Mitchell:
The Leaning Tower of Babel (2000)

I recently, and unfortunately only rather belatedly, came across an online review by Joe Celko of my book *SQL and Relational Theory: How to Write Accurate SQL Code* (O'Reilly, 2009).[1] The review in question was prefaced by the following introductory paragraph (I don't know who wote it):

SQL and Relational Theory, by Chris Date, isn't likely to be a book that SQL's greatest defender, Joe Celko, would agree with. However, following the debates between Date and Celko on the relational purity of SQL has all the fascination of watching Godzilla wrestling King Kong. [*Make of that what you will!*]

Well, there certainly wasn't any wrestling at the time, because as I've said I didn't even see Celko's review until comparatively recently. What's more, for reasons that should be clear from the epigraph to this chapter, I'm a little

---

[1] That was the first edition. The second edition was published by O'Reilly in 2012 and the third in 2015. Celko's review, dated September 26th, 2012—in other words, when the first edition had already been superseded by the second!—can be found on the website *www.red-gate.com*.

reluctant to start wrestling now ... But there are so many issues arising from that review that cry out for a response that I feel I simply have to try to defend myself, even though it's so belatedly. In any case, I do think the record needs to be set straight as well. So here goes. I'll begin by giving Celko's review in its entirety, quoted absolutely verbatim except for a few trivial (mostly formatting) edits by myself.

CELKO'S REVIEW, VERBATIM

The title of this book is *SQL and Relational Theory*. It is subtitled *How to Write Accurate SQL Code* and it is part of a *Theory in Practice* series.

Chris Date has produced a collection of books on RDBMS and SQL from various publishers over several decades. His *An Introduction to Database Systems* (ISBN 0-321-19784-4, Addison-Wesley, 2004) is now in its eighth edition and was the standard college textbook for years. His claim to fame in the RDBMS world is that he worked with, and then partnered with, Ted Codd for many years to create the consulting company (Codd & Date).

Going back to the early days of RDBMS, when there was not so much internet, we had things made out of paper that we called magazines. In particular, there were newsstand computer magazines devoted to the "new" and exciting topic of databases. They were *DBMS* from M&T Publishing and *Database Programming & Design* from Miller Freeman. The publishing industry is volatile and there are buyouts and cancellations. Thanks to something happening to a parent company in Germany, *both* magazines wound up belonging to Miller Freeman.

So for a few years, Chris Date and I each had columns in a different magazine from the same publisher! Chris would write a piece on topic X and I would respond the next month with an anti-X piece. If you are really old or are a radio nostalgia buff, you will remember the Jack Benny & Fred Allen mock feud. They sniped at each other back and forth on their respective radio shows and boosted the audience for both shows.

We did the same thing; people had to buy *both* magazines to get the full story. Without that incentive, would you have bought two separate magazines on the same topic otherwise? Perhaps the best part of the series was "Dueling Medians"; each of us would offer a solution for finding the Median in SQL and the other would reply with another approach, other people joined in. I gave the various solutions in my *SQL for Smarties*.

Chris Date collected his columns and some other material into a series of books for Addison-Wesley in 1986, 1990, 1992 and 1994, then a collection from Apress in 2006 of articles written after the magazine columns were gone.

To this day, I still get asked if I hate Chris Date. Of course not! I buy and read every one of his books. But we do disagree on technical issues. The super short version is that I am the great defender of SQL and data standards; Chris is the defender of a **Tutorial D** and his school of Relational Theory. I am more hands-on and Chris is more theory.

The bad news is that large amounts of the discussion are about how SQL does not subscribe to the Date Relational Model, and much of the code is in **Tutorial D**. If you are not familiar with **Tutorial D**, I ought to explain that it is a relational programming language that is directly based on the relational calculus. The reader has to learn enough **Tutorial D** to read the comparisons between SQL and **Tutorial D**. Date uses his famous Suppliers and Parts database for the examples. He does not spend a lot of time on the DDL and moves to DML. But 80-95% of the work in SQL is done in the DDL, not the DML. And his examples are done with very simple code at the SQL-92 level. Let me be more specific:

The Parts table P (I will get to the DDL for it shortly) gives the weight of a part in pounds and we want it in grams. The **Tutorial D** version is:

```
EXTEND P ADD ( weight * 454.0 AS gm_wt )
```

The SQL is:

```
SELECT  P.* , ( weight * 454.0 ) AS gm_wt
FROM    P ;
```

Now let's go to the next step. Write a query to give us all parts with a weight greater than 7000.0 gm. The **Tutorial D** version Date gives is:

```
( ( EXTEND P ADD ( weight * 454.0 AS gm_wt ) )
          WHERE gm_wt > 7000.0 ) { pno , gm_wt }
```

The SQL he gives is:

```
SELECT  P.* , ( weight * 454.0 ) AS gm_wt
FROM    P
WHERE   ( weight * 454.0 ) > 7000.0 ;
```

His point is that you have to re-use the computation in the WHERE clause. But that is not the case; it can be done with a derived table or CTE if you want to avoid using a VIEW:

```
SELECT X.*
FROM   ( SELECT pno , ( weight * 454.0 ) AS gm_wt
          FROM   P ) AS X ( pno , gm_wt )
WHERE  gm_wt > 7000.0 ;
```

This is a direct translation of the first query into SQL. The inner SELECT is a derived table that mimics the function of the EXTEND in **Tutorial D**.

Going further, an SQL programmer would probably say to himself, "I am going to need to do this conversion in a lot of places" and he then does the computation in the DDL with a VIEW or with a computed column.

```
CREATE VIEW Metric_Parts
AS
SELECT pno , pname, color, city, ( weight * 454.0 ) AS gm_wt
FROM   P ;
```

Alternatively, the computed column will act like a VIEW; the syntax is just a little different.

```
CREATE TABLE Metric_Parts
( pno CHAR(2) NOT NULL PRIMARY KEY ,
  pname VARCHAR(10) NOT NULL ,
  color VARCHAR(10) NOT NULL ,
  city VARCHAR(10) NOT NULL ,
  weight DECIMAL(5,2) NOT NULL ,
  COMPUTE ( weight * 454.0 AS gm_wt ) ) ;
```

In fairness, Date also has complaints about **Tutorial D** because it lacks a Relational Division and introduces his DIVIDEBY operator from his previous books. Unfortunately, Relational Division come in many flavors—Codd's original division, Todd's division, with and without remainders and probably others.

Some statements are incorrect. In Chapter 8 on constraints, on page 100, he states that "Transition constraints aren't current supported in either **Tutorial D** or SQL (other than procedurally)." His discussion uses a transition from "never married" to "married" and you cannot go back to a status of "never married" again.

I published the DDL code for state transition constraint in an article entitled "Constraint Yourself" in Simple Talk. I used (born, married, divorced, dead) as my status values.

In a footnote, he says:

> The semantics of WITH LOCAL CHECK OPTION are far too baroque to be spelled out in detail here. In any case, it's hard to see why anyone would ever want such semantics; indeed, it's hard to resist the suspicion that this alternative was included in the standard for no other reason than to allow certain flawed implementations, extant at the time, to be abler to claim conformance.

ANSI tries to get all of the membership to agree on a common abstract model of how SQL works. We then create features on that model. By now, you should know that the clauses of a basic SELECT.. FROM.. WHERE.. GROUP BY.. HAVING.. statement start with the from clause and end with the select clause. We had to work out those rules in the committee because not all products did it that way. At one point, the GROUP BY implementations either put the NULLs in one group or put each NULL in its own group. Sybase did the ALL () and ANY () predicates wrong. Oracle had to add the CHAR2(n) because they got the CHAR(n) wrong; Microsoft added DATETIME(2) to implement the ANSI Standard TIMESTAMP. Did you notice that *= is long gone from products? The truth is that when the standards change, the vendors change their products, not the other way around. As the standards have progressed, we have fewer and fewer "implementation defined" features.

All that said, yes, the WITH [LOCAL | CASCADE] CHECK OPTION is baroque when you nest VIEWs inside each other. But it can be very powerful and enforce complex relationships that would otherwise have to be done with triggers or worse. It how you can express multi-table joins in SQL when you do not have a CREATE ASSERTION statement.

Chapter 11 is "Using Logic to Formulate Expressions" which introduces two-valued predicate logic and quantifiers. The explanations are done with **Tutorial D**, and then translated into SQL. That is confusing. **Tutorial D** is like classic (i.e. NULL free) predicate logic but it is still another language to learn. But SQL does have NULLs and we need to consider them from the start. This is one reason that minimal Netiquette on SQL Forums requires that you post DDL even for the simplest SQL problems.

For example, Date gives one of his classic tables:

```
CREATE TABLE Parts
( pno CHAR(2) NOT NULL PRIMARY KEY ,
  pname VARCHAR(10) NOT NULL ,
  color VARCHAR(10) NOT NULL ,
  weight DECIMAL(5,2) ,
  city VARCHAR(10) NOT NULL ) ;
```

Please notice that the weight is NULL-able, but the first sample data is like this:

```
INSERT INTO Parts
VALUES
( 'P1' , 'nut' , 'red' , 12.0 , 'London' ) ,
( 'P2' , 'bolt' , 'green' , 17.0 , 'Paris' ) ,
( 'P3' , 'screw' , 'blue' , 17.0 , 'Oslo' ) ,
( 'P4' , 'screw' , 'red' , 14.0 , 'London' ) ,
( 'P5' , 'cam' , 'blue' , 12.0 , 'Paris' ) ,
( 'P6' , 'cog' , 'red' , 19.0 , 'London' ) ;
```

Given the problem "find the parts that have a weight that is different from the weight of any part in Paris."

```
SELECT P1.pname
FROM   Parts AS P1
WHERE  NOT EXISTS
       ( SELECT *
         FROM   Parts AS P2
         WHERE  P2.city = 'Paris'
         AND    P2.weight = P1.weight ) ;
```

Produces the same results, but only if there are no NULL weights in the table.

```
SELECT P1.pname
FROM   Parts AS P1
WHERE  P1.weight NOT IN
       ( SELECT P2.weight
         FROM   Parts AS P2
         WHERE  P2.city = 'Paris' ) ;
```

The EXISTS () predicate is always TRUE or FALSE, but the IN () predicate is a shorthand for a chain of OR-ed predicates. The IN () predicate can return UNKNOWN if there are NULLs. We would need get rid of the NULLs:

```
SELECT  P1.pname
FROM    Parts AS P1
WHERE   P1.weight IS NOT NULL
AND     P1.weight NOT IN
        ( SELECT  P2.weight
          FROM    Parts AS P2
          WHERE   P2.weight IS NOT NULL
          AND     P2.city = 'Paris' ) ;
```

And we now the "IS [NOT] DISTINCT FROM" comparison operator that will treat NULLs as if they are equal:

```
SELECT  P1.pname
FROM    Parts AS P1
WHERE   NOT EXISTS
        ( SELECT  *
          FROM    Parts AS P2
          WHERE   P2.city = 'Paris'
          AND     P2.weight IS NOT DISTINCT FROM P1.weight ) ;
```

Summary: I do not feel the book lived up to its title. Someone trying to improve his SQL or find a systematic approach to constructing a query has to first predicate logic and **Tutorial D**. Date's dislike of SQL shows up everywhere in the book; he was looking for ways to make SQL look bad. Much of his SQL code is dated and fails to use newer features.

While you expect some repetition, the material was a re-arrangement of his older material without adding anything new. If you have not read Date's other books, then this might not be a problem.

I feel that a better approach would have been to show dangerous or shoddy SQL, demonstrate the problems, explain the math, relational algebra and logic that was ignored and then solve the problems with better SQL. The "Paris-weights" example I showed would be the start of such a detailed analysis. The reader would not be confused by **Tutorial D** code and would have come away with a better understanding for the limits and power of SQL.

"A BETTER APPROACH?"

How to respond to all of the above? Well, the first thing I want to say is this: It seems to me that if you're going to write a book review, then you do owe it to your readers—not to mention the author—to read the book in question carefully. Celko has clearly not done so in the case at hand. I'll give examples in support of this claim in the next section; before then, however, I'd like to address Celko's suggestion, in his summary, regarding a possible "better approach" (meaning, presumably, a "better approach" to doing what I was trying to do with my book). I disagree with that suggestion, of course, and I'd like to take a moment to explain why.

My overall aim with the book (as the title and subtitle, not to mention the preface, surely make clear) was to provide readers with an understanding of both relational concepts in general and the relational model in particular—an understanding that could help them in their task of writing accurate SQL code. To elaborate briefly:

- It's my claim and firm belief that SQL is a very difficult language,[2] and hence that writing accurate SQL code requires discipline.

- The book proposes such a discipline. The discipline in question consists in using SQL as if it truly were a concrete realization of the abstract principles of the relational model: in particular, in avoiding aspects of the language that flout those principles.

- In order to follow that discipline, of course, you need to know what those principles are. In other words, you need to know the relational model. The book explains that model, and shows how to use SQL in accordance with it.

- In order to explain that model, I have to use some concrete syntax. SQL is unsuitable for that purpose, precisely because it fails in so many ways to abide by the prescriptions of that model. (If it didn't, the book wouldn't have been necessary in the first place!) So instead I use **Tutorial D**, which does faithfully abide by those prescriptions.

So it's certainly true as Celko claims that readers have to learn, or at least understand, aspects of the **Tutorial D** language as they work through the book— but what he doesn't say, when he complains about this state of affairs, is that the aspects in question are blindingly simple, and the process of learning or at least understanding them as the book proceeds is utterly trivial. And by the way, **Tutorial D** is directly based, not on the relational calculus as Celko states, but instead on the relational algebra—as would be obvious to any database

---

[2] Strong evidence in support of this claim can be found in Chapter 16 of the present book, as well as in the *SQL and Relational Theory* book that's the subject of Celko's review and in numerous other writings by myself and others.

professional who examined it for even just a few seconds would immediately see. Evidence right there, in my opinion, that Celko can't have read the book very carefully.

Note: I also offer, in Chapter 11 of the book, an alternative discipline for formulating queries specifically (meaning SQL queries specifically, of course, and especially ones that might otherwise seem a little complicated), based not on **Tutorial D** but rather on predicate logic. It's my claim that users who have to deal with this problem—viz., formulating complicated queries in SQL—owe it to themselves to have some reasonable familiarity with predicate logic and the discipline proposed. Indeed, if they aren't familiar with such matters, then I for one won't trust the formulations they come up with or the answers those formulations produce.

Now I want to turn to some more specific aspects of Celko's review. In fact, what I plan to do is this: I'll repeat Celko's review in its entirety, but this time interspersed and annotated with comments of my own (in the form of added asides, footnotes, and so on). In other words, I plan to engage in the delicate art of *deconstruction* ... In case you're not familiar with this splendid term of art, let me explain that what it means—as far as I'm concerned, at any rate!—is that you can judge a writer's intent only by what he or she has actually said, not by what you might possibly think he or she might possibly have wanted to have possibly said, but didn't.

CELKO'S REVIEW, ANNOTATED

The title of this book is *SQL and Relational Theory*. It is subtitled *How to Write Accurate SQL Code* and it is part of a *Theory in Practice* series.

Chris Date has produced a collection of books on RDBMS and SQL from various publishers over several decades. His *An Introduction to Database Systems* (ISBN 0-321-19784-4, Addison-Wesley, 2004) is now in its eighth edition and was the standard college textbook for years. His claim to fame in the RDBMS world is that he worked with, and then partnered with, Ted Codd for many years to create the consulting company (Codd & Date). [*It's just a matter of wounded pride, perhaps, but I'd like to think my "claim to fame"—such as it is—is a little more than just reflected glory from Ted Codd!*]

Going back to the early days of RDBMS, when there was not so much internet, we had things made out of paper that we called magazines. In particular, there were newsstand computer magazines devoted to the "new" and exciting topic of databases. They were *DBMS* from M&T Publishing and *Database Programming & Design* from Miller Freeman. The publishing industry is volatile and there are buyouts and cancellations. Thanks to something happening to a parent company in Germany, *both* magazines wound up belonging to Miller Freeman.

So for a few years, Chris Date and I each had columns in a different magazine from the same publisher! Chris would write a piece on topic X and I would respond the next month with an anti-X piece. If you are really old or are a radio nostalgia buff, you will remember the Jack Benny & Fred Allen mock feud. They sniped at each other back and forth on their respective radio shows and boosted the audience for both shows.

We did the same thing; people had to buy *both* magazines to get the full story. Without that incentive, would you have bought two separate magazines on the same topic otherwise? [*Probably yes, if they were any good.*] Perhaps the best part of the series was "Dueling Medians"; each of us would offer a solution for finding the Median in SQL and the other would reply with another approach, other people joined in. I gave the various solutions in my *SQL for Smarties.*[3]

Chris Date collected his columns and some other material into a series of books for Addison-Wesley in 1986, 1990, 1992 and 1994, then a collection from Apress in 2006 of articles written after the magazine columns were gone. [*Just to set the record straight: The books in question appeared in 1986, 1990, 1992, 1995 (not 1994 as Celko states), and 1998, respectively (there were five of them, not four, published prior to the Apress book Celko mentions). Columns from the magazine Database Programming & Design appeared in the 1992 and 1995 books only.*]

To this day, I still get asked if I hate Chris Date. Of course not! I buy and read every one of his books.[4] But we do disagree on technical issues. The super short version is that I am the great defender of SQL and data standards; Chris is the defender of a [*sic*] **Tutorial D** and his school of Relational Theory. I am more hands-on and Chris is more theory.

---

[3] Note the first word ("We") of this paragraph, which implies that Celko and I somehow conspired in a plot to sell magazines. Really? In my opinion the whole paragraph is ridiculously overblown, with respect to both (a) the specific example it cites ("Dueling Medians," a very trivial issue—and by the way, there never was any kind of "duel," as such, on that issue) and (b) the broader suggestion that we had an ongoing "series" of "debates" in those magazines. I think we had at most three disagreements in print (they were hardly debates as such). Maybe it was only two.

[4] Well, that's gratifying to know. But if it's true, then I have to say I'm really disappointed to see how little he seems to have learned from all of that reading. PS: For the record, I don't hate Joe Celko either.

Comment: There are a couple of things I want to say in connection with the foregoing paragraph. First, Celko describes himself as "more hands on" and myself as "more theory." Well, that's probably true; however, he certainly likes to air his theoretical erudition in his writings, thereby prompting the possibly unworthy suspicion that he's just trying to blind his readers with science. For example, in his attack on *The Third Manifesto*'s prescriptions regarding types (something I'll be discussing in detail in the planned follow-on to the present book, viz., *Stating the Obvious, and Other Database Writings*), he makes reference to all of the following: Peano's Postulates; Aleph Null; Cantor sets; Julia sets; the "3*n* + 1 problem" set (actually I think that should be sequence, not set); a proof that there are more irrational than rational numbers; and possibly more. These are all fairly abstruse theoretical topics, and I would guess that not too many people in his target audience would be familiar with them—not to mention the fact that none of the topics mentioned has any real relevance anyway to the issue he's supposed to be discussing (viz., type theory). So I could be wrong, but it looks to me as if Celko is trying to have his cake here and eat it too.

Second, I really object to the phrase "his [*i.e., my*] school of Relational Theory," as if there might be many such "schools," all competing with one another and all of them equally valid. And other writings of Celko's do indeed suggest he thinks there are. To be specific, in Chapter 18 ("Different Relational Models") of his book *Joe Celko's Data and Databases: Concepts in Practice* (Morgan Kaufmann, 1999), he says this: "There is no such thing as *the* relational model for databases anymore [*sic*] than there is just one geometry." And he goes on—rather curiously, in my opinion—to list six such "models," as follows:

1. Chris Date = No Duplicates, No NULLs[5]
2. E. F. Codd, RM Version I
3. E. F. Codd, RM Version II
4. SQL-92 = Duplicates, One NULL
5. Duplicates, One NULL, Non-1NF Tables
6. Rick Snodgrass = Temporal SQL

I touched on this issue in Chapter 2 of the present book, as you might recall. Elsewhere, in fact, I've done my best to debunk it, too—see, e.g., Chapter 19 ("There's Only One Relational Model") of the Apress book mentioned earlier, *Date on Database: Writings 2000-2006* (Apress, 2006). So I won't go into

---

[5] For reasons unexplained Celko always sets the word *null* in all caps.

further details on the matter here but will content myself with referring you to this latter book for further discussion. *End of comment.*

The bad news [*i.e., as far as the subject book is concerned, presumably*] is that large amounts of the discussion are about how SQL does not subscribe to the Date Relational Model [*sic*], and much of the code is in **Tutorial D**. If you are not familiar with **Tutorial D**, I ought to explain that it is a relational programming language that is directly based on the relational calculus. [*No, it's not! As noted in the previous section, what it's "directly based" on is the relational algebra.*] The reader has to learn enough **Tutorial D** to read the comparisons between SQL and **Tutorial D**.

> *Comment:* Personally, I would have said the real "bad news" here isn't (a) the fact that "large amounts of the discussion are about how SQL does not subscribe to the Date Relational Model [*sic*]," but rather (b) the fact that large amounts of SQL do not subscribe (better: *conform*) to the relational model. It's this state of affairs that accounts not only for why the book is the way it is but also for the book's existence in the first place. As for that "Date Relational Model," I've already criticized Celko's use of the essentially similar and equally objectionable phrase "his [*i.e., my*] school of Relational Theory.") And as for "much of the code is in **Tutorial D** ... The reader has to learn enough **Tutorial D** to read the comparisons between SQL and **Tutorial D**": Well, this claim is correct, of course, but as I've already explained it's a criticism that counts for very little in the larger scheme of things. *End of comment.*

Date uses his famous Suppliers and Parts database for the examples. He does not spend a lot of time on the DDL and moves to [*focuses on?*] DML. But 80-95% of the work in SQL is done in the DDL, not the DML. And his examples are done with very simple code at the SQL-92 level.

> *Comment:* One of the strengths of relational languages (SQL too, come to that) is that there's really no hard and fast dividing line between DDL and DML. For example, a view definition would probably be thought of as "DDL," but a large part of such a definition consists of the view defining expression, which is "DML." That said, my book says exactly as much about DDL as is necessary. Celko's claim that "80 to 95 percent of the work in SQL is done in the DDL, not the DML" is absurd on its face.
>
> As for my limiting myself to "very simple code at the SQL-92 level," the point is irrelevant! Later "levels" of the standard certainly haven't done anything

to make SQL "more relational." In fact, of course, they can't, thanks to what Hugh Darwen calls *The Shackle of Compatibility*. For example, because the very first version of the standard allowed tables to contain duplicate rows, all later versions have to do so too, for fear of causing existing programs to fail.[6]

Finally, I note for the record that the official name for what Celko calls "SQL-92" is SQL:1992. It's a very small point, of course, but we're supposed to be talking about a standard here. *End of comment*.

Let me be more specific: The Parts table P (I will get to the DDL for it shortly) gives the weight of a part in pounds and we want it in grams. The **Tutorial D** version is:[7]

```
EXTEND P ADD ( weight * 454.0 AS gm_wt )
```

The SQL is:

```
SELECT P.* , ( weight * 454.0 ) AS gm_wt
FROM   P ;
```

Now let's go to the next step. Write a query to give us all parts with a weight greater than 7000.0 gm. The **Tutorial D** version Date gives is:

```
( ( EXTEND P ADD ( weight * 454.0 AS gm_wt ) )
          WHERE gm_wt > 7000.0 ) { pno , gm_wt }
```

The SQL he gives is:

```
SELECT P.* , ( weight * 454.0 ) AS gm_wt
FROM   P
WHERE  ( weight * 454.0 ) > 7000.0 ;
```

---

[6] To put the point another way, languages (even bad ones like SQL) do "live forever"—so do their mistakes!—which is precisely why it's so important to get them right the first time.

[7] I note in passing that what Celko calls "the **Tutorial D** version" in this example is an *expression* but his SQL version is a *statement* (it was an expression in my book). There's a logical difference between statements and expressions!—I was going to say a big logical difference, but all logical differences are big differences by definition. PS: The syntax of EXTEND has been improved since the first edition of the *SQL and Relational Theory* book, and the example under discussion here would now look like this: EXTEND P: {gm_wt := weight * 454.0}. (In fact this change was reflected in the second edition of the book, which as noted in footnote 1 was already available when Celko's review was published.) But I'll stay with the earlier syntax for the purposes of this chapter.

His point is that you have to re-use the computation in the WHERE clause. [*No, the point is that you have to **redo** it, not reuse it.*] But that is not the case; it can be done with a derived table or CTE if you want to avoid using a VIEW:[8]

```
SELECT X . *
FROM ( SELECT pno , ( weight * 454.0 ) AS gm_wt
       FROM   P ) AS X ( pno , gm_wt )
WHERE  gm_wt > 7000.0 ;
```

This is a direct translation of the first query into SQL. The inner SELECT is a derived table that mimics the function of the EXTEND in **Tutorial D**.

> *Comment:* Several points here. First of all, I believe Celko's unexplained abbreviation CTE stands for *common table expression*.[9] If so, then it's hardly a very appropriate name for the construct, at least in the case at hand. Why? Because it's used just once, not several times (which it would need to be to in order to be considered "common" to all of those uses). Anyway, I think what Celko means by his CTE remark is that all we need in the example is the ability to use a subquery in the FROM clause—which was a large part of my point in the first place, and brings me to my next response.
>
> Second, then (and much more important), my book does give an SQL formulation of the query that's essentially identical to the one Celko gives, and it's dishonest to imply otherwise (which I certainly think is what Celko's text does). What I was trying to say with my whole discussion was (a) that in order to avoid the repetition you need support for subqueries in the FROM clause (support that was absent from the standard prior to SQL:1992, incidentally), and (b) that even with such support, the rigidity of the SQL SELECT – FROM – WHERE template has the undesirable consequence that it forces you to reference something (X, in the example) before—possibly a long way before—it's defined. Celko's review does address my point (a), albeit in what seems to me a dishonest manner, but ignores my point (b) entirely.
>
> Third, I don't really know what Celko means by "the first query" here, nor what he means when he says his SQL formulation is a "direct translation" of it.
>
> Fourth, it's not really accurate to say either that (a) "the inner SELECT is a ... table" (derived or otherwise) or that (b) it "mimics the function of the EXTEND"

---

[8] For reasons unexplained Celko always sets the word *view* in all caps. PS: In any case, using a view won't avoid the repeated computation, it'll only conceal it (see Celko's view definition on the next page).

[9] I could be wrong on this. The version of the standard that was current at the time Celko was writing his review (viz., SQL:2011) doesn't seem to mention either the phrase *common table expression* or the abbreviation *CTE*.

in the **Tutorial D** formulation. Regarding point (a), the inner SELECT is an expression that evaluates to a table but isn't itself a table as such. Regarding point (b), the table that the inner SELECT evaluates to has two columns while the relation the **Tutorial D** EXTEND expression evaluates to has six attributes, so they're certainly not equivalent. Small points, perhaps, but sloppiness in writing can be a sign of sloppiness in thinking, and it can certainly give rise to errors in programming. *End of comment.*

Going further, an SQL programmer would probably say to himself [*sic*], "I am going to need to do this conversion in a lot of places" and he [*sic*] then does the computation in the DDL with a VIEW or with a computed column.

```
CREATE VIEW Metric_Parts
AS
SELECT pno , pname, color, city, ( weight * 454.0 ) AS gm_wt
FROM    P ;
```

Comment: "Going further" is right—Celko is going off on a tangent that has nothing to with the part of my book he's supposed to be discussing at this point, and accordingly nothing to do with the subject matter at hand (viz., the EXTEND operator and what has to be done in SQL to "mimic the function" of that operator). Detailed discussion of views is deferred in my book—deliberately, of course—to a later chapter; at this point, they're nothing but a red herring. *End of comment.*

Alternatively, the computed column will act like a VIEW [*but how can a column "act like" a view?—a column is a column and a view is a table!*]; the syntax is just a little different.

```
CREATE TABLE Metric_Parts
( pno CHAR(2) NOT NULL PRIMARY KEY ,
  pname VARCHAR(10) NOT NULL ,
  color VARCHAR(10) NOT NULL ,
  city VARCHAR(10) NOT NULL ,
  weight DECIMAL(5,2) NOT NULL ,
  COMPUTE ( weight * 454.0 AS gm_wt ) ;
```

Comment: Celko uses the COMPUTE keyword in this example, but I don't know where he got it from; I don't see any reference to it, nor to the concept it apparently corresponds to, in my copy of the SQL:2011 standard.

Incidentally, I note that Celko's Metric_Parts table is in second normal form and not third, and hence that it's subject to a variety of interesting update anomalies, which would have to be explained to the user. I note too that there appears to be a syntax error in Celko's CREATE TABLE statement (final closing parenthesis missing). *End of comment.*

In fairness, Date also has complaints about **Tutorial D** because it lacks a Relational Division and introduces his DIVIDEBY operator from his previous books. Unfortunately, Relational Division come in many flavors—Codd's original division, Todd's division, with and without remainders and probably others.

> *Comment:* Here Celko is being truly outrageous in several different ways at once. Here's the opening paragraph of my section on "Relational Division":
>
> > I include the following discussion of divide in this chapter only to show why (contrary to conventional wisdom, perhaps) I don't think it's very important; in fact, I think it should be dropped. You can skip this section if you like.
>
> To me, that hardly looks like a "complaint [that] **Tutorial D** ... lacks ... Relational Division"! Indeed, my text continues:
>
> > I have several reasons (three at least) for wanting to drop divide. One is that any query that can be formulated in terms of divide can alternatively, and much more simply, be formulated in terms of image relations instead, as I'll demonstrate in just a moment. Another is that there are at least seven different divide operators anyway!—that is, there are, unfortunately, at least seven different operators all having some claim to be called "divide," and I certainly don't want to explain all of them. Instead, I'll limit my attention here to the original and simplest one.
>
> And a little later I give my third reason:
>
> > In other words, the divide operator not only suffers from problems of complexity and lack of succinctness—it doesn't even solve the problem it was originally, and explicitly, intended to address.
>
> Thus, I fail to understand how *anyone* could construe my text as "complaining that **Tutorial D** lacks support for relational division."
>
> As for "Unfortunately, Relational Division comes in many flavors": Well, my text explicitly makes that point, as you can see. What's more, Celko's "Unfortunately" tends—perhaps is intended?—to suggest that he's aware of this state of affairs but I'm not, and hence that it's no good my "complaining" about

that "lack of support"! With respect to those many flavors, in fact, ("Codd's original division, Todd's division, with and without remainders and probably others"): Obviously I don't know where Celko gets his information, but the only publication I'm aware of that actually discusses all of those different divide operators is one I wrote myself with Hugh Darwen ("Into the Great Divide," in our joint book *Relational Database Writings 1989-1991*, Addison-Wesley, 1992). So it looks to me very much as if he's trying to blind his readers with science once again—science that he probably got from me in the first place!—and doing so without acknowledging the source of his information. *End of comment.*

Some statements are incorrect.[10] In Chapter 8 on constraints, on page 100,[11] he states that "Transition constraints aren't current[ly] supported in either **Tutorial D** or SQL (other than procedurally)." His discussion uses a transition from "never married" to "married" and you cannot go back to a status of "never married" again.

I published the DDL code for state transition constraint[s] in an article entitled "Constraint Yourself" in Simple Talk. I used (born, married, divorced, dead) as my status values.

Comment: What Celko actually does in the article he mentions is as follows (I'll explain it in terms of my own example): First, he sets up an SQL table containing all legal transitions, in the form of old-value / new-value pairs; in my simple example, the legal pairs are "never married / never married," "never married / married," and "married / married" (the only illegal one is "married / never married"). Then the PERSON table is defined to have both an "old value" column and a "new value" column (thus, each PERSON row has to contain not just the pertinent current value but the pertinent previous value as well), and the old-value / new-value column pair is then defined to be a foreign key referencing the "legal transitions" table. The net effect is thus that the transition constraint is enforced. But it's not enforced by merely stating the constraint and telling the DBMS that it's a transition constraint; rather, it's enforced, at least in part, by designing the database in a way that seems to me neither obvious nor natural, and one that's likely to contain a lot of redundancy. Note in particular that every row that contains a new value of "never married" must also contain an old value

---

[10] Celko says "some statements are incorrect" and proceeds to give just one example of what he says is such a statement, one that I don't agree is incorrect at all. If he thinks there are others, he owes it to all of us to say what they are. If he doesn't, then that "some" is misleading and very unfair. My own suspicion is that the latter is the case, because if he could point to other "incorrect" statements I'm pretty sure he would.

[11] Actually it's page 180.

of "never married," and every row that contains an old value of "married" must also contain a new value of "married." Note too the consequent implications for INSERT and UPDATE operations—DELETE operations too, possibly, though not in the simple example under discussion.

So yes, you can *simulate* transition constraint support in the manner outlined, but as far as I'm concerned such simulated support is a very different thing from what might be called direct, native support for the functionality in question. I stand by my original claim. *End of comment.*

In a footnote, [Date] says:

The semantics of WITH LOCAL CHECK OPTION are far too baroque to be spelled out in detail here. In any case, it's hard to see why anyone would ever want such semantics; indeed, it's hard to resist the suspicion that this alternative was included in the standard for no other reason than to allow certain flawed implementations, extant at the time, to be abler to claim conformance. [*Actually I wrote "able," not "abler."*]

ANSI tries to get all of the membership to agree on a common abstract model of how SQL works. We then create features on [*the basis of?*] that model. By now, you should know that the clauses of a basic SELECT.. FROM.. WHERE.. GROUP BY.. HAVING.. statement [*expression, rather*] start with the from clause and end with the select clause. We had to work out those rules in the committee because not all products did it that way. At one point, the GROUP BY implementations either put the NULLs in one group or put each NULL in its own group. Sybase did the ALL () and ANY () predicates wrong. Oracle had to add the CHAR2(n) because they got the CHAR(n) wrong; Microsoft added DATETIME(2) to implement the ANSI Standard TIMESTAMP. Did you notice that *= is long gone from products? The truth is that when the standards change, the vendors change their products, not the other way around. As the standards have progressed, we have fewer and fewer "implementation defined" features.

All that said, yes, the WITH [LOCAL | CASCADE] CHECK OPTION is baroque when you nest VIEWs inside each other. But it can be very powerful and enforce complex relationships that would otherwise have to be done with triggers or worse. It [*is?*] how you can express multi-table joins in SQL when you do not have a CREATE ASSERTION statement.

Comment: These two paragraphs of Celko's demand almost a blow by blow response—there are so many things wrong with them!—that I think I'd better go through them more or less one sentence at a time:

- ANSI tries to get all of the membership to agree on a common abstract model of how SQL works.

   The reference to ANSI here is revealing. The SQL standard is supposed to be an *international* standard, and the relevant standards body is ISO (International Organization for Standardization). ANSI ("American National Standards Institute"), representing the U.S., is just one voting member body within the ISO SQL committee; others represent the U.K., Germany, Japan, and so on. However, it's unfortunately true that the ANSI tail does often wag the ISO dog.

- [The] clauses of a basic SELECT.. FROM.. WHERE.. GROUP BY.. HAVING.. statement [*expression, rather*] start with the from clause and end with the select clause. We had to work out those rules in the committee because not all products did it that way.

   Really? I find the final claim here ("not all products did it that way") extremely hard to believe, and very surprising if true. The clauses were *always* evaluated in SQL in that order, right from Day One—which is to say, right from 1974, and probably earlier than that.

- Did you notice that *= is long gone from products?

   Really? The syntax "*=" was a highly flawed attempt on the part of one particular product (not products, plural, so far as I know) at supporting a highly flawed notion, and I'm glad it's gone. If it has! *The Shackle of Compatibility* makes me suspicious of Celko's claim here.

- The truth is that when the standards change, the vendors change their products, not the other way around.

   Really? See the discussion of "Darwen's last straw" in Chapter 2.

- As the standards have progressed, we have fewer and fewer "implementation defined" features.

Really? The fact is, the SQL:2011 standard has some *22 pages*—very detailed pages at that—of "implementation dependent" (i.e., undefined) features, and "undefined" is surely even worse than just "implementation defined."

■ All that said, yes, the WITH [LOCAL | CASCADE] CHECK OPTION is baroque when you nest VIEWs inside each other.

First, the keyword is CASCADED, not CASCADE. Second, I wasn't claiming in my original complaint that [the semantics of] WITH [LOCAL | CASCADED] CHECK OPTION were baroque, I was claiming that the semantics of WITH *LOCAL* CHECK OPTION (emphasis added) were baroque—and they are (see further explanation below, following this bullet list). Third, Celko apparently agrees with my complaint "when you nest views inside each other" [*sic*]—but that's exactly when the choice between LOCAL and CASCADED is relevant! If there's no such nesting, LOCAL and CASCADED have effectively identical semantics, and the baroque nature of LOCAL is immaterial.

■ But [LOCAL vs. CASCADED] can be very powerful and enforce complex relationships that would otherwise have to be done with triggers or worse.

I have no idea what this sentence means.

■ It [*is?*] how you can express multi-table joins in SQL when you do not have a CREATE ASSERTION statement.

I have even less idea what this sentence means. I assume the initial "It" refers to WITH CHECK OPTION—but as far as I know, WITH CHECK OPTION has absolutely nothing to do with either "expressing multi-table joins" or the CREATE ASSERTION statement, and neither of these latter has anything to do with the other.

Let me get back to my original complaint. Here again is what I wrote in my book:

[It's] hard to resist the suspicion that [WITH LOCAL CHECK OPTION] was included in the standard for no other reason than to allow certain flawed implementations, extant at the time, to be able to claim conformance.

Well, allow me to indulge in a small personal reminiscence here ... I believe I was the one who discovered that IBM's DB2 product in particular was a case in point—I mean, it was an example of what I referred to in my text as a "flawed implementation." (I was still working in IBM at the time, and this all happened in, I think, 1982, just prior to DB2's first release.) Let me explain the flaw. Suppose we have a view PS ("Paris suppliers") defined as follows:

```
CREATE VIEW PS AS
       SELECT * FROM S WHERE CITY = 'Paris' ;
```

Now suppose we define a further view LPS ("low status Paris suppliers") on top of—i.e., in terms of—view PS, and this time we specify WITH CHECK OPTION:

```
CREATE VIEW LPS AS
       SELECT * FROM PS WHERE STATUS < 20
       WITH CHECK OPTION ;
```

And now suppose we try to insert a row into LS with status less than 20 but city not Paris. Do you think that INSERT should succeed?

Well, I certainly don't think it should, but in the first release of DB2 it did. (The new row wouldn't be visible via view PS, of course, and hence not via view LPS either, but it *would* be inserted into table S.) In other words, the check option defined for view LPS wasn't "inherited" (as it were) by view PS. Which to my mind was clearly a bug—and I reported it to the powers that be in IBM at the time, and they agreed it was a bug; but it was too late to fix it, and so the first release went out to the waiting world with the bug unfixed.[12]

Now, the SQL standards bodies were busy working at the time on what became the first version of the standard ("SQL/86"), and I think it's fair to say that, other things being equal, they wanted the standard to be as close as possible to the DB2 version of the language. Anyway, whether that's so or not, the first version of the standard certainly did include that same bug. And it remained in place until SQL:1992, when the LOCAL vs. CASCADED option was added to the language. (Loosely speaking, CASCADED is the sensible or "inheriting" option, while LOCAL means you like the bug.)[13] *End of comment.*

---

[12] It was finally fixed several years later, in DB2 Version 1 Release 3 (1987).

[13] The CHECK option is discussed in excruciating detail in the planned follow-on to the present book, *Stating the Obvious, and Other Database Writings.*

Chapter 11 is "Using Logic to Formulate Expressions" which introduces two-valued predicate logic and quantifiers. The explanations are done with **Tutorial D**, and then translated into SQL. That is confusing. **Tutorial D** is like classic (i.e. NULL free) predicate logic but it is still another language to learn. But SQL does have NULLs and we need to consider them from the start. This is one reason that minimal Netiquette on SQL Forums requires that you post DDL even for the simplest SQL problems.

> *Comment:* Again there's so much I want to say in response that I think I'd better take Celko's paragraph one point at a time:

- Chapter 11 ... introduces two-valued logic and quantifiers.

   No, it doesn't—that's already been done in Chapter 10.

- The explanations are done with **Tutorial D**.

   No, they're not—they're done with predicate logic.

- That is confusing.

   I don't think it's confusing at all, I think it's a useful and valid approach to formulating accurate SQL expressions. (Well, Celko himself is clearly confused here, since he thinks "the explanations are done with **Tutorial D**," but I don't see how he can reasonably accuse me of being the cause of his confusion.)

- **Tutorial D** is like classic (i.e., null free) predicate logic.

   It's true that **Tutorial D** and "classic predicate logic" are both null free, but **Tutorial D** is based on relational algebra, not on "classic predicate logic."

- [**Tutorial D**] is still another language to learn.

   I believe I've already dealt with this objection.

- But SQL does have NULLs and we need to consider them from the start.

Using SQL relationally—which is what my book is all about—implies among other things rejecting nulls 100 per cent. Chapter 4 of that book ("No Duplicates, No Nulls") explains in some detail why rejecting nulls is necessary: not just for what might be termed "relational purist" reasons, but for very solid practical reasons as well. (But of course Celko loves SQL and SQL loves nulls, so Celko loves nulls. Despite all of those theoretical *and practical*—yes, "hands on," 100 percent solid, practical—reasons to reject them.) So yes, I did "consider nulls from the start" (that's *exactly* what I did), and I rejected them.

■ This is one reason that minimal Netiquette on SQL Forums requires that you post DDL even for the simplest SQL problems.

Of course you should always show the pertinent data definitions, with or without nulls—I have no objection to following such a discipline. But all nulls do in this connection is make the problem worse.

End of comment.

For example, Date gives one of his classic tables:

```
CREATE TABLE Parts
( pno CHAR(2) NOT NULL PRIMARY KEY ,
  pname VARCHAR(10) NOT NULL ,
  color VARCHAR(10) NOT NULL ,
  weight DECIMAL(5,2) ,
  city VARCHAR(10) NOT NULL ) ;
```

Please notice that the weight is NULL-able, but the first sample data is like this:[14]

```
INSERT INTO Parts
VALUES
( 'P1' , 'nut' , 'red' , 12.0 , 'London' ) ,
( 'P2' , 'bolt' , 'green' , 17.0 , 'Paris' ) ,
( 'P3' , 'screw' , 'blue' , 17.0 , 'Oslo' ) ,
( 'P4' , 'screw' , 'red' , 14.0 , 'London' ) ,
( 'P5' , 'cam' , 'blue' , 12.0 , 'Paris' ) ,
( 'P6' , 'cog' , 'red' , 19.0 , 'London' ) ;
```

---

[14] I'm sure you'll believe me when I tell you the WEIGHT column certainly wasn't "nullable" in my version of the table. What's more, my version of the table was called not Parts but simply P. As for that "but" that opens the second part of Celko's sentence, it's rather an odd word in context; I assume it's there simply because Celko wants to draw attention to the fact that even though WEIGHT is "nullable" (according to him, that is), no part in the sample data actually has a null weight.

Given the problem "find the parts that have a weight that is different from the weight of any part in Paris," [the following code will suffice]:

```
SELECT  P1.pname
FROM    Parts AS P1
WHERE   NOT EXISTS
      ( SELECT *
        FROM    Parts AS P2
        WHERE   P2.city = 'Paris'
        AND     P2.weight = P1.weight ) ;
```

Comment: The query as Celko states it is basically Example 3 from Chapter 11 of the *SQL and Relational Theory* book, except that Celko asks for parts as such but my Example 3 asked for part names—as indeed his SQL formulation does. That formulation is basically the same as the one I give in my book, except that Celko forgets the all important DISTINCT that ought by rights to be included in the outer SELECT clause.

PS: It's very naughty of me, I know, but I can't help deriving just a tiny bit of *schadenfreude* from seeing such a well known SQL apologist make such an elementary mistake over such a well known SQL trap (viz., duplicates). *End of comment.*

[The following formulation produces] the same results, but only if there are no NULL weights in the table.

```
SELECT  P1.pname
FROM    Parts AS P1
WHERE   P1.weight NOT IN
      ( SELECT P2.weight
        FROM    Parts AS P2
        WHERE   P2.city = 'Paris' ) ;
```

The EXISTS () predicate is always TRUE or FALSE,[15] but the IN () predicate is a shorthand for a chain of OR-ed predicates. The IN () predicate can return UNKNOWN if there are NULLs. We would need [*to*] get rid of the NULLs:

---

[15] The fact that EXISTS in SQL never returns UNKNOWN is a flaw in itself, inasmuch as it shows that EXISTS in SQL isn't a faithful realization of the existential quantifier of the three-valued logic on which SQL is allegedly based. It's not a flaw I want to complain about too much, though, because I object more fundamentally to SQL's use of that logic. I mean, if we got away from that logic, then there'd obviously be no question of EXISTS ever returning UNKNOWN, and that "flaw" would then not be a flaw after all.

```
SELECT  P1.pname
FROM    Parts AS P1
WHERE   P1.weight IS NOT NULL
AND     P1.weight NOT IN
      ( SELECT  P2.weight
        FROM    Parts AS P2
        WHERE   P2.weight IS NOT NULL
        AND     P2.city = 'Paris' ) ;
```

Comment: All that Celko is doing here, it seems to me, is this: He's trying to explain certain points—in fact, certain problems caused by nulls, would you believe—and not making a very good job of it. (I believe my book explains them better.) Moreover, it's not at all clear *why* he's doing what he's doing. I mean, what does it all have to do with reviewing my book? Especially since, as I've explained in detail already, we're not supposed to be talking about nulls at this point anyway.

Celko complains that I go out of the way in my book to make SQL look bad (see his "Summary" paragraph below), but in this particular instance I think his own text actually makes it look worse. Especially when his next point, regarding IS [NOT] DISTINCT FROM, is taken into account as well. And he still omits that DISTINCT that's required in the outer SELECT! *End of comment.*

And we now [*need?*] the "IS [NOT] DISTINCT FROM" comparison operator that will treat NULLs as if they are equal:[16]

```
SELECT  P1.pname
FROM    Parts AS P1
WHERE   NOT EXISTS
      ( SELECT  *
        FROM    Parts AS P2
        WHERE   P2.city = 'Paris'
        AND     P2.weight IS NOT DISTINCT FROM P1.weight ) ;
```

Summary: I do not feel the book lived up to its title. Someone trying to improve his [*sic*] SQL or find a systematic approach to constructing a query has to first [*learn?*] predicate logic and **Tutorial D**.[17] Date's dislike of SQL shows up

---

[16] I love that "as if"! Are two nulls equal or aren't they?

[17] *The gentle art of deconstruction once again:* What Celko meant to say with this sentence is presumably that the someone in question will have difficulty with my book because he or she will have to learn predicate logic and **Tutorial D**. However, what he actually says is that anyone who wants to improve his or her use of SQL must first learn predicate logic and **Tutorial D**—which is the message of my book, almost exactly! Couldn't have said it better myself.

everywhere in the book; he was looking for ways to make SQL look bad.[18] Much of his SQL code is dated [*ha ha*] and fails to use newer features.[19]

While you expect some repetition, the material was a re-arrangement of his older material without adding anything new.[20] If you have not read Date's other books, then this might not be a problem.

I feel that a better approach would have been to show dangerous or shoddy SQL, demonstrate the problems, explain the math, relational algebra and logic that was ignored and then solve the problems with better SQL. The "Paris-weights" example I showed would be the start of such a detailed analysis. The reader would not be confused by **Tutorial D** code and would have come away with a better understanding for the limits and power of SQL.

> *Comment:* Well, I've tried to explain in some detail why I reject this conclusion of Celko's. Whether you do so too is a matter for you to decide, of course. *End of comment.*

CONCLUDING REMARKS

The one thing a book review is surely supposed to do is give readers an idea of what the book in question is all about. Did you notice that Celko's review doesn't do that at all? It begins by giving a little bit of not entirely accurate background about myself, plus a bit about Celko himself, and then launches into a series of mostly unjustified gripes regarding **Tutorial D** and a few—*very few*—of the SQL examples I use. It never mentions the book's thesis or core argument (summarized earlier in the present chapter, on page 164). Nor does it give any kind of table of contents (listing chapter titles at the very least). Nor

---

[18] I'm sorry, but there's no need to "look for" ways to make SQL look bad. Almost everything makes SQL look bad.

[19] "Newer features" are irrelevant. As I've already said (more or less), "newer features" can't make SQL more relational. And in any case, if those "newer features" are truly desirable, then why weren't they already in SQL in the first place?

[20] This criticism is rather grossly, and grotesquely, unfair. (And Celko's next sentence—"If you have not read, etc."—just looks like a put-down to me.) No previous publication of mine explicitly considered the question of expressing truly relational functionality in SQL, or imposing some relational discipline on the use of SQL. In fact the opposite is the case, in a sense—the book under review grew out of an earlier one (*Database in Depth: Relational Theory for Practitioners*, O'Reilly, 2005), where I explained relational theory and left it to the reader to map that theory into concrete SQL, as it were. Subsequent experience led me to realize that many people needed guidance on how to perform that mapping, and that's why I wrote the newer book.

does it mention the fact that the book explains the relational model in detail, as well as giving reasons for why the model is the way it is. Nor does it mention the fact that for each aspect of the model it shows, in detail, how to realize that aspect in SQL. Nor does it have anything to say about various other major features of the book, such as:

- The discussion of the crucial logical differences between values and variables in general and between relations and relvars in particular

- The in-depth explanations of why duplicates and nulls should be avoided

- The careful examination of types in general and relation types (and relation type inference) in particular

- The detailed consideration of integrity constraints and *The Assignment Principle* and **The Golden Rule**[21]

- The extensive set of exercises, with answers explained in detail

and on and on (the foregoing list is far from exhaustive). In fact, it probably didn't escape your notice that Celko's review has nothing positive to say about my book at all!—a state of affairs that, I think it's fair to say, is somewhat unusual regarding book reviews in general.

Well, I don't think I can do better by way of closing this chapter than by citing the following quote (it's from one of my personal heroes, Jean Sibelius):

> *Never pay any attention to what the critics say.*
> *No one ever put up a statue to a critic.*

---

[21] Loose definitions: *The Assignment Principle* says that after assignment of value v to variable V, the comparison $v = V$ must give TRUE; **The Golden Rule** says that integrity constraints must never be violated. Both have numerous important implications, some of them far from obvious.

Part III

FREQUENTLY ASKED

QUESTIONS

Chapter 7

R e l a t i o n a l   T e r m i n o l o g y

One cannot present a science
without at the same time defining its terms.
> —Gottfried Wilhelm Leibniz:
> "On the Division of the Sciences" (1765)

Ask an impertinent question,
and you are on the way to a pertinent answer.

> —Jacob Bronowski:
> *The Ascent of Man* (1973)

Every chapter in this part of the book represents an attempt on my part to respond to a question or series of questions having to do with relational database management. The questions are genuine, in the sense that they're all based on real ones that I've been asked over the years, but I've edited them for style, flow, nomenclature, and so forth. Also, I should state for the record that my answers aren't necessarily meant to be definitive! Back in the early years of the relational era Codd himself undertook a similar exercise, contributing a series of columns under the generic title "Understanding Relations" to the ACM publication *FDT*.[1] In the first installment, he wrote the following:

Q: Does the fact that you are launching this column mean you think you know everything there is to know about relations and databases?

A: Normally we shall not deal with such personal questions, but in this case we'll make an exception. Our answer is "Lord, no." We have a lot to learn in both areas ... Occasionally, we may have to say "we don't know." (Have you noticed, incidentally, how seldom other column writers say this?)

---

[1] "FDT" stood for File Definition and Translation. *FDT* was the predecessor to what's now called *SIGMOD Record*. The first installment of "Understanding Relations" appeared in *FDT 5*, No. 1 (June 1973).

My sentiments exactly! Now read on ...

The purpose of this first chapter in the series is simply to explain the origin and meaning of certain relational terms, including in particular the term *relation* itself. It was motivated by an email request from Jonathan Gennick dated August 29th, 2016, which read in part as follows:

> I have a question. I'm planning a short blog post on the term "relational." I understand the term comes from set theory. I further recall being told once that the term "relational" derives from the fact that all the elements in a tuple are related to each other.
>
> Is my understanding correct?
>
> Is there a reference you can point me toward, that I might be able to quote in my post?

In my response (August 31st, 2016) I said this:

> The short answer is: Yes, your understanding is correct, at least to a first approximation. A much longer—but still somewhat informal—answer follows!

What follows is basically just a revised and considerably extended version of that longer answer. (As for Jonathan's request for a reference I could "point him toward," I'll get to that later.)

Note: Before I present that detailed explanation, however, the foregoing brief overview might help. Jonathan says he recalls being told once that the term *relational* derives from "the fact that all the elements in a tuple are related to each other." Well, I was the one who told him that. In one of my books[2] (a draft of which Jonathan reviewed, and he and I discussed at the time), I wrote the following:

> Basically, each tuple in a relation represents an *n*-ary relationship, in the ordinary natural language sense of that term, interrelating a collection of *n* values (one such

---

[2] *Database in Depth: Relational Theory for Practitioners* (O'Reilly, 2005).

value for each tuple attribute); the full set of tuples in a given relation represents the full set of such relationships that happen to exist at some given time;[3] and, mathematically speaking, that set of tuples is a relation. Thus, the explanation often heard, to the effect that the relational model is so called because it lets us "relate one table to another," though accurate in a kind of secondary sense, really misses the point; the relational model is so called because it deals with certain abstractions that we can think of informally as "tables" but are known in mathematics, formally, as relations.

———— ♦ ♦ ♦ ♦ ♦ ————

The term *relation* itself derives, at least primarily, not so much from set theory as it does from logic (more precisely, *predicate* logic—but I'll use the unqualified term *logic* to mean predicate logic specifically throughout this chapter). In fact, it's tightly bound up with the logic concept of a predicate as such. By way of example, consider the following statement (let's call it *P*):

```
X gave Y to Z
```

This statement *P* is an example of a predicate—more precisely, a 3-place predicate, because it has three *parameters X*, *Y*, and *Z*.[4] Predicates in general can conveniently be categorized according to the cardinality of their set of parameters. Note right away that *X*, *Y*, and *Z* in this example can reasonably be said to be *related* to one another by the very fact of their being parameters to the same predicate.

> *Aside:* Actually (and contrary to what I've just claimed!), a predicate isn't really a statement as such; rather, it's the assertion that the statement in question denotes. For example, "*X* gave *Y* to *Z*," "*Z* was given *Y* by *X*," and "*X* a donné *Y* à *Z*" are three different statements, but they all denote the same predicate.
>
> That said, however, it's often convenient to pretend—and for the remainder of this chapter I will pretend—that predicates simply are statements

---

[3] I'm assuming here, tacitly and for simplicity, that the relation in question is "a relation in the database" and is thus the current value of some particular relation variable, or relvar, in the database in question. See elsewhere in this book (e.g., Chapter 2) for an informal explanation of what a relvar is.

[4] Logicians would refer to *X*, *Y*, and *Z* not as parameters but rather as *free variables*, or sometimes as *placeholders*. I prefer the term *parameters* because parameters, in the usual computer or programming language sense of that term, is exactly what they are, and computer professionals are my target readership.

as such. For present purposes, moreover, I'll assume that the statements in question are expressed in English.

Note: All of the foregoing applies to propositions as well as predicates, of course, mutatis mutandis. See the paragraph immediately following for more specifics regarding propositions. *End of aside.*

Next, if we substitute *arguments* for the parameters of a given predicate—for all of them, that is—then the effect is to transform the predicate in question into a *proposition*, which in logic is a statement that's categorically either true or false.[5] In the case of predicate P, for example, substituting Jonathan for X, *The Wind in the Willows* for Y, and Chris for Z yields the proposition

```
Jonathan gave The Wind in the Willows to Chris
```

And the X value Jonathan, the Y value *The Wind in the Willows*, and the Z value Chris here can also reasonably be said to be related to one another by the fact of their being part of the same proposition—assuming, that is, that the proposition in question is a true one.

Aside: An example of a statement that's not categorically either true or false, and is therefore not a proposition, is "It will rain tomorrow." Note that predicates in particular (most predicates, at any rate) aren't propositions—they aren't categorically either true or false, precisely because they're parameterized. More precisely, a predicate is categorically either true or false if and only if it's 0-place (i.e., if and only if the cardinality of its set of parameters is zero), in which case the predicate is in fact a proposition. Thus, a proposition can be regarded as a degenerate predicate—all propositions are predicates, but "most" predicates aren't propositions. *End of aside.*

Now, the foregoing proposition, like all propositions, can be represented by a tuple—in the case at hand, by the 3-tuple

```
{ X Jonathan , Y The Wind in the Willows , Z Chris }
```

Let me immediately clarify a couple of points:

---

[5] Some writers are a little sloppy in their use of the terms *argument* and *parameter*, so let me spell out what I mean by them. A parameter is a formal operand, used in the definition of some operator (and note that a predicate can indeed be regarded as an operator, one that returns a truth value when it's invoked). An argument is an actual operand, used to replace some parameter when the operator in question is invoked.

■ First, a tuple is just a set[6] of elements, or *components*, where each component in turn, in the notation I'm using here, is an ordered pair consisting of a component name and a value for that component. (In the case at hand, of course, those component names are X, Y, and Z, and they correspond to the pertinent parameters.)

   Note: A tuple of n components is sometimes referred to more specifically as an n-tuple. In fact, the term *tuple* is really just an abbreviated form of that extended term.

■ Second, when I say a proposition can be represented by a tuple, I'm being a bit sloppy. What I mean a little more precisely is that the *arguments*—the arguments, that is, that are used to obtain the proposition in question from the pertinent predicate—can be represented by a tuple. To put it another way, if we think of a proposition as a sentence, then the nouns in that sentence, but not the verb, can be represented by a tuple. (Of course, this latter statement is pretty sloppy too!—but I think it can be helpful from an intuitive point of view.)

Next, let S be the set of all propositions that can be obtained, or *derived*, from predicate P in the foregoing manner (i.e., by substituting arguments for the parameters X, Y, and Z); in other words, let S be the set of all propositions of the form "x gave y to z," such that x is a legitimate value for X, y is a legitimate value for Y, and z is a legitimate value for Z. *More terminology:* The set of all possible legitimate values for a given parameter is referred to as the *type* of that parameter, also known as its *domain*. For example, parameters X and Z might both be of type PNAME, where PNAME is the set of all person names, and parameter Y might be of type BTITLE, where BTITLE is the set of all book titles.

Now let T be the set consisting of all propositions in S that are true and let F be the set consisting of all propositions in S that are false (so S is the disjoint union of T and F). Finally, let RT be the set of all tuples corresponding to propositions in T. Then RT is a *relation*—specifically, the relation representing what's called the *extension* of predicate P.[7]

---

[6] So here's one point where set theory does come in after all. A couple more such will show up in just a moment.

[7] Please note immediately that this definition (such as it is) is still quite loose. I'll make it more precise later.

———— ♦♦♦♦♦ ————

Of course, the set *RF* of all tuples corresponding to propositions in *F* is a relation also—it's the relation corresponding to the extension of the predicate NOT *P*, or in other words the predicate "It's not the case that *X* gave *Y* to *Z*" (or, more colloquially, just "*X* didn't give *Y* to *Z*").[8] Note carefully, however, that all of the tuples in *RT*, and indeed all of the tuples in *RF* as well, are 3-tuples specifically; moreover, each such 3-tuple consists specifically of an *X* component, a *Y* component, and a *Z* component. (In other words, those tuples are all of the same tuple *type*—see further discussion below.) So not every set of tuples is a relation. In fact, a set of tuples is a relation *if and only if* the tuples in question are all of the same tuple type. Of course, distinct relations can contain tuples of distinct tuple types, though they don't have to; in other words, two distinct relations might both, and sometimes will, contain tuples of the same tuple type (just as *RT* and *RF* do, in fact).

To summarize to this point, then: Every predicate has an extension, viz., the set of all true propositions that can legitimately be derived from the predicate by substituting arguments for all of its parameters, and the set of tuples corresponding to such an extension is a relation. However, it's important to understand that the converse is true as well—that is, *every* relation represents the extension of some predicate in the foregoing sense.[9] In other words, relations and predicates are indeed, as I claimed earlier, tightly bound up with one another.

At the same time, it's important to understand too that the same relation can represent the extension of any number of distinct predicates. As a trivial example, let *t* be a tuple—in fact, the unique tuple—containing just one component *N*, of type INTEGER and with the value 1, and let *r* be the unique relation containing just that tuple *t*. Then *r* represents the extension of both "Planet Earth has *N* moons" and "The U.S. has *N* presidents at any one time."

———— ♦♦♦♦♦ ————

---

[8] Note that *RF* is likely to have many more tuples than *RT* does (why, exactly?).

[9] In fact this statement is *obviously* true so long as tuples contain a finite number of components and relations contain a finite number of tuples (why, exactly?). In particular, therefore, it's certainly true in the database context.

Now I need to confess that I've cheated slightly in my explanations so far. To be specific, logicians, and mathematicians too, typically wouldn't refer to parameters by name as I've been doing; rather, they'd refer to them by ordinal position, thereby referring to *X*, *Y*, and *Z* in our running example as the first, second, and third parameter, respectively, to predicate *P*. As a consequence, logicians and mathematicians would think of the tuple corresponding to the sample proposition quoted earlier ("Jonathan gave *The Wind in the Willows* to Chris") not as

```
{ X Jonathan , Y The Wind in the Willows , Z Chris }
```

but rather as just

```
< Jonathan , The Wind in the Willows , Chris >
```

Observe that I've replaced the braces by angle brackets, in order to show that what they contain is a sequence—i.e., an ordered collection of elements—rather than a set.

The advantage of using parameter names is, of course, precisely that then there's no need to identify those parameters by ordinal position. To spell the point out, the following would be regarded as distinct tuples in mathematics:

```
< Jonathan , The Wind in the Willows , Chris >

< Chris , The Wind in the Willows , Jonathan >
```

By contrast, the following—

```
{ X Jonathan , Y The Wind in the Willows , Z Chris }

{ Z Chris , Y The Wind in the Willows , X Jonathan }
```

—are regarded as identical tuples in the relational model.

> *Aside:* Perhaps I need to clarify the foregoing point. Of course, the two lines of text just shown are obviously not identical. But those lines of text aren't tuples!—rather, they're just *pictures* of tuples on some flat medium, such as paper or a display screen. So what I'm saying is, those two pictures need to be understood just as different pictures of the same thing. *End of aside.*

Now, the advantages, at least in the computing context, of defining tuples to be sets and not sequences are overwhelming, which is why the relational model does so.[10] But doing so does mean there's a certain discrepancy, or logical difference, between the relational model as such, on the one hand, and the logical or mathematical theory of relations on the other. To spell the point out one more time:

- In logic and mathematics, tuples have a left to right ordering to their components, and those components are unnamed.

- In the relational model, tuples have no ordering to their components, and those components are therefore (and necessarily, and uniquely) named.[11]

And it follows immediately, of course, that the foregoing remarks are true of relations as well, mutatis mutandis.

Another importance difference between the relational model and the logical or mathematical theory of relations (and another way I cheated in my earlier explanations) is this: Logicians and mathematicians don't usually consider parameters and arguments as having types—or, more precisely, they consider them as all being of the same type, often referred to as *the universe of discourse* (also known as the *domain* of discourse). This simplification might be acceptable from a strictly logical or mathematical point of view, but it's obviously not acceptable in the computing context.

Yet another difference is an immediate consequence of the previous point. A relation in mathematics is basically just a set of tuples, where the tuples in question all have the same number of components or, equivalently, are all of the same *degree* (also known as *arity*). As I've already mentioned, however, in the relational model the tuples in any given relation are required to be, not just all of the same degree, but all of the same *type*, where the type in question is at

---

[10] Yes, the relational model does so, but SQL doesn't (rows in SQL have a left to right ordering to their fields)—just one of the many unfortunate differencs between the relational model and SQL. As for the advantages mentioned, I refer you to Chapter 9 ("A Sweet Disorder") of my book *Date on Database: Writings 2000-2006* (Apress, 2006) for a detailed explanation.

[11] There's another minor discrepancy too, viz.: In the relational model, the components of a tuple are called *attributes* instead of parameters, even though they correspond to parameters, as such, of the pertinent predicate (and corresponding argument values in tuples are then called *attribute values* accordingly). However, the reasons for this shift in terminology are primarily historical in nature, and they're not very important; they have to do with the fact that tuples look—not accidentally!— a bit like what certain programming languages call "structs" or "structures," and those languages in turn typically use the term "attributes" to refer to the components of those structures.

least partly a function of the types of the pertinent parameters (or *attributes*, rather, in the relational model context). For example, in the case of relation *RT*—i.e., the relation representing the extension of predicate *P* ("*X* gave *Y* to *Z*")—the tuples are all of this type:

```
TUPLE { X PNAME , Y BTITLE , Z PNAME }
```

The text following the keyword TUPLE here denotes the common *heading*—let's call it *H*—of all of those tuples. As you can see, therefore, a heading consists of a set of ordered pairs, each such pair consisting of an attribute name and a corresponding attribute type (and no significance attaches to the sequence in which those ordered pairs are specified, of course, when the heading in question is specified in written form as above). Thus, tuple types in general can be regarded as having names of the form TUPLE *H*, where *H* is the pertinent heading.

Following on from the foregoing, it clearly makes sense to say that relations too have a type—viz., the type (in the case of relation *RT*)

```
RELATION { X PNAME , Y BTITLE , Z PNAME }
```

—or, more generally, RELATION *H*, where *H* is a heading as previously defined. Thus, a relation in the relational model isn't, as it is in mathematics, just a set of tuples; rather, it's a pair <*H,B*>, where *H* is a heading and *B* is a set of tuples—the *body*—all of which are of type TUPLE *H*.

I give the following precise definitions for purposes of reference:

> **Definition (heading):** A *heading H* is a set, the elements of which are *attributes*. Let *H* have cardinality *n* ($n \geq 0$); then the value *n* is the *degree* of *H*. A heading of degree zero is *nullary*, a heading of degree one is *unary*, a heading of degree two is *binary*, ..., and more generally a heading of degree *n* is *n-ary*. Each attribute in *H* is of the form <*Aj,Tj*>, where *Aj* is the *attribute name* and *Tj* is the corresponding *type name* ($0 < j \leq n$), and the attribute names *Aj* are all distinct. *Note:* In contexts where the type names *Tj* are unimportant, a heading can be denoted (loosely) as just the set of attribute names *Aj*.

Definition (tuple): Let heading *H* be of degree *n*. For each attribute *<Aj,Tj>* in *H*, define a *component* of the form *<Aj,Tj,vj>*, where the *attribute value vj* is a value of type *Tj*. The set—call it *t*—of all *n* components so defined is a *tuple value* (or just a *tuple* for short) over the attributes of *H*. *H* is the *tuple heading* (or just the heading for short) for *t*, and the degree and attributes of *H* are, respectively, the degree and attributes of *t*.

Definition (body): Given a heading *H*, a *body B* conforming to *H* is a set of *m* tuples ($m \geq 0$), each with heading *H*. The value *m* is the *cardinality* of *B*.

Definition (relation): Let *H* be a heading, and let *B* be a body conforming to *H*. The pair *<H,B>*—call it *r*—is a *relation value* (or just a *relation* for short) over the attributes of *H*. *H* is the *relation heading* (or just the heading for short) for *r*, and the degree and attributes of *H* and the cardinality of *B* are, respectively, the degree, attributes, and cardinality of *r*.

———— ◆◆◆◆◆ ————

Given all of the above, it should be clear how the operators of the relational algebra—join, projection, union, and so on—can also all be understood in logical terms; in other words, they all have logical interpretations. For example, let *P* and *Q* be the predicates "*X* gave *Y* to *Z*" and "*Y* was published by *W*," respectively. Then:

■   The join of the relations corresponding to the extensions of *P* and *Q* represents the extension of the predicate *P* AND *Q*, which can be spelled out as follows—

```
X gave Y to Z and Y was published by W
```

—or (simplifying slightly) "*X* gave *Y*, which was published by *W*, to *Z*." In other words, the join operator is the analog in the relational model of the AND operator, or *connective*, in logic.

■   The projection on attributes *X* and *Y* of the relation corresponding to the extension of *P* represents the extension of the predicate EXISTS *Z* (*P*), which can be spelled out as follows—

```
EXISTS Z ( X gave Y to Z )
```

—or (simplifying slightly) "*X* gave *Y* to some unspecified *Z*," or (simplifying a little further) "*X* gave *Y* to someone." In other words, the projection operator is the analog in the relational model of the *existential quantifier* EXISTS in logic.

And so on.

I think the best way to bring these explanations to a close is by simply quoting more or less verbatim from my original response to Jonathan Gennick:

> I hope all this helps. One last point: Be aware that the logic literature is far from consistent in its use of terminology. The terms I've used above are the ones we find most useful and have settled on in the relational context, but I don't think you'll find *any* logic text that uses or agrees with those terms 100%. Which brings me to your request for "a reference I can point you toward": Well, if you want a reference that conforms to the terminology I've been using, then I'm afraid it has to be something by either Hugh Darwen or myself: e.g., Hugh's book *An Introduction to Relational Database Theory* (2010), available as a free download from *http://bookboon.com*, or either of my own books *Relational Theory for Computer Professionals* (2013) and *SQL and Relational Theory* (3rd edition, 2015), both from O'Reilly. If you want something from the logic literature, you might try *Set Theory and Logic*, by Robert R. Stoll (Dover, 1973)—though I feel compelled to quote some text from that book, just to illustrate my point that it might not be the kind of thing you're looking for:
>
> > The following partial sentences (or predicates) are examples of relations:
> >
> > > is less than
> > > divides
> > > ...
> > > is the mother of
>
> So according to Stoll (a) a predicate and a relation are the same thing, and (b) neither of them has parameters (or attributes). Perhaps you can begin to see the difficulties!
> I really like logic a lot, but I don't think I like logicians very much.

———— ♦ ♦ ♦ ♦ ———

A much more extensive investigation into what predicates really are—perhaps I should rather say, what various logicians seem to think they are, because in fact there doesn't seem to be very much in the way of consensus—can be found in my paper "What's a Predicate?" I originally wrote that paper several years ago and included it in the book *Database Explorations: Essays on The Third Manifesto and Related Topics*, by Hugh Darwen and myself (Trafford, 2010). However, I came to the conclusion that it would be useful to revise and extend that paper, and I've done so (see Chapter 3 of this book's predecessor *Logic and Relational Theory: Thoughts and Essays on Database Matters*, Technics Publications, 2020).

Chapter 8

Drawing Relations as Tables

[A] drawing should have no unnecessary lines.
—William Strunk, Jr.:
The Elements of Style (1918)

Drawing is the true test of art.
—Jean-Auguste-Dominique Ingres:
Pensées d'Ingres (1922)

I don't understand your double underlining convention. I mean, when I see pictures of relations in your books, sometimes some of the columns have double underlining, and I think it means the columns in question are key columns. Sometimes, however, there's no double underlining at all—but I thought relations always had keys. Please explain! What exactly are the rules?

I don't blame you for finding the situation confusing; indeed, it's not nearly as straightforward as one might think. Let's see if I can clarify matters.

To begin with, everyone knows that when it's necessary to represent relations in some reasonably "user friendly" form—e.g., on paper or a display screen—it's usual to draw them as *tables*. Fig. 8.1 gives a simple example.

DEPT

DNO	DNAME	BUDGET
D1	Marketing	12M
D2	Training	5M
D3	Research	10M

EMP

ENO	ENAME	DNO	SALARY
E1	Lopez	D1	40K
E2	Cheng	D1	42K
E3	Finzi	D2	30K
E4	Saito	D2	35K

Fig. 8.1: Departments and employees—sample values

Let me take care of one potential confusion right away. It's unfortunately the case that the term *table* has two quite distinct meanings in the database world—it's used to mean both (a) the SQL counterpart to a relation, on the one hand, and (b) a picture of a relation on paper or some other "flat" or two-dimensional medium, on the other.[1] *Let me make it absolutely clear, therefore, that in this chapter I'll be using the term exclusively in this latter sense.* In other words, a table as far as I'm concerned here is definitely not a relation (nor the SQL counterpart to a relation) but is, rather, a picture of a relation—and, of course, there are any number of logical differences between a thing and a picture of that thing.

Now, the following points are—or should be!—widely understood, but I want to spell them out anyway, just to be definite:

- In any given table, the row at the top is special—it represents the *heading* of the pertinent relation. I'll have more to say about headings in a few moments, but for now please just note that the heading row specifies a name for each column of the table.

- In any given table, each row below the heading row represents a *tuple* of the pertinent relation. Moreover, those rows appear in the table in a certain top to bottom order (necessarily so, of course), but no significance attaches to that order—the tuples of a relation have no such ordering. (This is just one of the many logical differences between a table and a relation.) Taken together, those rows represent the *body* of the pertinent relation.

- In any given table, each column represents an *attribute* of the pertinent relation. Moreover, those columns appear in the table in a certain left to right order (again, necessarily so), but no significance attaches to that order—the attributes of a relation have no such ordering. This is another logical difference between a table and a relation.

---

[1] Two points here: First, a confusion between relations as such and those tabular pictures probably accounts for the popular misconception that relations per se are flat or two-dimensional. While it's obviously true that the pictures are two-dimensional, relations in general aren't; rather, a relation of degree n is n-dimensional, in the sense that its tuples correspond to points in some n-dimensional space (one dimension for each attribute of the relation in question). Second, such tabular pictures can obviously be used to represent SQL tables as well as relations; in this chapter, however, I want to focus on relations specifically.

■ In any given relation, each attribute is of some *type*.[2] For present purposes, a type can be thought of just as a conceptual pool of values from which attributes take their actual values. With reference to Fig. 8.1, for example, there might be a type called DNO ("department numbers"), which is the set of all valid department numbers, and then the attribute called DNO in the DEPT ("departments") relation and the attribute called DNO in the EMP ("employees") relation would both contain values from that conceptual pool.[3] Now, it's usual to omit the type names—i.e., to show just the attribute names—in pictures like Fig. 8.1; however, it wouldn't be wrong to include them as shown in Fig. 8.2 (a revised version of the departments table from Fig. 8.1, showing that attributes DNO, DNAME, and BUDGET of the departments relation are of types DNO, NAME, and MONEY, respectively).

```
DEPT
┌─────────────┬───────────────┬─────────────────┐
│ DNO  :  DNO │ DNAME  : NAME │ BUDGET  : MONEY │
├─────────────┼───────────────┼─────────────────┤
│    D1       │ Marketing     │            12M  │
│    D2       │ Training      │             5M  │
│    D3       │ Research      │            10M  │
└─────────────┴───────────────┴─────────────────┘
```

Fig. 8.2: Departments with attribute type names shown

Note: To repeat, it's usual when depicting relations as tables to omit the type names.[4] For reasons that should become clear later, however, in this chapter I'll generally show them explicitly from this point forward.

■ Regardless of whether they're shown explicitly, those type names must certainly be understood to be part of the heading as such (even though they can indeed be ignored in informal contexts, and in practice often are). Thus, the heading for the departments relation of Figs. 8.1 and 8.2 is:

```
    { DNO DNO , DNAME NAME , BUDGET MONEY }
```

---

[2] Types are also referred to in the relational world (especially in early writings) as *domains*.

[3] Of course, attributes don't necessarily have to have the same name as the corresponding types, although they happen to do so in this particular example. I'll give some counterexamples in just a moment.

[4] The practice of omitting the type names from those tabular pictures can be traced—perhaps unfortunately!—all the way back to Codd's very first (1969 and 1979) papers on the relational model.

This example illustrates the syntax used for headings in the language **Tutorial D**. For reference purposes, here's the relevant portion of the **Tutorial D** grammar (slightly simplified here):

```
<heading>
      ::=    { <attribute commalist> }

<attribute>
      ::=    <attribute name> <type name>
```

In other words, a heading is denoted in **Tutorial D** by a commalist of attributes (where an attribute in turn is denoted by an attribute name followed by a type name), the whole commalist being enclosed in braces.[5] As you can see, therefore, **Tutorial D** uses spaces instead of colons as in Fig. 8.2 to separate attribute names from their associated type names, and commas to separate each attribute from the next.

Of course, relations have no left to right ordering to their attributes, and so no significance attaches to the order in which the attributes are specified in a heading in **Tutorial D**. For example, the following is equally valid as a **Tutorial D** representation of the heading of the departments relation:

```
{ BUDGET MONEY , DNAME NAME , DNO DNO }
```

And if we want to ignore those type names, we might even represent that heading thus—

```
{ BUDGET , DNAME , DNO }
```

—though I must emphasize that this latter isn't valid **Tutorial D** syntax for a heading as such, nor is it meant to be.

---

[5] This notation is in conformance with normal mathematical convention, according to which a set is typically represented on paper by a comma separated list, or *commalist*, of items denoting the elements of the set in question, the whole commalist being enclosed in braces. *Note:* Within a given commalist, spaces appearing immediately before the first item or any comma, or immediately after the last item or any comma, are ignored.

RELATIONS vs. RELVARS

As I hope you know—though, sadly, the point is still not as widely appreciated as it should be—there's a logical difference between relation values (*relations* for short) and relation variables (*relvars* for short). The tables in Figs. 8.1 and 8.2 depict certain relation values, but in all probability those relation values are just possible values for certain relation variables. In fact, let's assume they are; i.e., let's assume that two relvars, DEPT and EMP, have been defined, perhaps as follows (**Tutorial D** again):

```
VAR DEPT BASE
   RELATION { DNO DNO , DNAME NAME , BUDGET MONEY }
   KEY { DNO } ;

VAR EMP BASE
   RELATION { ENO ENO , ENAME NAME , DNO DNO , SALARY MONEY }
   KEY { ENO }
   FOREIGN KEY { DNO } REFERENCES DEPT ;
```

Explanation (for simplicity I'll focus on the first of these definitions specifically, but of course the following points all apply equally well to the second, mutatis mutandis):[6]

- The keyword VAR means that what's being defined is a variable—DEPT is the name of the variable being defined, and the keyword BASE means the variable is a base relvar specifically. (For the purposes of this chapter I assume you're familiar with the difference between base relvars and other kinds, such as views, which are virtual relvars.)

  > *Aside:* Variables are *always* named in **Tutorial D**; values, by contrast, aren't, and in fact can't be. Thus, the names DEPT and EMP shown in Figs. 8.1 and 8.2 aren't names of the pertinent relations—rather, they're the names of the relvars of which the relations depicted are sample values. *End of aside*.

- The second line of the definition specifies the type of that variable—the keyword RELATION shows it's a relation type, and the commalist in

---

[6] The definitions differ, however, in that the one for relvar EMP includes a foreign key specification. Foreign keys aren't relevant to the topic of this chapter, however, and I'll ignore them from this point forward.

braces specifies the set of attributes that make up the corresponding heading. Of course, to say it again, no significance attaches to the order in which those attributes are specified.

> *Aside:* In other words—and indeed as already noted in Chapters 3 and 7— **Tutorial D** represents relation types by means of syntax of the form RELATION *H*, where *H* is the pertinent heading. If *R* is a relvar, then every relation *r* that's ever assigned to *R* is of course required to have the heading specified in the definition of *R*. *End of aside.*

■ The last line defines {DNO} to be a key for that relvar.

In connection with this last point, I assume you're familiar with the notion of a key, as that term is used in the relational model; in particular, I assume you know that (a) a key is a *set* of attributes of the pertinent relvar (hence the braces), and that (b) key values are therefore *tuples*. Once again, however, there are a few points that I think are worth spelling out explicitly:

■ Key declarations constitute a certain kind of integrity constraint (a "key constraint," also known as a uniqueness constraint); integrity constraints constrain updates; and if something can be updated, then by definition that something is a variable specifically. It follows that it's relvars, not relations, that have keys.
  Note: If *R* is a relvar and *KC* is a key constraint that applies to *R*, then every relation *r* that's ever assigned to *R* is certainly required to satisfy constraint *KC*. But of course there's a logical difference between (a) the concept of some variable being *subject to* some constraint, on the one hand, and (b) the concept of some value *satisfying*—or *violating*, come to that— that same constraint, on the other.

■ It's customary when depicting a relation on paper—at least when the relation in question is supposed to be a value or "state" for some relvar—to indicate attributes that participate in some particular key of that relvar by using double underlining beneath the pertinent column names (see, e.g., Figs. 8.1 and 8.2).[7] However, such double underlining must be clearly

---

[7] Of course, a relvar can have any number *n* of keys ($n \geq 1$)), though $n = 1$ is common in practice. If a relvar has two or more keys, though, the double underlining convention obviously can't be used for more than one of them.

understood as indicating that the attributes in question constitute a key, not for the relation being depicted (relations don't have keys), but rather for the pertinent relvar.

■ Such double underlining is usually taken to mean that what I've just called the "particular key" of the pertinent relvar is actually the *primary* key of that relvar. However, **Tutorial D** deliberately provides no way of—in particular, no syntax for—distinguishing between primary and other keys, referring to them all as just keys.

    Note: Arguments in favor of not making a formal distinction between primary and other keys can be found in Appendix C, "Primary Keys Are Nice but Not Essential," of my book *Database Design and Relational Theory: Normal Forms and All That Jazz*, 2nd edition (Apress, 2019).

Given all of the above, however, what are we to make of Fig. 8.3, which shows the result of restricting the current value of relvar DEPT as shown in Fig. 8.2 to just those departments with budget less than $10M? Specifically, what are we to make of the double underlining in that figure?

DNO : DNO	DNAME : NAME	BUDGET : MONEY
D3	Training	5M

Fig. 8.3: Result of evaluating DEPT WHERE BUDGET < 10M
on departments as shown in Fig. 8.2

What Fig. 8.3 shows is just a relation as such, not the relation that happens to be the current value (or "current state") of some relvar, and—to say it again—relations don't have keys. So, again, what's the appropriate interpretation of the double underlining in that picture, or in other pictures like it? My answer to this question is as follows:

■ Such pictures can be regarded as showing a sample value for some relational expression *rx* (viz., DEPT WHERE BUDGET < 10M, in the case of Fig. 8.3). That expression *rx* in turn can be regarded as the defining expression for some temporary relvar *R* (e.g., *rx* could be a view defining expression and *R* the corresponding view). So the double underlining indicates that a key K could in principle be declared for R and the pertinent attribute is part of K.[8]

An alternative but equivalent way of saying the same thing is this: The relation depicted certainly doesn't "have" the indicated key—in fact, it would be logically incorrect to say it "has" that key—but it does satisfy the corresponding key constraint.

A Remark on Empty Keys

Any key for relvar R must be a subset of the heading of R. In other words, as I've already said, a key is a *set* of attributes of the pertinent relvar—and since the empty set is certainly a legitimate set (and in fact a subset of every set), we can define an *empty key* to be a key where the pertinent set of attributes is empty. What are the implications of such a concept?

Well, to say that relvar R has an empty key is to say that R can never contain more than one tuple. Why? Because *every* tuple has the same value for the empty set of attributes: namely, the empty tuple. Thus, if R had an empty key, and if R were to contain two or more tuples, we'd have a key uniqueness violation on our hands! Here's a simple example of such a relvar:

```
VAR COMPANY BASE
    RELATION { CNAME NAME , BUDGET MONEY }
    KEY { } ;
```

At all times this relvar contains exactly one tuple—the CNAME value in that tuple is the company name, and the BUDGET value is the total budget for the entire company. Here's a sample value:

COMPANY

CNAME : NAME	BUDGET : MONEY
RDB Inc.	27M

As you can see, the COMPANY relvar has an empty key, and empty keys obviously can't be depicted using the double underlining convention; thus, no

---

[8] Of course, SQL in particular doesn't allow keys to be declared for views, but it should, and **Tutorial D** does. Certainly views *have* keys, just as base relvars do.

column in the table just shown, which depicts a sample COMPANY value, involves any double underlining.

EFFECTS OF TYPE INHERITANCE

So far, so good (I hope!—in particular, I hope you don't think I've been making extraordinarily heavy weather of what is, after all, a pretty simple idea). Unfortunately, however, the situation gets rather more complicated when we bring type inheritance into the picture (I choose my words carefully). The basic reason for the increase in complexity is that, with type inheritance, it's no longer the case that every value necessarily has just one type. For example, every circle is also an ellipse, and so a value of type CIRCLE is necessarily also a value of type ELLIPSE (assuming for the sake of the example that such types have been appropriately defined, of course). Let's take a closer look.

Background

By the term *type inheritance*, I mean more specifically the model of type inheritance developed by Hugh Darwen and myself in connection wth our work on *The Third Manifesto*. That model is discussed in detail in my book *Type Inheritance and Relational Theory: Subtypes, Supertypes, and Substitutability* (O'Reilly, 2016),[9] and the following brief explanations are taken from that book.

First of all, the term *type inheritance*, or just *inheritance* for short, refers to that phenomenon according to which we can sensibly say that (e.g.) every circle is an ellipse, and hence that all properties that apply to ellipses in general apply to—i.e., "are inherited by"—circles in particular. For example, every ellipse has an area, and therefore every circle has an area also. More precisely, we can say that:

- Types ELLIPSE and CIRCLE are such that type ELLIPSE is a *supertype* of type CIRCLE, and type CIRCLE is a *subtype* of type ELLIPSE.

- There's an operator—AREA_OF, say—that returns the area of a given ellipse, and that operator can be invoked with an argument of type CIRCLE, precisely because circles are ellipses.

---

[9] There's a video based on that book too, also available from O'Reilly. See also Chapter 2 of the present book.

Of course, the converse is false—the subtype will have properties of its own that don't apply to the supertype. For example, circles have a radius, but ellipses in general don't; in other words, there's an operator that returns the radius of a given circle, but that operator can't be invoked with an argument that's "just an ellipse" (meaning an ellipse that's not a circle), because such ellipses don't have a radius.

Now let me introduce the running example that I'll be using as a basis for numerous individual examples later. That example is, I hope, self-explanatory; it involves several geometric types, arranged into what's called a *type hierarchy*, as shown in Fig. 8.4:

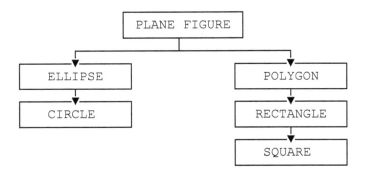

Fig. 8.4: A sample type hierarchy

The directed arrows in the figure can be read as "is a supertype of" (more precisely, "is an *immediate* supertype of"—further explanation to follow). For example, the arrow from ELLIPSE to CIRCLE means that type ELLIPSE is a supertype of type CIRCLE (equivalently, of course, type CIRCLE is a subtype of type ELLIPSE). *Note:* All of the types in the figure are, specifically, *scalar* types, meaning they have no user visible components. Our inheritance model does deal with tuple and relation subtypes and supertypes as well, but I don't want to get into such nonscalar types just yet. (It also deals with both single and multiple inheritance, but for the purposes of this chapter it's sufficient to consider single inheritance only.)

Now I need to introduce a few more terms and concepts that I'm going to be needing later on. Let *T* be a type. Then:

- A subtype of a subtype of *T* is a subtype of *T*. For example, SQUARE is a subtype of POLYGON.

- In mathematics, every set is a subset of itself; analogously, every type is a subtype of itself. For example, ELLIPSE is a subtype of ELLIPSE.

- If *T'* is a subtype of *T* and *T'* and *T* are distinct, then *T'* is a *proper* subtype of *T*. For example, SQUARE is a proper subtype of POLYGON.

Analogous remarks apply to supertypes, of course. Thus:

- A supertype of a supertype of *T* is a supertype of *T* (e.g., POLYGON is a supertype of SQUARE).

- Every type is a supertype of itself (e.g., ELLIPSE is a supertype of ELLIPSE).

- If *T* is a supertype of *T'* and *T* and *T'* are distinct, then *T* is a *proper* supertype of *T'* (e.g., POLYGON is a proper supertype of SQUARE).

Moreover:

- If *T'* is a proper subtype of *T* and there's no type that's both a proper supertype of *T'* and a proper subtype of *T*, then *T'* is an *immediate* subtype of *T* and *T* is an *immediate* supertype of *T'*. For example, SQUARE is an immediate subtype of RECTANGLE, and RECTANGLE is an immediate supertype of SQUARE. Note that if *T'* is an immediate subtype of *T* then it's certainly a proper subtype of *T*, but the converse is false (a proper subtype of *T* isn't necessarily an immediate subtype of *T* (and similarly for supertypes, of course, mutatis mutandis).

- A type with no immediate supertype is a *root* type (e.g., PLANE_FIGURE is a root type), and a type with no immediate subtype is a *leaf* type (e.g., SQUARE is a leaf type).

Aside: More correctly, a scalar root type has no immediate supertype except for the maximal scalar type *alpha*, and a scalar leaf type has no immediate subtype except for the minimal scalar type *omega*. Type *alpha* contains all scalar values and type *omega* contains no values at all (no scalar values in particular). It's conventional to exclude these types from figures like Fig. 8.4; however, I'm going to have to make use of them later in this chapter, which is why I mention them here.

Note: The foregoing remarks do assume the only types we have to deal with are scalar types specifically (as indeed they are, as far as the present discussion is concerned); they'd need some refinement if we wanted them to take nonscalar types into account as well. *End of aside.*

Now, if T' is a subtype of T, then all operators that apply to values of type T apply to values of type T' as well, necessarily.[10] For example, as mentioned earlier, if AREA_OF (e) is valid, where e is an ellipse, then AREA_OF (c), where c is a circle, must be valid as well. In other words, wherever the system expects a value of type ELLIPSE, we can always *substitute* a value of type CIRCLE, because, to repeat, circles are ellipses. (Indeed, for reasons beyond the scope of this chapter, this business of "substitutability" is in many ways the whole point of inheritance.) As a consequence of such considerations, we need to be particularly careful over yet another logical difference—viz., the logical difference between:

a. The parameters in terms of which an operator is defined, with their *declared* types, and

b. The corresponding arguments to some invocation of that operator, with their *actual* types (better: their *most specific* types).

In the AREA_OF example, for instance, the operator is presumably defined in terms of a parameter of declared type ELLIPSE, but the most specific type of the argument in an of invocation AREA_OF might be CIRCLE. So now I need to say a little more about this question of declared types vs. most specific types:

■ Let V be a variable; then the type specified in the definition of V is the *declared type* of V. Analogously, let A be an attribute of relvar R; then the type specified in the definition of A (as part of the definition of R) is the

---

[10] Note that "operators that apply to values" are read-only operators by definition. Inheritance does apply to update operators as well, but the picture is more complicated in that case. Perhaps fortunately, however, there's no need to discuss that case here.

declared type of *A*. In what follows, I'll use the notation *DT*(*X*), where *X* is either a variable or an attribute of a relvar, to refer to the declared type of *X*.

■ Let *v* be a value of type *T* and not of any proper subtype of *T*; then *T* is the *most specific type* of *v*. (Note that the most specific type *T* of any given value *v* is unique—i.e., every value has exactly one most specific type— and the set of types possessed by that value *v* is, precisely, the set of all supertypes of *T*. For example, if *v* is of type RECTANGLE and not of any proper subtype of RECTANGLE, then the most specific type of *v* is RECTANGLE, and the set of types possessed by *v* is RECTANGLE, POLYGON, and PLANE_FIGURE.)[11] In what follows, I'll use the notation *MST*(*x*) to refer to the most specific type of the value *v* denoted by expression *x*; in particular, if *x* is simply a reference to some variable *V*, I'll use the notation *MST*(*V*) to refer to the most specific type of the value *v* currently contained in that variable *V*.

By way of illustration, let E and F be variables of declared type ELLIPSE, thus—

```
VAR E ELLIPSE ;
VAR F ELLIPSE ;
```

—and let *cx* be an expression (perhaps just a literal) denoting a value *c* of most specific type CIRCLE. Then the following assignment is certainly legitimate:

```
E := cx ;
```

After this assignment, the variable E, of declared type ELLIPSE, contains the value *c*, of most specific type CIRCLE. In other words, *DT*(E) is still ELLIPSE, of course, but *MST*(E) is now CIRCLE. And if we now assign E to F, thus—

```
F := E ;
```

—F will of course contain that same value *c*, and *DT*(F) and *MST*(F) will be ELLIPSE and CIRCLE, respectively.

---

[11] And the maximal scalar type *alpha*, discussed in an aside earlier.

Headings Revisited

So far we've seen that (a) a given scalar value might have any number of different types, but that (b) it always has exactly one most specific type. But precisely analogous remarks naturally apply to nonscalar values as well, of course. In particular, they apply to relation values; that is, any given relation might have any number of different types, but it always has exactly one most specific type (where the types in question are relation types, of course). So the question arises: How is the concept of "most specific type" concept defined, when the types involved happen to be relation types? Well, let's consider a few examples.

First of all, let relvar ERV be defined as follows:

```
VAR ERV BASE
    RELATION { E ELLIPSE , R RECTANGLE }
    KEY { E , R } ;
```

The declared type *DT*(ERV) of relvar ERV is, of course, RELATION {E ELLIPSE, R RECTANGLE}. But I hope it's at least intuitively obvious that, e.g., the following relation—let's call it *cs*—can legitimately be assigned to relvar ERV:

E : CIRCLE	R : SQUARE
c1 : circle	s1 : square
c2 : circle	s2 : square

I'm assuming here that $c1$ and $c2$ are values of most specific type CIRCLE and $s1$ and $s2$ are values of most specific type SQUARE (as I've tried to suggest in the picture by annotating the values accordingly). Thus, I hope it's also intuitively obvious that the most specific type *MST*(*cs*) of relation *cs* is as follows (as I've also tried to suggest in the picture by specifying attribute type names in the heading row accordingly):

```
RELATION { E CIRCLE , R SQUARE }
```

What's more, I hope it's intuitively obvious as well that this latter type is a proper subtype of the declared type of relvar ERV, so that assigning relation *cs* to relvar ERV is indeed legitimate as claimed. (Certainly it's true that every value of the type just shown—viz., type RELATION {E CIRCLE, R SQUARE}—is also a value of the declared type of relvar ERV, and that state of affairs effectively makes the former a subtype of the latter, by definition.)

To repeat, then, the most specific type $MST(cs)$ of relation cs is the type just shown. But of course that relation is also of all types that are proper supertypes of that type, and so the full set of types possessed by that relation is as follows (*alpha*, I remind you, is the maximal scalar type and contains all scalar values):

```
RELATION { E CIRCLE       , R SQUARE }
RELATION { E ELLIPSE      , R SQUARE }
RELATION { E PLANE_FIGURE , R SQUARE }
RELATION { E alpha        , R SQUARE }

RELATION { E CIRCLE       , R RECTANGLE }
RELATION { E ELLIPSE      , R RECTANGLE }
RELATION { E PLANE_FIGURE , R RECTANGLE }
RELATION { E alpha        , R RECTANGLE }

RELATION { E CIRCLE       , R POLYGON }
RELATION { E ELLIPSE      , R POLYGON }
RELATION { E PLANE_FIGURE , R POLYGON }
RELATION { E alpha        , R POLYGON }

RELATION { E CIRCLE       , R PLANE_FIGURE }
RELATION { E ELLIPSE      , R PLANE_FIGURE }
RELATION { E PLANE_FIGURE , R PLANE_FIGURE }
RELATION { E alpha        , R PLANE_FIGURE }

RELATION { E CIRCLE       , R alpha }
RELATION { E ELLIPSE      , R alpha }
RELATION { E PLANE_FIGURE , R alpha }
RELATION { E alpha        , R alpha }
```

And since the relation has all of these different types, it effectively has many different headings as well—though just one of those headings (viz., the first in the foregoing list) corresponds to that relation's most specific type.

By way of another example, consider the following relation (let's call it cr):

E : CIRCLE	R : RECTANGLE
c1 : circle	s1 : square
c2 : circle	r2 : rectangle

Note that the most specific type $MST(cr)$ of this relation is

```
RELATION { E CIRCLE , R RECTANGLE }
```

—even though one of the tuples has a square (*s1*) as its value for attribute R. The point is, the type of attribute R in *MST*(*cr*) can't be SQUARE,[12] because one of the values in that attribute position in relation *cr* is "just a rectangle," and a rectangle that's "just a rectangle" isn't a square.[13] Nevertheless, relation *cr* can still be assigned to relvar ERV, because *MST*(*cr*) is still a subtype—in fact, a proper subtype—of *DT*(ERV).

One further example: Let relation *er* be as follows:

E : ELLIPSE	R : RECTANGLE
e1 : *ellipse*	s1 : *square*
c2 : *circle*	r2 : *rectangle*

The most specific type *MST*(*er*) of this relation is

```
RELATION { E ELLIPSE , R RECTANGLE }
```

—even though no tuple in relation *er* has both "just an ellipse" as its value for attribute E and "just a rectangle" as its value for attribute R. (The type of attribute E in *MST*(*er*) can't be CIRCLE, because one of the values in that attribute position in relation *er* is "just an ellipse," and an ellipse that's "just an ellipse" isn't a circle; likewise, the type of attribute R in *MST*(*er*) can't be SQUARE, because one of the values in that attribute position in relation *er* is "just a rectangle," and a rectangle that's "just a rectangle" isn't a square.) But of course relation *er* can certainly be assigned to relvar ERV, because *MST*(*er*) is certainly a subtype—though not a proper subtype—of *DT*(ERV).

From the foregoing examples, I hope it's clear that the most specific type of a relation can be (in fact, has to be) defined as follows:[14]

---

[12] Nor any proper subtype of SQUARE, if any such subtype existed other than *omega*.

[13] Loosely, squares can be substituted for rectangles, but rectangles can't be substituted for squares. Equivalently (but still loosely), a square can appear where a rectangle is expected, but a rectangle can't appear where a square is expected.

[14] I note in passing that this definition is sufficiently general to take care of both (a) nonscalar as well as scalar attributes and (b) multiple as well as single inheritance. For further specifics, I refer you to the book mentioned earlier, *Type Inheritance and Relational Theory: Subtypes, Supertypes, and Substitutability* (O'Reilly, 2016).

Definition (most specific type of a relation): Let relation r be of type

```
RELATION { A1 T1 , A2 T2 , ... , An Tn }
```

and let its body consist of tuples $t1$, $t2$, ..., tm. Within tuple ti, let attribute Aj have value vij, of most specific type $MSTij$ ($i = 1, 2, ..., m$; $j = 1, 2, ..., n$). Note that $MSTij$ will in general be different for different tuples ti, but will always be a subtype of Tj. Then the most specific type of r is

```
RELATION { A1 MST1 , A2 MST2 , ... , An MSTn }
```

where, for all j, $MSTj$ is the most specific common supertype of those most specific types $MSTij$, taken over all tuples ti.

Now, the foregoing definition might look a little daunting, but basically all it's saying is something like this:

■ If attribute A of relation r contains (for example) squares in some tuples, "just rectangles" in others, and "just polygons" in the rest, then the most specific type of r must have POLYGON as the type for attribute A— because POLYGON is "the most specific common supertype" for types SQUARE, RECTANGLE, and POLYGON.

■ Likewise, if attribute A of relation r contains (for example) squares in some tuples and "just rectangles" in the rest, then the most specific type of r must have RECTANGLE as the type for attribute A—because RECTANGLE is "the most specific common supertype" for types SQUARE and RECTANGLE. (Of course, POLYGON is also a common supertype for types SQUARE and RECTANGLE, but it's not the *most specific* common supertype for those types.)

Aside: For the record, here's another—perhaps simpler, and certainly more succinct—definition of the concept of most specific type of a relation:

Definition (most specific type of a relation, alternative definition): Let relation r have attributes $A1$, $A2$, ..., An (only). Then the most specific type of r is the type RELATION H such that each tuple of r is of type TUPLE H and there's no heading *H'* such that (a) TUPLE *H'* is a proper subtype of TUPLE *H* and (b) each tuple of *r* is of type TUPLE *H'*.

Note, however, that this definition relies on the concepts of tuple types and subtypes, which I deliberately haven't discussed in this chapter at all prior to this point (nor do I plan to). *End of aside.*

Here then are some more examples of relations, all of which have most specific type some subtype of the declared type *DT*(ERV) of relvar ERV and can thus certainly be assigned to that relvar. In each case, the heading row shows the most specific type of the relation in question.

E : ELLIPSE	R : RECTANGLE
e1 : ellipse	r1 : rectangle
c2 : circle	r2 : rectangle
e3 : ellipse	s3 : square
c4 : circle	s4 : square

E : ELLIPSE	R : RECTANGLE
e1 : ellipse	r1 : rectangle
c4 : circle	s4 : square

E : ELLIPSE	R : RECTANGLE
e1 : ellipse	r1 : rectangle
c3 : ellipse	s4 : square

E : CIRCLE	R : RECTANGLE
c2 : circle	r2 : rectangle
c4 : circle	s4 : square

E : ELLIPSE	R : RECTANGLE
c2 : circle	r2 : rectangle
e3 : ellipse	s3 : square

E : ELLIPSE	R : SQUARE
e3 : ellipse	s3 : square

E : CIRCLE	R : SQUARE
c4 : circle	*s4 : square*

These examples are, I think, self-explanatory. However, there's still one issue to address: Relations can, of course, be empty (i.e., they can have a body that contains no tuples at all). Here by way of example is the (unique) empty relation that can legitimately be assigned to relvar ERV:

E	R

But what's the most specific type of this relation? From the "most specific type of a relation" definition given earlier, we see that the most specific type in question must have as its type for attribute E "the most specific common supertype" of an empty set of types (and analogously for attribute R). So what's the most specific common supertype for an empty set of scalar types? As it turns out, this question is slightly tricky, and I don't propose to consider it in detail here; rather, I'll simply claim without attempting to prove it that the answer is *omega* (the empty scalar type).[15] So we can complete the previous picture as follows:

E : *omega*	R : *omega*

By the way, the following point is worth making explicitly. By definition, no scalar value can have most specific type *omega*. Likewise, no scalar variable can have declared type *omega* (because no value could ever be assigned to such a variable!). However, a relation *can* have an attribute of most specific type *omega* (as indeed the example illustrates), and a relvar can have an attribute of declared

---

[15] A proper treatment of this issue can be found in the book mentioned several times already, *Type Inheritance and Relational Theory: Subtypes, Supertypes, and Substitutability*(O'Reilly, 2016). However, it might help to point out that if *S* is an empty set of scalar types, then clearly there's no type in *S* that's *more specific* than *omega* (right?).

type *omega*. However, any such relation will necessarily be empty, and any such relavar can only have the unique corresponding empty relation as its value.[16]

Drawing Pictures

What are the implications of all of the above for drawing relations as tables? A sensible answer to this question (or so it seems to me) is as follows:

- When the table depicts a relation that's meant to be a possible or actual value for some relvar, the table should be labeled with the name of the pertinent relvar, and the columns of that table should be labeled with the names of the corresponding attribute declared types.

- When the table depicts just a relation as such (that is, just a relation value, independent of any specific relvar), the columns of that table should be labeled in accordance with the most specific type of that relation, and no relvar name should appear at all.

To illustrate the difference between the two cases, Fig. 8.5 shows a relation that's meant to be a possible value for relvar ERV, while Fig. 8.6 shows that same relation as "just a relation as such" (i.e., independent of any relvar).

```
ERV
```

E : ELLIPSE	R : RECTANGLE
c1	s1
c2	s2

Fig. 8.5: A sample value for relvar ERV

E : CIRCLE	R : SQUARE
c1	s1
c2	s2

Fig. 8.6: The relation of Fig. 8.5 considered as "just a relation"

---

[16] So the value of such a "variable" is in fact constant! Note too that if *omega* is the declared type of any scalar attribute of such a relvar, it might as well be the declared type of all such attributes.

Note: As earlier in this chapter, I adopt the convention in these figures that values of the form *ci* denote circles and values of the form *si* denote squares. However, I no longer show any accompanying annotation to that effect because we don't usually bother to do so in practice (though I suppose it wouldn't hurt if we did, at least in the inheritance context). Note too that (as recommended) Fig. 8.5 includes the pertinent relvar name, whereas no such name would be either appropriate or applicable in Fig. 8.6.

A MATTER OF DEFINITION

To close this chapter, I'll leave you with something to think about. The previous section mentioned in passing the notion that two relation types, *RT* and *RT'*, say, could be such that *RT* is a proper supertype of *RT'* and *RT'* is a proper subtype of *RT*. But how exactly do you think these concepts—i.e., proper supertype, proper subtype—might reasonably and rigorously be defined, if the types in question are indeed relation types?

Chapter 9

Mathematics and
the Relational Model

Mathematics, rightly viewed,
possesses not only truth, but supreme beauty.
—Bertrand Russell:
Philosophical Essays (1910)

Mathematics may be defined as the subject
in which we never know what we are talking about,
nor whether what we are saying is true.
—Bertrand Russell:
Mysticism and Logic (1918)

SOME LOGICAL DIFFERENCES

Relational advocates are always claiming that the relational model is based on mathematics. Yet I see many differences between relations as understood in mathematics and relations in the relational model. Can you comment?

It's certainly true that such differences exist. I think it's fair to say the following: While Codd used the concept of a mathematical relation, together with various related concepts from set theory (including operators such as union), as a basis on which to define his relational model, he deliberately didn't limit himself in his definition to those concepts as they were known at the time. Rather, what he did was use those concepts to develop, or begin to develop, a whole new branch of mathematics in its own right—because that's what relational theory, in the database sense, is: a new, albeit small, part of mathematics. Thus, while that theory is certainly based on relations in their original mathematical sense, it goes a long way beyond just classical mathematical relations as such. Here are some of the principal points of difference between the two:

■ Database relations are typed—they emphasize, much more than mathematical relations do, the significance of the pertinent heading. In fact, I think it's fair to say that mathematics scarcely includes any notion of relations having a "heading" (and hence a type) in the first place. Thus, the relational model requires a supporting theory of types, while classical relation theory doesn't. See reference [7] for further discussion.

■ Database relations have no left to right ordering to their attributes; mathematical relations do have such an ordering. (In fact, of course, the term "attribute," in the database sense, is never used at all in the mathematical context.) More specifically, attributes of database relations are *named*, while attributes of mathematical relations aren't (so in the database case every attribute can be identified by its name, and we don't need to talk in that context about, e.g., the third attribute, or the last attribute, or whatever). Those names in turn play an essential role in the relational algebra, with respect to the critically important notion of result type inference in particular. What's more, those attribute names are conceptually distinct from the underlying domain names.
    Note: Domain was the term Codd originally used for the type concept; myself, I very much prefer the term *type*, and these days I almost always use this latter term, except when I'm quoting from other writers.

■ The emphasis in mathematics is on binary relations specifically. Database relations, by contrast, are *n*-ary, where *n* can be any nonnegative integer (0, 1, 2, 3, ...). It was one of Codd's many great contributions to show that *n*-ary relations for $n \neq 2$ are interesting in their own right—i.e., they enjoy interesting formal properties that aren't apparent if they're regarded merely as "nests" (as it were) of binary relations. Note the cases $n = 0$ and $n = 1$ in particular! The case $n = 0$ turns out to be crucially important for all kinds of fundamental reasons (see references [3], [4], and [6]).
    Note: In the interest of historical accuracy, I should add that Codd himself never had much to say concerning the case $n = 0$. The first paper I'm aware of that did so is reference [2].

■ *Relational algebra:* Very little work seems to have been done in mathematics on general *n*-ary relational operators, presumably because of the emphasis already noted on binary relations specifically. For example, reference [8], a textbook on logic, defines an operator it calls *relative product*.[1] Here's a definition, paraphrased from that reference:

> **Definition (relative product):** Let $r(A,B)$ and $s(B,C)$ be binary relations. Then their relative product $t(A,C)$ is the binary relation consisting of all pairs $<a,c>$ such that, for some b, the pair $<a,b>$ appears in r and the pair $<b,c>$ appears in s.

In relational model terms, this operation corresponds to the projection on A and C of the join of r and s on B. But notice how the operation is specifically defined to produce a binary relation as its result; the ternary relation that's the intermediate result—i.e., the join—is never explicitly mentioned. (Note too how the definition relies on the fact that attributes of mathematical relations have a left to right ordering.)

Thus, although operators such as join (and all of the other operators of the relational algebra) are clearly applicable—albeit with certain modifications, in some cases—to mathematical relations, it's fair to say for the most part that they were first defined in the context of relations in the database sense. Indeed, the theory of such operators (including the laws of expression transformation and the associated principles of optimization, as well as the rules already mentioned for determining result types) can reasonably be regarded as part of that "new branch of mathematics" I referred to earlier—a part that was developed in response to the needs and problems of database management specifically.

■ *Dependency theory:* To repeat, the emphasis in mathematics is on binary relations, whereas the emphasis in the relational model is on *n*-ary relations instead. And the entire field of what's now usually called dependency theory—the large body of theorems and techniques concerning such matters as redundancy, keys, functional dependence, multivalued dependence, join dependence, higher normal forms, and so forth—is crucially dependent on this difference in emphasis. For example, the concept of Boyce/Codd normal form (BCNF) is relevant for the most part

---

[1] More usually called *composition*.

only to relations of degree three or more,[2] because "almost all" relations of degree less than three are necessarily in BCNF.[3] In fact, the entire field of dependency theory, like the theory of *n*-ary relational operators mentioned previously, can be regarded as another new branch of mathematics, one that was brought into being by the special requirements of a theory of data and a theory of *n*-ary relations (as opposed to a theory of binary relations merely).

■ *Relation values vs. relation variables:* So far as I'm aware, mathematics has no notion of a relation variable, in the database sense, at all—it deals with relation values only. Database theory, by contrast, is crucially dependent on relation variables, at least if we ever want to be able to update the database <*joke*>. In fact, the dependency theory mentioned under the previous bullet item only makes sense if we're dealing with relation variables specifically—it would be pretty pointless if we had relation values only.

　　Note: As in numerous other writings by myself and others, from this point forward I'll take the unqualified term *relation* to mean a relation value specifically, and I'll use the abbreviation *relvar* to refer to a relation variable.

■ *Integrity:* It's a logical consequence of the previous point that everything having to do with data integrity in any way also makes sense only if we are dealing with relation variables specifically. In particular, integrity constraints apply to relation variables specifically.

■ *Views* and *view updating theory* are further aspects of database relations (or relvars, rather) that depend at least in part on integrity theory and have no counterpart in traditional mathematics, so far as I'm aware.

RELATIONS vs. RELATIONSHIPS

What's the difference between a relation and a relationship?

---

[2] The reference to relations in this sentence, and all subsequent such references in the rest of this paragraph, ought really to be references to relation *variables*. See the bullet item immediately following regarding the logical difference between relations and relation variables.

[3] *Almost* all, please note, not all. Finding one that isn't is left as an exercise!

Well, of course, that depends on how you define the term *relationship*! Personally, I try to avoid that term as much as I can (in particular, I was never much of a fan of "entity / relationship modeling"—E/R modeling for short). The term was introduced, it seems to me, primarily by people without a mathematical background, or at least by people who prefer fuzzy concepts to precise ones. Though in fairness perhaps I should add that in Codd's famous 1970 paper on the relational model [1], we find the following:

> [We] propose that users deal, not with relations which are domain-ordered, but with *relationships* which are their domain-unordered counterparts ... [Users] should interact with a relational model of the data consisting of a collection of time-varying relationships (rather than relations).

In other words, the domains, and hence the attributes, of a (database) relation were originally considered by Codd to have a left to right ordering, but the relational model as such was supposed to be concerned with "relationships," not relations. In the rest of that same paper, however, and indeed in all of his subsequent writings, Codd used the term *relation* to mean what he originally called a relationship. So I suppose it's possible, though I think it's a bit of a stretch, to lay part of the blame for "relationships" at Codd's door.

So how do I define the term *relationship?* Well, here's what I say in reference [5]:

> **Definition (relationship):** 1. A term used briefly in Codd's earliest papers (but quickly discarded) to mean what we would now call either a relation or a relvar, as the context demands. It was used to distinguish relations in the relational model sense (which don't have a left to right ordering to their attributes) from their mathematical counterparts (which do). 2. In E/R modeling, "an association among entities" (this extremely imprecise definition is taken from Chen's original E/R paper, "The Entity-Relationship Model—Toward a Unified View of Data," *ACM TODS 1*, No. 1, March 1976). 3. More generally, given two sets (not necessarily distinct), a rule pairing elements of the first set with elements of the second set; equivalently, that pairing itself. *Note:* This last definition can easily be extended to three, four, ..., or any number of given sets.

Note that the last of these definitions can be regarded as a very loose definition of a relation in the database sense, except for (a) its reliance on ordinality ("first" set, "second" set, and so forth) and (b) the fact that it assumes that "relationships" must have degree at least two.

REFEXIVITY, SYMMETRY, TRANSITIVITY

The mathematical theory of relations includes certain concepts—reflexivity, symmetry, and transitivity—that I never see mentioned in discussions of the relational model. Don't those concepts have any role to play in connection with database relations?

Reflexivity, symmetry, and transitivity are properties possessed by, specifically, certain *binary* relations. Loosely, a mathematical binary relation r is:

- *Reflexive* if and only if, for all x, the tuple $\langle x,x \rangle$ appears in r

- *Symmetric* if and only if, for all x and y, if the tuple $\langle x,y \rangle$ appears in r, then so does the tuple $\langle y,x \rangle$

- *Transitive* if and only if, for all x, y, and z, if the tuples $\langle x,y \rangle$ and $\langle y,z \rangle$ both appear in r, then so does the tuple $\langle x,z \rangle$

Note: Since the relation r is (as stated) a mathematical relation specifically, the tuples mentioned in the foregoing definitions have a first and second attribute. Thus, for example, the phrase "for all x" in the definition of reflexivity can be understand as meaning "for all x appearing in the first attribute position in r." Similarly for the phrases "for all x and y" and "for all x, y, and z" in the other two definitions.

In the database context, of course, it's more interesting if the three properties are supposed to be satisfied, not just by some given binary relation r, but by all possible values r of some given binary relvar R. If they are, then they're integrity constraints on that relvar, defined perhaps as follows:

```
VAR R BASE
    RELATION { X ... , Y ... }
    KEY { X , Y } ;

CONSTRAINT R_IS_REFLEXIVE
   ( EXTEND R { X } : { Y := X } ) ⊆ R ;
```

```
CONSTRAINT R_IS_SYMMETRIC
   ( R RENAME { X AS Y , Y AS X } ) = R ;

CONSTRAINT R_IS_TRANSITIVE
   ( ( R JOIN ( R RENAME { Y AS Z , X AS Y } ) { X , Z } )
              RENAME { Z AS Y } ) ⊆ R ;
```

Of course, it would be possible to define shorthands for these constraints that would enable us to define such a relvar much more simply, perhaps like this:

```
VAR R BASE
     RELATION { X   , Y   }
     KEY { X , Y }
     REFLEXIVE SYMMETRIC TRANSITIVE ;
```

Such shorthands, like the familiar KEY shorthand, could have the additional advantage that they would enable the system to implement both (a) the relvar itself, and (b) the specified constraints on that relvar, more efficiently; in particular, they might allow the system to avoid certain obvious redundancies in the data as stored. That said, however, I'm not sure I'd support such shorthands if they really did apply to binary relvars only. Perhaps there's a way to generalize the ideas to apply to *n*-ary relvars for arbitrary nonnegative integer *n*. Perhaps more research is required.

REFERENCES AND BIBLIOGRAPHY

1. E. F. Codd: "A Relational Model of Data for Large Shared Data Banks," *CACM 13*, No. 6 (June 1970).

2. Hugh Darwen (writing as Andrew Warden): "TABLE_DEE and TABLE_DUM," in C. J. Date, *Relational Database Writings 1985-1989*. Reading, Mass.: Addison-Wesley (1990).

3. Hugh Darwen: "The Nullologist in Relationland," in C. J. Date and Hugh Darwen, *Relational Database Writings 1989-1991*. Reading, Mass.: Addison-Wesley (1992).

4. C. J. Date: "Tables with No Columns," in *Relational Database Writings 1991-1994*. Reading, Mass.: Addison-Wesley (1995).

5. C. J. Date: *The New Relational Database Dictionary*. Sebastopol, Calif.: O'Reilly Media Inc. (2016).

6. C. J. Date: "Why Is It Called Relational Algebra?" in *Logic and Relational Theory: Thoughts and Essays on Database Matters* (Technics Publications, to appear 2020).

7. C. J. Date and Hugh Darwen: *Databases, Types, and the Relational Model: The Third Manifesto* (3rd edition). Boston, Mass.: Addison-Wesley (2007).

8. Patrick Suppes: *Introduction to Logic*. Princeton, N.J.: Van Nostrand (1957).

Chapter 10

R e l a t i o n a l   A l g e b r a

*In poetry and algebra we have the pure idea
elaborated and expressed through the vehicle of language.*
—James Joseph Sylvester
(*attrib.*)

*In real life, I assure you,
there is no such thing as algebra.*

—Fran Lebowitz:
"Tips for Teens," in *Social Studies* (1981)

ALGEBRA vs. CALCULUS

**I often hear claims to the effect that relational algebra and relational
calculus are logically equivalent. What exactly do such claims mean?**

Relational algebra and relational calculus are both formalisms for writing
relational expressions—expressions, that is, that evaluate to, or in other words
denote, relations. Such expressions can be used for a variety of purposes, of
which the most obvious is perhaps the formulation of queries. For example, here
are algebraic and calculus formulations of the query "Get supplier numbers for
suppliers who supply at least one red part," given the familiar suppliers-and-parts
database:

Algebra:

```
( S { SNO } ) MATCHING
                ( SP MATCHING
                      ( P WHERE COLOR = 'Red' ) ) )
```

Calculus:

```
( S.SNO ) WHERE EXISTS SP
                ( EXISTS P
                     ( S.SNO = SP.SNO AND
                       SP.PNO = P.PNO AND
                       P.COLOR = 'Red' ) )
```

The two formalisms are logically equivalent because every algebraic expression has an exact counterpart in the calculus and vice versa; that is, every relation that can be defined by means of some algebraic expression can also be defined by means of some expression in the calculus, and vice versa. Given this state of affairs, the choice between the two comes down in some ways to a mere matter of personal preference. (Which of the two formulations shown above for the query "Get supplier numbers for suppliers who supply at least one red part" do you prefer? Why?)

Now, it's often suggested that programmers prefer the algebra while end users prefer the calculus—indeed, I've been known to suggest as much myself. However, it might be closer to the truth to say that the algebra is better suited to some tasks while the calculus is better suited to others. Codd himself, in the paper in which he defined the two formalisms [3], gave arguments for regarding the calculus as superior (or at least more user friendly), and he even claimed in reference [2] that the calculus was at a higher level of abstraction than the algebra. In reference [7], however, I give my own reasons for thinking those arguments don't really stand up; in other words, I stand by my position that the choice is essentially arbitrary.

One more thing: The algebra, consisting as it does of explicit operators, is more obviously implementable than the calculus (albeit not necessarily more efficiently so!); the calculus looks a little bit more like natural language, and its implementability is thus not so immediately apparent. Thus, by showing in reference [3] that any expression of the calculus could be mapped into a logically equivalent expression of the algebra,[1] Codd provided (among other things) a basis for implementing the calculus.

---

[1] Of course, the converse is true too; that is, any expression of the algebra can be mapped into a logically equivalent expression of the calculus. *Note:* Interestingly, this latter wasn't quite true of the algebra as originally defined in reference [3]—certain unions could be formulated in that paper's algebra but not in its calculus. However, this state of affairs was of course unintended, and the defect was quickly remedied.

Exercise: Because the algebra and the calculus are logically equivalent, the design of a database language can reasonably be based on either. Given that this is so, which do you think SQL is based on?[2]

ALGEBRAIC OPERATORS

I thought there was such a thing as "the" relational algebra—namely, the set of operators (restrict, project, join, and so forth) as originally defined by Codd. But in recent writings of yours I've seen you mention all kinds of other operators (group, ungroup, semijoin, semidifference, and many others) that you refer to as algebraic operators also. What's going on here? Is there or isn't there a unique true algebra?

I've discussed these matters in detail in this book's predecessor [8], and I won't repeat those details here. However, there's one point from that discussion that does effectively provide an overall answer to the reader's question—namely:

> *The relational algebra is required to be at least as powerful as the relational calculus.*

Equivalently, the relational algebra is required to be *relationally complete* [3]. What this means, essentially, is that it doesn't really matter what operators are included in "the" algebra, just so long as it can be shown that every calculus expression has a semantically equivalent algebraic counterpart—that is, every relation that can be defined by means of some calculus expression can also be defined by means of some expression of the algebra. In other words, the relational completeness requirement places a kind of lower bound on the functionality that *must* be provided; however, we're at liberty to include any operators we like in "our" algebra, just so long as that requirement is satisfied. In particular, we're at liberty to appeal to the principle of syntactic substitution [4]—see Chapter 2 for further discussion of this useful principle—and define "new" operators that aren't really anything but shorthand for certain combinations of existing operators. For example, the algebra of which **Tutorial D** is a concrete realization includes an attribute renaming operator, even though that operator can easily be defined in terms of the existing operators

---

[2] An extended discussion of this question can be found in Chapter 4 ("Redundancy in SQL") of the planned follow-on to the present book (*Stating the Obvious, and Other Database Writings*).

extend and project. Similarly, semijoin is just shorthand for a certain combination of join and projection; intersection is just a special case of join; and so on.[3]

ATTRIBUTE NAMING

Your version of the relational algebra relies heavily on attribute naming. For example, the expression *A* JOIN *B* is defined to do the join on the basis of just those attributes of *A* and *B* that have the same name. Isn't this approach rather fragile? For example, what happens to that join if we later add a new attribute to *B* (say) that has the same name as one already present in *A*?

First let me clarify one point. It's true, the version of the algebra I advocate does rely on attribute names; for example, *A* JOIN *B* is indeed defined to operate on the basis of attributes with the same name, as the reader says. (Note that this requirement imposes no limitation on functionality, thanks to the availability of the attribute RENAME operator.) However, it also requires those attributes with the same name to be of the same type (and hence in fact to be the very same attribute, formally speaking). Thus, an error would occur—at compile time, too, let me add—if, in the expression *A* JOIN *B*, *A* and *B* both had an attribute called *X* but the two *X*'s were of different types.

Now to the substance of the question. There's a popular misconception here, and I'm very glad to have this opportunity to dispel it. In current DBMSs, application program access to the database is provided either through a call level interface or else through an embedded, but conceptually distinct, data sublanguage. (Embedded SQL provides the standard example of the latter approach.) Of course, the embedded language approach is really just a call level interface with a superficial dusting of syntactic sugar, so to speak, and so the two approaches really come to the same thing from the DBMS's point of view, and indeed from the host language's point of view as well. In other words, the DBMS and the host language are typically only *loosely coupled* in most systems today. As a result, much of the advantage of using a well designed, well structured programming language is lost in today's database environment. As reference [11] puts it, "most programming errors in database applications would

---

[3] As a matter of interest, Appendix A of reference [9] shows that, rather surprisingly, it's possible to define a version of the relational algebra consisting of just two primitive operators. See also reference [8].

show up as *type errors* [if the database schema were] part of the type structure of the program."

Now, the fact that the database schema is not "part of the type structure of the program" in today's DBMSs can be traced back to a fundamental misunderstanding that existed in the database community in the early 1960s or so. The perception at that time was that, in order to achieve logical data independence, it was necessary to move the database definition out of the program so that (in principle) that definition could be changed later without changing the program. But of course that perception was incorrect. What was, and is, really needed is *two separate definitions*, one inside the program and one outside; the one inside would represent the programmer's view of the database (and would provide the necessary compile time checking on queries, etc.), the one outside would represent the database "as it really is." Then, if it subsequently becomes necessary to change the definition of the database "as it really is," logical data independence is preserved by changing the mapping between the two definitions.

Here's how the mechanism I've just briefly described might look in a real system. *Note:* The discussion that follows is based on *The Third Manifesto* [9], which requires such a mechanism to be supported. To be specific, the *Manifesto* prescribes support for what it calls *public relvars*. A public relvar represents the application's perception of some portion of the database. For example:

```
VAR A PUBLIC RELATION
  { SNO SNO , SNAME NAME , CITY CHAR }
    KEY { SNO } ;

VAR B PUBLIC RELATION
  { SNO SNO , PNO PNO }
    KEY { SNO , PNO } ;
```

These definitions effectively assert that "the application believes" there are relvars in the suppliers-and-parts database called A and B, with attributes and keys as specified. Such is not the case, of course—but there are database relvars called S and SP (with attributes and keys as specified for A and B, respectively, but with one additional attribute in each case), and we can clearly define mappings as follows:

$$A \stackrel{\text{def}}{=} S \; \{ \; \text{SNO, SNAME, CITY} \; \}$$

$$B \stackrel{\text{def}}{=} SP \; \{ \; \text{SNO, PNO} \; \}$$

These mappings are defined outside the application (the symbol "$\stackrel{\text{def}}{=}$" means "is defined as").

Now consider the expression A JOIN B; clearly, the join is done on the basis of the common attribute, SNO. And if, say, an attribute SNAME is added to the database relvar SP, all we have to do is change the mapping from SP to B accordingly—actually no change is required at all, in this particular example—and everything will continue to work as before; in other words, logical data independence will be preserved.

Note finally that (to make an obvious point explicit) today's SQL products don't work this way. Thus, for example, the SQL expression

```
SELECT * FROM S NATURAL JOIN SP
```

(which is an SQL analog of the join example discussed above) is, sadly, subject to exactly the "fragility" problem mentioned in the original question.[4] In other words, today's SQL products suffer from a very undesirable (and unfortunate, and unnecessary) loss of logical data independence.

THE JOIN TRAP (?)

I've heard people refer to something called "the join trap," suggesting (to me at least) that there's some flaw in the join operation that users need to know about. Can you elaborate?

Yes, I can. The first time I ever encountered this term was in a paper by an old U.K. acquaintance of mine, Adrian Larner, titled "A New Foundation for the ER Model." (The copy I have is undated, and I don't know where if anywhere it was published or if it was ever widely distributed. "The ER model" is the so called entity / relationship model, of course.[5]) The following is an extract from Adrian's paper. I've edited it for consistency with our usual terminology but haven't changed the sense.

---

[4] So too is the simpler expression SELECT * FROM S, come to that.

[5] That said, it's not clear that there's really such a thing as *the* entity / relationship model, anyway. The *term* "entity / relationship model" first appeared, albeit punctuated slightly differently, in the paper by Peter Chen mentioned in the previous chapter, viz., "The Entity-Relationship Model—Toward a Unified View of Data" (*ACM TODS 1, No. 1*, March 1976). Over the years, however, numerous variants on Chen's original proposal have been defined, all or most of them laying some claim to the original name.

Consider the following relvars, with sample values as indicated:

```
SP                        PJ
 ┌───────┬───────┐         ┌───────┬───────┐
 │ SNO   │ PNO   │         │ PNO   │ JNO   │
 ├───────┼───────┤         ├───────┼───────┤
 │ S1    │ P1    │         │ P1    │ J1    │
 │ S2    │ P1    │         │ P2    │ J1    │
 │ S2    │ P2    │         │ P1    │ J2    │
 └───────┴───────┘         └───────┴───────┘
```

The predicates are as follows:

SP: *Supplier SNO supplies part PNO.*

PJ: *Part PNO is used in project JNO.*

Now we form the composition of SP and PJ (i.e., the join of SP and PJ on PNO, projected on SNO and JNO). The predicate for the result is:

```
EXISTS pno ( sno supplies pno and pno is used in jno )
```

In English, one instantiation is: There is something supplied by S1 and used in J1; or, S1 supplies something used in J1. But this does *not* follow from our base data; it could be false while the base data (shown above) is true (if none of the P1's supplied by S1 are used in J1): the classic join trap.

Well, I'm sorry (and I don't mean to be disrespectful to Adrian), but this is really such nonsense. Values of attribute SNO are supplier numbers; they identify specific suppliers. Likewise, values of attribute JNO are project numbers, and they identify specific projects. But values of attribute PNO, though we do call them part numbers, do *not* identify specific parts—rather, they identify specific *kinds of* parts.[6] The interpretation as given in the sentence beginning "In English" should thus more correctly be:

There is some kind of part supplied by S1 and used in J1; or, S1 supplies some kind of part used in J1.

As far as I'm concerned, this interpretation is 100 percent correct.

---

[6] I should know!—I invented this example (though I did base it on an earlier one of Codd's), and I've been using it since 1972, if not earlier. Though in fairness I suppose I have to admit that my explanations of the example might not always have been as clear as they ought to have been.

What's more, it seems to me that the so called "join trap" is identical to what James Martin called, in reference [10] and possibly elsewhere, "semantic disintegrity." I wrote a short paper, reference [5], over 35 years ago (!) that tried, among other things, to debunk that notion. What follows is a lightly edited version of the relevant portion of that paper:

> A good illustration of lack of clear thinking—arising presumably from an inadequate understanding of the relational model and its interpretation—is provided by what's sometimes called *semantic disintegrity*. Here's an example, taken from a book by James Martin ... Consider the relvars:
>
> ```
> EMP  { ENO , DNO }
> DEPT { DNO , LOCATION }
> ```
>
> Suppose a given department can have any number of locations. Now consider the relvar:
>
> ```
> RESULT { ENO , DNO , LOCATION }
> ```
>
> (the natural join of EMP and DEPT, on DNO). Martin says this join is invalid, because if employee *e* works in department *d* and department *d* has locations *x* and *y*, it certainly doesn't follow that *e* is located in both *x* and *y*. The assumption seems to be that relation RESULT states otherwise. But of course it doesn't; it merely states what we already know—namely, that *e* works in *d* and *d* has locations *x* and *y*. Relation RESULT does represent the answer to a certain query, but that query is not "Get employee locations." Thus, it's definitely wrong to say the join is invalid (though it might be legitimate to warn against incorrect interpretation of that join).

I'd also like to comment on Adrian Larner's use of the term "classic join trap." First, I'm not aware of that term appearing anywhere else in the literature, so I'm not at all sure the epithet "classic" is warranted. More to the point, I think what Adrian is calling "the join trap" is essentially identical to—or at least is very closely related to—what Codd, in his 1970 paper [1], called the *connection trap*. In that paper, however, Codd was arguing *against* precisely the kind of confusion that Larner and James Martin are both guilty of! In reference [6] I commented on this issue as follows:

> [*Codd wrote:*] A lack of understanding of [the semantics of the relational operators] has led several systems designers into what may be called the *connection trap*. [For example, suppose we have a nonrelational system in which]

each supplier description is linked by pointers to the descriptions of each part supplied by that supplier, and each part description is similarly linked to the descriptions of each project which uses that part. A conclusion is now drawn which is, in general, erroneous: namely that, if all possible paths are followed from a given supplier via the [corresponding] parts ... to the projects using those parts, one will obtain a valid set of all projects supplied by that supplier.

[*To which I added:*] Of course, we don't have to be following pointers in order to fall into the connection trap—the very same logical error can unfortunately be made in a purely relational system too [*as the foregoing discussion of the writings of Larner and Martin demonstrates rather clearly!*]. Indeed, some writers have criticized relational systems on exactly these grounds ... I hope it's obvious, however, that such criticisms are invalid, betraying as they do a sad lack of understanding of the relational model.

The point is this (or at least, so it seems to me): We can never stop users from falling into errors of interpretation; but in a relational context, at least, the errors rise to the surface, as it were, and can thus be clearly identified, and perhaps avoided. So Adrian is effectively blaming the relational model for a problem that, at its worst, is more easily recognized and fixed in a relational system than it is in systems of other kinds. Such criticism seems less than fair.

REFERENCES AND BIBLIOGRAPHY

1. E. F. Codd: "A Relational Model of Data for Large Shared Data Banks," *CACM 13*, No. 6 (June 1970).

2. E. F. Codd: "A Data Base Sublanguage Founded on the Relational Calculus," Proc. 1971 ACM SIGFIDET Workshop on Data Description, Access and Control, San Diego, Calif. (November 1971).

3. E. F. Codd: "Relational Completeness of Data Base Sublanguages," in Randall J. Rustin (ed.), *Data Base Systems, Courant Computer Science Symposia Series 6*. Englewood Cliffs, N.J.: Prentice Hall (1972).

4. Hugh Darwen: "Valid Time and Transaction Time Proposals: Language Design Aspects," in Opher Etzion, Sushil Jajodia, and Suryanaryan Sripada (eds.): *Temporal Databases: Research and Practice*. New York, N.Y.: Springer Verlag (1998).

5. C. J. Date: "The Relational Model and its Interpretation," in *Relational Database: Selected Writings*. Reading, Mass.: Addison-Wesley (1986).

6. C. J. Date: *The Database Relational Model: A Retrospective Review and Analysis*. Reading, Mass.: Addison-Wesley (2001).

7. C. J. Date: *E. F. Codd and Relational Theory: A Detailed Review and Analysis of Codd's Major Database Writings* (Lulu Press, 2019).

8. C. J. Date: "Why Is It Called Relational Algebra?" in *Logic and Relational Theory: Thoughts and Essays on Database Matters* (Technics Publications, to appear 2020).

9. C. J. Date and Hugh Darwen: *Databases, Types, and the Relational Model: The Third Manifesto* (3rd edition). Boston, Mass.: Addison-Wesley (2007).

10. James Martin: "Semantic Disintegrity in Relational Operations," Chapter 18 of *Fourth-Generation Languages Volume I: Principles*. Englewood Cliffs, N.J.: Prentice-Hall (1985).

11. Atsushi Ohori, Peter Buneman, and Val Breazu-Tannen: "Database Programming in Machiavelli—A Polymorphic Language with Static Type Inference." Proc. ACM SIGMOD International Conference on Management of Data, Portland, Ore. (June 1989).

Chapter 11

Relvar Predicates

It Don't Mean a Thing If It Ain't Got That Swing
—Duke Ellington (1922)

The predicate for relvar S (suppliers) is:

> *Supplier SNO is under contract, is named SNAME, has status STATUS, and is located in city CITY.*

If we project suppliers on all but CITY, the predicate for the result is:

> *Supplier SNO is under contract, is named SNAME, has status STATUS, and is located in some city CITY.*

But why do we mention the city in this predicate at all, since it's not part of the result? We might as well include further arbitrary clauses such as "... and has been in business for some number of years, and employs some number of workers, and contributes to some political party" (and so on). Do we mention the city only because the projection is derived from a relvar that has a CITY attribute?

Imagine we had a relvar that has the same heading as relvar S except that it has no CITY attribute. This is the same as the result of the projection of S on all but CITY, yet I believe the correct predicate is simply:

> *Supplier SNO is under contract, is named SNAME, and has status STATUS.*

Am I right?

These are good questions! They're important—in some ways, in fact, they get to the heart of what databases are all about—so I'll do my best to answer them as carefully as I can. For that reason, I need to approach them slowly and lay quite a bit of groundwork first ... Please bear with me.

Essentially, your questions have to do with what the symbols that happen to appear in some database mean, or represent. Now, I hope you agree that the kinds of symbols we're talking about don't, in general, have any absolute or fixed meaning. Even a familiar symbol like "3" doesn't mean much in the absence of appropriate additional information (three whats?). Of course, if I'm a DBA, I might design a certain database in such a way that the appearance of that symbol "3" in a certain position is to be interpreted to mean that (for example) employee Joe has three weeks of vacation. And then, if you're a user of my database, I would have to explain that interpretation to you in order for you to be able to understand and use that piece of data correctly and effectively. Of course, I'd try to choose relvar and attribute names (among other things) that make that explanation as intuitively obvious as possible. For example, I might use names as indicated in the following picture:

VACATIONS

NAME	NO_OF_WEEKS
Joe	3

But the fact remains that I'd still have to explain the interpretation to you, even when it's "intuitively obvious" as in this example. (In any case, I'm sure we've all seen real world examples where the relvar and attribute names make the intended interpretation very far from obvious indeed.)

Now, the way to explain the interpretation of a given relvar—equivalently, the way to explain what that relvar means—is to state the corresponding *relvar predicate*. In the case at hand, that predicate looks something like this:

The employee called NAME has NO_OF_WEEKS weeks of vacation.[1]

Next, it's important to understand that *every* relvar has a corresponding predicate; the predicate *is* the intended interpretation. It's also important to

---

[1] Of course, such predicates are only informal (necessarily so), and they can be stated in any number of different ways. In the case at hand, for example, we might equally well say the predicate is *NO_OF_WEEKS is the number of weeks of vacation due to employee NAME*—or anything else that has the same informal meaning. What's more, of course, such predicates might equally well be stated in Spanish, or Russian, or Chinese (etc.)—they don't have to be in English.

understand that users must *always* be told the predicate for every relvar they want to use. (In practice, we don't often talk in such high flown terms, of course—that is, we don't often use the terms *predicate* or *interpretation* in the sense in which I'm using them here—but we do have to say what relvars mean, and however we choose to carry out that necessary task, whatever we do is logically equivalent to stating the predicate.)

Note very carefully too that the predicate for a given relvar is not innate (if it were, we wouldn't have to spell it out). Even the VACATIONS relvar might conceivably have a very different interpretation—for example: *The cat called NAME has had NO_OF_WEEKS visits to the vet.* Of course, if this latter is the intended interpretation, the names VACATIONS and NO_OF_WEEKS aren't very well chosen from an intuitive point of view, but so what? There's nothing *logically* wrong with them. Names are arbitrary—right?

Next, given some relvar, each tuple appearing in that relvar at some given time *t* represents some proposition that's true at that time *t* (more accurately, some proposition that *we believe* is true at that time *t*, but I'm going to ignore that little nicety here). The proposition in question is derived from the relvar predicate by substituting attribute values from the tuple in question for the parameters appearing in the predicate. In the case of relvar VACATIONS, for example, with its predicate *The employee called NAME has NO_OF_WEEKS weeks of vacation*, the tuple for Joe represents the proposition *The employee called Joe has 3 weeks of vacation* (and if that tuple appears in the relvar at a given time, then that proposition is supposed to be true at that time).

I turn now to the suppliers relvar that your questions are based on. I'll also make use of the shipments relvar, SP, with its attributes SNO and PNO (I'll ignore attribute QTY for simplicity). Suppose, then, that I'm the DBA and you're the user. So I tell you—and you have no choice but to believe me!—that the predicate for relvar S (suppliers) is:

> *Supplier SNO is under contract, is named SNAME, has status STATUS, and is located in city CITY.*

Moreover, I also tell you that the predicate for relvar SP (shipments) is:

> *Supplier SNO supplies part PNO.*

Armed with this information, you now know that, at any given time, the tuples in the relation that's the value of relvar S at that time represent propositions of a certain form that are true at that time, and similarly for relvar SP. *And you rely on that knowledge in a variety of ways—in particular, when you formulate queries.* As a simple example, suppose you form the join of suppliers and shipments:

```
S JOIN SP
```

Then—because you know what S and SP mean, and because you also know what JOIN "means" (in other words you know how to interpret each of these things)—you know that every tuple in the relation that's the output from that join (a) has attributes SNO, SNAME, STATUS, CITY, and PNO, and (b) represents a true proposition of the following form:

> *Supplier SNO is under contract, is named SNAME, has status STATUS, is located in city CITY, and supplies part PNO.*

Thus, this latter statement is (by definition) the predicate for the output from the join, and it effectively dictates how you interpret the result of the query. In fact, it's precisely because you understand that the result of the join is to be interpreted in this way that you formulated the query in the first place in the manner that you did. The natural language formulation of that query is "Get supplier number, name, status, city, and part number for each supplier under contract and each part supplied by the supplier in question."

> *Aside:* The result of any given query is a relation, of course, not a relvar—so what I referred to in the foregoing example as "the predicate for the output" isn't exactly a predicate for a relvar as such; rather, it simply tells us how to understand or interpret that result relation. But we might assign that result relation to a relvar *R*, say, and that "predicate for the output" would then be the predicate for that relvar *R*. (Of course, *R* would have to have been defined to have the same attributes—i.e., the same heading—as that result relation for that assignment to be legitimate in the first place.) Or we might use the expression S JOIN SP as the defining expression for a view *V*, and the "predicate for the output" would then be the predicate for that view *V*. *End of aside.*

By way of another example, suppose you restrict suppliers to just the ones in Paris ("Get supplier number, name, status, and city for suppliers under contract and located in Paris"):

```
S WHERE CITY = 'Paris'
```

The predicate for the output this time is:

> *Supplier SNO is under contract, is named SNAME, has status STATUS, is located in city CITY, and city CITY is Paris.*

Of course, there's little point in retaining the CITY attribute in the output in this example, because we know its value is Paris in every tuple. So a more reasonable form of the query is the following, which projects away the CITY attribute ("Get supplier number, name, and status, but not city, for suppliers under contract and located in Paris"):

```
( S WHERE CITY = 'Paris' ) { ALL BUT CITY }
```

And the predicate for the output is now, obviously enough:

> *Supplier SNO is under contract, is named SNAME, has status STATUS,* **and there exists some city CITY such that supplier SNO** *is located in city CITY, and city CITY is Paris.*

Or more simply:

> *Supplier SNO is under contract, is named SNAME, has status STATUS, and is located in Paris.*

What I'm trying to show by these simple examples is that for *every* relational operation (join, restrict, project, and so on), given the predicate(s) satisfied by the tuples of the input relation(s), *there's a well defined predicate that's satisfied by the tuples of the output relation*—and that "output predicate" is determined from the "input predicate(s)" by the semantics of the operation in question, as the examples illustrate.

Now, the particular case you ask about is the projection of suppliers on all but CITY ("Get supplier number, name, and status for suppliers under contract"):

```
S { ALL BUT CITY }
```

Adopting an intuitively obvious simplified notation for tuples, it's clear that the tuple *<sno,sn,st>* appears in the output here if and only if the tuple *<sno,sn,st,sc>* appears in the input for some city *sc.* So the output predicate is:

> *Supplier SNO is under contract, is named SNAME, has status STATUS, and is located in some (unspecified) city CITY.*

Now, you ask why we mention the city in this predicate at all, since it's not part of the result (i.e., the result has no CITY attribute). You go on to suggest that we might as well include further arbitrary terms such as "... and has been in business for some number of years, and employs some number of workers, and contributes to some political party" (and so on). However, later you say: "Do we mention the city only because the projection is derived from a relvar that has a CITY attribute?" I hope you can now see that the answer to this latter question is *yes. The output predicate depends on the input predicate* (or input predicates, plural, but there's only one in the example). If—but only if—the input predicate had mentioned "number of years in business" (for example), then the output predicate would have had to have done so too.

You also say:

> Imagine we had a relvar that has the same heading as relvar S except that it has no CITY attribute. This is the same as the result of the projection of S on all but CITY, yet I believe the correct predicate is simply:

> > *Supplier SNO is under contract, is named SNAME, and has status STATUS.*

I'm afraid you're under a serious misconception here. Your imagined relvar is *not* "the same as the result of the projection of relvar S on all but CITY." I agree it has the same attributes; it might even have the same tuples, at some particular time; but it doesn't follow that the two are the same (even if they do happen to "compare equal"). *It depends on the predicates*; in fact, the two relvars would be the same if and only if they had the same predicates. But we've already agreed (I hope!—see the VACATIONS example earlier) that the predicate for a given relvar is whatever the definer says it is—it's not innate. Thus, you're at liberty to say the predicate for your revised suppliers relvar is what you say it is:

> *Supplier SNO is under contract, is named SNAME, and has status STATUS.*

But even if you do, there's no contradiction or inconsistency with my claim to the effect that the predicate for the projection of the original suppliers relvar on all but CITY is what *I* say it is:

> *Supplier SNO is under contract, is named SNAME, has status STATUS, and is located in some (unspecified) city CITY.*

Or simplifying slightly:

> *Supplier SNO is under contract, is named SNAME, has status STATUS, and is located somewhere.*

Of course, you're also fully at liberty to say the predicate for your imagined relvar is something entirely different—perhaps:

> *Supplier SNO is a friend of mine, has a cat called SNAME, and lives STATUS miles outside town.*

Still no contradiction—though it's probably a bad design, if only because you've named the attributes so misleadingly. In fact, I'd like to close this discussion by following up on this latter point briefly. A good rule of thumb is this:

> Other things being equal, a given attribute name should have the same denotation wherever it appears.

That's why, for example, the "supplier number" attributes in relvars S and SP are both called SNO. In other words, I recommend rather strongly that you *not* do what I've seen other writers recommend you do: viz., play silly games in such cases by giving such attributes different names, such as SNO in relvar S but SNUM in relvar SP.

By the way, note that it follows from the foregoing recommendation that attributes having different denotations should have different names. That's why, if the predicate for your imagined relvar truly is "Supplier SNO is a friend of mine, has a cat called SNAME, and lives STATUS miles outside town," then I'd feel obliged to criticize your choice of attribute names. (Of course, I'm assuming here that we're talking about a design that includes both your imagined relvar and the original suppliers relvar. If it includes just one of the two, there's no problem—or not so much of a problem, at any rate.)

Chapter 12

Relation Valued Attributes

The sinister First Order ... the diabolical First Order ...
—Lawrence Kasdan, J J. Abrams, and Michael Arndt:
Star Wars VI: The Force Awakens (2015);
J. J. Abrams and Chris Terrio:
Star Wars IX: The Rise of Skywalker (2019)

A DETAILED EXAMPLE

In recent writings you seem to embrace the idea of relation valued attributes (RVAs). But don't RVAs violate first normal form?

The idea that relation valued attributes might violate first normal form (1NF for short) is based on a confusion between RVAs and repeating groups—a confusion to which I was subject myself for many years, I hasten to add. Well ... perhaps a better way to put it is: The RVA concept is well defined, the repeating group concept isn't (at least, it doesn't seem to have a unique definition that's universally accepted in the community at large). And while RVAs as such don't violate 1NF, repeating groups—depending on how that term is defined—might. For a detailed elaboration of this position, see reference [9].

Let's look at an example in which an RVA might be a good idea. Suppose we need to design a relvar to represent the predicate *X and Y live together—* which I take to mean, more precisely, *X and Y are distinct individuals, they live together, and nobody else lives with X and Y.* Perhaps the most obvious design involves a binary relvar R2 {X,Y}—I call it "R2" because it's of degree two— with the constraint, which I'll call C2, that the tuple $<x,y>$ appears in R2 if and only if the tuple $<y,x>$ also appears in R2 (in other words, R2 is *symmetric*, in the sense of that term explained in Chapter 9—but note the redundancy implied by that symmetry):

```
VAR R2 BASE
    RELATION { X ... , Y ... }
    KEY { X }
    KEY { Y } ;

CONSTRAINT C2
    ( R2 RENAME { X AS Y , Y AS X } ) = R2 ;
```

Here's a sample R2 value:

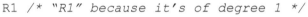

```
R2 /* "R2" because it's of degree 2 */
```

X	Y
Amy	Bob
Bob	Amy
Cal	Dee
Dee	Cal

However, I greatly prefer the alternative design illustrated below:

```
R1 /* "R1" because it's of degree 1 */
```

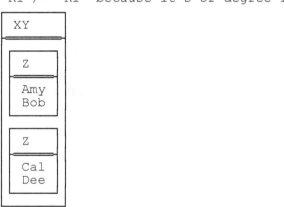

As you can see, my preferred design consists of a unary relvar R1 {XY} whose sole attribute XY has values that are unary relations containing exactly two tuples each. (The sample value just shown corresponds to the sample value for R1 shown above.) Here's the relvar definition:

```
VAR R1 BASE
    RELATION { XY RELATION { Z ... } }
    KEY { XY } ;
```

This design, it seems to me, more directly reflects the symmetric predicate *X and Y live together*—or, slightly more precisely, the predicate *XY is a pair of individuals who live together* (and note how it avoids the redundancy inherent in the R2 design). By contrast, the R2 design reflects the less obviously symmetric predicate *X lives with Y*, and it explicitly requires enforcement of constraint C2 in order to capture the symmetry property. Of course, both designs require a constraint to ensure that each "pair" does indeed contain exactly two persons, and another to ensure that no person is included in more than one pair. Here are suitable definitions for relvar R1 (the one with the RVA):

```
CONSTRAINT R1_PAIRS_HAVE_CARDINALITY_TWO
    IS_EMPTY ( R1 WHERE COUNT ( XY ) ≠ 2 ) ;

CONSTRAINT R1_PAIRS_ARE_DISJOINT
    COUNT ( R1 UNGROUP XY ) = 2 * COUNT ( R1 ) ;
```

For relvar R2, by contrast, life is arguably a little more complicated; we need the combination of (a) constraint C2 (the symmetry constraint), (b) a constraint to the effect that no tuple has X = Y (i.e., reflexivity does not apply), and (c) constraints to the effect that {X} and {Y} are both keys (incidentally implying that transitivity doesn't apply, either). Together, these constraints do the trick—though as already suggested the redundancy implied by constraint C2 is a little worrisome.

> *Aside:* You might be thinking there's still a third possible design, a binary relvar R3 with attributes PAIR and PERSON (where PAIR is a "pair identifier" of some kind). However, this design really represents a different predicate—*Person PERSON is a member of pair PAIR*—and for that reason I don't want to discuss it any further here. *End of aside.*

Of course, the R1 and R2 designs can each be derived from the other (i.e., they're information equivalent); I'll explain those derivations in just a moment. First, however, let me just mention that a particularly strong argument, it seems to me, in favor of the R1 design is that it extends gracefully to the case of *N* individuals living together for arbitrary *N* (with a predicate along the lines of *X, Y, et al., are all distinct, they live together, and nobody else lives with X, Y, et al.*). The R2 design does not extend analogously—at least, not well.

Now let me explain how each of R1 and R2 can be derived from the other. Here's a definition of R1 in terms of R2:

```
R1 ≝ ( EXTEND R2 :
          { XY := RELATION
                { TUPLE { Z X } , TUPLE { Z Y } } } { XY }
```

(Note, incidentally, how this definition ensures that the cardinality of R1 is exactly half that of R2.) Defining R2 in terms of R1 is rather more complicated, but the following does the trick:

```
R2 ≝ WITH
        ( T1 := EXTEND R1 : { XYZ := WITH
                ( T2 := RELATION { TUPLE { * } } ,
                  T3 := T2 UNGROUP XY ,
                  T4 := T3 RENAME { Z AS X } ,
                  T5 := T3 RENAME { Z AS Y } ,
                  T6 := T4 JOIN T5 ,
                  T7 := T6 WHERE X ≠ Y ) : T7 } ) :
    ( T1 { XYZ } ) UNGROUP XYZ
```

This needs a certain amount of explanation, I think! Let's start by considering the subexpression RELATION {TUPLE {*}}. First of all, the syntactic construct TUPLE {*} is a shorthand that can be used within any **Tutorial D** expression—but *only* within such an expression—that can be thought of as being evaluated for each tuple in turn of some relation, and it denotes "the current tuple" during the process of that evaluation.[1] In the case at hand, for example, it's being used in the context of an EXTEND on the current value (*r1*, say) of relvar R1; thus, it can be thought of as denoting the current tuple (*t1*, say) of that relation *r1* during evaluation of that EXTEND. So the subexpression RELATION {TUPLE {*}} denotes the unique relation containing just that tuple *t1*. For example, if *t1* is the first of the tuples in the picture of the sample value for relvar R1 on page 248, then that relation—referred to in the inner WITH clause, within the foregoing overall expression, as *T2*—looks like this:

---

[1] The shorthand in question is explained in detail in Chapter 13, "Image Relations," of this book's predecessor *Logic and Relational Theory: Thoughts and Essays on Database Matters* (Technics Publications, 2020). *Note:* Because relvar R1 has just one attribute, the "longhand" or expanded form (i.e., of the expression TUPLE{*}) in this particular case isn't actually very long!—it's just TUPLE {XY XY}, where the first XY is an attribute name and the second denotes the value of the attribute of that name within "the current tuple" of the relation that's the current value of relvar R1.

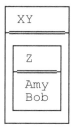

For that same tuple *t1*, therefore, relations *T3*, *T4*, *T5*, *T6*, and *T7* look like this (from left to right):[2]

Z
Amy
Bob

X
Amy
Bob

Y
Amy
Bob

X	Y
Amy	Amy
Amy	Bob
Bob	Amy
Bob	Bob

X	Y
Amy	Bob
Bob	Amy

For the other tuple in our sample R1 value, of course, the corresponding relations *T3*, *T4*, *T5*, *T6*, and *T7* look much the same except that Cal replaces Amy and Dee replaces Bob (or Cal replaces Bob and Dee replaces Amy, I suppose). So the EXTEND result, relation *T1*, looks like this:

XY	XYZ	
Z Amy Bob	**X** Amy Bob	**Y** Bob Amy
Z Cal Dee	**X** Cal Dee	**Y** Dee Cal

---

[2] Note how, since *T4* and *T5* have no attributes in common, the join in the definition of *T6* degenerates to cartesian product.

And projecting away attribute XY from this relation and ungrouping the result on XYZ yields the R2 value corresponding to our sample R1 value:

X	Y
Amy	Bob
Bob	Amy
Cal	Dee
Dee	Cal

————— ◆ ◆ ◆ ◆ ◆ —————

What follows is a kind of postscript to the foregoing discussion. *The Third Manifesto* [10] includes the following "very strong suggestion":[3]

> *The system should provide a mechanism by which an arbitrary relation can be extended to include an attribute whose values (a) are unique within that relation and (b) are supplied by the system.*

If this suggestion were adopted, defining R2 in terms of R1 could be done a little more straightforwardly as follows:

```
R2 ≝ WITH ( T1 := EXTEND R1 :
                    { XY' := XY RENAME { Z AS Z' } } ,
            T2 := TAG ( T1 , Q ) ,
            T3 := ( ( T2 UNGROUP XY ) UNGROUP XY' ,
            T4 := T3 WHERE Z ≠ Z' ,
            T5 := T4 RENAME { Z AS X , Z' AS Y } ) :
      T5 { ALL BUT Q }
```

Let's go through this definition one step at a time, again using the sample value for R1 shown on page 248 as a basis for explanations. First of all, *T1* looks like this:

---

[3] For present purposes I've simplified that "very strong suggestion" considerably. There's actually quite a lot more to it than my text and subsequent example might suggest.

XY	XY'

Z	Z'
Amy Bob	Amy Bob

Z	Z'
Cal Dee	Cal Dee

The next step is where the *Manifesto* "very strong suggestion" comes in. The basic idea behind the hypothetical operator TAG is as follows: It allows us to tag the tuples of the result of a given relational expression in such a way that each tuple in the result is given a unique numeric tag in the range 1 to N, where N is the cardinality of that result. In the example, therefore, *T2*—the result of the expression TAG(*T1*,Q)—might look like this:[4]

XY	XY'	Q

Z	Z'	1
Amy Bob	Amy Bob	

Z	Z'	2
Cal Dee	Cal Dee	

T3 thus looks like this:

---

[4] The result isn't unique, in general, because TAG involves a certain amount of unpredictability (that's why I say the result *might* look as shown). However, such results are at least required to be *repeatable*, in the sense that (other things being equal) a given expression should always return the same output given the same input, even if it involves an invocation of TAG. For more details, see reference [10].

Z	Z'	Q
Amy	Amy	1
Amy	Bob	1
Bob	Amy	1
Bob	Bob	1
Cal	Cal	2
Cal	Dee	2
Dee	Cal	2
Dee	Dee	2

The remainder of the definition is now straightforward. First, *T4* is the leftmost of the following three relations:

Z	Z'	Q
Amy	Bob	1
Bob	Amy	1
Cal	Dee	2
Dee	Cal	2

X	Y	Q
Amy	Bob	1
Bob	Amy	1
Cal	Dee	2
Dee	Cal	2

X	Y
Amy	Bob
Bob	Amy
Cal	Dee
Dee	Cal

T5 is the same, except that attributes Z and Z' are renamed X and Y, respectively (it's shown above in the middle), and the final result (the projection of *T5* on all but Q, shown above on the right) is clearly equal to R2 (again see page 248, or else page 252).

THE GUARANTEED ACCESS RULE

Following on from my previous question, what about Codd's "Guaranteed Access Rule"? Don't RVAs violate that?

Well, it depends on how you interpret that rule! I strongly suspect that Codd would have said that RVAs do violate it—see reference [2], where he at least suggested that RVAs should be eliminated if possible—but I don't agree. Here's the exact wording of the Guaranteed Access Rule as Codd originally formulated it in reference [3]:

Each and every datum (atomic value) in a relational database is guaranteed to be logically accessible by resorting to a combination of table name, primary key value, and column name.

The wording as he gave it later in reference [4] is almost but not quite identical:

Each and every datum (atomic value) stored in a relational database is guaranteed to be logically accessible by resorting to a combination of R-table name, primary key value, and column name.

The only differences are that (a) "datum ... in" has been replaced by "datum ... stored in" and (b) "table name" has been replaced by "R-table name."

Now, there are things I like about this rule as stated and things I don't (with, perhaps, the former outweighing the latter). I certainly like the idea that all access is associative—more specifically, I like the implication that columns are referenced by name and not by ordinal position—and I like the implication that no two rows in the same table are identical, and hence that every "datum" is logically accessible by, in effect, specifying the row and column intersection that contains it.[5] By contrast, here are some things I don't like so much:

■ I reject the notion of "each and every datum" being an "atomic value"; more precisely, I reject the notion of data value atomicity, at least if that notion is supposed to have any kind of absolute meaning (see, e.g., reference [9] for further explanation). That's why I don't agree that RVAs violate the rule—a "datum" that happens to be a relation value is still a perfectly valid "datum." (As noted in my answer to the previous question in this chapter, I might agree that repeating groups violate the rule, but that's not the same thing. Again, see reference [9] for further discussion.)

■ I reject the suggestion that "each and every datum" must be "stored." If the Guaranteed Access Rule applies to relations at all, it must apply to *all* relations, be they "stored relations" (whatever those might be), base relations, views, snapshots, intermediate results, final results, catalog relations, or whatever. (Actually I'm quite surprised to see Codd mentioning things being "stored" at all, since the relational model very deliberately has nothing to say about physical storage matters.)

---

[5] Although I usually prefer to use the terminology of relations, tuples, and attributes, I use the terminology of tables, rows, and columns here because Codd's rule does the same (in both versions).

■ I would vastly prefer to see the rule being formulated in terms of *relvars* rather than relations (or tables, or "R-tables"). It's true that *at any given time* a database can be thought of as containing relations as such (those relations being the values at that time of the relvars in the database), but we surely want a rule that applies at all times, not just at some given time. (I should explain that Codd's terminology of "R-tables" wasn't an attempt to get at the logical difference between relations and relvars; rather, it was intended to get at the logical difference between those tables that do faithfully represent relations and those—like SQL's, most of the time!— that don't.)

■ For reasons documented in reference [6], I reject the reference to primary keys as such. I do believe that every relvar has to have at least one candidate key (which for simplicity I usually abbreviate to just *key*). Moreover, I don't object to the idea of optionally allowing some key out of the set of keys that apply to a given relvar to be chosen as "primary." However, I do object to the idea that a primary key might be *required*, and I don't agree with any approach that gives primary keys some special semantic properties that don't apply to keys in general.

As you can see, therefore, on some of these points at least I find myself in disagreement with Codd. If you find this state of affairs surprising, let me also say this: Ted Codd was my friend and mentor, and I'll always be grateful to him for inventing the relational model and thereby giving me (and so many others) the basis for such an endlessly interesting and satisfying career. What's more, I worked directly with Ted for many years, first at IBM, and then subsequently in our joint consulting company Codd and Date, Inc. But these facts don't mean that we always saw eye to eye on technical matters, and sometimes we didn't.

SECOND ORDER LOGIC (?)

One more question on relation valued attributes: Don't such attributes take us into the realm of second order logic?

This is a big question! It's also one that's asked quite frequently. Unfortunately, I'm not a logician, so there's no way I can answer it definitively; however, I do know the relational model well, and I've been impressed—not positively, I should add—by the logicians I've discussed the issue with, who've universally failed to answer the question in a way that made any sense to me. More specifically, I've been impressed, again not positively, by the fact that none of those logicians has managed to demonstrate to me any actual problem that might be caused by the fact—if fact it is—that RVAs do mean second order logic. Nor have I seen anything close to a comprehensible account of the matter in the literature.

Given all of the foregoing, I think it's worth attempting to provide at least a kind of layperson's response to the question. In fact, I'd like to raise a few related questions of my own. Thus, what follows can be seen as a plea for somebody who really knows both logic and the relational model to come up with a coherent, comprehensible, and definitive statement on the issue. Indeed, the very fact that no such statement exists at the time of writing (so far as I know) is, I think, telling in itself. (Speaking purely for myself here, I'd like to add that what I'd really like to see is not just some kind of abstract discussion of the matter; rather, I'd like to see a concrete proposal for a second order relational language,[6] with concrete examples of the problems if any that arise with such a language and are due to its second order nature.)

I'll start with a little historical background. The debate in this context over first vs. second order logic goes all the way back to Codd's original papers. In 1969, in his very first paper on the relational model [1], Codd said the following:

> The adoption of a relational view of data ... permits the development of a universal retrieval sublanguage based on the second order predicate calculus.

(For the purposes of the present discussion, at least, the terms *predicate calculus* and *logic* can be taken as meaning the exact same thing.) In his better known 1970 paper [2], by contrast, he said the following:

> The adoption of a relational model of data ... permits the development of a universal data sublanguage based on an applied predicate calculus. A first order predicate calculus suffices if the collection of relations is in normal form.

---

[6] Unless **Tutorial D** already is such a language, I suppose I have to add.

Normal form, to Codd at that time, just meant "no RVAs"[7]—indeed, one of the biggest differences between the 1969 and 1970 papers was precisely that the 1969 paper permitted RVAs and the 1970 paper didn't. As you can see, therefore, Codd was effectively claiming that RVAs meant second order logic; what's more, he was apparently also claiming, at least implicitly, that second order logic was somehow undesirable and first order logic was to be preferred.

> *Aside:* It's relevant to mention here that when I drew the attention of one particular logician—one I do respect more than most, perhaps—to these remarks of Codd's (in particular, to the implication of those remarks spelled out in the second sentence of the foregoing paragraph), he instantly and simply replied "Oh, Codd was wrong." *End of aside.*

So what do the terms *first order logic* and *second order logic* mean? Well, here are some definitions (taken from reference [7] but slightly reworded here):

Definition (first order logic): A form of predicate logic in which the sets over which variables range aren't allowed to contain predicates.

Definition (second order logic): A form of predicate logic in which the sets over which variables range are allowed to contain predicates.

An example of a predicate that's definitely first order is the relvar predicate for the suppliers relvar S:

Supplier SNO is under contract, is named SNAME, has status STATUS, and is located in city CITY.

The variables here—variables in the sense of logic, that is, not programming language variables (see Chapter 15)—are SNO, SNAME, STATUS, and CITY, and they range over the set of all supplier numbers, the set of all names, the set of all integers, and the set of all character strings, respectively. Since the values in those sets certainly aren't predicates, we can say the predicate for S is first order.

---

[7] It doesn't mean that now! As explained in my book *Database Design and Relational Theory: Normal Forms and All That Jazz*, 2nd edition (Apress, 2019), *all* relations—or all relvars, rather—are "in normal form"; that is, they're all in first normal form at the very least, and often in some higher normal form as well. Even if they have RVAs.

An example of a second order predicate is the predicate that defines the fundamental notion of *equality*:

```
FORALL x FORALL y
              ( ( x = y ) ≡ FORALL P ( P ( x ) ≡ P ( y ) ) )
```

In somewhat stilted English: For all x and y, x and y are equal if and only if, for all predicates P, the effect of applying P to x and the effect of applying P to y are the same. So the parameter P ranges over the set of all monadic predicates (I assume P to be monadic here for simplicity), and the overall predicate is thus second order.

So one question that arises immediately is this: The relational model most certainly relies on the notion of equality; so doesn't this fact mean we're already relying on second order logic anyway, regardless of whether we allow RVAs or not?

Onward. I believe one simple way to point up the difference between first and second order logic in database terms is as follows (this characterization might help if, like me, you have no training in formal logic):

■ First order logic allows us to ask, for example, whether there exists a tuple for supplier S1 in the current value of the suppliers relvar.

■ Second order logic, by contrast, would enable us to ask whether there exists a tuple for supplier S1 in the current value of the entire database.[8]

So my next question is: Is the foregoing characterization accurate? If it is, it certainly suggests that support for second order logic might be a nice thing to have.

Aside: I should explain that second order logic isn't the end of the road. Here's a general definition (it's recursive, as you can see):

Definition (order of a predicate): Let P be a predicate. If P involves no variables (i.e., if it's a proposition), it's of order zero; otherwise, if it has at least one variable denoting some predicate of order N and no variable denoting some predicate of order greater than N, then it's of order $N + 1$.

---

[8] I.e., does there exist a relation r in the database right now such that there exists a tuple for supplier S1 in r? Since (in a sense) relations correspond to predicates, "does there exist a relation r ...?" suggests that the variable r ranges over a set of predicates. Maybe. Further discussion to follow almost immediately!

Note: With reference to the defining predicate I gave earlier for equality (which I said was second order), we have to assume that predicate *P* in that definition is first order; otherwise that defining predicate might be third or even higher order. *End of aside.*

Anyway, the question now arises: What exactly is the connection between second order logic as sketched above and RVAs? Well, every relvar *R* corresponds to some predicate *P*, and the attributes of *R* correspond to the parameters (free variables) of *P*; thus, if *R* has an RVA, the corresponding parameter is relation valued. Note carefully, however, that the corresponding parameter is indeed *relation* valued—it isn't *relvar* valued. If it were relvar valued (if such a possibility could somehow be made to make sense), then I suppose we might say that relvar *R* was "a second order relvar," since it would apparently correspond to a predicate one of whose parameters corresponded to a predicate in turn. But a relvar with an RVA is not, it seems to me, a "second order relvar"; in any given tuple of such a relvar, the attributes have values that are ... well, values, not variables. There's no such thing in the relational model as a "second order relvar."

Aside: To elaborate briefly: A "second order relvar"—i.e., a relvar with a relvar valued attribute—would be a variable with other variables nested inside itself. Now, I've argued elsewhere (see, e.g., reference [8]) that the idea of one variable being nested inside another makes no logical sense.[9] But maybe I was wrong. (This is another question for the logicians, perhaps, though I observe that logicians have no concept of variables at all in the sense in which I'm using that term here, so I'm not even sure it's a matter of logic anyway.) Be that as it may, it does seem as if "relvar valued attributes" might be what we'd have to add to the relational model in order to support second order logic. *End of aside.*

Onward again. Those who complain that RVAs mean second order logic often go on to claim that second logic can lead to a lack of decidability or the possibility of paradoxes or both. I respond to these claims as follows:[10]

---

[9] In case you were wondering, the possibility that *the database itself* might be thought of as "a variable containing variables" is explained (and explained away) in Chapter 4.

[10] Though honesty compels me to admit that we—where by "we" I mean those of us who embrace the idea of RVAs—might be in violation of *The Principle of Cautious Design* in this regard [5].

- *Undecidability:* Apparently we have this problem anyway, regardless of whether we support second order logic, and I've already dealt with it in Chapter 5 of this book.

- *Paradoxes:* As far as I know, the paradoxes in question all arise from some kind of self reference. I've already dealt with this issue too, in Chapter 3. Though perhaps I should add that, as I understand it, there are ways, even in second (and higher) order logic, of preventing paradoxes from occurring: Basically, all we have to do is enforce a rule to the effect that no predicate of order N is allowed to appear where a predicate of order M ($M < N$) is expected.

One last point: RVAs might not be the only point at issue here. To be specific, *The Third Manifesto* [10] embraces at least two other constructs that might be regarded as introducing some aspects of second order logic into the relational model. The first is the transitive closure operator, TCLOSE; the second is the *n*-adic versions of certain operators (for example, union and join). All of these operators have definitions that are essentially recursive and (so far as I know) can't be expressed in first order logic. Hence two final questions:[11] Does the availability of these operators have any negative implications for the model—with respect to second order logic in particular? And if so, what are they?

My apologies to all concerned if the foregoing discussion turns out to be nothing but muddle and confusion on my part.

REFERENCES AND BIBLIOGRAPHY

1. E. F. Codd: "Derivability, Redundancy, and Consistency of Relations Stored in Large Data Banks," IBM Research Report RJ599 (August 19th, 1969).

2. E. F. Codd: "A Relational Model of Data for Large Shared Data Banks," *CACM 13*, No. 6 (June 1970).

---

[11] For now!

3. E. F. Codd: "Is Your DBMS Really Relational?" and "Does Your DBMS Run by the Rules?" (*Computerworld*, October 14th and October 21st, 1985, respectively).

4. E. F. Codd: *The Relational Model for Database Management Version 2.* Reading, Mass.: Addison-Wesley (1990).

5. C. J. Date: "*The Principle of Cautious Design,*" in C. J. Date and Hugh Darwen, *Relational Database Writings 1989-1991.* Reading, Mass.: Addison-Wesley (1992).

6. C. J. Date: "Primary Keys Are Nice but Not Essential, in *Database Design and Relational Theory: Normal Forms and All That Jazz,* 2nd edition (Apress, 2019).

7. C. J. Date: *The New Relational Database Dictionary.* Sebastopol, Calif.: O'Reilly Media Inc. (2016).

8. C. J. Date: "On the Logical Differences Between Types, Values, and Variables," in *Date on Database: Writings 2000-2006.* Berkeley, Calif.: Apress (2006).

9. C. J. Date: "What First Normal Form Really Means," in *Date on Database: Writings 2000-2006.* Berkeley, Calif.: Apress (2006).

10. C. J. Date and Hugh Darwen: *Databases, Types, and the Relational Model: The Third Manifesto* (3rd edition). Boston, Mass.: Addison-Wesley (2007).

Chapter 13

Normalization and Keys

We are normal and we want our freedom
—Neil Innes and Vivian Stanshall
(from the album *The Doughnut in Granny's Greenhouse*
by The Bonzo Dog Doo Dah Band, 1968)

SECOND NORMAL FORM

I'm confused about normal forms. In your book *An Introduction to Database Systems* (8th edition), page 369, you give an example of a relvar you say is in 3NF but not BCNF. But it seems to me it isn't even in 2NF, and hence not in 3NF either, let alone BCNF. What's going on?

Let me begin by repeating the original example as given in that book (reference [2]). We're given a relvar SSP that looks like this (in outline):

```
SSP { SNO , SNAME , PNO , QTY }
     KEY { SNO , PNO }
     KEY { SNAME , PNO }
```

What's more, the following functional dependencies (FDs) hold in this relvar (in addition to ones implied by the keys, of course):

```
{ SNO } → { SNAME }
{ SNAME } → { SNO }
```

Now, in reference [2] I claim, correctly, that this relvar SSP is not in BCNF. But is it in 2NF? If it isn't, then I agree that, as the question says, it's not in 3NF either, a fortiori, let alone BCNF.

Well, the reason it might be thought not to be in 2NF is that:

a.   If we choose—arbitrarily—{SNO,PNO} as the primary key, then {SNAME}, though necessarily functionally dependent on that primary key, isn't *irreducibly* so,[1] and

b.   2NF is usually thought of as requiring every attribute to be irreducibly dependent on the primary key.

But point b. here is a misconception. Now, I fear this misconception is a common one, and it's partly my fault ... In the section of reference [2] that explains 2NF (also 1NF and 3NF), I deliberately indulged in some "creative lying," as it were; that is, I deliberately simplified some of the material for pedagogic reasons. In my own defense, however, let me note that I did call out that fact quite explicitly in that book! The very first paragraph of the section in question reads as follows (boldface and italics as in the original):

> *Caveat: Throughout this section, we assume for simplicity that each relvar has exactly one candidate key, which we further assume is the primary key. These assumptions are reflected in our definitions, which (we repeat) are not very rigorous. The case of a relvar having more than one candidate key is discussed in [a later section].*

And here's the "not very rigorous" definition of 2NF from that same section, also quoted more or less verbatim (please note the qualification in italics):

> **Definition (second normal form—*definition assuming just one candidate key, referred to here as the primary key*):** A relvar is in 2NF if and only if it is in 1NF and every nonkey attribute is irreducibly dependent on the primary key.

Two points arise immediately:

■   First, in a relvar with a primary key and no other candidate keys, a nonkey attribute is just an attribute that's not part of the primary key. More generally, though, a nonkey attribute is any attribute that isn't a key attribute, and a key attribute in turn is any attribute that participates in at least one candidate key.

---

[1] Because it's also functionally dependent on a proper subset of that key, viz., {SNO}. See later in this chapter for further discussion of this kind of irreducibility.

■ Second, if I were to rewrite that book today, I'd frame the foregoing definition of 2NF (and all other normal form definitions) in terms of *sets* of attributes, or equivalently in terms of subsets of the heading, instead of in terms of individual attributes per se.

Anyway, here by contrast is a precise definition (it's essentially the original definition as given by Codd in reference [1], back in 1971):[2]

> **Definition (second normal form per Codd):** A relvar is in 2NF if it's in 1NF and every nonkey attribute is irreducibly dependent on each candidate key.

Going back to the SSP example, then, the problem with that relvar is that attributes SNO and SNAME are both key attributes. Relvar SSP is thus in 2NF (3NF also, in fact) by Codd's original definition, even though it looks as if it isn't in 2NF, let alone 3NF, according to my (over)simplified definition.

By the way, Codd's 2NF definition is certainly correct, of course, but (with a great deal of hindsight) I don't care for it all that much. For one thing, I now think the various normal form definitions should all be independent of one another (i.e., I don't much care for definitions along the lines of "Relvar R is in $(n+1)$st normal form if it's in nth normal form and ...").[3] Here's a revised form of Codd's definition that avoids mention of 1NF:

> **Definition (second normal form):** Relvar R is in 2NF if and only if, for every key K of R and every nonkey attribute A of R, the FD $K \rightarrow \{A\}$ (which holds in R, necessarily) is irreducible.

In practice, however, I prefer the following definition:

> **Definition (second normal form, preferred):** Relvar R is in second normal form (2NF) if and only if, for every nontrivial FD $X \rightarrow Y$ that holds in R, at least one of the following is true:

---

[2] Codd used the term "nonprime attribute" in place of my "nonkey attribute," but the meaning is the same. *Note:* He also used "relation" in place of my "relvar"—but then he never used the term "relvar" at all, either in reference [1] or in any of his other writings.

[3] In a sense, though, this first criticism of mine is vacuous in the case at hand (i.e., as far as Codd's 2NF definition is concerned), because *all* relvars are in at least 1NF (see Chapter 12, footnote 7).

a. *X* is a superkey.

b. *Y* is a subkey.

c. *X* is not a subkey.

The two definitions are logically equivalent, of course (exercise for the reader!), but for reasons beyond the scope of the present discussion the second can sometimes be more useful. Further discussion and explanation can be found in reference [4]. Here let me just give for the record definitions of the useful concepts *superkey* and *subkey*:

Definition (superkey): Let *SK* be a subset of the heading of relvar *R*. Then *SK* is a superkey for *R* if and only if no legitimate value for *R* contains two distinct tuples with the same value for *SK*. (In other words, a superkey for *R* is a subset of the heading of *R* that includes some key of *R* as a subset.)

Definition (subkey): Let *SK* be a subset of the heading of relvar *R*. Then *SK* is a subkey for *R* if and only if it's a subset of at least one key of *R*.

FOURTH NORMAL FORM

In various writings you give as an example of a violation of fourth normal form (4NF) a relvar CTX with attributes C (course), T (teacher), and X (text). You say this relvar is all key. But a key by definition has to be the identifier of something, and there's no "something"—no entity—that's identified by the combination of C, T, and X. So making a relvar out of the three attributes was senseless and in my opinion wrong from the beginning. I believe a relvar should consist of a key and at least one additional attribute, functionally dependent on that key. For practical reasons, a relvar might consist of a key only (if we're not interested in any additional attributes), but surely it must be shown that conceptually there *exists* at least one attribute that depends on this key. I believe that with this definition every relvar is automatically in 4NF.

A lot to unpack here! First let me repeat in outline the example you mention, involving relvar CTX. As you say, that relvar has just three attributes, C, T, and X. The predicate is:

Course C can be taught by teacher T and uses text X as a textbook.

The example also stipulates that for a given course, the set of teachers and the set of texts are quite independent of each other; that is, no matter which teacher actually teaches some particular offering of some course, the same texts are used. As a consequence—indeed, as reference [2] shows—it turns out that the relvar is in BCNF but not 4NF.

Now I can respond to the various points in your question:

- First, and despite what your question claims, the relvar just *is* all key. Of course, I'm appealing here to the formal definition of the term *key*; after all, the relational model is a formal system, and all of its features or components thus have formal definitions—necessarily so. Now, we naturally hope those formal definitions have a good correspondence with certain informally defined constructs in the real world; to the extent such a correspondence can be found, the relational model will be a good basis for dealing with real world problems. Do please note, however, that the correspondence will be informal too!—we can't have a formal mapping between something formal and something informal, by definition.

- By contrast, you seem to think the term *key* should be used to mean something informal, not formal. Well, you're at liberty to use the term that way if you want to—but you're not then at liberty to criticize the relational model because its use of terminology is different from yours. You can't have your cake and eat it too.

- Even given your informal concept of what a key is, though, I can't believe you really want to insist that "entities" *must* have additional attributes. For example, consider the relvar HOLIDAYS, with just one attribute, DATE, which simply lists all the national holidays for some country. For another example, consider the relvar FRIENDS with two attributes A and B, with predicate "A and B are friends." And so on.

■ You say that "making a relvar out of attributes C, T, and X was senseless in the first place" (slightly paraphrased). Well, that might be true; in fact, the discussion in reference [2] goes on to make the same point (see page 386). But the point is an informal one ... The whole *raison d'être* of normalization theory is to come up with formal arguments to bolster up our informal intuition. Informally, we might say CTX is a bad design. Formally, normalization theory tells us exactly *why* it's a bad design. What's more, if we can formalize such matters, we can go on to mechanize them, too (i.e., we can get the machine to do the work). So your objection here really misses the point. (You're not alone here, by the way—most critics of normalization make exactly the same mistake.)

■ You also say "there's no entity that's identified by the combination of C, T, and X." But in any real world database of which relvar CTX might be a part, there'd almost certainly be a relvar for courses (with key {C}), and another for teachers (with key {T}), and another for texts (with key {X})— and then relvar CTX would denote a certain "relationship" among the course, teacher, and text "entities." Now, if you want to argue that "relationships" aren't "entities," you're entitled to your opinion; both terms are fuzzy, so you can make them mean pretty much whatever you want them to mean. But I don't think such an opinion constitutes a valid criticism of the idea that relvars like CTX can and do exist, in practice as well as in theory.

■ You also say you "believe a relvar should consist of a key and at least one additional attribute, functionally dependent on that key, [and] that with this definition every relvar is automatically in 4NF." Well, first, given a relvar *R*, every attribute of *R* is functionally dependent on every key of *R* by definition, so the qualification "functionally dependent on that key" is redundant. Second, here's a counterexample to your claim, viz., a relvar (with, I trust, self-explanatory semantics) that "consists of a key and at least one additional attribute" but isn't in 4NF:

```
EMP { ENO , DNO , BUDGET }
```

Here {ENO} is the key, and the functional dependencies (FDs)

```
{ ENO }  →  { DNO }
{ ENO }  →  { BUDGET }
```

therefore hold, necessarily. The trouble is, the FD

```
{ DNO } → { BUDGET }
```

holds as well; as a consequence, this relvar isn't even in 3NF, and so it certainly isn't in 4NF either.

■ Finally, you say "a relvar might consist of a key only (if we're not interested in any additional attributes), but surely it must be shown that conceptually there *exists* at least one attribute that depends on this key." OK: Let me add an attribute, N, to CTX, that depends on the key {C,T,X}; let me call this extended version of the relvar CTXN, and let the predicate for CTXN be:

> *Course C can be taught by teacher T and uses text X as a textbook, and teacher T spends N days on text X when teaching course C.*

So it can certainly be argued that "conceptually there exists at least one attribute that depends on the key" in this example. What's more, it's true that this extended version of the relvar is in 4NF: It can't be nonloss decomposed into projections in any nontrivial way, because N depends on the combination of all three of CNO, TNO, and XNO, and therefore can't appear in a relvar with anything less than all three. However, none of this alters the fact that the original relvar CTX *isn't* in 4NF! Your conclusion— "I believe that with this definition every relvar is automatically in 4NF"— simply doesn't follow.

DOMAIN-KEY NORMAL FORM

I have difficulty in understanding domain-key normal form (DK/NF). Can you help? In particular, if a relvar has an atomic key and is in 3NF, is it automatically in DK/NF?

I don't blame you for having difficulties here; there's certainly been some nonsense published on this topic in the trade press and elsewhere. Let me see if I can clarify matters.

First of all, DK/NF is best thought of just as a kind of trial balloon. It was introduced by Ron Fagin in reference [8]. In that paper, Fagin defined a relvar *R* to be in DK/NF if and only if every constraint on *R* is a logical consequence of what he called the domain constraints and key constraints on *R*, where:

- By *domain constraint*, he effectively just meant a constraint to the effect that some given attribute *A* of *R* takes its values from some given domain *D* (i.e., is of some given type *D*). *Note:* In my opinion, such a constraint is much better called an *attribute* constraint, and I'll use this latter term throughout the remainder of this discussion.

- By *key constraint*, he simply meant a constraint to the effect that some given subset of the heading of *R* constitutes a key for *R*.

If *R* is in DK/NF, therefore, it's sufficient to enforce the attribute and key constraints for *R*, and all constraints on *R* will be enforced automatically. And enforcing those particular constraints is, of course, very simple (I can't imagine there being a DBMS today that doesn't do it already). To be specific, enforcing attribute constraints just means checking that attribute values are always values from the applicable domain (i.e., are values of the right type), and enforcing key constraints just means checking that key values are unique.

So what's wrong with this idea? Well, there's nothing wrong with the idea as such, as far as it goes. However, it must be clearly understood that:

- First, all of the constraints mentioned in the DK/NF definition (and indeed all of the constraints mentioned anywhere in the present discussion) are *single relvar* constraints specifically. A single relvar constraint is any constraint that can be checked by examining just the pertinent relvar in isolation, i.e., without having to examine any other relvar in the database. Such constraints are to be contrasted with *multirelvar* constraints, which are constraints that involve two or more relvars. In the familiar suppliers-and-parts database, for example, the foreign key constraint from shipments to suppliers and the foreign key constraint from shipments to parts are both multirelvar constraints, and DK/NF has nothing to say about them.

- Second, lots of relvars simply aren't in DK/NF, anyway. For example, suppose there's a constraint on *R* to the effect that *R* must contain at least ten tuples (note that this is indeed a single relvar constraint). Then that constraint is certainly not a consequence of the attribute and key constraints that apply to *R*, and so *R* isn't in DK/NF. The sad fact is, not all relvars can be reduced to DK/NF; nor do we know the answer to the question "Exactly when *can* a relvar be so reduced?"

Now, Fagin does prove in his paper that if relvar *R* is in DK/NF, then it's automatically in 5NF (and hence in 4NF, BCNF, etc.) as well. However, it's wrong to think of DK/NF as another step in the progression from 1NF to 2NF to ... to 5NF. Why? Because the operation that takes us from 1NF to 2NF to ... to 5NF is projection, while the operation (if it even exists) that takes us from 5NF to DK/NF is certainly not projection. What's more, 5NF is always achievable, but (as we've just seen) DK/NF is not.

> *Aside:* A recent book by Darwen, Lorentzos, and myself [6] describes a new (well, fairly new) *sixth* normal form, 6NF. 6NF is "higher" than 5NF (meaning that all 6NF relvars are in 5NF, but the converse isn't true); moreover, 6NF is always achievable, but it isn't implied by DK/NF. In other words, there are relvars in DK/NF that aren't in 6NF. A trivial example is:
>
> ```
> EMP { ENO , DNO , SALARY } KEY { ENO }
> ```
>
> (with the obvious semantics). Thus, DK/NF doesn't imply 6NF. Nor does 6NF imply DK/NF; thus, a relvar can be in either of these two normal forms and not in the other, and so neither one is "higher" than the other. *End of aside*.

"If a relvar has an atomic key and is in 3NF, is it automatically in DK/NF?" Sadly, no.[4] If the EMP relvar just shown is subject to the constraint that there must be at least ten employees, then EMP is in 3NF, and in fact 5NF, but not DK/NF. (Incidentally, this example also answers another frequently asked question: "Can you give an example of a relvar that's in 5NF but not in DK/NF?") *Note:* I'm assuming here that the term "atomic key" means what would more correctly be called a *simple* key; a simple key is one that's not composite, and a composite key is one that consists of two or more attributes.

The net of this discussion is that DK/NF is (at least at the time of writing) a concept that's of some theoretical interest, but little practical interest. The reason is that while it might be nice if all relvars in the database were in DK/NF, we know that goal is impossible to achieve in general; moreover, we don't know

---

[4] Though if a relvar is such that *all* of its keys are "atomic" and it's in 3NF, it's at least in 5NF [7].

exactly when it *is* possible. For practical purposes, therefore, we have to stick to 5NF (or perhaps 6NF).

KEY IRREDUCIBILITY

Keys (i.e., candidate keys generally) are supposed to be unique and irreducible. I understand the uniqueness part, of course, but not the irreducibility part. Please explain.

Your opening statement here is correct—keys are indeed supposed to be both unique and irreducible, where *irreducible* means that if *K* is a key for relvar *R*, then no proper subset of *K* has the uniqueness property (recall that keys are *sets* of attributes, so that expressions like "subset of *K*" do make sense).[5] In other words, we require keys not to contain any attributes that aren't needed for unique identification purposes. For the record, here's a precise definition:

> **Definition (key):** Let *K* be a subset of the heading of relvar *R*; then *K* is a key for, or of, *R* if and only if (a) no possible value for *R* contains two distinct tuples with the same value for *K* (the uniqueness property), while (b) the same can't be said for any proper subset of *K* (the irreducibility property).

There are at least two reasons why key irreducibility is desirable. To see what they are, consider the usual suppliers relvar S and the set of attributes {SNO,CITY}. Let's call that set SC. Then SC certainly has the uniqueness property—no relation that's a possible value for relvar S has two distinct tuples with the same value for SC—but it doesn't have the irreducibility property, because we could discard the CITY attribute and what's left, the set {SNO}, would still have the uniqueness property. So we wouldn't regard SC as a key, because it's "too big" (i.e., it's reducible). By contrast, {SNO} is irreducible, and it's a key.

Why do we want keys to be irreducible? Well, here's one reason (it's not the only one): Suppose we were to specify a "key" that wasn't irreducible. Then the DBMS wouldn't be able to enforce the uniqueness constraint properly. For

---

[5] We've met the term *irreducible* before in this chapter, with a distinct (though related) meaning. To be specific, let *A* and *B* be subsets of the heading of some relvar *R*. Then *B* is *irreducibly dependent* on *A* if it's functionally dependent on *A* and not on any proper subset of *A*.

example, suppose we told the DBMS (lying!) that the combination SC (i.e., {SNO,CITY}) was a key for relvar S. Then the DBMS couldn't enforce the constraint that supplier numbers are "globally" unique; instead, it could enforce only the weaker constraint that supplier numbers are "locally" unique, in the sense that they're unique within city.

A second reason has to do with foreign keys. Suppose again that we specified the combination {SNO,CITY} as a key for relvar S. Now consider the corresponding foreign key in the shipments relvar SP. Clearly, that foreign key, in order to *be* a foreign key according to the formal definition, would also have to include the CITY attribute—and relvar SP would thus involve redundancy. To be specific, the functional dependency {SNO} → {CITY} would hold in that relvar; as a consequence, the relvar wouldn't even be in second normal form (let alone 3NF, BCNF, or any higher normal form).

By the way, it's worth pointing out explicitly that, while the DBMS can obviously enforce the uniqueness requirement on keys, it can't enforce the irreducibility requirement. As a consequence, it can't stop users from lying in this regard.[6] And I've even seen situations described in the literature in which such lying is positively encouraged! Such situations usually involve two relvars, *R1* and *R2* say, such that some subset of the heading of *R2* is required to match some proper superkey for *R1* (where (a) a superkey is a set of attributes of the pertinent relvar that form a superset of some key for that relvar, as we already know, and (b) a proper superkey is a superkey that's not a key). By way of example, suppose we're given the following relvars:

```
ED { ENO , DNO }
   KEY { ENO }

DE { DNO , ENO }
   KEY { DNO }
```

The predicates are as follows:

- ED: *Employee ENO works in department DNO.*

- DE: *Department DNO is managed by employee ENO.*

---

[6] Formally speaking, therefore, declaring the key constraint KEY{*K*} for relvar *R* doesn't necessarily mean that {*K*} is a key for *R*—it only means it's at least a superkey (proper or otherwise) for *R*. *Note:* As explained later in the paragraph, a proper superkey is a subset of the pertinent heading that's a proper superset of some key.

Clearly, {ENO} in DE is a foreign key matching the key {ENO} in ED. But suppose now that there's a constraint in effect that says that the manager of a given department must be an employee working in the department in question. In other words, if relvar DE shows department *d* as being managed by employee *e*, then relvar ED must show employee *e* as working in department *e*. Thus, if we could specify {ENO,DNO} as a "key" for ED, then we could formulate that constraint by simply specifying {DNO,ENO} as a matching "foreign key" for DE.

Well, I don't know what you think about this example. My own feeling is that such a comparatively trivial increase in functionality isn't worth destroying the (very well established, and very familiar) semantics of the key and foreign key notions for. And in any case, the increase in functionality isn't really an increase, anyway (I mean, we can easily obtain that "increased functionality" by some other means). In the case at hand, for example, we can easily specify the desired constraint as follows:

```
CONSTRAINT ... DE ⊆ ED ;
```

SIXTH NORMAL FORM

Talking of irreducibility, I've often heard people talking about irreducible relations. What do they mean?

Well, indeed you probably have heard people talking about "irreducible relations," but what they should probably have been talking about is irreducible *relvars*—irreducibility in the sense in which I'm sure they meant it is a property of relvars, not relations. To be specific, a relvar is irreducible if and only if it's in sixth normal form (in other words, *irreducible* in this context is just another term for 6NF). A 6NF relvar is irreducible because it can't be "reduced" or nonloss decomposed via projection into relvars of smaller degree.

However, there's a point worth making here: The "reducibility," or lack thereof, does refer to reducibility via projection specifically. It doesn't mean the relvar in question can't be "reduced" via some other operation. As a concrete example, consider the familiar shipments relvar SP:

```
SP { SNO , PNO , QTY }
```

This relvar is of degree three, and it's certainly irreducible in the 6NF sense; I mean, the relvar is indeed in sixth normal form. However, we could "reduce" it (in a nonloss way, moreover) to a relvar of degree two by means of the GROUP operator, thus:

```
SP GROUP { PNO , QTY } AS PQ
```

Given our usual sample data, this expression yields the result (let's call it *spq*) shown in the picture below. Observe that *spq* is indeed of degree two—its heading (ignoring attribute types as usual) is as follows:

```
{ SNO , PQ RELATION { PNO , QTY } }
```

Note in particular that attribute PQ is relation valued; in other words, it's an RVA. (RVAs are legal, as we saw in Chapter 12.)

SNO	PQ	

S1	PNO	QTY
	P1	300
	P2	200
	P3	400
	P4	200
	P5	100
	P6	100

S2	PNO	QTY
	P1	300

S2	PNO	QTY
	P1	300
	P1	300
	P1	300

S2	PNO	QTY
	P1	300
	P2	400

Note, moreover, that unlike relvar SP, a relvar of this type—equivalently, a relvar with this heading—can legitimately include tuples for suppliers who supply no parts at all. The PQ value in such a tuple would be an empty relation. Here's an example of such a tuple:[7]

---

[7] The absence of any double underlining under attribute SNO in this example isn't a mistake—the picture shows a tuple, not a relation.

SNO	PQ	
S5	PNO	QTY

The foregoing discussion touches on another important point, though. As you might know, many writers have argued over the years that binary relvars are all we need—general *n*-ary relvars are unnecessary. And the fact that a 6NF relvar of degree greater than two can always be "reduced" to a binary relvar in the manner suggested by the foregoing example might possibly lend some (very slight!) credibility to this position. As a matter of fact, several early systems—prototypes, at any rate, if not commercial products—were based exclusively on binary instead of *n*-ary relvars. I have in mind here the following systems among others:

- The Relational Data File (see R. E. Levein and M. E. Maron, "A Computer System for Inference Execution and Data Retrieval," *CACM 10*, No. 11, November 1967)

- TRAMP (see W. Ash and E. H. Sibley, "TRAMP: An Interpretive Associative Processor with Deductive Capabilities," *Proc. ACM 23rd National Conference*, 1968)

- LEAP (see J. A. Feldman and P. D. Rovner, "An Algol-Based Associative Language," *CACM 12*, No. 8, August 1969)[8]

These systems all predated the relational model as such. But I doubt very much whether they included proper support for RVAs! In fact, they would all typically use *three* binary relvars to represent shipment information (not one as in the *spq* example), like this:

---

[8] In connection with Algol, incidentally, I was interested—not to say intrigued—to discover quite recently that the name Algol (meaning the star, of course, not the programming language) derives from an Arabic word meaning "the ghoul."

```
XS { XNO , SNO }

XP { XNO , PNO }

XQ { XNO , QTY }
```

Here XNO is a shipment surrogate, and each real world shipment is represented by exactly one tuple in each of the three relvars XS, XP, and XQ.

So there are at least three approaches to representing shipment information, which I'll refer to for present purposes as "*n*-ary relvar," "binary relvar with an RVA," and "several binary relvars," respectively. Now I'd like to compare those three approaches from various points of view. The first is the number of names the user has to deal with:

- *n-ary relvar:* Four—one relvar name (S) and three attribute names (SNO, PNO, and QTY). In general, of course, an *n*-ary relvar without RVAs always involves $n + 1$ names.

- *Binary relvar with an RVA:* Five—one relvar name (SPQ, say), two attribute names (SNO and PQ), and two "nested" attribute names (PNO and QTY). But suppose the original relvar without RVAs had four attributes instead of three; for definiteness, consider the extended shipments relvar SPJ{SNO,PNO,JNO,QTY}, where JNO is a project number. If all relvars must be binary, we'll have to replace this relvar by one looking something like this, perhaps (I hope my slightly ad hoc notation here is sufficiently self-explanatory):

  ```
  SPJ { SNO , PJQ { PNO , JQ { JNO , QTY } } }
  ```

  Now the user has to deal with seven names instead of five. In general, in fact, it should be clear that this approach requires $2n - 1$ names instead of $n + 1$ (a factor of nearly double; if $n = 30$, for example, it means 59 names instead of 31).

- *Several binary relvars:* Seven (or, more generally, $2n + 1$ names instead of $n + 1$: the original *n* attribute names, *n* relvar names, and the surrogate name—though note too that this latter appears *n* times).

Next, let's think about constraints: specifically, the constraint that every shipment has exactly one supplier number, exactly one part number, and exactly one quantity. How is this constraint formulated in the three cases?

- *N-ary relvar:* The key constraint on SP suffices:

  ```
  KEY { SNO , PNO }
  ```

- *Binary relvar with an RVA:* First, we need the key constraint:

  ```
  KEY { SNO }
  ```

  But we also need a constraint to the effect that part numbers are "unique within supplier":

  ```
  CONSTRAINT ...
     COUNT   ( SPQ UNGROUP PQ ) =
     COUNT ( ( SPQ UNGROUP PQ ) { SNO , PNO } ) ;
  ```

  (Again I'm assuming that SPQ is the binary relvar name.)[9]

- *Several binary relvars:* First, the key constraint

  ```
  KEY { XNO }
  ```

  must be specified for each of XS, XP, and XQ. But we also need to say that each of XS, XP, and XQ contains exactly the same set of XNO values. Here's one way to do that:

  ```
  CONSTRAINT ...
     XS { XNO } = XP { XNO } AND XP { XNO } = XQ { XNO } ;
  ```

  Or we might make use of the system's foreign key mechanism. Note, however, that whatever formulation we choose does seem to involve (necessarily) either some redundancy or some arbitrariness or both.

---

[9] I'm on record (in reference [5] and elsewhere—in fact, in writings dating as far back as 1992) as suggesting that it might be nice if we could specify key constraints for general relational expressions. Such a mechanism would let us specify the constraint under consideration more simply thus: CONSTRAINT ... (SPQ UNGROUP PQ) KEY {SNO,PNO}.

Finally, I'd like to say a little more on the topic of arbitrariness (these observations apply specifically to the design involving an RVA). The fact is, there are three possible designs for shipments that involve just one binary relvar with an RVA. I'll call them SPX, SPY, and SPZ, respectively. In outline, they look like this:

```
SPX { SNO , PQ { PNO , QTY } }

SPY { PNO , QS { QTY , SNO } }

SPZ { QTY , SP { SNO , PNO } }
```

More generally, an *n*-ary relvar without RVAs can be replaced by any of $(n!)/2$ binary relvars with an RVA (where $n!$ = factorial $n = n \times (n-1) \times ... \times 2 \times 1$).[10]

The net of the foregoing analysis is surely obvious: Almost always, the simple *n*-ary relvar without RVAs is the best design. And now let me add the following further observations:

■ As should be clear from discussions in Chapter 3 and elsewhere, we certainly need relations of degree zero (viz., TABLE_DEE and TABLE_DUM), and possibly relvars of degree zero as well.

■ It's obvious that we also need both relations and relvars of degree one (e.g., consider the query "Get all currently assigned supplier numbers").

■ Relational operators (join and so on) are defined to work on operands of arbitrary degree and to produce results of arbitrary degree as well. If we're to limit ourselves to binary relations only, therefore, all of those operators will have to be redefined to take operands and produce results that are always binary relations specifically. (And it's therefore very tempting to add: So what's the point?)

■ Updates are *much* more complicated on the "binary relvar with an RVA" and "several binary relvars" designs than they are with the conventional relational design. I'll leave it as an exercise to think through the specifics

---

[10] Two points here: First, what makes the situation worse in the case at hand is that the first two of those three binary relvars (viz., SPX and SPY) treat suppliers and parts asymmetrically. Second, the number of alternative designs becomes much greater then $(n!)/2$ if the original relvar has enough attributes and we don't limit ourselves to replacing it by, specifically, either (a) binary relvars or (b) relvars with just one RVA or (c) relvars having no RVAs nested inside others.

of this point for yourself. However, some hint as to what's involved can be found in reference [3].

All of the foregoing points serve as strong arguments, I think, against the suggestion that we might want to deal with binary relations only, and I believe they give some idea as to why (at least in my opinion) the "binary relations only" movement has been thoroughly discredited over the years. Despite which, the notion that databases, or (worse) some proposed database "model," should be largely or even exclusively based on "binary relations only" is one that keeps surfacing in the literature, time after time after time[11] ... I leave you to draw your own conclusions.

MORE ON RELVAR IRREDUCIBILITY

All right, I believe you when you say we don't want binary relations only. But isn't there a good argument for saying that base relvars, at least, should always be binary?

Not quite. It's true there's a good argument for saying that base relvars should usually be irreducible, and it's also true that irreducible relvars are often binary. But there are some logical differences here!—between your suggested position, that is, and the true state of affairs. Let me elaborate.

Base relvars should usually be irreducible: Irreducibility means sixth normal form, and sixth normal form is the end of the normalization road (as normalization is usually understood), so all of the usual normalization advantages apply. I'll skip the details here (an extended discussion of such matters can be found in reference [4]).

But not always: Sometimes there's no good reason for breaking a 5NF relvar down into 6NF projections. Consider, for example, a relvar representing scheduled flights. Every flight always has both a scheduled departure time and a scheduled arrival time. Thus, there doesn't seem to be much point in replacing the 5NF relvar

```
FLIGHT { FNO , DEP , ARR }
```

---

[11] I could be wrong, but "RDF triples" in the "Resource Description Framework data model" (which is used, I believe, in the "Semantic Web") look to me very much like a case in point.

by its 6NF projections on {FNO,DEP} and {FNO,ARR}, respectively.

Irreducible relvars are often binary: A relvar R with just one key K and at most one attribute A not part of K is often irreducible—and if K consists of just one attribute, then R is binary. This is a common case. For example, the projections of the suppliers relvar S on {SNO,SNAME}, {SNO,STATUS}, and {SNO,CITY} are all irreducible, and they're all binary.

But not always: The shipments relvar SP is irreducible, too, but it's ternary, not binary. And some irreducible relvars are unary, or even have no attributes at all.

And not all binary relvars are irreducible: Consider the relvar R{X,Y}, with predicate *X and Y are both members of the Green Party*. This relvar can be nonloss decomposed into its projections on {X} and {Y}. (In fact, these two projections are identical! One of them could be discarded. I'll leave it as an exercise for you to find a more realistic example of a binary relvar that's not in 6NF.)

And a relvar with a key K and at most one attribute not part of K isn't necessarily in 6NF, either: Well, the Green Party example illustrates this point, too. But here's another example (taken from reference [2]): Relvar SJT{S,J,T} has predicate *Student S is taught subject J by teacher T*, and the following constraints apply:

- For each subject, each student of that subject is taught by only one teacher.

- Each teacher teaches only one subject (but each subject is taught by several teachers).

I'll leave it to you to work out the specifics of this example. In particular, what normal form is the relvar in?[12]

REFERENCES AND BIBLIOGRAPHY

1. E. F. Codd: "Further Normalization of the Data Base Relational Model," in Randall J. Rustin (ed.), *Data Base Systems: Courant Computer Science Symposia Series 6.* Englewood Cliffs, N.J.: Prentice-Hall (1972).

---

[12] Here's another interesting example for you to think about. Let view SCP be defined as the projection on {SNO, CITY, PNO} of the join of S, SP, and P. What normal form is SCP in? What dependencies hold? What are the keys?

2. C. J. Date: *An Introduction to Database Systems* (8th edition). Boston, Mass.: Addison-Wesley (2004).

3. C. J. Date: "What First Normal Form Really Means," in *Date on Database: Writings 2000-2006*. Berkeley, Calif.: Apress (2006).

4. C. J. Date: *Database and Relational Theory: Normal Forms and All That Jazz* (2nd edition). Berkeley, Calif.: Apress (2019).

5. C. J. Date: "Data Redundancy and Database Design: Further Thoughts Number One," in *Date on Database: Writings 2000-2006*. Berkeley, Calif.: Apress (2006).

6. C. J. Date, Hugh Darwen, and Nikos Lorentzos: *Time and Relational Theory: Temporal Data in the Relational Model and SQL*. Waltham, Mass.: Morgan Kaufmann (2014).

7. C. J. Date and Ronald Fagin: "Simple Conditions for Guaranteeing Higher Normal Forms in Relational Databases," *ACM Transactions on Database Systems 17*, No. 3 (September 1992). Republished in C. J. Date and Hugh Darwen, *Relational Database Writings 1989-1991*. Reading, Mass.: Addison-Wesley (1992).

8. Ronald Fagin: "A Normal Form for Relational Databases that Is Based on Domains and Keys," *ACM TODS 6*, No. 3 (September 1981).

Chapter 14

Missing Information

I call it my billion dollar mistake. It was the invention of the null reference in 1965. At that time, I was designing the first comprehensive type system for references in an object oriented language (ALGOL-W). My goal was to ensure that all use of references should be absolutely safe, with checking performed automatically by the compiler. But I couldn't resist the temptation to put in a null reference, simply because it was so easy to implement. This has led to innumerable errors, vulnerabilities, and system crashes, which have probably caused a billion dollars of pain and damage in the last forty years.

—Tony Hoare:
Presentation at a QCon conference (August 25th, 2009)

*Don't tell me there isn't one bit of difference
between null and [a] space,
because that's exactly how much difference there is.*

—Larry Wall:
Usenet article, *<10209@jpl-devvax.JPL.NASA.GOV>* (1990)

WHAT'S WRONG WITH NULLS?

Many of your writings attack the idea of nulls and three-valued logic (3VL) as a basis for dealing with missing information. In particular, you claim that nulls lead to wrong answers (you've referred to this state of affairs as a "showstopper"). But many people seem to be able to use nulls correctly and get answers they're perfectly happy with. So what's going on? Aren't you worrying about nothing *<joke>*? Conversely, if you're right and we do have to avoid nulls, what should we be doing instead?

Well, there are many issues all mixed together here. Let me take the last one first: If we do have to avoid nulls, what should we be doing instead? I wish I had a good answer to this question! To quote somebody or other—I forget who—I feel your pain ... In particular, I know that if you do make the (to me very sensible) decision not to use nulls, you'll have a hard row to hoe with today's products, because they (the products, I mean) have all been designed on the assumption that you *will* use them. As a result, those products don't just not help, they actively hinder, attempts to avoid such use. As a trivial but typical example of the point, they make it easier for a column to permit nulls than to prohibit them; *and*, just to rub salt into the wound, prohibiting nulls is likely to lead to worse performance than permitting them. Maybe.

All of that said, I still think you should avoid nulls. I'm not going to repeat all of the arguments here, since I've given them before in many, many places (see, e.g., references [2], [4], and [5]).[1] However, I'd like to summarize a few of the main points, in a form that's at least partly different from the way I've put them before:

■ It isn't up to me to prove that nulls can give wrong answers—I've already done that, many times and in many places. Rather, it's up to the nulls advocates to prove the converse: that is, they need to prove that, *at least in their particular situation*, nulls can't (or at least never do) give wrong answers.[2] Only if they can provide such a proof will it be safe for them to use nulls, and then again *only in their particular situation*. Of course, I venture to suggest that providing such a proof will be quite difficult, and very likely impossible.

■ Following on from the previous point, I have it on good authority that nulls really do give wrong answers in practice. In fact it's happened to me! Luckily, I was able to tell right away in the case in question that the answer was wrong, because it failed to include a particular "datum" (as Codd might have called it, per the discussions in Chapter 12) that I knew should have been included. But suppose I hadn't noticed?

---

[1] See also the discussion near the end of Chapter 2 of the present book.

[2] They obviously can't prove that nulls can't give wrong answers *in general*, since I've already proved the opposite (see, e.g., reference [4]).

Note: The cynic might say that if I hadn't noticed, then it wouldn't have mattered. The operational definition of an error is one that's noticed—if it isn't noticed, then it isn't an error. But I digress.[3]

- A related point, following on from both of the previous ones: Nulls can give right answers as well as wrong ones, of course, but in general we have no way of knowing which are right and which are wrong. Another showstopper, it seems to me.

- The questioner asserts that "many people seem to be able to use nulls correctly" and that they "get answers they're perfectly happy with." I'll consider these claims one at a time.

  1. I'm not sure what it might mean "to use nulls correctly." In particular, I've never claimed that three-valued logic can't be made to work correctly (though SQL's attempt to do so—to make it work correctly, that is—demonstrably fails, because it embodies various inconsistencies). But that's not the point. The point is that three-valued logic (3VL for short), even when "working correctly," doesn't solve the problem!—it yields answers to queries that are correct according to the logic but not correct in the real world. In other words, the nulls problem isn't a problem with SQL only (though SQL does exacerbate it).

  2. As for people being happy with the answers they're getting out of nulls, there are various possibilities: Either they're lucky, and they actually are getting right answers; or they're failing to notice the errors (see above); or—possibly for reasons that aren't technical in nature—they're keeping quiet about the errors; or they're just not thinking critically; or some combination of all of these possibilities. And, of course, even if it's true that some people are happy with the answers they're getting, it doesn't follow that other people aren't having the opposite experience ... The two aren't mutually exclusive. I believe that the defenders of nulls should be concerned with producing evidence that people never get incorrect results, not making

---

[3] It's true that if the wrong answer is literally never noticed, then it doesn't matter. But the real problem occurs with errors that *are* noticed, but noticed too late—i.e., only after some action has been taken based on the wrong answer, and the damage caused by that action can't reasonably be undone.

arm waving and unsupported statements to the effect that sometimes they get correct ones.

With respect to the point about keeping quiet for nontechnical reasons, by the way, I'm often asked to give concrete examples of practical situations where nulls and 3VL have given rise to genuine and perhaps costly errors in the real world. But a moment's thought should show why I won't do this, even if I could. Suppose I were to go around telling stories of how DBMS X caused Customer Y to commit some huge blunder, causing who knows what damage—bridges collapsing, planes falling out of the sky, vaccines becoming contaminated, and who knows what else besides—and costing money and possibly even lives. At best, I would surely be sued by the vendor or the customer or both. And I'm not going to do it! But the fact that I won't doesn't mean I can't, or that such situations can't occur, or indeed that they haven't occurred. You can probably supply your own examples.

A CLOSER LOOK

There are a few more points I'd like to make, a little more technical perhaps than the ones I've been making so far. First of all, it seems to me that a perceived need for nulls in a given database design often (perhaps always?) arises out of what I call "mixing predicates." The following example is based on a real application. The designer wanted to represent the results of a series of earth drilling experiments, in which some but not all of the holes drilled reached what I'll refer to here as "the green layer." So he—the designer was a he—came up with the following design (I'll use SQL here because the designer did so too):

```
CREATE TABLE H ( HOLE_ID ... , TOTAL_DEPTH ... , D_GREEN ...
     /* if D_GREEN is null, the green layer wasn't reached */
                                              ... ) ;
```

But there are really two distinct predicates involved here:

■ *Hole HOLE_ID of depth TOTAL_DEPTH reached the green layer at depth D_GREEN.*

■ *Hole HOLE_ID of depth TOTAL_DEPTH didn't reach the green layer.*

So there should clearly be two distinct relvars (sorry, tables). It's always a bad idea to mix—i.e., to "OR," as it were—two distinct predicates in one relvar in the way the designer has done in the example.[4] Of course, with two relvars there'd have to be an additional constraint to the effect that the same hole can't be represented in both; but at least now there wouldn't be any "need" for nulls in the database.

Note: The two-relvar design does also mean that some queries might now have to examine both relvars. However, if you think such queries are awkward, then of course you can always use views to conceal some of the awkwardness.

My second technical point is as follows. Many writers have argued that the real world isn't as black and white as two-valued logic (2VL) might suggest and that we need 3VL in order to get various kinds of "gray" answers to queries. As I've explained at length in reference [6], however, it isn't necessary to embrace nulls and 3VL in order to get "don't know" answers out of the database. The fact is, I can always write a query—even in SQL, and even limiting myself to 2VL— that returns the value "true" when true is the right answer, "false" when false is the right answer, and "unknown" when unknown is the right answer. The trick is to make these responses not truth values but character strings.[5] See reference [6] for further discussion.

My third point is that nulls and 3VL *completely undermine the relational model*. By definition, a null isn't a value. As a direct consequence of this fact:

- A "type" that contains a null isn't a type;

- An "attribute" that contains a null isn't an attribute;

- A "tuple" that contains a null isn't a tuple;

- A "relation" that contains a null isn't a relation; and

---

[4] By "two distinct predicates" here, what I mean a little more precisely is that one of the two has all of the parameters of the other, plus at least one additional one. But the situation can be more extreme than that. A more general statement is as follows: Let predicates *P1* and *P2* be such that *P1* has *n1* parameters that *P2* doesn't have and *P2* has *n2* parameters that *P1* doesn't have; then *P1* and *P2* can be involved in a "mixed predicate" situation if and only if at least one of *n1* and *n2* is greater than zero.

[5] In SQL, in fact, I'm more or less forced into using this trick anyway, even with 2VL, precisely because SQL (at least as implemented in the mainstream products) fails to support a truth value data type. It's odd, really: You'd think the very first thing a language would have to do, if it's going to claim to be founded on logic of any kind, would be to support a truth value data type. In fact the standard does (though it didn't do so originally), but SQL products typically don't. Oh well.

- A "relvar" that contains a null isn't a relvar.

The overall foundation for what we're doing, whatever else it might be, is thus no longer the relational model. I don't know what it is, but it isn't the relational model.

Following on from the previous point, incidentally, I'd like to caution you not to be blinded by science in connection with this topic. Several quite formal and academic texts on relational theory include detailed discussions of nulls and 3VL, and you might therefore be forgiven for thinking that nulls and 3VL are academically respectable after all. But it's all too easy to hide a paucity of thinking behind an excess of formalism. Just because ideas are presented with a lot of academic formalism, it doesn't necessarily mean the ideas in question are right! For example, one textbook on relational theory (title and author omitted to protect the guilty) includes an entire chapter—out of only nine altogether—titled "The Theory of Null Values." Now, there's a problem right there in the title, because a large part of the point about nulls is precisely that they aren't values; but that's not the point I want to make here. Rather, tucked away among the formalisms in that chapter (which is indeed quite formal) we find this sentence:

> The term *unknown* is used both for the null value and for the third truth value, since their respective meanings are identical.

But they aren't!—indeed, there's a serious logical difference between them.[6] So the chapter in question is founded on a serious logical error, and it and its formalisms are therefore irrelevant and can safely be ignored.

As an aside, I remark that I much prefer the treatment in another formal textbook, reference [7], which, though it does include a whole chapter on "null values" [*sic*], at least has the honesty to say—as indeed I already mentioned in passing in Chapter 2—"It all makes sense if you squint a little and don't think too hard." Precisely.

---

[6] Note in particular that (to state the obvious) one's a value and the other isn't. To elaborate briefly: Let X be a variable of type truth value. Then to say that X is unknown means that X has "the third truth value" as its value, whereas to say that X is null means that X doesn't have a value at all. Though perhaps I should add in fairness that Codd himself makes the very same mistake ... In the paper in which he—very regrettably, in my opinion—added nulls and 3VL to his relational model ("Extending the Database Relational Model to Capture More Meaning," *ACM TODS 4*, No. 4, December 1979), he said this (very slightly edited here): "We shall concern ourselves with only the *value at present unknown* type of null and denote it by ω ... We use the same symbol ω to denote the unknown truth value, because truth values can be stored in databases and we want the treatment of all unknown or null values to be uniform."

Finally, let me come back to the last part of the question: If we do have to avoid nulls, what should we be doing instead? As I've said, I don't have a definitive answer to this question. Nevertheless, there are still some things I want to say:

- Although I haven't given a good solution to the problem of "missing information," I've at least tried to convince you that nulls and 3VL are a disastrously bad one. Please don't use them.

- Elsewhere [3] I've described an approach based on "default values" (better called *special* values). I'm not particularly proud of that solution and would advocate its use only in very simple cases, but at least it does work sometimes, and you ought to be familiar with it.

- I rather like Hugh Darwen's approach as described in reference [1] (also in Chapter 2); given today's rather poor product architectures, however, it will probably cause performance and other problems.

- In reference [8] David McGoveran describes another approach (also discussed in Chapter 2), similar to Darwen's but not quite the same, to which similar remarks apply.

- Finally, I really think it's incumbent on users to educate themselves with respect to this matter and to lobby the vendors for better solutions ... and I offer discussions like the present one, and the one in reference [6], and the one in Chapter 2, as small contributions toward such efforts.

REFERENCES AND BIBLIOGRAPHY

1. Hugh Darwen: "How to Handle Missing Information Without Using Nulls" (presentation slides), *www.thethirdmanifesto.com* (May 9th, 2003).

2. C. J. Date: "NOT Is Not "Not"! (Notes on Three-Valued Logic and Related Matters)," in *Relational Database Writings 1985-1989*. Reading, Mass.: Addison-Wesley (1990).

3. C. J. Date: "Faults and Defaults" (in five parts), in C. J. Date, Hugh Darwen, and David McGoveran, *Relational Database Writings 1994-1997*. Reading, Mass.: Addison-Wesley (1998).

4. C. J. Date: *SQL and Relational Theory: How to Write Accurate SQL Code*, 3rd edition. Sebastopol, Calif.: O'Reilly Media, Inc. (2015).

5. C. J. Date: "Why Three- and Four-Valued Logic Don't Work," in *Date on Database: Writings 2000-2006*. Berkeley, Calif.: Apress (2006).

6. C. J. Date: *"The Closed World Assumption,"* in *Logic and Relational Theory: Thoughts and Essays on Database Matters* (Technics Publications, 2020).

7. David Maier: *The Theory of Relational Databases*. Rockville, Md.: Computer Science Press (1983).

8. David McGoveran: "Nothing from Nothing" (in four parts), in C. J. Date, Hugh Darwen, and David McGoveran, *Relational Database Writings 1994-1997*. Reading, Mass.: Addison-Wesley (1998).

Chapter 15

Values, Variables,

Types, and Constraints

*A value is a mathematical abstraction. Values do not have temporal
or spatial characteristics. They cannot be stored or changed in a
computer memory. They can be represented (by some encoding) in a
computer memory.*

—J. Craig Cleaveland:
An Introduction to Data Types (1986)

VARIABLES

**I've often heard you draw a distinction between what you call *variables in
the programming language sense* and *variables in the sense of logic*—but I'm
not clear what exactly the difference is that you're getting at here. Can you
please elaborate?**

Indeed yes; in fact, there's a huge logical difference between these two concepts,
and it's rather unfortunate that the same term is used with two such very different
meanings. Of course, I'm sure you know what a variable is in the programming
language sense, but let me spell it out for the record. Basically, a programming
language variable is a holder, or container, for a value (more precisely, for a
representation of a value)—different values at different times, in general, which
is why we call it a variable; its value varies over time. For example, in the code
fragment that follows, N is declared to be a variable of type INTEGER, and the
two assignment statements have the effect of assigning, first, the integer value
three, and then the integer value five, to that variable:

```
VAR N INTEGER ;

N := 3 ;
N := N + 2 ;
```

As this example suggests, the crucial thing about programming language variables is that they can be updated—that is, the current value of the variable in question can be replaced by another value. In other words, to be a variable is to be updatable (equivalently, to be a variable is to be assignable to), and to be updatable, or to be assignable to, is to be a variable. Indeed, that's more or less the *definition* of a variable in the programming language sense.

> *Aside:* You can think of a variable in the foregoing sense as an abstraction of a piece of storage, if you find that way of thinking helpful (since "pieces of storage" are what are used at the machine level to hold values). Personally, however, I prefer not to explain one level of abstraction in terms of another—I think it's better for each level to be self-contained, as it were. One important logical difference in the case at hand is that pieces of storage at the machine level are referenced by address, whereas variables are referenced by name.[1] *End of aside.*

Perhaps I should state explicitly that elsewhere in this book (and indeed throughout my writings in general), the term *variable* should be understood to mean a variable in the foregoing programming language sense, unless the context demands otherwise.

Turning now to variables in the sense of logic: There are two kinds of such variables, called free and bound, respectively. A free variable is basically just a parameter, or placeholder, to some predicate. For example, let COPRIME (x,y) denote the predicate *Integers x and y have no common factors*. This predicate has two parameters, or in other words free variables, viz., x and y. When we invoke or "instantiate" this predicate, we substitute arguments for the parameters, and we obtain a truth value—or, rather, we obtain a proposition, and that proposition then evaluates to either TRUE or FALSE, by definition. Thus, for example, the proposition COPRIME $(27,14)$ evaluates to TRUE, while the proposition COPRIME $(27,12)$ evaluates to FALSE. In programming language terms, we can think of COPRIME (x,y) as a truth valued read-only operator, or function, implemented as follows (pseudocode):

---

[1] Usually. In object systems, however, objects (which are the OO counterpart to conventional programming language variables) *are* typically referenced by address instead of by name. I'm on record elsewhere as criticizing object systems for exactly this reason, among others (see, e.g., reference [1]).

```
OPERATOR COPRIME ( X INTEGER , Y INTEGER ) RETURNS BOOLEAN ;
   RETURN ( IF X and Y have no common factors
              THEN TRUE ELSE FALSE ) ;
END OPERATOR ;
```

As for bound variables:[2] Like free variables, bound variables can appear within predicates—indeed, they can't appear anywhere else. Unlike free variables, however, they don't act as parameters; in fact, they have no exact counterpart in conventional programming terms at all—instead, they serve merely as a mechanism for constructing one predicate out of another, as it were. Consider the following example:

■ Again let COPRIME (x,y) stand for the predicate *Integers x and y have no common factors*. Note that this predicate is dyadic: It involves exactly two parameters.

■ Suppose we substitute the argument 27 for x but make no substitution for y. Clearly, we obtain the expression COPRIME $(27,y)$, which by definition stands for the predicate *Integers 27 and y have no common factors*. Note that this is a still a predicate (but now a monadic one); we can't meaningfully say that it returns any particular truth value until we substitute an argument for the parameter y.

■ Now, we can obtain a proposition from the predicate COPRIME $(27,y)$ by substituting an argument for y, as we already know. But we can also obtain a proposition from that predicate by *quantifying* over y. Here's an example: The expression

```
EXISTS y ( COPRIME ( 27 , y ) )
```

denotes the proposition *There exists an integer y such that integers 27 and y have no common factors* (which evaluates to TRUE, of course). Alternatively, the expression

```
FORALL y ( COPRIME ( 27 , y ) )
```

---

[2] As we'll soon see, a better term here might be *quantified* variables.

denotes the proposition *For all integers y, integers 27 and y have no common factors* (which evaluates to FALSE).

I don't want to go into lots of details on quantification here—I assume you're already familiar with the basic idea. I'd just like to make the following points:

■ In both of the foregoing examples, the effect of the quantification was to construct a niladic predicate out of a monadic predicate. More generally, given an *n*-adic predicate, if we quantify over *m* parameters ($m \leq n$), we obtain an *r*-adic predicate, where $r = n - m$.

■ As you can see (and as I've written elsewhere), bound variables behave as a kind of *dummy*—they serve only to link the predicate inside the parentheses to the quantifier outside, as it were. That's why they have no exact counterpart in conventional programming terms.

■ I've said that the crucial thing about variables in the programming language sense is that they can be updated. Bound variables, by contrast, can't; that is, they can't be the target of an assignment operation.

Finally, I do need to say that logicians, or logic texts at any rate, tend to be a bit slapdash regarding *exactly* what a bound variable is (or a free variable, come to that). Indeed, I think it's fair—not to mention more accurate—to say that the terms refer more specifically to certain *appearances* of certain symbols (within certain expressions that denote certain predicates). For example, consider the expression

```
EXISTS x ( COPRIME ( x , y ) ) AND EXISTS y ( x > y )
```

This expression contains three appearances each of the symbols *x* and *y*. Of these, the first two appearances of *x* and the last two appearances of *y* are all bound, while the last appearance of *x* and the first appearance of *y* are both free. In other words, there are really two different *x*'s and two different *y*'s in this example—that is, there are two distinct variables both called *x* and two distinct variables both called *y*. The following systematic renaming makes the point clear:

```
EXISTS a ( COPRIME ( a , y ) ) AND EXISTS b ( x > b )
```

Of course, such renaming is legitimate—i.e., it doesn't change the meaning of the overall expression—because bound variables (or bound variable appearances, perhaps I should say) are only dummies anyway.

CHARACTER STRING TYPES

Suppose some variable or some attribute is declared to be "of type CHAR(5)." I've always been a little unclear as to what such a specification truly signifies. Is the type really CHAR(5)? Or is CHAR the type, and the "(5)" just an integrity constraint—i.e., a constraint on the length of the pertinent character strings?

The answer to this question obviously depends to some extent on what language we're talking about, and in particular on whether the language in question supports type inheritance (and supertypes and subtypes) or not. However, I can offer some general remarks ... I'll assume until further notice that inheritance and supertypes and subtypes are *not* supported.

First of all, we need to agree on what the specification CHAR(5) actually means. Just to be definite, let's suppose it's some variable (as opposed to some attribute), V say, that's declared to be "of type CHAR(5)." If the pertinent language is SQL—to pick an example entirely at random, of course—that declaration would mean that legal values of V are character strings of length exactly five characters. In such a language, then, if CHAR(5) is indeed regarded as a type as such, we'll be forced to consider, e.g., CHAR(3) as a completely different type (since the set of strings of length five certainly isn't the same as the set of strings of length three).[3] As a consequence, a comparison of the form

```
'xyz  ' = 'xyz'
```

(note the trailing blanks in the left comparand) will either:

---

[3] In such a language, CHAR (unqualified) can and really should be regarded as a *type generator*, and such things as CHAR(5) and CHAR(3) can then be regarded as invocations of that generator, with parameters 5 and 3, respectively, that return certain specific character string types as such. A detailed explanation of such matters can be found in my book *SQL and Relational Theory: How to Write Accurate SQL Code* (3rd edition, O'Reilly, 2015).

a. Fail on a compile time type error, because the comparands are of different types;

b. Or compile successfully but return FALSE at run time, because the comparands are of different types;

c. Or compile successfully but cause implicit conversion, or *coercion*, of one comparand to the type of the other (and then return either TRUE or FALSE at run time as appropriate).

> *Aside:* Possibility b. is surely undesirable, though SQL does support it—there seems little point in allowing a comparison that we know will give FALSE at run time. As for possibility c., most writers agree that coercions are error prone and in general just a bad idea. Personally, I'd prefer it if they weren't supported at all; in other words, I think all type conversions should be done explicitly, perhaps using (as in SQL) some kind of explicit CAST operator. However, if we want the particular comparison under consideration to return TRUE—which SQL does want, sometimes—then coercions of some kind will have to be supported, and SQL does therefore support them.[4] *End of aside.*

Alternatively, the pertinent language might be such that the declaration— i.e., the declaration that variable V is "of type CHAR(5)"—means that legal values of V are character strings of length *at most* five characters.[5] Again, then, if CHAR(5) is indeed regarded as a type as such, we'll be forced to consider, e.g., CHAR(3) as a different type, since the set of strings of length at most five certainly isn't the same as the set of strings of length at most three. On the other hand, the set of strings of length at most five does include the set of strings of length at most three as a proper subset; under this interpretation, in other words, every value of type CHAR(3) is also a value of type CHAR(5), though the converse isn't true. But what happens to our sample comparison under this interpretation? As a moment's thought should make clear, the possibilities are

---

[4] In the case at hand that SQL coercion works as follows: The right comparand is extended at the right with two space characters—which has the effect of replacing that comparand by a different value, one of type CHAR(5)—before it does the comparison. Note, however, that the foregoing coercion occurs only if PAD SPACE applies to the pertinent "collation"; if PAD SPACE doesn't apply, no coercion is done, and the comparison returns FALSE (in effect, possibility c. reduces to possibility b.). *Note:* A detailed explanation of such matters and much else relevant can be found in C. J. Date and Hugh Darwen, *A Guide to the SQL Standard* (4th edition, Addison-Wesley, 1997).

[5] Like VARCHAR(5) in SQL, in other words.

exactly the same as before. Thus, the alternative interpretation, to the effect that, e.g., CHAR(5) is still a type but the specification "(5)" represents a maximum instead of an exact length, solves nothing. What's more, it leads to a rather strange situation in which supertypes and subtypes aren't supported—that was my assumption, remember—and yet some types are effectively subtypes of others, anyway. In fact, I think it unlikely that the alternative interpretation described in this paragraph would be supported at all unless supertypes and subtypes were supported as well.[6] So let's take a look at this possibility.

Again, then, let CHAR(3) and CHAR(5) denote the set of all character strings of length at most three and the set of all character strings of length at most five, respectively. Clearly, then, CHAR(3) is a proper subset of CHAR(5), as we've seen—every value in the set CHAR(3) is also a value in the set CHAR(5). So it seems eminently reasonable in this case, given our agreed assumptions, to say that CHAR(3) and CHAR(5) are different types—after all, a type *is* basically just a set of values—and to say further that CHAR(3) is a proper subtype of CHAR(5) and CHAR(5) is a proper supertype of CHAR(3). Now the comparison

```
'xyz  ' = 'xyz'
```

is certainly a legitimate expression, thanks to the type inheritance mechanism called *value substitutability* (which says that wherever a value of type *T* is permitted, a value of type *T'*, where *T'* is a subtype of *T*, can always be substituted—because a value of type *T' is* a value of type *T*). In the example, (a) the left comparand is of type CHAR(5), (b) the right comparand is of type CHAR(3) and therefore of type CHAR(5) as well, and therefore (c) the comparison is legal. (It should still return FALSE, of course, since the values in question are different, though in SQL it'll sometimes return TRUE.)

Note: In this approach the length specifications are indeed basically integrity constraints (as the original question suggested they might be), but they're constraints that are part of the pertinent type constraints specifically. I'll have a little more to say about type constraints later, as part of a discussion of integrity constraints in general.

All of that being said, I'd now like to add that I think the most elegant approach to the problem is (a) to regard the type as just CHAR, meaning

---

[6] Perhaps I shouldn't say it's unlikely, because in fact the situation described is exactly what SQL supports with its VARCHAR types. To spell the point out: In SQL, (a) VARCHAR(3) and VARCHAR(5) are different types; (b) every value of type VARCHAR(3) is also a value of type VARCHAR(5); and yet (c) the former isn't considered a subtype of the latter.

character strings of arbitrary length—which, not incidentally, is what **Tutorial D** does—and then (b) to regard the length specifications as (once again) constraints, but constraints not on the type as such but, rather, on the use of that type in various contexts. For example, defining attribute CITY of the suppliers relvar as, say, CHAR(10) would be shorthand for a constraint—actually a single relvar constraint—that might look like this:

```
CONSTRAINT ...
    IS_EMPTY ( S WHERE CHAR_LENGTH ( CITY ) > 10 ) ;
```

In this approach, the comparison

```
'xyz  ' = 'xyz'
```

again involves comparands of the same type—viz., CHAR—but now we don't need to appeal to the notion of value substitutability in order to show that the comparison is legitimate. (Though it still gives FALSE, of course.)

Incidentally, considerations very similar to those discussed above apply to types—or specifications, rather—of the form NUMERIC(p,q). I omit detailed discussion here, except to point out that, unlike the character string example discussed above, this case involves multiple inheritance (at least potentially). The reason is that, e.g., a number with no more than r significant digits before the decimal point ($r = p - q$) and no more than q significant digits after it is both:

a. A special case of a number with no more than $r + 1$ significant digits before the decimal point and no more than q significant digits after it, and

b. A special case of a number with no more than r significant digits before the decimal point and no more than $q + 1$ significant digits after it.

TUPLE CONSTRAINTS

In various writings you've classified integrity constraints into type, attribute, relvar, and database constraints. It seems to me there's an obvious omission here: tuple constraints. Aren't tuple constraints a legitimate and useful concept?

Let me begin by summarizing the constraint classification scheme you're referring to (see, e.g., reference [3] for further discussion):

- A *type* constraint is simply a definition of the set of values that constitute a given type.

- An *attribute* constraint is a constraint on the values a given attribute is permitted to assume.

- A *relvar* constraint—preferably referred to as a *single* relvar constraint, for emphasis—is a constraint on the values a given relvar is permitted to assume.

- A *database* constraint—which I now much prefer to call a *multirelvar* constraint, and from here on out I will—is a constraint on the values two or more given relvars are permitted to assume in combination.

> *Aside:* Two points here. First (and ignoring type constraints for the moment), the foregoing classification scheme does make a tacit assumption that the only constraints we're interested in are ones that have to do with data in the database specifically. What's more, I'll continue to make that assumption throughout the remainder of the present discussion. Second (and again ignoring type constraints for simplicity), the whole scheme is somewhat informal anyway, and (among other things) the distinction it makes between single relvar and multirelvar constraints shows why. The fact is, the very same business rule in the real world can map to a single relvar constraint with one design for the database and a multirelvar constraint with another! For example, consider the business rule "part numbers must be unique," given (a) a design involving just a single parts relvar vs. (b) a design in which there's one relvar for red parts, another for blue parts, and so on. *End of aside.*

For the purposes of the present discussion, it's single relvar constraints that we need to focus on. Such a constraint can be arbitrarily complex, just so long as it mentions exactly one relvar.[7] Here are some examples:

---

[7] Or, to be absolutely accurate, *at most* one relvar; for example, CONSTRAINT ... 1 > 0 and CONSTRAINT ... TRUE are both "single relvar constraints," technically speaking. *Note:* No constraint, be it single relvar or multirelvar, can mention any variables apart from relvars, of course.

```
CONSTRAINT SC1
   COUNT ( S ) = COUNT ( S { SNO } ) ;
```

This one just says that, within relvar S, supplier numbers are unique.

```
CONSTRAINT SC2
   IS_EMPTY ( S WHERE STATUS < 1 OR STATUS > 100 ) ;
```

This one says that supplier status values must be in the range 1 to 100 inclusive. Unlike the previous example, it has the property that it can be checked for a given supplier tuple by examining just that tuple in isolation—there's no need to look at any other tuples in the relvar or any other relvars in the database—and that's the definition (at least, the informal definition) of what might reasonably be called a "tuple constraint."[8] To spell it out:

> **Definition (tuple constraint):** Slightly deprecated term sometimes used to refer to a single relvar constraint of the form IS_EMPTY (*R* WHERE *bx*), where *R* is a relvar and *bx* is a restriction condition on *R* (and can therefore be evaluated for an individual tuple, proposed for entry into *R*, by examining just that tuple in isolation).

So what's a restriction condition? Here's the definition:

> **Definition (restriction condition):** Let *R* be a relvar; then a restriction condition on *R* is a boolean expression in which all attribute references are references to attributes of *R* and there are no relvar references.

In other words, tuple constraints as just defined are a special case of single relvar constraints; they can be arbitrarily complex, just so long as they can be checked for a given tuple by examining just that tuple in isolation. Here's another example:

```
CONSTRAINT SC3
   IS_EMPTY ( S WHERE CITY = 'London' AND
                       STATUS ≠ 20 ) ;
```

---

[8] But I note in passing that the constraint in question can also perfectly well be regarded as an attribute constraint—another illustration, therefore, of the general point that the entire classification scheme is only informal at best.

This one says that suppliers in London must have status 20. The constraint is more complicated than Constraint SC3 because it involves two distinct attributes, but it's clearly still a tuple constraint.

So, as the question says, aren't tuple constraints a legitimate and useful concept? Why aren't they included in the classification scheme? The short answer is: They might be legitimate, and they could have been included, and as a matter of fact they *were* included, originally.[9] As for their being useful, I've made use of them myself on occasion. For example, the view updating proposals of reference [5] can be understood in terms of them, at least in part—though I hasten to add that any such understanding is necessarily both informal and incomplete. (I mean, the proposals in question don't rely on tuple constraints in any formal sense; it's just that the tuple constraint concept can be used to make certain aspects of the proposals easier to understand, and possibly easier to implement as well.)

Incidentally, it's interesting to note that the SQL standard too used to call out tuple constraints as a special case; in fact they were the only kinds of constraints it supported, apart from primary and foreign key constraints, prior to SQL:1992, and it still provides special case syntax for them. It's also interesting to note that various SQL products adopted (and in some cases continue to adopt) very much the same position; in fact, I believe I'm right in saying that some—perhaps even most—of those products don't support anything much more sophisticated than simple tuple constraints, even today.

That said, I believe I'm also right in saying that the standard, and the products in question, adopted the position they did for implementation reasons, not model reasons (it's clear that tuple constraints are much easier to implement than single relvar or multirelvar constraints in their full generality). From a logical point of view, however, I see tuple constraints as just a simple special case of single relvar constraints in general. It might be pragmatically useful from the point of view of the user and/or the DBA and/or the DBMS to call out that special case and give it some special syntactic treatment, but (to say it again) I don't see such considerations as a model issue.

One last point: As noted previously (in an aside), a given business rule might map to a single relvar constraint with one design and a multirelvar constraint with another; that is, the distinction between single relvar and

---

[9] They don't fit very neatly into the overall classification scheme, though, at least from an intuitive point of view. A relvar constraint is a constraint on a relation variable. What's a tuple constraint a constraint on? It can't be a tuple variable, because there aren't any tuple variables in the relational model. And it certainly can't be a tuple value, because values never change, and the concept of a constraint applying to values therefore makes no sense.

multirelvar constraints is more a matter of pragma than it is of logic. In exactly the same way, a given business rule might become a tuple constraint with one design and a more general single relvar constraint (or even a multirelvar constraint) with another; that is, the distinction between tuple constraints and more general single relvar (or multirelvar) constraints is also more one of pragma than of logic. The only really hard and fast division between different kinds of constraints is that between type constraints and others.[10]

Note: Those other constraints—i.e., the ones that aren't type constraints—are sometimes referred to generically as *database* constraints (that term now being available, since what we used to call database constraints are now referred to, and much better referred to, as multirelvar constraints).

TYPE DESIGN

Following on from the previous question, could tuple constraints be useful in helping to decide when we need to introduce another type? For example, suppose I have an EMPLOYEE relvar with, among other things, attributes HIRE_YEAR, HIRE_MONTH, and HIRE_DAY, with the obvious semantics. There are clearly various tuple constraints involved here—for example, if HIRE_MONTH is April, then HIRE_DAY can't be 31. Does the existence of these constraints imply that we'd be better off introducing a HIRE_DATE type and treating HIRE_YEAR, etc., as operators that return the appropriate value from a given hire date?

If I understand you correctly, what I think you're trying to do is come up with some guidelines, if not formal principles, to help answer the question:

When I'm doing logical database design, what types do I need?

(Presumably you're talking too about a system in which we're not limited to system defined types but can introduce types of our own—so called user defined types or UDTs.)

I also understand you to be suggesting that if we find that a tuple constraint interrelates attributes *A1*, *A2*, ..., *An* of some relvar in some way, then we might be better off replacing that set of attributes by a single attribute *A* defined over

---

[10] Even an attribute constraint is conceptually just a "tuple constraint" (and therefore a single relvar constraint), as we saw in footnote 8.

some type *T* that has a possible representation ("possrep") whose components map one to one to those attributes *A1, A2, ..., An. Note:* See reference [2] for an informal discussion of the idea of "possreps," and reference [6] for a more detailed formal treatment.

I find myself in some sympathy with this suggestion. I also have to say that, sadly, I'm not aware of any formal work that has been done on the issue. Deciding types has always seemed to me just as difficult as deciding entities! (I hasten to add, probably unnecessarily, that the two issues are certainly not the same.) As far as I'm concerned, therefore, the field is wide open for new contributions ... So I guess your question becomes: How can we precisely characterize those "tuple constraints" that mean we should be thinking about a new type instead? That looks like a research topic to me.

Note: I observe that if your hunch is right—i.e., that the existence of certain tuple constraints suggests that we might have done the design wrong and we should be thinking about a new type instead—then presumably the pragmatic usefulness of tuple constraints will be diminished somewhat, since they'll effectively become type constraints instead.

QUERYING TYPES (?)

I think it should be possible to query types as well as relations. For example, suppose we're given type COLOR; how can we get a list of all valid colors?

I agree it could be useful to be able to ask questions of the database like the one you mention. At the same time, I certainly don't want to makes types "queryable objects" like relations; as I'm sure you can see, to do that would effectively double the size of the query language at a stroke—perhaps more than double it—and would lead to all kinds of problems that we don't need (or have, in the relational world). Indeed, it would be the first step on a road that could, I suspect, eventually lead to all of the complexities and redundancies of OO languages.

So what we have to do is find a way of getting the information we want to query—the type information, if you like—into relational form. Are you familiar with the concept of a universal relation? Here's a definition:

Definition (universal relation): Given a relation type RELATION *H*, where *H* is a heading, the universal relation of that type is the relation with heading *H* and body consisting of all possible tuples of type TUPLE *H*. Note, therefore, that there's exactly one universal relation for each relation type, and every relation of a given type is what might be called a subrelation of the pertinent universal relation.

So suppose we had a relvar defined as follows:

```
VAR COLORS BASE RELATION { COLOR COLOR } KEY { COLOR } ;
```

Now if we had a way of assigning to relvar COLORS the universal relation of type RELATION {COLOR COLOR}, our job would be almost done (the relational expression COLORS—or the SQL expression SELECT * FROM COLORS—would then yield the desired result). So let me now extend the language **Tutorial D** by adding a new kind of relational expression (actually a new kind of "relation selector") of the form

```
U_RELATION <heading>
```

This expression is defined to evaluate to the (unique) universal relation corresponding to the specified *<heading>*. (Simplifying just slightly, a *<heading>* in **Tutorial D** is a commalist of *<attribute>*s enclosed in braces, and an *<attribute>* is a pair consisting of an attribute name and a type name, in that order.) Thus, for example, the following statement will have the effect of assigning the desired universal relation to relvar COLORS:

```
COLORS := U_RELATION { COLOR COLOR } ;
```

Let me now add that—as you've probably realized already—we don't actually need relvar COLORS at all for the purpose at hand (I introduced it purely as a prop for the argument). Rather, the query "List all valid colors" can be formulated just as:

```
U_RELATION { COLOR COLOR }
```

I hope this answers your original question. But there's one more point I want to make ... If we did indeed extend **Tutorial D** in the manner I've suggested, we'd certainly want to be very circumspect in our use of this new feature! Imagine, for example, what would happen if we asked the system to evaluate any of the following expressions:

```
U_RELATION { X INTEGER }

U_RELATION { Y RATIONAL }

U_RELATION { Z CHAR }
```

THE MOST FUNDAMENTAL CONCEPT OF ALL (?)

I've seen claims to the effect that *type* is the most fundamental concept of all. Can you explain this claim?

Yes, I can. Here's a lightly edited extract from reference [6], by Hugh Darwen and myself:

> For definiteness, we assume throughout *The Third Manifesto* that the language **D** is imperative in style. Like all such languages, therefore, it's based on the four core concepts *type, value, variable,* and *operator* ... For example, we might have a type called INTEGER; the integer 3 might be a value of that type; N might be a variable of that type, whose value at any given time is some integer value (i.e., some value of that type); and "−" (negation) might be an operator that applies to integer values (i.e., to values of that type) ... We remark that if it's true that the *Manifesto* can be regarded as defining a foundation for database technology, then the concepts of type, value, variable, and operator can be regarded as providing a foundation for that foundation. And since the value, variable, and operator concepts in turn all rely on the type concept, we might go further and say the type concept can be regarded as a foundation for the foundation for the foundation. In other words, *type is the most fundamental concept of all*.

I think the foregoing text answers the question as stated. But there's more I want to say; in fact, I want to introduce what might be regarded as a kind of reductionist argument and use it to raise an additional question or two of my own.

Reference [6] adopts as one of its philosophical starting points the position that all values simply exist, a priori. In other words, values aren't—can't be—created or changed or destroyed; instead, they're simply available for use, by anyone, anywhere, for any purpose, at any time. For example, I might use the integer value 3 to assert that three is my lucky number, while you might use that same integer value 3 to assert that you have three dependents. In effect, I'm talking here about two distinct variables, representing lucky number and number of dependents, respectively, both of which happen to be of type INTEGER and to have the integer 3 as their current value. (Of course, the current value of such a variable can be replaced by another, but—to repeat—*those values as such* can never change, and they never do.)

If you can accept the foregoing position (that all values do indeed exist a priori), then consider this series of logical consequences of that position:

■ Names are values, so all names exist a priori.

■ Sets are values, so all sets exist a priori.

■ Pairs (by which I mean, at least for present purposes, *ordered* pairs specifically) are sets, so all pairs exist a priori.[11]

■ Types are *<name, set>* pairs, so all types exist a priori.

■ Relation headings are sets, so all headings exist a priori.

■ Relation bodies are sets, so all bodies exist a priori.

■ Relations are *<heading, body>* pairs, so all relations exist a priori.

■ Operators are relations, so all operators exist a priori.

■ Variables are *<name, value>* pairs (though the pairs contain different value components at different times), so all variables exist a priori too, in a sense.

And so on. So all we really need is values!

Now, I have to admit that I find this conclusion, if valid, a little startling, not to say troubling. One question I want to ask is: What type are those values?

Moreover—again, if the foregoing conclusion is valid—an appropriate rhetorical question to ask is this: By what criteria exactly do we decide (as we do in reference [6]) that we should construct our scheme on the basis of the four "primitive" notions *type, value, variable,* and *operator*? The answer, presumably, is that the "extra"—i.e., actually nonprimitive (?)—notions *type, variable,* and *operator,* though perhaps logically unnecessary, are of enormous

---

[11] The ordered pair *<a,b>* is defined to be equal to the set {{*a*},{*a,b*}}. *Exercise:* Show that this definition preserves all of the characteristic properties of an ordered pair. What happens if *a = b*?

pragmatic usefulness; they represent certain highly important bundles of concepts that could otherwise be discussed only in terms of inordinately longwinded circumlocutions. But is this the only answer? Or the best? And is it even correct?

REFERENCES AND BIBLIOGRAPHY

1. C. J. Date: "Why the Object Model Is Not a Data Model," in C. J. Date, Hugh Darwen, and David McGoveran, *Relational Database Writings 1994--1997*. Reading, Mass.: Addison-Wesley (1998).

2. C. J. Date: *SQL and Relational Theory: How to Write Accurate SQL Code*, 3rd edition. Sebastopol, Calif.: O'Reilly Media, Inc. (2015).

3. C. J. Date: "Constraints and Predicates," in *Logic and Relational Theory: Thoughts and Essays on Database Matters* (Technics Publications, 2020).

4. C. J. Date: "*The Closed World Assumption*," in *Logic and Relational Theory: Thoughts and Essays on Database Matters* (Technics Publications, 2020).

5. C. J. Date: *View Updating and Relational Theory: Solving the View Update Problem*. Sebastopol, Calif.: O'Reilly Media, Inc. (2013).

6. C. J. Date and Hugh Darwen: *Databases, Types, and the Relational Model: The Third Manifesto* (3rd edition). Boston, Mass.: Addison-Wesley (2007).

Chapter 16

Some SQL Criticisms

The sequel will be the biggest, the best, the greatest ever. By FAR.
Never happened before, ever in history. Totally unprecedented. Believe me.
—Lord Ant-Dump
(*attrib.*)

SELECT EXPRESSIONS

You're very critical of SQL. But to me SQL's SELECT statement seems so much simpler and easier to understand than relational algebra or relational calculus! How do you respond?

It's tempting to respond just by saying there's no accounting for taste and leaving it at that. But I think there's quite a lot more that can usefully be said, so let me give it a try.

SQL was originally intended to be different from both the relational algebra and (perhaps more particularly) the relational calculus. Indeed, the suggestion that SQL's SELECT statement might be "simpler and easier to understand than relational algebra or relational calculus" reminds me of certain remarks in the paper [2] that first unleashed SQL on an unsuspecting world. To quote:

> Consider the [query] "Find the total volume of items of type A sold by departments on the second floor" ... The calculus programmer must be concerned with:
>
> 1. Setting up three variables ... to sequence through [three separate tables]
>
> 2. The notions of existential quantifiers and bound variables
>
> 3. The explicit linking terms ... [to specify cross references from one table to another]

4.   The actual matching criteria for membership in the output set

[But] this query could be expressed in [SQL] simply by composing three mapping blocks.

Aside: A "mapping block" is basically what's nowadays usually referred to as a *subquery,* and "composing" such blocks means combining those subqueries in various ways—in particular, by allowing a comparand in a WHERE clause to be denoted by such a subquery. The subquery in question can then be regarded as being "nested" within the "outer" query expression.
   Note: Such nesting is discussed further later in this chapter. There's just one point I'd like to make here: In a well designed languge, that outer query expression would surely be regarded as a subquery in turn. In SQL, however, it isn't (not exactly), owing to SQL's rather bizarre syntax rules. *End of aside.*

Elsewhere in the same paper [2], the authors also say:

We believed that the applied predicate calculus with its concepts of variables and quantifiers required too much sophistication for the ordinary user.

In other words, one of the motivations for creating SQL in the first place was a perception that the relational calculus was what might be called "user hostile." However, I believe quite strongly that such a perception was, and is, rather seriously mistaken; to be specific, I believe it displays a confusion between syntax and semantics. I observed in Chapter 10 of this book that the calculus "looks a little like natural language"—and what I meant by that remark is that the semantics of the calculus are rather close to the semantics of (precise) natural language, and are hence not too difficult to teach or learn. (I speak from experience here.) As for the syntax, I believe it's easy enough to come up with a language design that hides most of the syntactic complexities, if complexities they truly are, of "the applied predicate calculus." In support of this contention, I might point to Query-By-Example [7]; Query-By-Example, better known as QBE, is essentially nothing more than a specific concrete syntax for relational calculus, and most users will surely agree that the syntax of QBE is nothing if not user friendly. *Note:* If you're not familiar with QBE, you can find a brief tutorial, with plenty of examples, in reference [4].
   Now, the authors of reference [2] didn't say as much explicitly, but I believe it can fairly be inferred from their paper that they had misgivings with respect to the relational algebra similar to those they had in connection with the

calculus. (For otherwise why not just use the algebra and be done with it?) If so, however, then I have to say that, again, I think they were confusing syntax and semantics. The algebraic syntax in Codd's early papers (and indeed in most treatments of the algebra in the literature right up to this day) might fairly be described as not very user friendly, or (again) even "user hostile"—but again I don't believe this state of affairs reflects anything intrinsic. The language **Tutorial D** is algebraic, and experience suggests that it's very easy to understand (and use) indeed.

To summarize so far, then:

- First, if you want to claim something is complex, you'd better be very clear as to exactly what it is you're imputing that quality of complexity to—in particular, you'd better be very clear as to whether the complexity you're claiming is intrinsic or merely an artefact of the way that "something" is presented. In other words: Complexity (or alleged complexity, rather) can be spurious. And in the case at hand—whether it's relational calculus or relational algebra that we're talking about—I think it is.

- Second, *exactly the same is true of simplicity:* Simplicity, or alleged simplicity, can be spurious too—and in the case of SQL in particular, I think it is. Although it's true that very simple queries can look simple when they're expressed in SQL, I really don't think SQL is simple at all; it doesn't take much in the way of "intrinsic query complexity" to get us into serious, and in my view quite unnecessary, SQL complexities.[1]

So much for generalities; now let's get a little more specific. The question talks in terms of what it refers to as "SQL's SELECT statement" specifically, so I'll concentrate on that construct too throughout what follows. After all, it's certainly true that most SQL queries are formulated as SELECT expressions (not *statements*, please)[2]—by which I mean expressions that involve, in sequence, a SELECT clause (with an optional DISTINCT specification), a FROM clause, a

---

[1] In any case, simple queries probably look simple no matter what language they're expressed in.

[2] An expression is basically just a read-only operator invocation; in effect, it's a rule for computing a value, and it can thus be said to denote the value in question. (Also, very importantly, expressions can be nested; that is, the arguments to a given expression can themselves be denoted by further operational expressions, also known as subexpressions.) By contrast, a statement is a construct that causes some action to occur, such as defining or updating a variable or changing the flow of control. Unlike expressions, statements can't be nested, at least not in general. (There are exceptions, of course—for example, IF and WHILE statements do contain other statements nested inside them—but these exceptions don't invalidate the general point.)

WHERE clause, a GROUP BY clause, and a HAVING clause (the last three of which, like that DISTINCT specification, are optional). And I'm going to assume you're familiar with the semantics of such expressions, at least in general terms. (The *detailed* semantics are quite complex, and I venture to suggest that not one SQL user in a thousand would be able to say exactly what they are. For the record, the relevant portion of the SQL:2011 standard occupies around one hundred very detailed pages.)

To repeat, the DISTINCT specification is optional. If it's omitted, however, the result of the SELECT expression might contain duplicate tuples (or duplicate rows, rather), which from a relational point of view should never be allowed to happen. Now, sometimes other factors are at work and the DISTINCT can safely be omitted—perhaps the query is such that the result can't possibly contain duplicate rows anyway, or perhaps the context is such that a temporary appearance of duplicate rows in the middle of processing the query has no effect on the overall result. In my opinion, however, it's far too much trouble to work out when it's safe to omit the DISTINCT and when it isn't. For that reason, the SELECT clauses in the examples in this chapter will always include the DISTINCT option, even when it's logically unnecessary. And if the implementation isn't smart enough to optimize away such DISTINCTs when they're unnecessary, then I regard that state of affairs as a deficiency of the implementation in question (also, and more important, as a criticism of SQL as such, of course).

To begin my analysis, then, let me remind you of a crucial property of the algebra (I choose the algebra just to be definite, though I could frame my remarks in terms of the calculus instead if I had to): viz., *orthogonality*. To elaborate: The algebra consists of a set of operators, of course, and—thanks to the well known algebraic closure property—*those operators can be combined to form expressions in arbitrary ways*. For example, we can do a restriction, then form the join of that restriction with some other relation, then project the result over certain attributes, then form the union of that projection with some other relation, and on and on. In other words, the operators are mutually orthogonal, in the sense that (a) the semantics of any given operator are independent of context, and hence that (b) the input(s) to any such operator can be denoted by essentially arbitrary algebraic (sub)expressions. It's this orthogonality property that makes the algebra easy to learn and use—once you've learned how to write (e.g.) a join expression, you know without any need for further study that such an expression can be used in any context where a relation of the applicable type is required. What's more, the semantics of that join expression, or whatever other kind of

expression we happen to be talking about, are totally independent of context—
JOIN {*A,B*} means JOIN {*A,B*}, no matter where it happens to appear.

So does SQL display these same nice properties? No, it doesn't, as I'll now
proceed to show.

Consider first the following generic example, which is close to being the
simplest possible example of a general SELECT expression:

```
SELECT DISTINCT X , Y
FROM    A , B
WHERE   c
```

Speaking *very* loosely, this expression is the SQL counterpart to the
following algebraic expression:

```
( ( A TIMES B ) WHERE c ) { X , Y }
```

In other words—and still speaking very loosely—the FROM clause
corresponds to cartesian product, the WHERE clause to restriction, and the
SELECT clause (with its DISTINCT specification) to projection. And the
clauses are evaluated, not in the order in which they're written, but rather in this
order: first FROM, then WHERE, then SELECT.

Observe now, however, that those clauses *must* be written in the order
shown (SELECT, then FROM, then WHERE)—which is, to repeat, not the order
in which they're evaluated. Thus, even if we limit ourselves to the corresponding
algebraic operators (i.e., product, restriction, projection, and nothing else), it's far
from obvious how to write the SQL analog of an algebraic expression that uses
just these operators but applies them repeatedly and/or in a different sequence—
for instance (to pick an example more or less at random):

```
( TIMES { A ,
         B { X } ,
         C WHERE cc ,
         TIMES { ( D { Y } ) WHERE cd ,
                 ( E WHERE ce ) { Z } } } ) { X , Y , Z }
```

Here for the record is a possible SQL analog (at least, I think it's such an
analog, though I'm far from certain—and, of course, that lack of certainty on my
part is precisely part of my point):

```
SELECT DISTINCT X , Y , Z
FROM ( SELECT DISTINCT *
       FROM A ) AS POINTLESS1 ,
```

```
( SELECT DISTINCT X
  FROM    B ) AS POINTLESS2 ,
( SELECT DISTINCT *
  FROM    C
  WHERE   cc ) AS POINTLESS3 ,
( SELECT DISTINCT Y , Z
  FROM  ( SELECT DISTINCT Y
          FROM    D
          WHERE   cd ) AS POINTLESS4 ,
        ( SELECT DISTINCT Z
          FROM    E
          WHERE   ce ) AS POINTLESS5 ) AS POINTLESS6
```

Observe that in order to come up with this formulation, the user must among other things:

- Be able to nest subqueries in the FROM clause (an ability that wasn't even supported in SQL for the first 15 years or so of its existence, and might not be supported in all SQL products even today)

- Be aware of the pointless rule that tables resulting from subqueries in the FROM clause must explicitly be assigned associated correlation names (*POINTLESS1*, *POINTLESS2*, etc.), even when—as in the example—those names are never referenced[3]

- Not forget to include at least some of those DISTINCTs—possibly not all, but if not, then the user must additionally be aware of when it's safe to omit them

- Be prepared to deal with the fact that it's often necessary to reference something in the SELECT clause (such as Z in the example) that doesn't make much sense until it's defined somewhere deep down in the overall expression, a *long* way after that clause

All in all, it seems to me that—to paraphrase that sentence I quoted earlier from reference [2]—these requirements taken together mean "the ordinary user" of *SQL*—never mind the algebra or the calculus—is surely going to need quite a lot in the way of "sophistication."

---

[3] Implying, therefore, that the user has to know about correlation names in general, of course. It's relevant to remind you here of the complaint in reference [2] to the effect that "the calculus programmer" has to be concerned with "setting up variables to sequence through tables."

Still staying with product, restriction, and projection only, let me now make a couple of additional points (speaking somewhat loosely in both cases):

- I've said that FROM is the rough analog of product, but note that the FROM clause can't appear in isolation—there must always be an accompanying SELECT clause (even if it's only "SELECT *").[4] Thus, SQL doesn't *really* support the product operation; instead, it supports only "projection of product." *Note:* Here and elsewhere I rely on the fact that the "product" of a single relation (or table, in SQL terms) *r* is just *r*.

- I've said that WHERE is the rough analog of restriction, but of course it too can't appear in isolation—there must always be an accompanying FROM clause, and hence an accompanying SELECT clause as well. In other words, SQL doesn't really support restriction; instead, it supports only "projection of restriction of product."

So much for orthogonality, then!—at least so far as projection, restriction, and product are concerned.

Now I observe that matters are actually much more complicated, and much less orthogonal, than I've been pretending so far. The fact is, the SELECT clause isn't just "the SQL analog of projection"—it's the SQL analog of, in general, some combination of at least all of the following:

- Projection, as already discussed;

- Attribute or column renaming (RENAME in **Tutorial D**); and

- Extension (EXTEND in **Tutorial D**).

For example, the SQL expression

```
SELECT DISTINCT
       SNO AS SUPPLIER , SNAME , STATUS , CITY AS LOCATION
FROM   S
```

is the SQL analog of this algebraic expression:

---

[4] I observe too that the FROM clause isn't "just" the rough analog of product—it also acts as the SQL mechanism for defining range variables or "correlation names" (at least implicitly, and often explicitly). Further awkward bundling, in my opinion.

```
S RENAME ( SNO AS SUPPLIER , CITY AS LOCATION )
```

Likewise, the SQL expression[5]

```
SELECT DISTINCT P.* , WEIGHT * 454 AS GMWT
FROM   P
```

is the SQL analog of this algebraic expression:

```
EXTEND P : { GMWT := WEIGHT * 454 }
```

Obvious questions thus arise in connection with the SQL analog of an algebraic expression that uses some combination of product, restriction, projection, extension, and renaming but applies them repeatedly and/or in a different sequence. As a trivial example, consider this query: "Get part numbers and gram weights for parts with weight greater than 7000 grams."[6] Here's an algebraic formulation:

```
( ( EXTEND P : ( GMWT := WEIGHT * 454 ) ) { PNO , GMWT }
                                    WHERE GMWT > 7000 )
```

And here's an SQL analog (note the need to repeat the subexpression WEIGHT * 454 in this SQL formulation):

```
SELECT DISTINCT PNO , WEIGHT * 454 AS GMWT
FROM   P
WHERE  WEIGHT * 454 > 7000
```

Alternatively, here's another SQL analog that (unlike the previous one) makes use of a subquery in the FROM clause:

```
SELECT DISTINCT PNO , GMWT
FROM ( SELECT DISTINCT PNO , WEIGHT * 454 AS GMWT
       FROM   P ) AS POINTLESS
WHERE  GMWT > 7000
```

---

[5] Here and elsewhere in this discussion I assume for definiteness that attribute WEIGHT gives part weights in pounds avoirdupois. However, the question of units in general (e.g., pounds vs. grams) is discussed in detail in the planned follow-on to the present book (*Stating the Obvious, and Other Database Writings*).

[6] This example is also discussed in Chapter 6, as you might recall.

The latter formulation does avoid the need to repeat the subexpression, but it raises another point (actually the point I touched on in the fourth bullet item in that list on page 314): The opening SELECT clause mentions an attribute (or column) called GMWT, *but that attribute isn't defined until we get some way down into the FROM clause.* In other words, the (desirable) ability to include subqueries in the FROM clause implies that, frequently, attributes will have to be referenced a long time before they're defined. By way of example, consider a SELECT expression of the following form:[7]

```
SELECT DISTINCT Z ...
FROM ( humongous great expression that, somewhere down
       in its depths, defines Z )
 . . .
```

The foregoing state of affairs means that SELECT expressions can't always be understood in a single "reading" from beginning to end. Of course, the objection I'm raising here is only a psychological one—but remember that we're supposed to be talking about "simplicity" (or alleged simplicity) and ease of use, which are surely nothing if not psychological issues. In fact, I think one trivial fix that would help matters quite a bit, psychologically speaking, would simply be to move the SELECT clause to the very end of the overall SELECT expression; then we could at least say, loosely, that the various clauses are evaluated in the order in which they're written. But as I've already indicated, I also think there are much bigger problems with SELECT expressions in general than just the sequence of the clauses.

Now I turn to the GROUP BY clause. Consider the following SQL expressions (shown side by side to facilitate comparison):

```
SELECT DISTINCT QTY        SELECT DISTINCT QTY
FROM    SP                 FROM    SP
                           GROUP   BY SNO
```

The expression on the left is straightforward. By contrast, the one on the right is illegal! Loosely speaking, it's illegal because the expression QTY in the SELECT clause isn't "single valued per group." However, it's not so much the legality or illegality of the two expressions that concerns me here; rather, it's the fact that *the two SELECT clauses are syntactically identical but semantically very different.* In other words, the semantics of the SELECT clause can't be

---

[7] See pages 313-314 for a concrete example of such an expression.

defined in isolation; they vary, depending on whether a GROUP BY clause is present or not.

> *Aside:* It follows from the example that omitting the GROUP BY clause is certainly not equivalent to specifying "GROUP BY no columns at all." Why not? Because the latter would—or should!—either produce no groups at all, if the table being grouped is empty, or consider the entire table as a single group otherwise, and in the example QTY is certainly not single valued with respect to the entire table (and so specifying "GROUP BY no columns at all" would cause a run time error).
>
> Let me explain why grouping by no columns should produce a result consisting of either a single group or no groups at all. The reason is that every row of every table always has the same value for no columns: namely, the empty row.[8] So if there are any rows at all in the input, there should be one group in the output; otherwise, there should be no groups in the output. However, that's *not* what SQL will produce; instead, it always produces a "grouped table" containing exactly one group, even if there are no rows in the input (that group will be empty, of course, in this latter case). That's why I said "or should!" in the foregoing paragraph.
>
> PS: The SQL syntax for grouping by no columns is GROUP BY ( ). In fact the commalist of GROUP BY operands can always optionally be enclosed in parentheses, and it *must* be so enclosed if it's empty. *End of aside.*

Here's a slightly more realistic example to illustrate the same point:

```
SELECT  DISTINCT                    SELECT  DISTINCT
        SUM ( QTY ) AS TQTY                 SUM ( QTY ) AS TQTY
FROM    SP                          FROM    SP
                                    GROUP   BY SNO
```

Now both expressions are legal, but of course they have different semantics: The one on the left gives the total of quantities taken over all shipments, the one on the right gives total quantities per supplier (with duplicate totals eliminated).[9] Again, therefore, the semantics of the very same SELECT clause—in this case, SELECT DISTINCT SUM(QTY) AS TQTY—depend on whether the GROUP BY clause is present or not.

---

[8] SQL effectively agrees with this point, even though it doesn't actually support empty rows.

[9] *Exercise:* What do the two expressions return if table SP happens to be empty? Do you think the two results should be the same in that case? *Are* they the same?

Next, I observe that the expression on the right (the one with the GROUP BY) isn't a very sensible query, anyway! Given our usual sample data values, for example, here's what it returns:

```
TQTY
────
1300
 900
 200
 700
```

The query isn't very sensible because the result fails to indicate which total quantity belongs to which supplier (the predicate is just *Some supplier—we don't know who!—supplies parts in total quantity TQTY*).[10] So another criticism of SQL's SELECT ... GROUP BY ... construct is that it permits the formulation of queries that aren't very sensible, and the user therefore has to take care to avoid them. *Note:* I should explain that the same criticism doesn't apply to the relational algebra "analog"—the relation that results from the expression

```
SUMMARIZE SP BY { SNO } : { TQTY := SUM ( QTY ) }
```

includes (by definition) both the "BY attribute" SNO and the "new attribute" TQTY:[11]

```
SNO │ TQTY
────┼─────
S1  │ 1300
S2  │  900
S3  │  200
S4  │  700
```

The SQL analog of this "sensible" query is, of course, as follows:

───────────────────

[10] Matters would be even worse if two or more distinct suppliers had the same total quantity (right?).

[11] Another relational algebra expression that gives the same result is this: EXTEND SP{SNO}: {TQTY := SUM (IMAGE_IN (SP), QTY)}. In fact, for reasons beyond the scope of this chapter, I prefer this latter formulation over its SUMMARIZE equivalent. For further discussion and explanation, see this book's predecessor *Logic and Relational Theory: Thoughts and Essays on Database Matters* (Technics Publications, 2020).

```
SELECT DISTINCT SNO, SUM ( QTY ) AS TQTY
FROM   SP
GROUP  BY SNO
```

But now there's another problem! To be specific, the SELECT clause shown here—SELECT DISTINCT SNO, SUM(QTY) AS TQTY—would be illegal if we were to delete the GROUP BY clause. (And I remind you in passing that the same was not the case when the specification SNO was omitted from the SELECT clause.) Yet again, therefore, we see that the semantics of the SELECT clause can't be defined in isolation but depend on context.

I haven't finished with the GROUP BY clause. My next point is that it doesn't really do the job it's supposed to do, anyway. Consider again the query "For each supplier, get the supplier number and the corresponding total quantity." The desired result is:

SNO	TQTY
S1	1300
S2	900
S3	200
S4	700
S5	0

As we've already seen, however, the SELECT ... GROUP BY ... expression doesn't deliver this result—it misses supplier S5, with total quantity zero. A relational algebra formulation that does give the desired result is:

```
SUMMARIZE SP PER ( S { SNO } ) : { TQTY := SUM ( QTY ) }
```

I've replaced the BY specification by a PER specification (shown above in **bold**), and that does the necessary.[12] By contrast, an "equivalent" SQL formulation is considerably more complex:

---

[12] An EXTEND equivalent of this revised SUMMARIZE expression—which again I prefer—is: EXTEND S{SNO}: {TQTY := SUM (IMAGE_IN (SP), QTY)}. *Note:* SUMMARIZE expressions can *always* be replaced by a semantically equivalent EXTEND expression, and for that reason we're actively considering dropping SUMMARIZE from **Tutorial D**. Note that we're at liberty to do this latter if we want to, because **Tutorial D** is still partly a work in progress. Indeed, it's precisely part of the point of **Tutorial D** that it's by way of an experiment in relational language design.

```
SELECT DISTINCT SNO , COALESCE ( TQTY , 0 ) AS TQTY
FROM    S , LATERAL ( SELECT DISTINCT SUM ( QTY ) AS TQTY
                      FROM    SP
                      WHERE   SP.SNO = S.SNO ) AS POINTLESS
```

Note in particular that this latter formulation doesn't involve a GROUP BY clause at all—a fact that might reasonably raise questions in your mind as to why GROUP BY is supported in the first place.[13] I'll come back to this point when I discuss the HAVING clause, later.

Still another point on GROUP BY: GROUP BY might be thought to be the SQL analog of the algebraic GROUP operator—and so it is, in a way. For example, GROUP BY SNO applied to SP is roughly analogous to the algebraic expression SP GROUP {PNO,QTY} AS *name*—PNO and QTY being the attributes of SP not mentioned in the GROUP BY clause (the algebraic GROUP operator specifies the attributes to be grouped, not the ones by which the grouping is to be done).[14] However:

- Unlike GROUP, GROUP BY can't appear in isolation—there must always be, among other things, an accompanying SELECT clause. And one of the effects of that SELECT clause is precisely to undo the effects of the grouping (i.e., to perform a corresponding UNGROUP, in algebraic terms).[15] In SQL, therefore, UNGROUP can't appear in isolation either— GROUP and UNGROUP always appear together, in effect, and any given grouping operation is followed immediately (well, almost immediately) by a corresponding ungrouping operation.

- Once again, questions arise regarding SQL analogs of algebraic expressions involving arbitrary mixtures of (now) summarizing, grouping, and ungrouping, in addition to all of the operations discussed previously (product, restriction, projection, extension, and renaming).

---

[13] It also illustrates two further SQL complications—a COALESCE invocation in the SELECT clause, and a LATERAL specification in the FROM clause. I'll leave it to you to figure out what these constructs do and why they're necessary. (*Are* they necessary?) *Note:* In case you're not familiar with them, COALESCE and LATERAL are both discussed in my book *SQL and Relational Theory: How to Write Accurate SQL Code*, 3rd edition (O'Reilly, 2015).

[14] The algebraic expression SP GROUP {PNO,QTY} AS *name* can alternatively be expressed thus: SP GROUP {ALL BUT SNO} AS *name*. This latter form is a little closer to the GROUP BY analog.

[15] So now we see the SELECT clause isn't just the SQL analog of some combination of projection and/or extension and/or renaming—it might involve some ungrouping too, in general.

And then there's the HAVING clause ... The HAVING clause is a kind of "WHERE clause for groups";[16] in other words, if the overall expression includes a HAVING clause, it usually includes a GROUP BY clause as well. However, that GROUP BY clause can be omitted, in which case it's as if "GROUP BY no columns at all" had been specified, and SQL then treats the entire table as a single group as explained earlier.

> *Aside:* Here let me repeat, but in different words, what I said in this connection in a previous aside: namely, that treating the entire table as a single group is logically incorrect if the table in question happens to be empty (i.e., contains no rows). In that case there obviously shouldn't be any groups at all; however, SQL says there's exactly one group (necessarily empty, of course). Note that there *is* a logical difference here: It's exactly the difference between the empty set and what the empty set contains. (What the empty set contains is nothing at all, but the empty set as such isn't nothing but something—if you see what I mean.) *End of aside*.

It isn't easy to say exactly what the algebraic analog of the HAVING clause is. However, it's certainly the case that any relation that can be obtained by means of an SQL expression that involves a HAVING clause can also be obtained by means of some algebraic expression. In fact, I've shown elsewhere (see reference [5]) that HAVING is effectively redundant in SQL, anyway; that is, any sensible SQL expression that involves a HAVING clause is logically equivalent to one that doesn't. (The same is true of GROUP BY, incidentally, as that same reference [5] also shows.) Which isn't to say that HAVING and GROUP BY can easily be defined in terms of syntactic substitution [3]; if they could, they wouldn't be so difficult to teach, learn, and use. *Au contraire*, in fact: The mappings are actually quite complicated, and vary from case to case; I mean, they suffer from the "large number of special cases" syndrome. Again, see reference [5] for further discussion.

Well, I think I've covered enough territory to show that SQL's SELECT expressions in general are very far from being as simple as they're often claimed

---

[16] Well, no, it isn't—not exactly. Simplifying somewhat, the regular WHERE clause involves, or at least permits, boolean expressions of the form *<row> <comparison op> <row>*; thus, a WHERE clause for groups would presumably involve, or at least permit, boolean expressions of the form *<group> <comparison op> <group>*. In fact, however, the HAVING clause typically involves boolean expressions of the form *<summary> <comparison op> <scalar>*, where *<summary>* is some expression such as SUM(QTY) that's single valued per group.

to be—and let me stress that my treatment has been very far from exhaustive. Anyway, let me summarize the main points I've been trying to make:

- The SELECT, FROM, WHERE, GROUP BY, and HAVING clauses don't correspond to distinct relational operations. Instead, various combinations of those clauses correspond, in no very straightforward or systematic manner, to various combinations of those operations. In other words, the precise effect of any individual clause is highly context sensitive, and the various clauses are a long way from being mutually orthogonal.

- This lack of orthogonality among the clauses contrasts strongly with the orthogonality of the relational operations. Note in particular that it's that lack of orthogonality that, quite apart from anything else, makes SQL so hard to *define*, as well as to document, teach, learn, remember, and use.[17] (That's one reason why the SQL standard is such an enormous document— not to mention the fact that it's also so full of errors.) In effect, that lack of orthogonality means that SQL is rife with special cases. As a consequence, we might say, loosely but not entirely incorrectly, that if we try to measure the relative complexity of relational algebra and SQL in terms of the number of concepts they involve, then the algebra is linear (additive), while SQL is multiplicative, in nature. Orthogonality means, among other things, that there's less for the user to learn, and in effect more functionality ("more bang for the buck") in what's learned.

ARE WE TALKING SCIENCE?

With regard to that business of always specifying DISTINCT, I've heard some people refer to the debate over duplicate rows as "religious." What do they mean? Do you agree with them?

No, I most certainly don't! Let me explain. First of all, of course, you're absolutely correct when you say some people characterize the debate as religious in nature. For example, here's what Don Chamberlin has to say on the matter:

---

[17] It's also what makes it virtually impossible to define a WITH clause feature for SQL that even begins to compare in usefulness with the WITH feature of **Tutorial D**. (In fact, the only kind of expression that can be "factored out," as it were, via WITH in SQL is—perhaps unsurprisingly—an entire SQL subquery.)

During the early development of SQL ... some decisions were made that were ultimately to generate a great deal more controversy than anyone anticipated. Chief among these were the decisions to support null values [*sic*] and to permit duplicate rows to occur in tables and in query results. I will devote a small amount of space here to examining the reasons for these decisions and the context in which they were made. My purpose here is historical rather than persuasive—I recognize that nulls and duplicates are religious topics, and I do not expect anyone to have a conversion experience after reading this chapter.

Don Chamberlin is, of course, widely recognized as the inventor (along with Raymond Boyce) of the SQL language, and this is the opening paragraph of a section titled "Some Controversial Decisions" in Chapter 1 ("A Brief History of SQL") of his book on DB2 [1].

> *Aside:* It's a little tangential to the main point at issue here, but I do have a couple of technical quibbles with the quoted paragraph. First, note the reference to "null values" once again. To say it one more time, a very large part of the point about nulls is precisely that they're not values. Second, note the reference to "tables and ... query results," a phrase that suggests fairly strongly that query results and tables are different things; yet a very large part of the point about the relational model is precisely that query results are tables (or, as I would prefer to say, relations). *End of aside.*

Be that as it may, there's clearly at least one writer who thinks that duplicates are a religious topic. So what does it mean to make such a claim? All it can possibly mean, it seems to me, is that the writer believes that:

a. There are no *scientific* reasons in favor of either side of the argument (i.e., in favor of either permitting or prohibiting duplicates), it's just a matter of faith—some people believe in duplicates and some don't, and that's all there is to be said.

And as a consequence:

b. It's just as scientifically respectable to permit duplicates as to prohibit them, and so it's a waste of time trying to have a scientific debate on the issue.

I reject this position absolutely. There are all kinds of solid and, yes, scientific reasons for prohibiting duplicates (see, e.g., reference [6]). By contrast, I'm not aware of *any* good reasons—emphasis on good—for permitting them. Note that it's only those in the "duplicates permitted" camp who describe the issue as religious!—nobody on the other side of the question does so. In fact, I suspect that those who describe the issue as religious do so precisely because they know they have little science to support their position. (Alternatively, I suppose, they might simply be unaware of, or might not understand, the scientific counterarguments. If so, however, then I don't think they have any right to foist their lack of knowledge or understanding on the community at large. Though I suppose there's plenty of precedent for *that*, in other disciplines as well as our own. Examples that come to mind include *<please supply your own>*.)

> *Aside:* Time to quote Bertrand Russell once again, I think (the quote is from the preface to *The Bertrand Russell Dictionary of Mind, Matter, and Morals* (Lester E. Denonn, ed., Citadel Press, 1993):
>
>> The kind of philosophy that I value and have endeavoured to pursue is scientific, in the sense that there is some definite knowledge to be obtained and that new discoveries can make the admission of former error inevitable to any candid mind. For what I have said, whether early or late, I do not claim the kind of truth which theologians claim for their creeds. I claim only, at best, that the opinion expressed was a sensible one to hold at the time ... I should be much surprised if subsequent research did not show that it needed to be modified. [Such opinions were not] intended as pontifical pronouncements, but only as the best I could do at the time towards the promotion of clear and accurate thinking. Clarity, above all, has been my aim.
>
> *End of aside.*

Incidentally, I'd like to add that one good philosophical argument against duplicates is that if you use *position* as the sole distinguishing feature of some object—which is effectively what you're forced to do if you "permit duplicates" [6]—then changing an object's position apparently changes its identity! But surely identity is, or should be, intrinsic to the object in question, not a mere quirk of where that object happens to be located. I'm still me, regardless of whether I happen to be in California, or Australia, or Mexico, or anywhere else. *Note:* Of course, I'm using the term *object* here in its generic sense, not its specialized OO sense. But this argument is in fact a good argument against object IDs, at least as a concept for use in "modeling reality." One of the reasons objects and databases are such a bad fit is that OO people want to write programs and chase pointers, while database people want to model reality. Two different objectives, and two different mindsets, and two different problems—and two different sets of tools are appropriate.

MORE ON GROUP BY

I've heard you complain that SQL's GROUP BY construct is "too procedural." Can you elaborate?

Well, I can try. First, though, I think I should say it seems to be quite difficult to pin down the meaning of *procedural* in any very precise manner; I think the best we can say is that some language *A* is either more or less procedural than some other language *B* ... or, perhaps better, that some formulation *A* of some given problem (e.g., some database query) is either more or less procedural than some other formulation *B* of the same problem. As a consequence, it's quite difficult to pin down the precise meaning of *declarative*, too, since *declarative* (whatever else it might mean) is usually equated with *nonprocedural*.

That said, yes, I do think GROUP BY is more procedural than certain other parts of SQL, in a sense. To my mind, an expression like (say)

```
SELECT DISTINCT SNO , SUM ( QTY ) AS TQTY
FROM    SP
GROUP   BY SNO
```

seems to me to be saying to the system: First, rearrange the rows of table SP into groups such that (a) all rows in the same group have the same SNO value and (b) rows in distinct groups have distinct SNO values; then, for each such group, extract the common SNO value and the total TQTY of the quantities in the rows in that group; then what results from the foregoing process is what I want. To me, this looks more like a recipe—i.e., a step by step algorithm, or procedure—for solving the problem, not just a simple declarative statement of what the problem is. I think a declarative statement would look more like this:

Get supplier numbers and corresponding total quantities.

It's not immediately obvious from this declarative statement that GROUP BY is what's required to solve the problem, and of course it's not required: I mean, we can certainly formulate the query without it, even in SQL—e.g., as follows:

```
SELECT DISTINCT SPX.SNO ,
               LATERAL ( SELECT DISTINCT SUM ( SPY.QTY )
                                AS TQTY
                         FROM   SP AS SPY
                         WHERE  SPY.SNO = SPX.SNO )
                       AS POINTLESS
FROM    SP AS SPX
```

Or in relational calculus:

```
( SPX.SNO ,
      TQTY := SUM ( SPY WHERE SPY.SNO = SPX.SNO , QTY ) )
```

I've assumed in this calculus formulation that SPX and SPY have both been defined to be range variables that range over the relation that's the value of relvar SP at the time the overall expression is evaluated:

```
RANGEVAR SPX RANGES OVER SP ;
RANGEVAR SPY RANGES OVER SP ;
```

(See, e.g., reference [4] for further explanation.) By the way, which of these two formulations of the query do you think is the simpler—the SQL expression, or the relational calculus counterpart?[18]

REFERENCES AND BIBLIOGRAPHY

1. Don Chamberlin: *Using the New DB2: IBM's Object-Relational Database System.* San Francisco, Calif.: Morgan Kaufmann (1996).

2. Donald D. Chamberlin and Raymond F. Boyce: "SEQUEL: A Structured English Query Language," Proc. 1974 ACM SIGMOD Workshop on Data Description, Access, and Control, Ann Arbor, Mich. (May 1974).

---

[18] When I wrote the first draft of this chapter the SQL standard didn't allow subqueries in the SELECT clause, and thus the SELECT expression shown at the top of this page wasn't even legal. What's more, I wasn't sure at that time, and I'm still not sure now, whether the LATERAL specification is required in this context, nor whether it's even permitted. What's more, I don't very much care.

3. Hugh Darwen: "Valid Time and Transaction Time Proposals: Language Design Aspects," in Opher Etzion, Sushil Jajodia, and Suryanaryan Sripada (eds.): *Temporal Databases: Research and Practice*. New York, N.Y.: Springer Verlag (1998).

4. C. J. Date: *An Introduction to Database Systems* (8th edition). Boston, Mass.: Addison-Wesley (2004).

5. C. J. Date: "Redundancy in SQL," Chapter 4 of the planned follow-on to the present book, viz., *Stating the Obvious, and Other Database Writings* (tentative title, to appear).

6. C. J. Date: "Double Trouble, Double Trouble," in *Date on Database: Writings 2000-2006*. Berkeley, Calif.: Apress (2006).

7. Moshé M. Zloof: "Query-By-Example," Proc. NCC *44*, Anaheim, Calif. (May 1975). Montvale, N.J.: AFIPS Press (1977).

Part IV

INTERVIEWS

Chapter 17

N o   t o   S Q L !

N o   t o   N o S Q L !

There are two ways of constructing a software design:
One way is to make it so simple
that there are obviously no deficiencies,
and the other way is to make it so complicated
that there are no obvious deficiencies.

—Tony Hoare:
The Emperor's Old Clothes
(Turing Award lecture, 1980)

This chapter consists of the text, very lightly edited here, of an interview
with Hugh Darwen and myself that appeared in the NoCOUG
Journal 27, No. 3 (August 2013) and was conducted by the editor of that
journal, Iggy Fernandez (who also chose the title and epigraph shown
above). [1] *My thanks to Hugh and Iggy for allowing me to republish the*
interview in its present form.

Iggy: It was more than 40 years ago that Edgar "Ted" Codd invented the
relational model. In that period, the DBMS market has come to be dominated by
the DBMS vendors and products—such as Oracle, DB2, SQL Server, MySQL,
and PostgreSQL—who adopted Codd's visionary ideas. But a small band of
relational purists have been complaining that the DBMS vendors have deviated
from the teachings of Codd. Two members of that band are Chris Date and Hugh
Darwen. Chris Date is the author of *An Introduction to Database Systems*, which
has sold some 900,000 copies since its first edition in 1975, and the author and

---

[1] The *NoCOUG Journal* is an official publication of the Northern California Oracle User Group.

coauthor of many other books, too numerous to list here. Hugh Darwen, working for IBM in the U.K., was an active participant in the development of the ISO SQL standard from 1988 until his retirement from that company in 2004. He has coauthored a number of books with Chris Date.

NO TO SQL!

Iggy: Most database practitioners would be surprised to hear your claims that the major database management systems of today are not fully relational. The logical first question is: What is the yardstick of "relationality"? I know that the creator of the relational model, Edgar Codd, wrote an article in *Computerworld* magazine in 1985 titled "Is Your DBMS Really Relational?" in which he said:

> In this paper, I supply a set of [twelve] rules with which a DBMS should comply if it is claimed to be fully relational. No existing DBMS product that I know of can honestly claim to be fully relational, at this time.

But, only five years later, he raised the bar higher and went on to list 333 rules—a suspiciously neat and tidy number—in his 1990 book *The Relational Model for Database Management Version 2* (RM/V2). Then there are the standards produced by the ISO committee on which Mr. Darwen was the IBM representative in the U.K. delegation from 1988 until 2004. The 2011 version of the ISO SQL standard has almost 4000 pages. Is it fair to keep moving the target from twelve conformance rules to 333 and then to 4000 pages of specifications? Isn't an RDBMS "relational enough" if it abides by Codd's original Twelve Rules, especially since he originally [*and, let me add, explicitly*] considered such products to be "fully relational"?

Chris: To be relational (even "fully" relational) is only a *minimum* requirement for a DBMS—the relational model addresses only what might be called core DBMS functionality. With respect to that core, the model serves as an abstract recipe for what the user interface should look like. And what that recipe says is basically two things:

1. The data should be presented to the user as relations (and nothing but relations).

2. The operators available to the user should be ones that operate on relations (and that set of operators should be "relationally complete").

Incidentally, let me point out right away that SQL fails on both counts. First, its basic data object is the SQL table, and there are at least seven points of difference (real logical difference, I mean) between SQL tables in general and relations. Second, its operators are, by definition, operators that work on SQL tables, not relations. [*They also fail the completeness test—if "relational completeness" can even be said to make sense in the SQL context, that is.*]

Now, the relational model isn't a totally static thing—it has evolved over time—so critics who accuse us of moving the goalposts do have a point, in a way. But the criticism is academic, because none of the mainstream SQL products supports even the original (1969) version of the model! And in any case, the changes that have occurred since then are, as I said, evolutionary; the model does grow, but it doesn't gyrate. It resembles mathematics in that respect; in fact, it's fair to say the model is itself a tiny piece of mathematics, in a way.

A word on Codd's Twelve Rules: I'm sorry to have to say this, but it's my honest opinion that the Twelve Rules paper simply wasn't up to the standard of Ted's earlier relational writings. In fact, I criticized it at the time.[2] This isn't the place to go into details; suffice it to say the rules weren't all independent of one another, some of them didn't make sense, some were unachievable, and some I think were simply wrong. Given this state of affairs, I really think it's a pity so many people pay attention to those rules (or say they do, at any rate).

As for RM/V2, I'm afraid the same applies, only more so.

What about SQL's 4000 pages? Well, I'll say one small thing in SQL's defense here. To repeat, the relational model as such is only a minimum requirement. You can define that requirement in just a few pages. But SQL, rightly or wrongly, is trying to deal with a lot more than that minimum (for example, it has all of those OLAP functions). So that's one reason why the specification is so big. That said, however, I do also believe that if you could somehow carve out just the pages that deal with SQL's "relational" functionality—such as it is—you'd still have several hundred pages on your hands, because SQL is, quite frankly, a horrendously and unnecessarily complicated language.

---

[2] See C. J. Date. "Notes Toward a Reconstituted Definition of the Relational Model Version 1 (RM/V1)," in C. J. Date and Hugh Darwen. *Relational Database Writings 1989-1991* (Addison-Wesley, 1992). *Note added on republication:* This reference has since been superseded by Chapter 7. "The Relational Model Version 1." of my book *E. F. Codd and Relational Theory: A Detailed Review and Analysis of Codd's Major Database Writings* (Lulu Press, 2019).

The net of all this is: To be fully relational, it's necessary and sufficient that you support the relational model. And *The Third Manifesto*—see the website *www.thethirdmanifesto.com*—is our attempt to spell out in detail exactly what that means. [*I'll leave it to Hugh elaborate.*]

Hugh: As far as we're concerned, the yardstick of "relationality" has to be *The Third Manifesto*, which first appeared, as a paper in a journal, in 1994 but has been subject to minor revisions on several subsequent republications. The most up-to-date version is available at our website, *www.thethirdmanifesto.com*. It's a detailed prescription to be followed in the design of a relational database language, and the few prototype implementations of it that have become available indicate to us that it does succeed in serving that purpose. Its first section consists of 26 numbered points, referred to as RM Prescriptions, where RM stands for Relational Model, of course. These 26 can be taken as our yardstick as such. The second section, RM Proscriptions, mentions some violations of the RM Prescriptions commonly found in attempts to implement the relational model, mostly in SQL. Other sections are devoted to (a) database issues that have nothing to do with the relational model as such and (b) strong suggestions that for one reason or another we can't regard as *sine qua nons*. The *Manifesto* is consistent with Codd's 1969-70 definition of the relational model, but it clarifies several points that, because he didn't make them very clear himself, have resulted in a certain amount of confusion over the years.

Sadly, Codd's 1985 observation concerning the nonexistence of "fully relational" DBMS products still holds good today as far as the commercial scene is concerned. However, at least we do now have a few prototype implementations of our *Manifesto*, made by individual enthusiasts. These are available as free downloads and can be thought of as setting the bar for putative commercial implementations.

As for Codd's famous "Twelve Rules" of 1985 (actually there were thirteen, because the numbering started at zero): Well, they certainly excluded quite a few important points and overemphasized others. Also, they omitted much essential detail, and they weren't expressed very precisely. (Contrariwise, his 1990 book suffered from overkill in our view, as well as including many features—Codd's term—with which we firmly disagree.) So is a DBMS "relational enough" if it abides by those Twelve Rules? No, it isn't. For one thing, they aren't detailed enough. For instance—and this is just one small but extremely important example—they don't make it clear, and nor did his original papers, that the attributes of a relation must be distinguished by *name*. In fact, there's no definition of the term *relation* in those rules, so when we criticize SQL for allowing two or more columns of a table to have the same name, for example (or for allowing the same row to appear several times in the same table, for another example), we can't merely cite the Twelve Rules to justify our criticism.

For our second point, there's at least one of those rules that we can't accept, and that's Rule 3, *Systematic treatment of null values*; in fact, we categorically reject it. Our reasons for doing so have been given over and over again, in numerous publications, over the past 30 years or so (and I think Chris will have a little more to say in a moment in this connection).[3] Most recently, I included a comprehensive treatment of the effects of nulls on SQL operations in my book, *SQL: A Comparative Survey*, available as a free download from *bookboon.com*. That exercise, possibly the first of its kind, was salutary. I can now point to my findings in that book when somebody accuses me of exaggerating when I complain about the adhocery that null gives rise to in SQL and the inconsistency [*we might even say the lack of that required "systematic treatment"*] it displays from one operation to the next.

———— ◆ ◆ ◆ ◆ ———

Iggy: The logical second question is: What benefits will a fully relational DBMS give to users? The need of the hour is performance and scalability to manage the explosion of data in a wired world. Will fully relational database management systems deliver the performance and scalability that today's users are clamoring for? And the logical third question is: Why are DBMS vendors not exactly rushing to make their products fully relational?

Chris: I think we need to disentangle a few issues here. First of all, your line of questioning tends to suggest that if those relational benefits don't include performance and scalability, then they're irrelevant. Forgive me, but that's like suggesting mathematics is irrelevant because it's not engineering. In fact, as I've already said, the relational model *is* a little piece of mathematics, while performance and scalability are engineering issues. Let me elaborate.

It's well known—or, at least, it should be well known—that the relational model is silent on everything to do with matters of physical implementation.

---

[3] I suppose one approach to "treatment of null values" that would certainly be "systematic" would be to reject them entirely. What's more, we'd be very much in favor of that particular approach! If Codd's Rule 3 had called for a systematic treatment of *missing information*, well, that would have been a different matter. What we "categorically reject" is "null values" as such. As Hugh says, I'll be coming back to that issue later.

That silence is deliberate, of course. The idea was to give implementers the freedom to implement the model in whatever way they saw fit (in particular, in whatever way seemed likely to yield good performance) and not to constrain them unnecessarily. Thus, performance and scalability, and other similar issues, are all matters for the implementation—they have nothing to do with whether or not the DBMS is relational. Well ... that said, let me now add that:

a. To the extent nonrelational systems achieve performance and scalability, they do so, at least in part, by muddying the distinction between model and implementation—in effect, by exposing part of the implementation to the user, thereby undermining the important goal of data independence.

b. Precisely because the relational model doesn't unnecessarily constrain the implementer, there's actually good reason to believe a relational DBMS should be able to do better than nonrelational systems on performance and related matters. In this connection, I'd like to mention Steve Tarin's work on The TransRelational™ Model, which is a radically novel and highly promising implementation technology for relational DBMSs.[4] (When I say it's radically novel, I mean it's quite dramatically different from all of today's mainstream SQL implementations.)

So what are (or would be) the benefits of a truly relational DBMS? Well, I've already mentioned data independence (which, as I've explained elsewhere in many different places, translates into *protecting user investment*). Another is simplicity—something that most certainly can't be claimed for SQL systems (I can show you examples of queries that take many lines of SQL code but can be expressed in one short line in a well designed relational language). And a third is, of course, the strong theoretical foundation the relational model provides. You wouldn't tolerate flying in a plane that wasn't built in accordance with the principles of physics and aerodynamics. You wouldn't tolerate living or working in a high rise building that wasn't built in accordance with sound architectural principles. Why would you tolerate using a DBMS that hasn't been built in accordance with solid database principles? In other words, I don't think people should ask "What are the benefits of being relational?" Rather, I think they should ask—or perhaps try to explain—what the benefits are of *not* being relational.

---

[4] See mv book *Go Faster! The TransRelational™ Approach to DBMS Implementation*, available as a free download from *bookboon.com*.

Finally: Why are DBMS vendors not rushing to make their products fully relational? Obviously, because customers aren't asking them to. And why aren't they asking? Because of the failure, I suppose, of relational advocates like ourselves to educate those customers adequately. But it's not for want of trying, I can assure you. Believe me, we find the situation frustrating in the extreme.

Hugh: What benefits would a fully relational DBMS give to users? Well, let me start by citing the objectives that Codd himself gave for his relational model in his 1974 invited paper "Recent Investigations into Relational Database Systems":[5]

1. To provide a high degree of data independence

2. To provide a community view of the data of spartan simplicity, so that a wide variety of users in an enterprise, ranging from the most computer naïve to the most computer sophisticated, can interact with a common model (while not prohibiting superimposed views for specialized purposes)

3. To simplify the potentially formidable job of the DBA

4. To introduce a theoretical foundation, albeit modest, into database management (a field sadly lacking in solid principles and guidelines)

5. To merge the fact retrieval and file management fields in preparation for the addition at a later time of inferential services in the commercial world

6. To lift database application programming to a new level—a level at which sets (and, more specifically, relations) are treated as operands instead of being processed element by element

However, there was no recognized distinction, in 1974, between "fully relational" and "not fully relational" systems. So we might add:

7. Not to compromise these objectives by failing to adhere strictly to the foundation defined to meet them

---

[5] E. F. Codd: "Recent Investigations into Relational Data Base Systems," Proc. IFIP Congress, Stockholm, Sweden (August 5th-10th, 1974).

8. Not to mess things up even further by violating generally accepted principles of good language design

My book *SQL: A Comparative Survey*, mentioned above, systematically compares SQL feature by feature with a language, **Tutorial D**, that has been designed to meet all eight of the above objectives (especially the last two).

In pursuit of these aims, the relational model as defined by *The Third Manifesto* offers the following significant features, for example:

- *Physical data independence:* the user interface excludes all reference to the way data is physically encoded in recording media

- *Uniformity of representation* of data at the user interface (in the form of relations) and concomitant uniformity in the way data is accessed

- *Completeness* of the set of operators for deriving relations from relations, for purposes such as expressing queries and defining integrity constraints

- *Absence of pointers* in the user interface—pointers effectively mean the IT department has to intervene between the database and its real (i.e., end) users, because, as Codd himself said in this connection, fewer people understand pointers than understand simple value comparisons

- *Obviation of the need for loops and branching* in application programs when accessing the database—these, like pointers, being a frequent cause of errors, especially when they're nested

——— ♦ ♦ ♦ ♦ ♦ ———

Iggy: I understand that a number of smaller players are attempting to build fully relational products. The Ingres Project D effort sounds particularly interesting because Ingres is already an enterprise level DBMS with all the bells and whistles needed by the enterprise. What is the current status of Ingres Project D?

Hugh: You're referring to the few prototype implementations of our *Manifesto* made by individual enthusiasts that I mentioned in my answer to your first question. The implementations are listed as Projects at our website, *www.thethirdmanifesto.com*. Unfortunately Ingres Project D was abandoned unfinished in 2011, for a number of unrelated reasons that had nothing to do with the *Manifesto* as such. Until you asked this question, we had omitted to update the information at the website. That omission has now been rectified, but we've retained the description of the project's aims, for interest's sake.

By the way, Ingres Project D isn't exactly the only one inspired by our *Manifesto* that you would describe as enterprise level. There's also Alphora's product, Dataphor (see *www.alphora.com*), which was the first commercial implementation to come to our attention. Dataphor is built as a relational front end to SQL systems. The initial aim was for its language, D4, to be in full conformance with the *Manifesto*, but unfortunately its developers eventually had to compromise over support for SQL's nulls. (It was fully compliant in Version 1, but that meant that existing SQL databases were incompatible with it, and so they had to capitulate to user demand.)

———— ♦ ♦ ♦ ♦ ♦ ————

Iggy: You are on record as vigorously opposing nulls and duplicate rows in SQL. On the other side of the debate, of course, is Don Chamberlin, the coinventor of SQL. In *A Complete Guide to DB2 Universal Database*, he says that *"model the real world"* and *"trust the user"* were guiding principles of SQL. He also points out that systematic treatment of null values was one of Codd's requirements, and, in fact, Rule 3 of Codd's set of 12 rules states:

> Null values (distinct from the empty character string or a string of blank characters and distinct from zero or any other number) are supported in fully relational DBMSs for representing missing information and inapplicable information in a systematic way, independent of data type.

Chamberlin concludes his defense by saying:

> In the end, I believe that the true arbiters of the null and duplicate-row issues will be users of database systems. If users find that these concepts are helpful in solving real problems, they will continue to use them. If on the other hand, users are convinced that nulls and duplicates are harmful, they will avoid these features and scrupulously use options such as NOT NULL, PRIMARY KEY, and SELECT DISTINCT. By supporting these options, DB2 makes it easy for users to "vote with their data."

Your latest books suggest that you have become resigned to the fact that SQL—for all its flaws—is widely used and that, if one cannot avoid using it, then one should use it correctly. Please tell us about your recent books and your reluctant rapprochement with SQL.

Chris: A strong and sufficient reason for opposing nulls and duplicates is simply that—Codd's Rule 3 notwithstanding—they represent a clear and major violation of relational principles, with all that such violation implies. But if you want a more "practical" reason, then how about the fact that they lead to wrong answers? (Wrong answers to queries, I mean.) Space doesn't permit a detailed explanation of this point here, but in any case we've gone into great depth on this issue, and related issues, in many other places.

As for Chamberlin's arguments: Well, Chamberlin is also on record as saying "I recognize that nulls and duplicates are religious topics." We think the issues are scientific, not religious. Moreover, we reject the idea that users should or will "vote with their data." First of all, SQL syntax and defaults are such as to make it hard to do the right thing and easy to do the wrong thing—they give you rope to hang yourself with, as it were. Second, we can expect users to do the right thing only if they're fully aware of all of the arguments on both sides, which in most cases they're demonstrably not. And if they do the wrong thing and then discover their mistake later, the damage is already done. What's more, it might not be possible, for all kinds of reasons, to correct the mistake later, either.

"Model the real world" is good, by the way. That's exactly what nulls and duplicates don't do.

Of course, you're absolutely right to say SQL is widely used, and obviously that situation isn't going to change any time soon. So what we have to do is try to educate SQL users to use the language wisely and well. Two of my most recent books from O'Reilly address this issue (and thanks for the chance to plug them!):

- *Relational Theory for Computer Professionals* is an attempt to explain relational principles as such. (Without a knowledge of those principles, there's no chance you'll be able to use SQL "wisely and well.")

- *SQL and Relational Theory* then goes on to show, for each aspect of relational theory, how to use SQL appropriately. In other words, it tells you what you should be doing. (It tells you what you shouldn't be doing, too!)

Hugh: Regarding books, I've already mentioned *SQL: A Comparative Survey.* That book is designed to be studied in parallel with another book of mine, *An Introduction to Relational Database Theory*, available from the same source.

As for that text by Don Chamberlin, an obvious response would be: "Well, he would say that, wouldn't he?" We find it rather annoying that Codd's own writings are so often cited in arguments like Chamberlin's. The tenor of such citations smacks of "Codd wrote this, so it must be right." Why isn't Codd allowed to have made a mistake here and there? The rest of us do. If somebody wishes to express agreement with something Codd wrote, then they should say why they agree with it. After all, we've stated very clearly why we disagree with Rule 3, and Chamberlin doesn't explicitly refute, or even dispute, any of our points of disagreement. In any case:

a. SQL's support for nulls isn't "systematic" as Codd's Rule 3 requires. The behavior of null in various operations, notably explicit comparisons, is consistent with its denotation as "value unknown," but SQL gives it various other meanings, depending on context, with which that behavior is not consistent at all. For example, the SUM of no numbers is null instead of being zero, the SOME of no truth values is null instead of FALSE, and the AVG of no numbers is null instead of being undefined. Also, its treatment in certain implicit comparisons is inconsistent with its treatment in explicit ones. For example, the result of SELECT DISTINCT on a table consisting of two rows that compare equal on all but one of their columns and each have null for the remaining column contains just one of those two rows. There's no other reasonable choice, of course—the problem lies in the treatment of *ex*plicit comparisons, which in turn arises from the very appearance of null in the first place.

b. SQL's treatment of nulls is loosely based on an early proposal by Codd that Codd himself later abjured (albeit in favor of something even worse, involving two different kinds of null and a fourth truth value).

Note also that Chamberlin doesn't cite Codd in connection with the duplicate row issue. Presumably that wouldn't have been convenient, given Codd's publicly stated bitter opposition to SQL's duplicate row support. We find that people who like to defend SQL against our criticisms are often prone to this kind of cherry picking in their choice of citations.

Chamberlin appeals to the users of database systems as the "true arbiters of the null and duplicate row issues." One problem I have with such statements is that the real end users aren't the ones the big SQL vendors take guidance from. Instead, they talk to the people who develop applications for those end users. Application developers are computer programmers. As such, they like to be in control (and thus maintain their job security); they don't like yielding control to the DBMS over matters they feel competent to deal with themselves. Moreover, developers tend to be more concerned with convenience in database definition and updating than with the ease of deriving useful and reliable information from the database.

In any case, I would argue that the choice offered to users isn't a genuine one, as no attempt has been made in SQL systems (as far as I know) to address perceived performance problems that might arise when a single base table containing nulls is decomposed into several base tables in order to eliminate those nulls.[6]

Chamberlin offers SELECT DISTINCT as a partial solution to the duplicate row problem, but this is a mite disingenuous. Most SQL systems make little or no attempt to take note of cases where SELECT ALL and SELECT DISTINCT are equivalent, even though the technology needed to detect such cases was known before the appearance of the first SQL products. As a consequence, SELECT DISTINCT usually runs a lot slower than SELECT ALL even when they're guaranteed to deliver the same result. SQL implementations thus force the user to work out if DISTINCT is needed (not always a trivial matter), as well as giving rise to traps for the unwary who accidentally leave it out when it's definitely needed. Hence there's no possibility for users to arbitrate between a system that always gives duplicate-free results and one that does so only on demand.

In any case, nulls and duplicate rows are by no means SQL's only harmful departures from relational theory. For example, whereas that theory places no significance on the order in which the attributes of a relation might appear, many SQL operations depend on an ordering to the columns of a table. How are users to express a preference (or otherwise) for a system in which every column in every table has a name unique to that column, thus obviating the need for an ordering, when no such system exists on the commercial scene?

---

[6] See Hugh Darwen's presentation slides ("How To Handle Missing Information Without Using NULL"), *www.dcs.warwick.ac.uk/~hugh/TTM/Missing-info-without-nulls.pdf*, also Chapter 2 of the present book.

NO TO NoSQL!

Note: This section previously appeared in slightly different form as one section out of four in Appendix F ("NoSQL and Relational Theory") of my book SQL and Relational Theory: How to Write Accurate SQL Code (3rd edition, O'Reilly, 2015).

Iggy: The archetypal NoSQL product is Dynamo from Amazon.com. The 2007 ACM paper by Amazon.com states:

> Customers should be able to view and add items to their shopping cart even if disks are failing, network routes are flapping, or data centers are being destroyed by tornados. Therefore, the service responsible for managing shopping carts requires that it can always write to and read from its data store, and that its data needs to be available across multiple data center ... There are many services on Amazon's platform that only need primary-key access to a data store. For many services, such as those that provide best seller lists, shopping carts, customer preferences, session management, sales rank, and product catalog, the common pattern of using a relational database would lead to inefficiencies and limit scale and availability. Dynamo provides a simple primary-key only interface to meet the requirements of these applications.

The Dynamo paper is where the popular claim originated that NoSQL products are faster, more scalable, and more available than relational products in certain clearly delineated scenarios such as online shopping carts. But is there any merit to the claim at all?

Chris: First off, let me make it very clear that I know almost nothing about Dynamo (or any other NoSQL product, come to that). But if the statement is correct that it provides "a simple primary-key only interface to meet the requirements of [certain rather simple] applications"—well, fine. I have no problem with that. If there's a class of applications that (a) are important for some pragmatic reason and (b) require only a limited subset of the system's full functionality, then I think it's perfectly reasonable for the system to provide a special interface tailored to just those requirements. Why, that's exactly what IMS did, with its Fast Path option! That special interface would support a carefully chosen subset of the full relational interface, and the implementation would be able to take advantage of the fact that the interface is circumscribed in just such a way. It might be able to make use of its own special stored data formats as well. And—just to spell the point out—I see no reason why the provision of that special interface and those special stored data formats should have any negative effect at all on users who want to use the regular "full function" relational interface.

That said, if there's a suggestion that Amazon's various disaster scenarios, regarding tornados and the rest, are somehow more of a problem for relational systems than they are for nonrelational ones, then of course I reject that suggestion one hundred percent. As so often, I strongly suspect that what's going on here is some kind of confusion between what truly relational systems ought to be capable of and what today's mainstream SQL products can actually do. If today's SQL products fail to meet Amazon's requirements, well, that might be a valid criticism of those products—but it's not a valid criticism of relational systems in general.

To sum up: I do think we should discard SQL, as quickly as we can, and replace it by something better. Unfortunately, however, most of the people who currently want to discard SQL (or, at least, those who are most vocal about doing so) seem to want to do so for the wrong reasons. And there's a strong likelihood that they'll replace it, not by something better, but by something worse.

Hugh: So Amazon is using a Dynamo key value to access a giant blob whose structure is understood only by the applications. In that case they're happy to forgo all of those aforementioned six advantages given by Codd in 1974, not all of which are properly delivered by SQL products in any case. If the people at Amazon are satisfied that Dynamo provides everything they need, and they feel they have good reason to reject the use of any SQL products, then who are we to argue? The indictment seems to be of SQL products, not relational databases.

It's easy to understand why the mainstream SQL products might be too "heavy" for Amazon's needs. Those products have become extremely cluttered up with all sorts of features that would be of little or no use in the Amazon scenario: baroque support for user defined data types, pointers (in the form of REF values), BLOBS and CLOBs, subtables and supertables, sequence generators, datalinks, locators, system versioned tables, and on and on.

Rel (*dbappbuilder.sourceforge.net/Rel.html*) is an implementation by Dave Voorhis of the University of Derby, U.K., of the relational language **Tutorial D** that Chris and I devised for teaching and illustrative purposes. *Rel* is a very simple DBMS that meets all the criteria for being fully relational. If *Rel*, or one of the other prototype implementations of our *Manifesto*, were dressed up sufficiently for commercial purposes—including in particular the performance enhancements to be obtained by implementation of established optimization techniques and sophisticated storage structures—then it would be interesting to see if Amazon still preferred Dynamo.

All of that said, we admit that full scalability might be hard to achieve with a fully relational system. That's because we require such a system to support expressions of arbitrary complexity for deriving whatever results might be desired from the database and for expressing whatever integrity constraints might be needed. Let's suppose there are extreme cases where what runs in acceptable time with small databases is simply not feasible with large ones. Such cases would militate against the declaration of certain integrity constraints that current SQL products don't even support. They also militate against the use of certain queries, in an OLTP context, that SQL products *do* support, but that problem can of course be avoided simply by not doing such queries. We conjecture that such cases would be unlikely to arise in Amazon's shopping scenario. In any case, if they would still prefer Dynamo to a putative souped-up *Rel*, then so be it. If the benefits of a relational system we described in answer to one of your previous questions aren't all needed in Amazon's particular situation, and provision of a more tailored solution in that situation is found to be cost effective, then who could argue that Amazon would have made a bad choice?

By the way, the bogey of scalability is sometimes advanced as justification for failing to provide any solution at all. A pertinent example is the lack of full support for integrity constraints in SQL systems (where something close to full support could be achieved by implementing the ISO standard's CREATE ASSERTION statement, for example).[7] But some databases are quite small and subject to quite infrequent updates. I use *Rel* for several small databases that I maintain for domestic and hobby purposes on my home computer. I have benefited significantly from the ability to define constraints that would be impossible to define in SQL without CREATE ASSERTION. Without those constraints, certain errors by me would have gone undetected, resulting in incorrect databases. I'm typically dealing with relations consisting of a few hundred tuples, and in some cases I'm updating no more than once per month. It seems unfair that small organizations, which have little clout with the SQL vendors, can't also enjoy the benefits of such solutions, just because those solutions might not be practical for large organizations (with deep pockets, therefore listened to by the DBMS vendors) using OLTP on enormous databases. In this connection, one SQL DBMS implementer once told me privately that he

---

[7] See "CREATE ASSERTION: The Impossible Dream?" by Toon Koppelaars, which appeared in the same issue of the *NoCOUG Journal* (*Vol. 27*, No. 3, August 2013) as the present interview.

agreed with me in principle, but tellingly added that (a) supporting CREATE ASSERTION would be very difficult in his product and (b) lack of scalability for some kinds of constraints would give him a good get-out clause!

———— ♦ ♦ ♦ ♦ ♦ ————

Iggy: Another breed of NoSQL products that has gained considerable commercial momentum is "graph databases" such as Neo4J. In "Normalized Database Structure: A Brief Tutorial," Codd carved out a special exception for such products:

> It may be argued that in some applications the problems have an immediate natural formulation in terms of networks. This is true of some applications, such as studies of transportation networks, power-line networks, computer design, and the like. We shall call these network applications … Except in network applications, links should not be employed in the user's data model.

Since the problems addressed by these products (e.g., shortest path) have no solution in relational calculus, do these products have a legitimate case to be nonrelational?

Chris: Several points here. Yes, Codd did "carve out a special exception" for what he called network applications. But I'm not sure he was right to do so. As a simple counterexample, a company's organization chart has "an immediate natural formulation in terms of networks" (in fact, often—though not always—in terms of a hierarchy, which is a simple special case). But it doesn't follow that we need a network DBMS (i.e., one that exposes "links" or pointers to the user) in order to deal with corporate organizations, and of course we don't.

Second, I'd like to point out that in the paper you reference, Codd also said this:

> [Users often have] occasion to require tables to be printed out or displayed. What could be a simpler, more universally needed, and more universally understood data structure than a table? Why not permit ... users to view all the data ... in a tabular way?

Third, any graph can always be represented—quite succinctly, in fact—in relational form. As for "shortest path" and other such problems, I say again that the relational model is only a minimum requirement. Even if you're right when you suggest that the shortest path problem can't be formulated in relational calculus—I presume you're referring to the fact that the relational calculus as originally defined had no support for the famous "ancestral" problem—well, that's not to say it never will have such support. In fact, a great deal of research has been done on adding such support (and implementing it efficiently, too).

Fourth, let's agree for the sake of the argument that there are some problems that graph-based DBMSs can solve better than relational ones. I don't have an issue with that. My position is this: We know the class of problems for which relational systems are suited is very large—but it's not necessarily universal. But I very much doubt whether any other approach is universal either. So my objection isn't to using, e.g., graph-based DBMSs to solve problems that they solve well; rather, my objection is to attempts to solve by nonrelational means problems that can reasonably, perhaps better, be solved by relational means. In other words, graph-based DBMSs (for example) might well have a role to play, but that role is *not* to take over the entire database world. To repeat something I've said elsewhere: I've never seen a proposal for "taking over the database world"—i.e., for replacing the relational model—in which the person doing the proposing really understood the relational model. Surely, if you want to claim that Technology *A* is no good and needs to be replaced by Technology *B*, then it's incumbent on you to understand Technology *A* in the first place? And, more specifically, to demonstrate that Technology *B* solves not only all of the problems that Technology *A* does, but also some problem that Technology *A* doesn't?

Hugh: Well, graph DBMSs and the like simply are nonrelational. Of course we don't suggest that *all* databases should be relational—only that all general purpose ones should be. But if you were to ask if it's legitimate to claim that solutions to problems like "shortest path" are inherently unobtainable with a relational system, then the answer is an emphatic "No!" As Chris has effectively already said, having no solution in relational calculus doesn't mean it's impossible for a relational DBMS to provide the necessary operators. For example, **Tutorial D** already includes an operator, TCLOSE, for deriving a relation representing the transitive closure of its operand, a recursive relation. And even SQL includes support—rather elaborate support, in fact—for recursive table expressions in general. Any operator that's closed over relations is admissible in a relational database language.

Now, the proponents of graph databases might wish to argue that their systems can provide much faster solutions to such problems than could ever be obtained by implementations of suitable relational operators. But suppose the graph DBMS were the *engine* of a relational DBMS, such that a relational expression is mapped under the covers to an equivalent expression or procedure in the graph DBMS's language. Wouldn't we then see the relational DBMS performing pretty much as well—or as badly!—as the graph DBMS on its own? And wouldn't its user then be receiving all the benefits claimed for relational DBMSs in general *in addition to* those claimed for graph DBMSs in particular? It's interesting to see in this connection that some of the DBMSs listed in the Wikipedia article "Graph database," notably those available from Oracle, use some form of SQL as their query language.

———— ♦ ♦ ♦ ♦ ♦ ————

Iggy: Another breed of NoSQL products that has gained considerable commercial momentum is the so called "Big Data" products like Hadoop that aim to process nontransactional data outside the transactional DBMS. It was apparent that the glaring drawback of this class of NoSQL products was the absence of SQL, and so there has been a rush to provide SQL-like functionality in this space, with Impala from Cloudera leading the way. Which leads to the question: Is it kosher to decouple relational algebra and relational calculus from the DBMS as Impala has done?

Chris: Before I became "a database person," I was a languages person. I worked for several years at IBM Hursley (in the U.K.), which in those days was the home of PL/I. (Of course, you might never have heard of PL/I, and I'll be the first to admit that as a language it looks a little antiquated now. But it was a big deal at the time—and a big revenue earner for IBM, I might add.) So when I first learned about Ted Codd's relational model, I wanted to add relations and relational operators to PL/I—in order that PL/I would be able to operate on data in a relational database, of course, but not only for that reason; I always thought it would be useful to have "local" relations, meaning ones that weren't in the database, and to be able to operate on those relations by means of joins and unions and so on. So if that's what you mean by "decoupling relational algebra and relational calculus from the DBMS," then I'm all for it.

But you touch on something else here: Big Data. Sorry if I'm beginning to sound like a broken record—I guess that metaphor is pretty antiquated too!—but I see no reason why a relational system shouldn't be able to handle "big data" perfectly well. Data size is, of course, an implementation concern, not a model concern. As I said in answer to your second question, the relational model is deliberately silent on all matters of physical implementation. Just because the implementation has to deal with enormous volumes of data, that's no reason, as far as I can see, why the user interface has to be anything other than relational.

Hugh: My observations on graph databases seem applicable here too. Couldn't Impala be thought of as the DBMS and Hadoop as Impala's database engine? Well, up to a point, perhaps, but if Impala users have to use Hadoop itself for certain purposes (perhaps database definition? updating? constraint enforcement?), then we could hardly call Impala a fully relational DBMS, even if its language, as far as it goes, were in keeping with the relational model. In any case, there have been many examples over the years of the need being perceived for a "decoupled" relational front end to a nonrelational system. For example, in the early 1980s a group in IBM U.K. developed an SQL front end to IBM's ancient and still running hierarchical system IMS. There can be no objection to such products; on the contrary, if the front end were fully relational (as opposed to SQL), we would encourage them to be provided where the need arises.[8]

PARTING ADVICE

Iggy: Thank you for spending so much time with us today. Most *NoCOUG Journal* readers have long careers ahead of them in the relational field. Do you have any parting advice for them?

Chris: As for the time, you're more than welcome. I'm always happy to do anything I can to help dispel all the myths that are out there regarding relational systems. Parting advice? Well, if you're right that they have long careers ahead of them in the *relational* field—my italics—then I congratulate them; the subject is intellectually stimulating, and pragmatically important, and it can be *fun*. One piece of advice I can offer is this (and I'm sorry if this sounds a little self-serving—I don't mean it to be):

1. Learn the relational model, by reading the right books and/or attending the right courses.

---

[8] For a detailed discussion of some of the technical issues involved, I refer you to the paper "Why Is It So Difficult to Provide a Relational Interface to IMS?" in my book *Relational Database: Selected Writings* (Addison-Wesley, 1986).

2. Go out and get your hands dirty working on a real project for a year or three.

3. Come back and read those books and/or attend those courses again.

A related piece of advice is: Learn the relational model first, SQL second (doing it the other way around is *hard*). Finally: Read either or both of Ted Codd's first two papers every year.[9]

Hugh: Yes, please do your best to become properly informed about what "relational" really means. In our experience, those who disparage relational are almost invariably very far from being properly informed and almost invariably equate "relational" with SQL and its implementations. If the NoSQL movement were to advocate relational as one of its proposed alternatives to SQL, then we would sign up ourselves!

---

[9] *Derivability, Redundancy, and Consistency of Relations Stored in Large Data Banks*, IBM Research Report RJ599 (August 19th, 1969), reprinted in ACM *SIGMOD Record 38*, No. 1 (March 2009); *A Relational Model of Data for Large Shared Data Banks*, *Communications of the ACM 13*, No. 6 (June 1970), reprinted in numerous places, including in particular the 100th issue of the *NoCOUG Journal* (*www.nocoug.org/Journal/NoCOUG_Journal_201111.pdf*).

Chapter 18

The SimpleTalk Interview

Sweet Reason, the newest and rarest thing in human life,
the most delicate child of human history
—Edward Abbey: "Science with a Human Face"
Abbey's Road (1979)

*This chapter consists of the text, very lightly edited here, of an interview
with myself that appeared online at SimpleTalk (August 22nd, 2014),[1]
under the title "Chris Date and the Relational Model." The interview
was conducted by Richard Morris. My thanks to Richard for allowing
me to republish it in its present form.*

RM: Chris, can you talk about the influence of Ted Codd on your work?

Before I respond to this question, I simply can't resist the temptation to note that
in my world, "RM" always stands for the relational model! So I'm truly honored
to be interviewed by someone with such auspicious initials. Anyway, what was
Ted's influence on my work? Well, of course it was huge. Let me explain how I
got into this business. My background is in mathematics. When I left university,
the only job that seemed to be available to mathematicians at the time that didn't
sound totally boring—I recall one possibility was time and motion study, can you
imagine?—was this new thing called computing. (This was back in 1962, and
we certainly didn't have any computer science in our curriculum in those days;
very few people even knew what a computer was.) So I became a computer
programmer. And that was fun and interesting for a while, but quite frankly it
didn't seem to have much to do with the mathematics I had learned at university,
in Cambridge. And then, in 1970, two things happened:

---

[1] *http://www.red-gate.com/simple-talk/*.

- First, a colleague and myself were given the job of figuring out what the language PL/I should do about another new thing: namely, databases. (I was working for the IBM lab in Hursley, U.K., by this time, which was the home of PL/I.)

- Second, Ted Codd's famous paper was published: namely, "A Relational Model of Data for Large Shared Data Banks," *Communications of the ACM 13*, No. 6 (June 1970).

So I read that paper—in among a lot of other database stuff, I should quickly add—and I discovered it was all about set theory and logic, stuff I did know and love from my time at Cambridge. So at last I had found an aspect of computing, database technology, where my mathematical background was relevant. I got in touch with Ted, and we became friends and colleagues—first within IBM, later in a consulting company that we started, along with Sharon Weinberg, in 1985 or so. And I've been working in that field (database technology, that is) all through that time, for something like 50 years now.

To get back to your question, I don't think I can do better than quote from the tribute piece I wrote for Ted when he died, back in 2003.[2] (Of course, it's very conceited to quote from oneself, but in the circumstances I hope you'll forgive me.)

> Dr Codd, known universally to his colleagues and friends—among whom I was proud to count myself—as Ted, was the man who, singlehanded, put the field of database management on a solid scientific footing. The entire relational database industry, now worth many billions of dollars a year, owes its existence to Ted's work, and the same is true of all of the huge number of relational database research and teaching programs under way worldwide in universities and similar organizations. Indeed, all of us who work in this field owe our career and livelihood to the giant contributions Ted made during the late 1960s and early 1970s. We all owe him a huge debt. This tribute to Ted and his achievements is offered in recognition of that debt.

In other words, Ted's influence on me was, as I've said, huge, but it wasn't just me—it was all of us in the database field. Though perhaps it was a little more directly on me than it was on a lot of other people.

---

[2] I've made a few minor editorial changes in the text of this quote as given here.

That said, I should say too that Ted and I certainly didn't see eye to eye on everything—we did have our disagreements. I say this because the idea seems to exist in certain circles that Ted's writings are and must forever be the final arbiter on all things relational. ("This must be right because it's what Ted Codd said.") I think such an attitude is quite dangerous. Science is a social activity; it's also an activity that's always in an ongoing state of development; and I don't think scientists in general—true scientists, that is—would ever claim that their own opinion is the absolute last word on any scientific subject. Critical thinking is just as important in the database field as it is everywhere else.

RM: Do you think we're taken a huge step backwards in terms of how SQL has developed? Do you think people have the intellectual curiosity about where the idea of relational databases came from? Are people aware of the history?

Oh dear. There's so much I want to say here! Let me see if I can put it all into some kind of sensible order. Perhaps the first item to address is: Why did SQL happen at all? I mean, why was it developed in the first place? The answer to this question can be found, I think, in the very first SQL paper: viz., Donald D. Chamberlin and Raymond F. Boyce, "SEQUEL: A Structured English Query Language," Proc. 1974 ACM SIGMOD Workshop on Data Description, Access, and Control, Ann Arbor, Mich., May 1974 (the name SEQUEL was subsequently changed to SQL for legal reasons). In that paper, the authors claimed, in effect, that their language was more user friendly than predicate calculus, and in particular that it didn't need what they called "the mathematical sophistication" of predicate calculus. You see, Ted's 1970 paper had proposed, among other things, that predicate calculus might reasonably be used as a basis for a database language (or data sublanguage, as Ted called it), and it gave examples of what expressions in such a language might look like. Unfortunately, it did so using the formal notation of predicate calculus, notation that many people in the computing world at the time—now too, probably—were quite unfamiliar with. So the idea arose that predicate calculus was just too difficult for ordinary mortals, and something simpler was needed. Ergo, SQL.

Now I think this was all a confusion on the part of the SQL folks. It's true that the notation—the syntax—of predicate calculus might look a little strange and complicated to many people; but the concepts expressed by that notation—the semantics—are actually quite simple, and can be explained quite simply too. In other words, it's not difficult to wrap some nice syntactic sugar around those concepts and make them very palatable indeed. Do you happen to be familiar with Query-By-Example (QBE)? QBE is exactly predicate calculus! In my opinion, it's a very user friendly syntactic sugarcoating of the semantic ideas embodied in predicate calculus. (Of course, QBE, like so many other proposals, was subsequently overwhelmed by the SQL juggernaut. I know one of your later questions has to do with such matters, so we'll come back to that issue later.)

Anyway, the SQL folks didn't do that (I mean, they didn't do what QBE did)—instead, they invented something different, based on what they called a subquery. I don't want to get into details of SQL's subqueries here; I just want to note that they're actually one hundred percent redundant! By which I mean, there's nothing relational you can do using SQL subqueries that you can't also do without them. It's ironic, really—the single biggest innovation in the SQL language could actually be thrown away without any serious loss of function.[3]

What's more, I seriously question whether SQL is more user friendly than predicate calculus, anyway. In fact I think it's what might reasonably be described as user hostile ... In my seminars—which are mostly intended these days for SQL professionals specifically—I make a point of showing a set of SQL queries, or would-be queries, and asking the class which ones are legal and which illegal. And *nobody* gets them all right the first time around. As a matter of fact I can never remember the answers myself either, because the pertinent syntax rules are just so convoluted and intertangled. You know, it's very easy to make something complicated; it's very hard to make something simple. (Parenthetically, part of the beauty of the relational model is precisely that it's fundamentally so simple.)

> *Aside:* For the record, here are those "SQL queries, or would-be queries" (better: SQL expressions, or would-be expressions) that I mentioned in the previous paragraph:

```
A NATURAL JOIN B

A INTERSECT B

SELECT * FROM A NATURAL JOIN B

SELECT * FROM A INTERSECT B
```

---

[3] I was referring here not to subqueries as they subsequently become but merely to subqueries as they were originally defined, where they could be used in a WHERE clause but not in a SELECT or FROM clause. See the planned follow-on to the present book, *Stating the Obvious, and Other Database Writings*, for more on this redundancy issue.

```
SELECT * FROM ( A NATURAL JOIN B )

SELECT * FROM ( A INTERSECT B )

SELECT * FROM
        ( SELECT * FROM A INTERSECT SELECT * FROM B )

SELECT * FROM ( A NATURAL JOIN B ) AS C

SELECT * FROM ( A INTERSECT B ) AS C

TABLE A NATURAL JOIN TABLE B

TABLE A INTERSECT TABLE B

SELECT * FROM A INTERSECT SELECT * FROM B

( SELECT * FROM A ) INTERSECT ( SELECT * FROM B )

( SELECT * FROM A ) AS AA
        INTERSECT ( SELECT * FROM B ) AS BB
```

You might like to have a go yourself at deciding which of the above are legal and which illegal. Answers if you're interested can be found in Chapter 12 ("Miscellaneous SQL Topics") of my book *SQL and Relational Theory: How to Write Accurate SQL Code*, 3rd edition (O'Reilly, 2015). *Note:* Perhaps I should remind you that, relationally speaking, intersection is a special case of natural join. *End of aside.*

There's more, a lot more. SQL isn't just user hostile, it involves some very serious departures from relational theory. I don't think this is the place to get into specifics—I've written about those problems at great length elsewhere (as indeed other people have too, including in particular my friend and colleague Hugh Darwen). Suffice it to say that those departures are so serious that I honestly believe SQL has no real right to be called relational at all. As a consequence, SQL DBMSs have no real right to be called relational at all, either. The truth is, there never has been a mainstream DBMS product that's truly relational.

There's something else I'd like to say in connection with all this. People who don't accept our criticisms of SQL often describe the points on which we disagree as "religious issues"—implying, I suppose, that a proper resolution of those issues is a matter of faith, not science. Our position is exactly the opposite: Proper resolution is a matter of science, not mere faith. For example, take nulls. The simple *scientific* fact is that an SQL table that contains a null isn't a relation;

thus, relational theory doesn't apply, and all bets are off. (Of course there's a lot more I could say here, but for present purposes I think that should be enough. Well, I'll just say one thing: If you'd prefer to replace the words *science* and *scientific* in the foregoing by *logic* and *logical*, respectively, then I won't argue with you. I mean, I don't think it makes any difference to the issue.)

You also ask whether people are aware of the history here, and whether they have the intellectual curiosity to want to be aware. Well, I don't think I should generalize too much here. At least I can say that the people who attend my seminars do seem to take an interest in this stuff. On the other hand, we live for better or worse in a world where the market is king, and a lot of people seem to take it as an article of faith (there's that word again!) that if something's new it must be better than what we had before: a position that seems to me to demonstrate a considerable *lack* of historical perspective, or historical interest. In connection with this point, I note that Lou Gerstner—IBM chairman at the time—was once quoted in *Informationweek* (February 9th, 1998) as saying the following:

> All large companies know today that speed and being early to market are often more important than being right.

Make of that what you will. Myself, I regard it as a giant indictment.

RM: What was key to SQL becoming the standard language for relational databases in the mid 1980s? Was it all down to good marketing?

To paraphrase your question: Why did SQL became so popular? Especially given all its faults? Well, I think this is rather a sorry story. I said earlier that there's never been a mainstream DBMS product that's truly relational. Thus, the obvious question is: Why not? So I think a good way for me to answer your questions here is to try to answer this latter question in their place, which I'll try to do by indulging in a kind of Socratic dialog. Like this:

Q: Why has no truly relational DBMS has ever been widely available in the marketplace?

A: Because SQL gained a stranglehold very early on, and SQL isn't relational.

Q: Why does SQL have such a stranglehold?

A: Because SQL is "the standard language for relational DBMSs."

Q: Why did the standardization body (viz., ISO) endorse SQL as such and not something else, something better?

A: Because IBM endorsed SQL originally, when it decided to build the product that became DB2.

Q: Why was that significant?

A: Because IBM used to be much more of a force in the marketplace than it is today. One effect of that state of affairs was that competitors— especially Relational Software Inc., which later became Oracle Corp.— simply assumed that SQL was destined to become a big deal, and so they jumped on the SQL bandwagon very early on (before IBM did, in fact, with its product DB2), with the consequence that SQL became a kind of de facto standard anyway.

Q: Why did IBM choose to support SQL in DB2?

A: Because IBM Research had running code for a prototype called System R which supported SQL, and the people in IBM management who made the decision to use System R as a basis on which to build DB2 didn't understand that there's all the difference in the world between a running prototype and an industrial strength product. They also, in my opinion, didn't understand software (they certainly didn't understand programming languages). They thought they had a bird in the hand.

Q: Why did the System R prototype support SQL?

A: My memory might be deficient here, but it's my recollection that the System R implementers were interested primarily in demonstrating that a relational (or would-be relational) DBMS could achieve reasonable performance. (Recall that it was widely believed at the time that "relational will never perform.") They weren't so interested in the form or quality of the user interface. In fact, some of them, at least, freely admitted that they weren't language designers as such. I'm pretty sure they weren't all totally committed to SQL specifically. (On the other hand, it's true that at least one of the original SQL language designers, Don Chamberlin, was a key player in the System R team.)

Q: Why didn't "the true relational fan club" in IBM—Ted and yourself in particular—make more fuss about SQL's deficiencies at the time, when the DB2 decision was made?

A: We did make some fuss, but not enough. The fact is, we were so relieved that IBM had finally agreed to build a relational, or would-be relational, product that we didn't want to rock the boat too much. At the same time, I have to say too that we didn't realize how truly awful SQL was or would turn out to be. (I note in passing that it's much worse now than it was then, though it was pretty bad right from the outset.) But I'm afraid I have to agree, somewhat, with the criticism that's implicit in the question; that is, I think I have to admit that the present mess is partly my fault. Certainly I did my bit in the early days to help push SQL on to an unsuspecting public. In my defense, let me say that the battles inside IBM to get management to commit to building a product at all were both bloody and exhausting, and I don't think we had much energy left to fight the battle that said "Well, we're pleased you've agreed to build a product, but don't you see you're still not doing it right?" As I've said, we made some fuss but not enough, and in fact I don't think the people who were making the decisions at that time cared very much what we thought, anyway. (I could cite some examples here but probably shouldn't.)

Well, you see what I mean by a sorry story. What makes it even sorrier is that a vastly preferable alternative to SQL existed *inside IBM at the time!* I'm referring here to ISBL ("Information System Base Language"), which was developed by Stephen Todd and others at the IBM Peterlee Scientific Centre in England.[4] The trouble was, California was the center of the world for database work at the time. Certainly all mainstream database work inside IBM in particular was being done in California. Thus, through no fault of the ISBL team as such, the ISBL work was marginalized at best, if not overlooked entirely, by the IBM decision makers. I don't think it's an exaggeration to say that we—by

---

[4] See P. A. V. Hall, P. Hitchcock, and S. J. P. Todd, "An Algebra of Relations for Machine Computation," Conference Record of the 2nd ACM Symposium on Principles of Programming Languages (Palo Alto, Calif., January 1975).

which I mean the database community in particular, and in fact society at large—are still paying the price for this state of affairs.

RM: **You've said that Ted was a genius but he wasn't too good at communicating his ideas to ordinary mortals, so you took over this area. Your writing style is very coherent. Did you learn to write in this style or do you write as you talk?**

I didn't exactly "take over this area," as you put it—it would be more accurate to say it fell in my lap. So much always depends on happenstance, doesn't it: the chance, or good luck, of being in the right place at the right time. I've explained how I first came across Ted's ideas in 1970, and I've said, or at least implied, that they seemed right to me because of their mathematical foundation. I've also talked about how we (i.e., my colleague in IBM Hursley and myself) were thinking about how to incorporate Ted's ideas into PL/I. What I didn't say before was that Ted was fighting very much of a lone battle in IBM at the time; he was up against some rather powerful vested interests. So in order to show that he wasn't completely alone, Ted invited IBM Hursley to send someone to California (where he was) to talk to various people about what we were doing. And that someone turned out to be me. And I flatter myself that my presentations went down well—I mean, I was able to make people understand what we were doing—and I began to get more requests to talk about relational technology, both to IBM folks and to IBM customers (and to technical audiences outside IBM as well, come to that). Then I got an IBM assignment to California (this was in 1974) and, well, one thing led to another, and Ted and I found ourselves increasingly being seen as a team.

Thank you for saying my writing style is "coherent"! But I think I can explain that, too. The truth is, I'm a rather slow learner. As a consequence, I think I can be a good teacher, because I can identify places where students are likely to have trouble. The truth is, all of my books are essentially written for *me* ... What I mean is, I try to write the book I would have liked to have read myself when I was learning the subject at hand. But I've never taken any formal lessons in how to write. (It's relevant to add, though, that I've always loved books, and I've always been interested in words, and language, and languages. Not just or even primarily computer books, I hasten to add; and not just or even primarily computer languages, either.)

As for "Do I talk the same way?": Well, I certainly try to when I'm teaching a class. Probably not, in unprepared conversation! In fact, certainly not. I need time to get my thoughts in order. So I'm often unable to answer a question coherently right away, for example. But then again, I tend to be rather suspicious of people who have an immediate opinion on every subject and are never at a loss for words.

RM: Even with added features over the years the code is still not completely portable among different database systems.

I don't follow the products much any more—they're too depressing—so I can't really answer product related questions. With reference to this specific comment of yours, however, I could point out the obvious, which is that even if everyone implemented the SQL standard (which they don't), you still wouldn't have portability, because:

a. The standard explicitly includes numerous "implementation dependent" features, which are things that are actually *un*defined in the standard but obviously have to be defined in any actual implementation (and the chance of all implementations defining such things in the same way is vanishingly small).

b. In any case, the standard as such is unimplementable—it's full of holes and inconsistencies and contradictions—so implementations have to do something about those holes etc. too.

c. "Added features" actually make matters worse, not better, because every implementation has its own—in fact, that's part of what the vendors market their product on.

So everyone implements what you might call a proper superset of a proper subset of the standard. I think it's all a bit of a confidence trick, really: Everyone talks about the standard, but nobody really cares about it. Especially since, as I've said, it's actually unimplementable.

RM: There's a common application language in D. Why in your view isn't this more widely used? Is there a possibility that in say five years, SQL will become what COBOL is to programmers, very much the last resort? If SQL is demoted to a language of last resort what will have been its legacy?

Apologies, but I'm going to ignore your last question here—the topic is too big. And I'd like to change your second question to say "Is there a possibility that in say five years, SQL will be displaced by **D**?" At any rate, that's the question I'll try to answer here.

First let me correct a misconception. **D**—the name is always set in boldface, by the way—isn't a language; rather, it's a generic name for any language that conforms to the principles laid down by *The Third Manifesto*. Perhaps you could say it's a family of languages. *The Third Manifesto* in turn is a set of prescriptions for future data and database management systems; it consists essentially of a precise though somewhat terse definition of the relational model and a supporting type theory (including a comprehensive model of type inheritance). It's described in detail in the book *Databases, Types, and the Relational Model: The Third Manifesto* (3rd edition), by Hugh Darwen and myself (Addison-Wesley, 2007).[5] Now, Hugh and I needed a generic name for a language that we could reference in the prescriptions of the *Manifesto*, just so that we could save ourselves a great deal of circumlocution in writing those prescriptions, and for reasons of our own we chose the name **D**. Any number of distinct languages could qualify as a valid **D**, though it goes without saying that SQL isn't one of them.

Of course, we also needed a concrete language that we could use in the *Manifesto* book in examples and so forth, and so we invented a concrete **D** that we called, for obvious reasons, **Tutorial D**. (**Tutorial D** is, of course, a valid **D**; in fact, it was expressly designed to be suitable as a vehicle for illustrating and teaching the ideas of *The Third Manifesto*, though Hugh and I, and others, have since used it as the basis for examples and the like in numerous other books and papers and presentations.) And implementations of **Tutorial D**, or something very close to it, do exist, though not in product form. One in particular I'd like to mention is *Rel*, by Dave Voorhis, which you can access by going to the website *www.thethirdmanifesto.com*.

So now let me reinterpret your question: Why isn't **Tutorial D** more widely used? Well, I think I've already answered that when I talked earlier about "the SQL stranglehold." But it's also true that there's something you might call "the *Third Manifesto* community," which consists of people all over the world who do indeed use **Tutorial D** (or something like it) for various practical and theoretical purposes.

---

[5] The type inheritance portion is described in detail in a more recent book by myself, *Type Inheritance and Relational Theory: Subtypes, Supertypes, and Substitutability* (O'Reilly, 2016).

That said, I should also admit that **Tutorial D** is, in a sense, only a toy language. To be specific, it has no I/O, and it has no exception handling. On the other hand, it *is* well designed, as far as it goes, and one of the things we'd like to do (in among a very long list of things we'd like to do) is beef it up to become what you might call **Industrial D**. And yes, we'd like **Industrial D** to be considered—under a much better name, I would assume!—for implementation in an industrial context. (As a matter of fact, we've already given some thought to the question of implementing **Tutorial D**, at least, on top of SQL.) But even if **Industrial D** is implemented in product form, will it displace SQL? Well, obviously not for many years, if ever (certainly more than five years, I'm quite sure of that). But we're optimists; we're in this for the long haul; we take the view that if we do nothing, then nothing will happen, but if we do something, then something might happen.

RM: The World Wide Web Consortium (W3C) enthuses about XQuery saying it's replacing proprietary languages, is much simpler to work with and easier to maintain than many other alternatives. Is XQuery a better alternative to SQL?

No.

Well, you probably wanted more than just a flat *no* here, so let me try the following. XQuery is designed to work with XML data, of course. Now, I haven't taken a close look at either XML or XQuery for some years now, so the following remarks might no longer be totally appropriate. If they aren't, then I apologize. But here's what I believe. First of all, XML structures are fundamentally hierarchic; thus, all of the intrinsic difficulties with hierarchies that we experienced all those years ago, with IBM's IMS product in particular, are rearing their ugly head again. (I often characterize XML, perhaps a little unfairly, as "IMS warmed over.") At least two serious problems arise immediately:

- First, the innate lack of symmetry in hierarchies means the structure might be suitable for some problems but will certainly be unsuitable for others.

- Second, many to many relationships will have to be dealt with in some ad hoc and probably unsatisfactory fashion.

In fact, XML structures aren't just hierarchies, they're linearizable hierarchies—there's a linear sequence to the nodes (I think I'm right in saying it's top to bottom, left to right sequence). As a consequence, when W3C tried to define an XML algebra (allegedly as a basis for XQuery, though I think it was defined after XQuery was defined), they had to base it on the sequence abstraction. But sequences aren't a *good* abstraction! I mean, they're unnecessarily complicated. Sets (which the relational model is based on) are so much better. One immediate consequence is that XQuery is necessarily much more complicated than a relational language. In particular, it includes support for iteration, which relational languages don't need, or have.

To sum up: I'm obviously no fan of SQL, but no, I don't think XQuery is better than SQL. In fact, I think it suffers from some of the same problems that SQL does, and maybe more. At least SQL, with all its faults, can be used—with a *lot* of discipline, like avoiding duplicates and nulls—almost as if it were relational; but the same clearly can't be said of XQuery.

RM: Can you identify any big changes in the way you think about relations and relational databases since your early days? Do you still enjoy your work as much as you used to when you first started?

In answer to your first question, yes. One big change is that in the early days, when we were still trying to convince people that relational was real (or at least could be real), we—and especially I—necessarily got into the business of comparing the relational model with the systems (primarily hierarchic and network systems) that existed at the time. Typically, we would take sample problems and show how and why the relational solutions were so much better than the hierarchic and network solutions. But in doing that, we unwittingly did ourselves, and the cause, a huge disservice: We effectively spread the idea, or perception, that relations were "the same kind of animal" as hierarchies and networks, and in particular that even if relations did replace hierarchies and networks as we said they would, so relations in turn would sometime be replaced by something better. But I've since come to believe that that perception was very wrong. I now believe—and I've explained this belief in detail in writing, as well as in my live lectures—that a database, in order to be a truly general purpose database within the meaning of the act, *must* be relational. Relational really is different.

I've lost count of the number of times someone has come up to me and said "I've got something that's better than the relational model." (For a good example of the kind of thing I mean, take a look at the letters column in the January 2013 issue of *Communications of the ACM*.[6] I might also mention the truly appalling preamble to a book I read recently extolling the virtues and "advantages" of graph databases.[7] And look at all the nonsense we were hearing a few years ago about how object databases were going to take over the world. At least we don't hear so much about this last one any more, do we?) It seems to me that if you want to replace Technology *A* by Technology *B*, then it's incumbent on you, first, to understand Technology *A* properly; second, to show that Technology *B* can solve all of the problems that Technology *A* solves; and third, to show there's some problem that Technology *B* solves and Technology *A* doesn't. And I can state categorically that, in my experience, people always fall at the first of these hurdles: They don't understand the relational model in the first place. In fact, I'd like to offer a challenge: Show me one problem that the relational model ought to be able to solve but can't.[8] But I warn you, if whatever you come up with here demonstrates a failure to understand the relational model, then I probably won't bother to respond.

In connection with the foregoing, I'd like to mention one of my current database interests, temporal data. There's been a lot of research into this subject over the years, and a lot of solutions proposed—but most of those solutions are nonrelational. I don't want to get into details here of just exactly how they're nonrelational; let me just say that the researchers often don't seem to realize what they're proposing is indeed nonrelational, because their papers have titles like "Temporal Extensions to the Relational Model" or "Adding the Time Dimension to the Relational Model." I believe this is more evidence of the general lack of understanding of the relational model in the database community at large. In strong contrast to the foregoing, I'm very pleased to be able to tell you that the relational model needs no extension, and no subsumption, and no correction, and above all no *perversion*, in order to incorporate temporal support. In fact, Hugh

---

[6] The letter in question was from Carl Hewitt, and it's discussed in detail in the planned follow-on to the present book (*Stating the Obvious, and Other Database Writings*).

[7] *Graph Databases*, by Ian Robinson, Jim Webber, and Emil Eifrem (O'Reilly, 2013). Here are some actual quotes from that preamble: "Relational databases lack relationships"; "Relational databases were initially designed to codify paper forms and tabular structures"; "Relationships do exist in the vernacular of relational databases, but only as a means of joining tables"; "[As] outlier data multiplies, ... the relational model [*sic*] becomes burdened with large join tables, sparsely populated rows, and lots of null-checking logic"; "Join tables add accidental complexity—they mix business data with foreign key metadata"; "Foreign key constraints add additional ... overhead *just to make the database work*" (italics in the original); "Relational databases struggle with highly connected domains"; and on and on.

[8] No one has yet risen to this challenge.

Darwen, Nikos Lorentzos, and I have just (July 2014) published a book that clearly demonstrates this very point (*Time and Relational Theory: Temporal Data in the Relational Model and SQL*, Morgan Kaufmann, 2014).

I have another reason for answering *yes* to your question, too ("Have I changed the way I think about relations and relational databases since the early days?")—and here I must credit several people: my friends David McGoveran, Hugh Darwen again, and a late colleague Adrian Larner. Together, these friends and colleagues made me realize that the best way to think of a relation is not just as an abstraction of the classical concept of a file (with its records and fields), but rather as the extension of a predicate. Once again, I don't think this is the place to get into details—I'll just to have to point you to any of my recent writings (e.g., the book on temporal databases just mentioned), where this perception is explained in depth (and the reason why it's important is explained in depth, too).

By the way, as a kind of PS to both of the foregoing responses, I'd like to mention that the SQL standard does now include some support for temporal data. But it seems to us—i.e., my coauthors and myself—that the support in question manages to violate the idea that a relation is supposed to be the extension of a predicate![9] In other words, it involves yet another rather large departure from relational theory. I don't know what the consequences of that departure are likely to be, but as far as I'm concerned it looks like yet another nail in the "SQL is relational" coffin.

My answer to your second question ("Do you still enjoy your work as much as you used to when you first started?") is yes. In many ways, in fact, I enjoy it more, especially since I now work for myself instead of some corporation. But the real point here is this: The relational model, although it's fundamentally so simple (you can explain the basic idea in five minutes), has amazing depths. You can peel away layer after layer of meaning and keep on discovering more and more. Thus, I'm still learning things about it myself, even after all these years. (If I wasn't, I would probably have given up this career years ago and become a park ranger or something.)

RM: Do you feel there were times in your life where your passion for work ran contrary to or to the detriment of other parts of your life?

---

[9] See Chapter 19, "The SQL Standard," of the book by Hugh Darwen, Nikos Lorentzos, and myself mentioned previously (*Time and Relational Theory: Temporal Data in the Relational Model and SQL*, Morgan Kaufmann, 2014) for arguments in support of this strong, serious, and perhaps rather surprising criticism.

Well, I think I need to challenge the premise of your question. I do enjoy my work, very much; it's challenging and creative and (I believe) useful. But I don't live to work, I work to live. I have absolutely no difficulty in switching off work-related thinking when (for example) I'm hiking the desert—which, parenthetically, is something I really enjoy doing. I have many interests outside of work: birdwatching, wildlife in general, music, politics, hiking, cosmology, art, and so on. Work is one of my interests, but it's not number one in the list. (I don't think I *have* a number one.)

RM: Do you consider yourself a scientist, an engineer, a writer or a craftsman?

Scientist: Yes (at least if you consider mathematics a science; I know some people don't, but I do). Engineer: No. Writer: Yes (though I might prefer "teacher"). Craftsman: Don't know! I'm not sure what you're getting at here.

RM: Do you have any recommendations for people who want to follow in your footsteps?

I don't know about "following in my footsteps," but if you're talking about people who want to work in the relational field—let me stress that word *relational*, though!—then, well, I don't think I can do better than repeat some remarks I made in another recent interview:[10]

> First, if people are serious about going into this field, then I congratulate them; the subject is intellectually stimulating, and pragmatically important, and it can be *fun*. As for advice, one thing I can say is this (and I'm sorry if this sounds a little self-serving—I don't mean it to be):
>
> 1. Learn the relational model, by reading the right books and/or attending the right courses.
>
> 2. Go out and get your hands dirty working on a real project for a year or three.
>
> 3. Come back and read those books and/or attend those courses again.

---

[10] Namely, the one in Chapter 17 of the present book.

A related piece of advice is: Learn the relational model first, SQL second (doing it the other way around is *hard*).

Finally, read either or both of Ted Codd's first two papers every year. (Those papers are "Derivability, Redundancy, and Consistency of Relations Stored in Large Data Banks", IBM Research Report RJ599, August 19th, 1969, reprinted in *ACM SIGMOD Record 38*, No. 1 (March 2009), and "A Relational Model of Data for Large Shared Data Banks", *Communications of the ACM 13*, No. 6, June 1970, which you can easily find online.)

RM: Is there anything I haven't asked about your work that you thought I might?

This is a dangerously open ended question! But I think I've been quite self-indulgent enough already, about quite enough different topics, so I think I'd better just stop here. Thank you for the opportunity to air my opinions.

Chapter 19

Looking Backward,

Looking Forward

I'm walking backwards for Christmas,
To prove that I love you

—Spike Milligan:
The Goon Show (1956)

It's a poor sort of memory that only works backwards.

—Lewis Carroll:
Through the Looking-Glass
and What Alice Found There (1872)

Backward ran sentences until reeled the mind.

—Wolcott Gibbs:
Time ... Fortune ... Life ... Luce (1958)

This chapter consists of the text, very lightly edited here, of an interview
with myself that was published in the NoCOUG Journal 33, No. 4
(November 2019)[1] *under the title "Down Memory Lane with*
C. J. Date." The interview was conducted by the editor of that journal,
Iggy Fernandez (and I thank Iggy for allowing me to republish it in its
present form). The trigger for the interview was the publication of a
new book by myself, viz., E. F. Codd and Relational Theory: A Detailed
Review and Analysis of Codd's Major Database Writings (Lulu Press,
2019).

---

[1] The *NoCOUG Journal* is an official publication of the Northern California Oracle User Group.

Iggy: **Your new book, *E. F. Codd and Relational Theory*, has just been published. Tell us about it: What does it cover? Why did you write it, and what exactly are you trying to achieve with it? Who's your target audience?**

Thanks for giving me the chance to answer these questions! What does the book cover? Well, first, notice my title. E. F. ("Ted") Codd was the original inventor of the relational model, of course, and it was that invention that turned databases into an academically respectable field and at the same time made them a truly practical and commercially viable proposition. All of us who work on databases today owe our professional existence, and indeed our very livelihoods, to the work that Ted did in the late 60s and early 70s. Yet in my experience very few database professionals nowadays are aware of what he actually did—in fact, I've met many who've never even heard of Ted Codd! So one thing I wanted to do with the book was give readers some sense of the historical foundations of their field. To do this, in the book I examine in considerable detail what seem to me (for one reason or another) to be the most significant of Ted's writings, explaining in each case what the contribution was, and in particular highlighting not only the many things he got right but also some of the things he got wrong. (No one is perfect, and I have to say Ted did make a few mistakes. But we can forgive him those mistakes in view of the one thing he did get superlatively right—his gift to the world—namely, his wonderful relational model.)

By the way, I hope you don't mind me constantly referring to him as "Ted." Of course, I don't mean to be either presumptuous or disrespectful here, but the fact is that he and I were friends and professional colleagues for many years, and "Ted" is how I always think of him.

Why did I write the book? Well, I've effectively answered this already, in part. Generally speaking, I've been troubled for years by the widespread lack of understanding of relational matters on the part of people who really ought—and need—to know better. (As an aside, I note that the book includes a short list of relational questions that I used to ask attendees at the beginning of my live seminars. What I found was that most of those attendees—all of whom were database professionals, by the way, typically DBAs or database application developers—were unable to answer *any* of those questions completely correctly.)

More specifically, I've been troubled by how few people seem to have actually read Ted's writings or have any kind of proper understanding or appreciation of his work. So I wanted to produce something that people could read and refer to as a useful summary and analysis of those writings and that work. At the same time I wanted to set the historical record straight here and there ... I mean, I have a huge admiration for what Ted did—as we should all have!—but it's important not to be blinded by such feelings into uncritical acceptance of everything he said or wrote. Nor do I feel it appropriate to accept him as the sole authority on relational matters. The fact is, he did get some things wrong, and I feel those things need to be documented too, as well as all the things he got right.

As for my target audience: Of course I'd like *everyone* to read it ... More seriously, I believe the material the book covers is something that all database professionals should have tucked away in their brain, as it were, as part of their general background knowledge. So my audience is anyone with a professional interest in relational databases—including, of course, anyone with a professional interest in SQL.

There are a few more things I'd like to say in connection with your original question here. In fact I'd like to quote some text from the book itself. (Very conceited to quote from oneself, I realize!—please forgive me.)

> [Ted's] papers were staggering in their originality. Among other things, they changed, and changed permanently, the way database management was perceived in the IT world; more specifically, they transformed what had previously been nothing but a ragbag of tricks and ad hoc techniques into a solid scientific endeavor. They also, not incidentally, laid the foundation for an entire multibillion dollar industry. Together, they provided the basis for a technology that has had, and continues to have, a major impact on the very fabric of our society. Thus, it's no exaggeration to say that Codd is the intellectual father of the modern database field.
>
> To the foregoing, I'd like to add this: Codd's relational model has been with us now for over 50 years. And I for one think it very telling that, in all that time, no one has managed to invent any kind of new theory, one that might reasonably supplant or seriously be considered superior to the relational model in any way. In my opinion, in fact, no one has even come close to inventing such a theory (though there have been many attempts, as I'm sure you're aware, but attempts that in my opinion have universally failed).
>
> And yet ... And yet, here we are—as I've said, over 50 years later—and what do we find? Well:
>
> ■ First, the teaching of relational theory, in universities in particular, seems everywhere to be in decline. What's more, what teaching there is seems not to have caught up—at least, not fully, and certainly not properly—with the numerous developments in relational theory that have occurred since publication of those early papers of Codd's.

■ Second, no truly relational DBMS has ever been widely available in the commercial marketplace.

So here are a couple more reasons why I wrote the book ... First, I wanted to provide something that might help spur educators, in universities and elsewhere, to get back to teaching relational theory properly (paying attention in particular to some of the work done by others since Ted's early papers). Second, I wanted to suggest some answers to the question implicit in the second of the foregoing bullet points. But I see you're going to ask essentially that same question explicitly later, so let me defer further discussion to my response to that later question.

***Iggy:* Can you say something about the book's structure?**

The book's subtitle is "A Detailed Review and Analysis of Codd's Major Database Writings." Obviously, the question arises: Which of Ted's writings qualify as major? In my opinion, the following ones do:

■ His 1970 paper "A Relational Model of Data for Large Shared Data Banks" and its 1969 predecessor "Derivability, Redundancy, and Consistency of Relations Stored in Large Data Banks"

■ His 1971 papers "A Data Base Sublanguage Founded on the Relational Calculus" and "Further Normalization of the Data Base Relational Model"

■ His papers "Relational Completeness of Data Base Sublanguages" (1972) and "Interactive Support for Nonprogrammers: The Relational and Network Approaches" (1974)

■ His 1985 two-part Computerworld article, "Is Your DBMS Really Relational?" and "Does Your DBMS Run by the Rules?"

■ His 1990 book *The Relational Model for Database Management Version 2*

My book takes seven long chapters to consider the foregoing publications in detail. It also has a "Setting the Scene" chapter that explains exactly what a relational DBMS is—or ought to be, at any rate. (Incidentally, that chapter includes a detailed list of SQL departures from the relational model.) And the book also has three appendixes: one containing the text of the piece I wrote in connection with Codd's 1981 Turing Award for the pertinent section of the ACM website (*amturing.acm.org*); one containing a set of formal definitions; and the last consisting of a consolidated list of references for the entire book.

Iggy: **What's the competition for your book?**

I don't mean to sound arrogant, but I don't think there are any books out there that cover exactly the same material in exactly the same way. In fact I don't really think there could be, given that Ted and I were friends and colleagues for so many years, first in IBM and then in a variety of companies with names like Codd & Date International, Codd & Date Limited, and so on; I mean, I believe I can claim certain unique insights in this area that other writers simply can't.

That said, the closest competitor is probably a book of my own anyway: viz., *The Database Relational Model: A Retrospective Review and Analysis* (Addison-Wesley, 2001). Let me explain. Some 20 years ago or so I wrote a series of twelve articles for the Miller Freeman monthly magazine *Intelligent Enterprise*, beginning with the October 1998 issue. The overall title for the series was "30 Years of Relational," because they were written in part to celebrate the relational model's forthcoming 30th birthday (August 19th, 1999). As I wrote at the time:

> [These articles are intended] to serve as a historical account and ... analysis of E. F. Codd's (huge!) contribution to the field of database technology. Codd's relational model, [described in] a startlingly novel series of research papers, was a revolution at the time, albeit one that was desperately needed. Now, however, it seems that—despite the fact that the entire multibillion dollar database industry is founded on Codd's original ideas—those ideas are in danger of being ignored or forgotten (or, at best, being paid mere lip service to). Certainly we can observe many examples today of those ideas being flouted in (among other things) database products, database designs, and database applications. It thus seems appropriate to take another look at Codd's original papers, with a view to assessing their true significance and restating, and reinforcing, their message for a new generation of database professionals ... So I thought it would be interesting, and (I also thought) useful, to devote a short series of articles to a careful, unbiased, retrospective review and assessment of [those] papers.

And I subsequently collected those articles into the "Retrospective" book mentioned above. However, while I still believe that book provides a useful overview of Ted's achievement overall (and the new book certainly isn't meant to replace it or displace it), I must make it clear that the new book goes into a much greater level of detail than the earlier book did, and it's really aimed at a different—perhaps a slightly more sophisticated—audience.

Iggy: **I'm intrigued by your reference above to a list of questions that you said attendees on your seminars couldn't answer. Can you tell us more about them?**

I'd be happy to—but I must stress that the book isn't aimed primarily at answering them, though in fact it does answer most of them in passing. Let me say first that the seminar on which I asked these questions was called "SQL and Relational Theory," and attendees were certainly supposed to be pretty familiar with SQL ahead of time. Anyway, here are the questions:

1. What exactly is first normal form?

2. What's the connection between relations and predicates?

3. What's semantic optimization?

4. What's an image relation?

5. Why is semidifference important?

6. Why doesn't deferred integrity checking make sense?

7. What's a relation variable?

8. What's prenex normal form?

9. Can a relation have an attribute whose values are relations?

10. Is SQL relationally complete?

11. Why is *The Information Principle* important?

12. How does XML fit with the relational model?

Twelve questions, of course (as you know, everything in the relational world has to come in twelves).

By the way, I complained earlier that university education these days doesn't seem to be all that it might be as far as relational matters are concerned. In particular, I frankly doubt whether the average university class deals with the foregoing issues properly (perhaps not at all, in some cases). What's more, much the same can be said of the majority of the numerous database textbooks currently available—at least the ones I'm aware of.

Iggy: **Personally I found portions of your book simply delightful. But I have to ask: Why bother analyzing papers and publications that today's practitioners and even today's researchers have not read and probably never will read?**

Thank you for your kind words ... Over the years I've had many adjectives used to describe my various writings as you can surely imagine, but I don't think "delightful" was ever one of them before. Anyway, you ask (paraphrasing): Why analyze writings that today's practitioners and researchers have never read and probably never will read? Well, I've tried to answer this question in part already, but let me say a bit more about it.

First, researchers. Personally, I'd be ashamed to call myself a researcher of any kind if I wasn't thoroughly familiar with the foundational writings in my field. For example, can you imagine someone calling himself or herself a cosmologist and not being familiar with Einstein's original papers? In other words, database researchers simply owe it to themselves to read Ted's original writings. They have no excuse not to! And then I'd like to think that my book could serve those researchers as a useful explanation of, and commentary on, and even a guide to, those writings—rather like the numerous books extant today that serve as an explanation of and commentary on and guide to Einstein's original writings.

Turning to practitioners: Actually, I don't really blame practitioners (as opposed to researchers) if they haven't read Ted's writings. Ted was a mathematician originally, and his first few papers tended to reflect that fact—the writing was terse and a little dry, the style theoretical and academic, the notation and examples mostly rather mathematical in tone, and it wasn't easy to relate what they had to say to practical day-to-day concerns. In a word, they weren't easy to read. So here I see my book as serving another, slightly different purpose: I see it as explaining what those papers of Ted's were all about, but in a way that's less formal than the originals wherever possible, with simple and practical examples. But I'd like to stress that the book isn't meant to be a substitute for Ted's originals. Rather, I'd like readers to read Ted's originals alongside my chapters, or after them, if they can. (Most of those writings of Ted's can now be found online, by the way.)

***Iggy:* Put another way, Codd's vision was never fully implemented, correct? Why not?**

I think this is a sad story. It's true that no fully relational commercial DBMSs exist today, so far as I'm aware. (Of course, people can and will argue about what "fully relational" means, but I don't want to get into that debate here.) Sadly, it seems to me that a small part of the blame for this depressing state of affairs has to be laid at Ted's own door. The fact is, those early writings of his, brilliantly innovative though they undoubtedly were, did suffer from a number of defects, as I've already indicated. And it's at least plausible to suggest that some of the sins to be observed in the present database landscape—sins of both omission and commission—can be regarded, with hindsight (always perfect, of course), as deriving from the defects in question.

A much bigger part of the blame, though, has to be laid at SQL's door. SQL was, of course, designed in IBM Research, and it's quite clear that the people responsible for its design never understood the relational model as well as they should have done. (I have clear written evidence of this claim which this margin is unfortunately too small to contain.) As a consequence, SQL was a long, long way from being what it ought to have been, viz., a true concrete realization of the abstract ideas of the relational model. Nevertheless, when IBM management finally decided—after delaying for far too long—that IBM should build a relational product, they grabbed on to SQL as the user language for that product, because SQL did at least already exist, albeit only in prototype form. Never mind that there were people in IBM at the time pointing out the problems with SQL, and pointing out too that it would be better and easier, and probably even cheaper, to support a truly relational language! All that those IBM managers could see was that SQL was light years better than DL/I, the language used with IBM's hierarchic product IMS; thus, arguments that there could be something light years better than SQL simply cut no ice.

So IBM ran with SQL; and given IBM's prominence in the computing world in those days, everyone else decided they needed to have SQL too in order to compete. Also a standard was developed that (at least in its initial manifestations) was essentially IBM SQL, warts and all. And so here we are now, stuck with it. As I say, I find this a very sad story; we had a once-in-a-lifetime opportunity to do it right, and we blew it.

Iggy: You're quite dismissive of SQL too. But you claim that SQL can be used safely, is that correct?

I'm not "dismissive" of SQL. It would be absurd to dismiss something so widespread and so (within its own lights) successful! Rather, I regard it as a clear and present evil, something that exists and so has to be dealt with appropriately. And yes, I do believe it can be used more or less "safely," as you put it. In a nutshell, I believe it's possible to limit your use—more or less—to what might be called "the relational kernel" of SQL. If you do that, you can behave as if SQL truly were relational—more or less—and you can enjoy the benefits of working with what is in effect a truly relational system.

Of course, if you're going to follow such a discipline, you need to know what that relational kernel is, which means in effect that (a) you need to know the relational model and (b) you need to know exactly how every aspect of that model materializes in SQL. In fact I wrote an entire book based on these ideas—*SQL and Relational Theory: How to Write Accurate SQL Code* (3rd edition, O'Reilly, 2015). But now I'm beginning to stray somewhat from the book I'm supposed to be talking about ... Let me just say in conclusion that the new book will certainly give you a good idea of what the relational model is all about, but it doesn't have much to say about SQL as such. After all, Ted Codd never had very much to do with SQL as such—though (like me) he did subsequently become very critical of it.

Iggy: Thank you for giving us so much of your time. One final question. This issue of the *NoCOUG Journal* includes a reprint of the ACM Turing Award Lecture delivered by Codd at ACM '81. Do you have any memories or stories about that lecture to share with us?

As a matter of fact I do. As I mentioned earlier, Ted did indeed receive the 1981 ACM Turing Award for his invention of the relational model, and nobody was more pleased about that than me. (Well, perhaps Ted was.) Actually I was the one who nominated him for that award; and there's a story there ... I'm sure you understand that putting a proper Turing Award nomination together is a lot of work. You need to provide detailed statements of who the nominee is, and why you think he or she deserves the award; what the person has achieved (i.e., what the contribution is); why the work is significant and novel, and in fact outstanding; what its relationship is to previous work in the field; and what the implications of the work are for computing as such, and for industry, and possibly even for society at large. You also need to provide a list of publications and citations, and letters from recognized authorities in the field supporting the nominee's candidacy, and a whole host of other things besides. And ideally you need to put all this material together without giving the nominee any hint of what's going on (for fear of raising false hopes, perhaps).

Well, I wanted Ted to get the award. I certainly felt he deserved it, and I was prepared to do the work of putting the nomination package together, and so I went to see my IBM manager Jim to get permission to spend maybe a week of my time doing so. (Ted and I were both still working in IBM in those days.) Jim was in charge of the DB2 Technical Planning Department—think about that as you hear what happened next—and my conversation with him went like this:

Me: "Jim, I'd like to take some of my time to work on nominating Ted Codd for the Turing Award. I think it'll take about a week of my time, though it'll probably continue at noise level over the next few weeks as well."

Jim: "What's the Turing Award?"

Me (slightly taken aback): "*Jim!* It's the top award in computing! It's not quite the Nobel prize, but it's kind of like a mini Nobel prize. It's awarded every year by the ACM."

Jim: "What's the ACM?"

Me (even more taken aback, jaw dropping): "?!?!?"

At least he didn't ask who Ted Codd was.

Well, anyway, I did do the nomination, and of course Ted did get the award, and that was great. *But* ... Ted was certainly a genius, but he was also a great procrastinator. The conference was getting nearer and nearer, and Ted was going to have to give his Turing lecture and write a paper to go with it, and repeated efforts by myself (to some extent) and Sharon Weinberg (to a much greater extent) to get him to prepare something seemed to run up against a brick wall every time. Ted didn't even have a theme in mind! Eventually Sharon suggested the theme of productivity, and Ted agreed to it. But he still seemed not to understand that the presentation was needed *right now* (the paper could wait a while, of course). In fact, I'm pretty sure I'm right in saying that most of the slides Ted used in his presentation were actually prepared by Sharon, and prepared quite literally just the night before.

I was there, of course—in fact I was the one who introduced Ted,[2] and it was very tempting to tell the audience the two stories above, but I very nobly didn't.

One last point: You'll notice that I don't include Ted's Turing Award paper in my list of what I called his major writings. That's because that paper wasn't truly theoretical or innovative like the ones my book deals with—it was more a kind of summary of where relational systems had come from and where they going, with the emphasis on why they could indeed serve as the advertised "practical foundation for productivity." All of which was perfectly right and proper, of course, given the context. In particular, I was very glad to see Ted attack a certain rather common but head-in-the-sand belief—one that we both ran up against repeatedly in the early days—namely, the one summed up in the ignorant phrase "If it's theoretical, it can't be practical!"

At the same time I do have to say there are aspects of the paper that I don't agree with. To get into details of such aspects would probably need another interview, though, or even another book, so I think I'd better stop while I'm ahead.

---

[2] On reflection I'm not sure this is true—I might be misremembering. I certainly did introduce Ted when he gave a repeat of his lecture at the VLDB Conference in Mexico City in September 1982. I was also at the ACM Conference in Los Angeles in November 1981 when he was presented with the award. But I'm not sure whether I actually did the introduction at the Los Angeles event—at this distance I might be conflating the two occasions in my mind.

Index

For alphabetization purposes, (a) differences in fonts and case are ignored; (b) quotation marks are ignored; (c) other punctuation symbols—hyphens, underscores, parentheses, etc.—are treated as blanks; (d) numerals precede letters; (e) blanks precede everything else.

www.ingramcontent.com/pod-product-compliance
Lightning Source LLC
Chambersburg PA
CBHW080607060326
40690CB00021B/4616